Critical Clinical
Social Work

Critical Clinical Social Work

Counterstorying for Social Justice

Edited by **Catrina Brown** and **Judy E. MacDonald**

Foreword by Donna Baines

CANADIAN
SCHOLARS

Toronto | Vancouver

Critical Clinical Social Work: Counterstorying for Social Justice
Edited by Catrina Brown and Judy E. MacDonald

First published in 2020 by
Canadian Scholars, an imprint of CSP Books Inc.
425 Adelaide Street West, Suite 200
Toronto, Ontario
M5V 3C1

www.canadianscholars.ca

Library and Archives Canada Cataloguing in Publication

Title: Critical clinical social work : counterstorying for social justice / edited by
    Catrina Brown and Judy E. MacDonald ; foreword by Donna Baines.
Names: Brown, Catrina, editor. | MacDonald, Judy E., 1961- editor. |
    Baines, Donna, 1960- writer of foreword.
Description: Includes bibliographical references and index.
Identifiers: Canadiana (print) 2020018086X | Canadiana (ebook) 20200180959 |
    ISBN 9781773381695 (softcover) | ISBN 9781773381701 (PDF) |
    ISBN 9781773381718 (EPUB)
Subjects: LCSH: Social service—Practice—Canada. | LCSH: Social service—
    Canada—Philosophy. | LCSH: Social service—Moral and ethical aspects—Canada. |
    LCSH: Social justice—Canada.
Classification: LCC HV40.8.C3 C75 2020 | DDC 361.3/20971—dc23

Page layout: S4Carlisle Publishing Services
Cover design: Rafael Chimicatti

Printed and bound in Ontario, Canada

Canadä

CONTENTS

PART III: CRITICAL SOCIAL WELFARE AND INSTITUTIONAL PRACTICES

PART IV: WORKING IN THE CONTEXT OF MARGINALIZATION, OPPRESSION, AND DIVERSITY

PART V: CONCLUSION

FOREWORD

This edited collection is a long-awaited, landmark work that reunites social justice with clinical social work skill. The authors included here effectively put to rest the notion that clinical work cannot and should not be politicized, instead showing that clinical social work practice is always political, always criss-crossed with power relations, and that clinical skills can be consciously and compassionately used to expose oppression and develop more livable conditions for service users and communities. Through tightly researched, theory-informed, cutting-edge arguments and research, the contributors convincingly demonstrate that clinical social work can and should be critically engaged and can consistently advance social justice through direct practice with individuals, families, couples, and groups.

Social justice holds a special place within social work practice, theory, and knowledge. Social work is the only profession with social justice as a central part of its code of ethics (Canadian Association of Social Workers, 2019). As a central value, it is not an optional add-on but something that should undergird every interaction, every relationship, every policy, and every aspect of the social work endeavour. However, social justice and "skills" are increasingly set up in opposition to each other, with measurable, "clinical" social work practices viewed as the only skills needed in today's underfunded, neoliberal workplace (Brown, 2016). This formulation views social justice practices as non-skills and an aspect of social work that is added on if time and resources permit. This marginalizes social justice social work practices as laudatory aspirations that are seen as largely unachievable and unaffordable in the current context.

The concept of "skills" needs to be problematized as it is not neutral. In actuality, the skills concept is central to powerful discourses that systemically undervalue the social work skills and practices associated with social justice, social change, policy analysis, community development and mobilization, grassroots services, social movements, and advocacy. What these social justice skills have in common is that they provide tools to question and challenge the status quo, expose inequities, produce empowering counterstories, and draw people together to redress injustices.

Though social justice skills are needed now more than ever before, they are frequently dismissed by underfunded, overloaded employers who insist that workers be job-ready and immediately able to take on large caseloads with little or no training or support. Within the skill debate, "skills" are generally held up as something that students do not have and must acquire in order to be successful in the job market. In contrast, adult learning models assert that adult students bring social experience, skills, self-awareness, and personal histories to learning that can act as resources on which new learnings can be built and applied (Pappas, 2018). Adults also tend to be more strongly motivated toward socially relevant learning including critical social analysis in its many forms (Korr, Derwin, Greene, & Sokoloff, 2012). This suggests that social justice analysis and practice is an essential plank in fostering students' understanding and interpretation of their own experience in ways that generate more effective, empathetic, and equitable social work practice (Pappas, 2018).

Skills are frequently discussed as if they are timeless and can be separated from the context in which they are used and taught. This decontextualizing is ahistorical and acts as a conservative force because it holds back the idea that skills should be continually developed and refined in response to emerging and unmet needs, new knowledge, and changing social conditions.

Neoliberalism's emphasis on narrowly quantifiable outcomes also means that certain social work skills (such as open-ended relationship building, critical social analysis, advocacy, policy analysis, organizational change, counter-storying, and critical reflexivity) are marginalized within a debate that views skills exclusively as depoliticized, easily measured, and used in fast paced, increasingly short-term direct interventions with individuals, families, and groups. As Fran Waugh and I (2019) argue, "One of the main victims of this rationalization of practice has been the hallmark trust-based, dignity-enhancing, time-intensive relationships generally thought to form the impetus and means for change within social work endeavor" (p. 250). Similarly, Brown and MacDonald argue in chapter 1 of this volume that rather than quietly accepting neoliberal social work practices as valid and skill-based, anti-oppressive social workers need to critique

> the neoliberal, managerialized approaches of agencies, hospitals, and government, which increasingly emphasize biomedical, decontextualized, depoliticized, diagnostic, pathologizing, one-size-fits-all, standardized, "evidence-based," short-term quick strategies. While these practices pose as objective and neutral, they do not address inequity and oppression.

Failure to problematize and politicize the skills debate, and the larger political economy that benefits from inequity and marginalization, produces social work practice that deepens and extends neoliberalism in the lives of service users, communities, and social work organizations, rather than challenging it.

This critical clinical social work collection provides much-needed, far-reaching remedies to this separation of social justice and skill. Instead of staking out clinical work as a realm in which politics and power play no part, this volume starts from a recognition that clinical practice and clinical skills are practices of power and an arena that is replete with possibilities for social justice practice, as well as for oppressive practice. This volume draws on a frame that emphasizes (1) depathologizing the service user's experience, (2) the unpacking and restorying of dominant and unhelpful social stories, and (3) fostering counterstories that highlight diverse experience and individual and social resistance.

Countering the claim that critical practice is not applicable to most practice settings, the collection explores social justice practice in clinical practice, community practice, social and individual advocacy, social activism, political change strategies, and social policy development. It also includes valuable contributions on teaching clinical work and advancing critical clinical practice through research and scholarship. The authors cogently analyze the critical clinical approach in areas such as complex trauma, sexual violence, addiction, HIV, child welfare, palliative care, aged care work, community work, men's use of violence, chronic pain and (dis)Ability, the value of animal/human bonds in social work practice, as well as critical clinical practices with racialized populations, specifically Africentric, Indigenous, and postcolonial practices. Some of the most powerful skills explored in this collection reflect the intersectional analysis undergirding the specific skills presented, and the many ways that an anti-oppressive perspective opens the door to social work practice that is deeply and radically humanist. It is also refreshing that social analysis is recognized as a pivotal social work skill that overlaps and links with so many other central social work skills, such as sharing knowledge and power in collaborative practice, depathologizing experience, and unpacking and restorying experience and emotion.

The social problems facing service users and communities are complex and often deeply rooted, requiring strong and far-reaching interventions. Fortunately, this collection provides the crucial link between critical theory and practice that generates thick and nuanced social justice–engaged solutions to the difficult questions facing social workers and service users in neoliberal times. As such, this book is likely to become a classic, as well as a much-needed catalyst to further writing, research, and theory on the compelling theme of critical clinical social work.

Donna Baines

REFERENCES

Baines, D., & Waugh, F. (2019). Afterword: Resistance, white fragility and late neoliberalism. In D. Baines, B. Bennett, S. Goodwin, & M. Rawsthorne (Eds.), *Working across difference: Social work, social policy and social justice* (pp. 247–260). London: Macmillan International.

Brown, C. (2016). The constraints of neo-liberal new managerialism in social work education. *Canadian Review of Social Work, 33*(1), 115–123.

Canadian Association of Social Workers. (2019). *Code of ethics.* Retrieved from https://www.casw-acts.ca/sites/default/files/attachements/casw_code_of_ethics.pdf

Korr, J., Derwin, E. B., Greene, K., & Sokoloff, W. (2012). Transitioning an adult-serving university to a blended learning model. *Journal of Continuing Higher Education, 60*(1), 2–11.

Pappas, C. (2018). Seven top facts about the adult learning theory. *Instructional Design.* Retrieved from https://elearningindustry.com/6-top-facts-about-adult-learning-theory-every-educator-should-know.

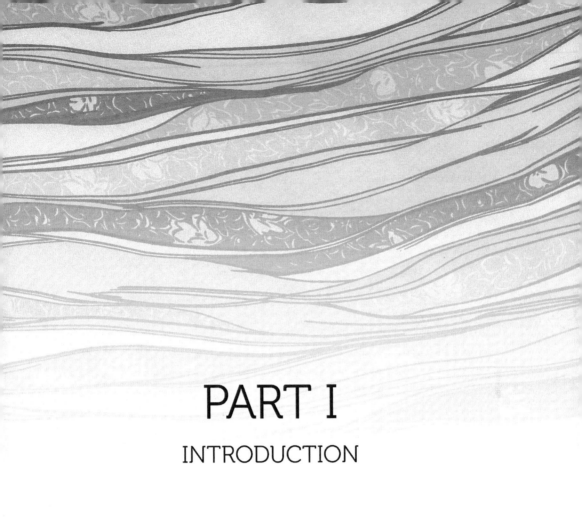

PART I

INTRODUCTION

INTRODUCTION

Critical Clinical Social Work: Counterstorying for Social Justice

Catrina Brown and Judy E. MacDonald

This book offers an original critical clinical approach to social work practice written by social work educators from the School of Social Work at Dalhousie University. Despite a long-standing history of anti-oppressive and social justice–based social work education and practice in Canadian social work, there has not been a substantial focus on the direct critical clinical application of these ideas. Since the 1970s, radical social work has tended to view clinical work as focusing on the individual and not contributing to social change, and aside from feminist, narrative, and empowerment-based practice, there has not been a significant focus on developing critical clinical approaches to practice.

In this book, we elaborate on critical clinical skills consistent with anti-oppressive and social justice paradigms of social work. These skills reflect post-modern critiques of central concepts such as power, knowledge, experience, self, emotion, and ethics, while recognizing the oppressive discursive and structural influences that shape people's lives. The neoliberal social and institutional context of social work practice today has demanded that social work education stress the development of stronger "clinical skills" (Brown, 2016). *Critical Clinical Social Work* focuses on integrating postmodern and critical frameworks, including feminist, narrative, antiracist, and postcolonial, with direct critical clinical practice. The critical clinical framework emphasizes non-pathologizing, discursive, contextual, and deconstructive narrative and collaborative strategies that aim to unpack dominant and unhelpful social stories through a variety of diverse and creative methods with a focus on counterviewing dominant problem stories and developing counterstories that participate in social resistance. In all of the chapters in this book, the writers emphasize the importance of unpacking clients' stories within the context of their history, experiences, and social location. The writers explore the impact of oppression, power, and dominant discourse in constraining and limiting people's voices and opportunities, and in often making it dangerous for people to tell their stories.

Within this book, the authors provide case histories and examples of direct critical clinical practice. Contributors tackle various substantive issues including coexisting mental health and addiction issues among women, working with complex trauma, men's use of violence, women's and girls' experiences of violence, unpacking pain through living with (dis)Ability, and the value of animal/human bonds in social work practice. Critical child welfare approaches are also explored, alongside working critically with aging populations within the context of palliative care. We explore intercultural, Africentric, and postcolonial practices, and practices that resist AIDS quarantine and treatment as prevention. Critical clinical work at Dalhousie University's School of Social Work Community Clinic is illustrated from the ground up. Finally, the book concludes with reflections on social resistance and transformation through counterstorying. The critical clinical approaches adopted move past abstract theoretical approaches or understandings of oppression and marginalization to specific and concrete clinical strategies for working with individuals, couples, families, and groups.

Key conceptual entry points to critical clinical social work practice are outlined to provide a foundation for this book. These include sharing of knowledge and power in collaborative practice; unpacking and restorying experience and emotion; depathologization and the social and historical contextualization of individuals' struggles; non-essentialized approaches to diverse and intersectional identities and the concept of self, challenging dominant and oppressive social discourses that reinforce negative identity conclusions; and creating counterstories that resist taken-for-granted, hegemonic, and unhelpful assumptions that often involve blaming, pathologization, and marginalization. Counterstories reflect preferred identities, alongside an integrated analysis of how discursive and institutional practices and structural systems of power and oppression are often co-implicated in people's struggles.

The emphasis and ethical stance in critical clinical practice involves equalizing power in the therapeutic context by stressing safety, client power and control over their own choices, and transparency throughout the work. This volume outlines an approach to addressing issues of power in therapeutic conversations, exploring how power and resistance play out in day-to-day life and in the problem stories people tell about themselves. We explore notions of the preferred self rather than the "real self." Clients' stories are contextualized and this collaborative approach emphasizes clients' strengths and agency alongside their vulnerability, marginalization, and pain. A central element of critical clinical practice involves the deconstruction of oppressive dominant social discourse, including dominant mental health and addiction discourse and others associated with pathologizing and medicalizing daily life and individual struggle. Critical clinical social work then involves a deconstruction of how problems have emerged from social contexts such as trauma, oppression, exclusion, colonization, discrimination, and marginalization, what realities and identities people prefer, and the restorying or creation of alternative stories of their identities and their lives. These ideas are discussed in greater depth in chapter 1, which orients the reader to the integration of critical conceptual and clinical practice within a critical clinical practice approach advanced at the School of Social Work. This chapter brings a clear focus to the book, acting as a conceptual frame from which to launch the chapters that follow.

In this book we provide an investigation and critical analysis of substantive areas within critical clinical practice (e.g., trauma, sexual violence, addiction, HIV, child welfare, palliative care, community work). We explore the linguistic, discursive, and narrative challenge(s) faced within and yet necessary to critical clinical practice, including hegemonic discourse, the absence of helpful linguistic framings of experience, epistemic gaps, and dangers in speech. We demonstrate how practice strategies can create more helpful stories of experience and contribute to counterstories and social resistance. We explore challenges to using a critical clinical approach such as the predominance of a biomedical model for practice, agency policies, and the limits of institutional practice and how they are addressed. The book advocates a move away from the medicalization of daily life and social problems; this can be seen, for instance, in the exploration of how the "borderline" diagnosis can often be counterstoried as a reflection of complex trauma, especially among women. We analyze the overall implications of a critical clinical approach in a substantive area of practice across dimensions of social work that may include social advocacy and activism, political change, community-based practice, enhancing clinical practice, policy development, teaching clinical work, and advancing critical clinical practice through research and scholarship. The concluding chapter provides analytic coherence across the preceding chapters and highlights implications for individual and social change efforts through practices of resistance through counterstorying for social justice.

OVERVIEW OF THE BOOK

This book begins by providing an overall conceptual lens for looking at critical clinical practice and ethical practice. In chapter 1, Catrina Brown elaborates on critical clinical social work principles and skills that involve the interpretation and integration of anti-oppressive and social justice paradigms of social work into direct practice, including feminist, queer, Africentric, postcolonial, and critical (dis)Ability. The integration of critical skills also reflects postmodern critiques of central concepts related to practice such as power, knowledge, experience, self, emotion, and ethics, while recognizing the oppressive discursive and structural influences that shape people's lives. Principles for critical clinical practice are offered.

Merlinda Weinberg offers an important discussion of ethics for critical clinical practice in chapter 2. Ethics in the field of social work practice has tended to focus on the dyad between worker and client, using a top-down decision-making model that emphasizes codes of ethics, universal principles, and rule following. However, this approach is insufficient to meet the needs of critical clinical ethics in practice. Weinberg makes a case for the inadequacy of a universalistic approach (Walker, 1998) as the primary vehicle for ethical deliberation and action. Ethics is understood as part of everyday clinical practice, in both the effort that practitioners make to see the salient aspects of ethics in their practice and to work toward doing their best as social workers (Banks, 2011), requiring a more situated approach to ethics. This chapter provides a framework for what constitutes good clinical practice in the realm of ethics by highlighting the need to politicize and bring in the contextual nature of clinical work. Social work is currently being practised in an era of neoliberalism (Mudge, 2008) and managerialism (Clarke, 2004; Rogowski, 2011); this chapter outlines the implications of these trends and how they contribute to the difficulty of acting ethically. Weinberg argues that since all practice is political and, consequently, all ethical decisions are as well, practices that focus on social justice, power dynamics, and inequities in society are required for sound critical clinical practice. Included in the discussion is an elaboration of structural paradoxes (Weinberg, 2016) and complexity of social work practice that result in ambiguity.

Part II of this book, "Critical Clinical Practice: Mental Health, Trauma, and Social Justice," focuses on trauma and its aftermath. Through engaging feminist narrative therapy as a form of critical clinical practice, Catrina Brown in chapter 3 illustrates the importance of the therapeutic relationship in complex trauma work, specifically focusing on restorying the "borderline" diagnosis many women receive who have complex trauma histories. These women are too often subsequently psychiatrized, with little attention to the impact that trauma has had on their lives. Here, Brown outlines the contribution that postmodern epistemology and critique can offer the direct critical clinical practice of social work. Through adopting a feminist narrative lens, she systematically illustrates critically based direct practice with a focus on gender and mental health coun-selling, drawing on a case example from the substantive practice areas of trauma and mental health diagnosis. As stories emerge in social, cultural, political, and historical contexts, they can challenge or reify harmful and unhelpful ideas. A feminist narrative lens offers a critical clinical approach to challenge the as-sumptions of this diagnosis and refocus therapeutic conversations on unpacking the meaning and construction of women's stories of trauma, the influence of the stories on their lives, and the creation of more helpful counterstories. The con-straints and dangers of telling a trauma story, dominant trauma discourses, and the importance of double listening are highlighted.

In chapter 4, Marion Brown explores direct practice with girls who have experienced sexualized violence. She argues that sexualized violence is a central organizing experience of teenaged girls, on the level of a public health concern in Canada. Prevailing therapeutic approaches tend to focus on the internalized effects of the violence, with emphasis on individualized coping strategies. While attention to the subjective experience is of course required, such approaches are typically depoliticized and decontextualized, thus reinscribing conventional scripts of binary gender power dynamics and leaving intact the cultural prac-tices that normalize male sexual violence. This is an injustice to all girls, both current and future, and dismisses a clear opportunity to disrupt the discourses that perpetuate rape culture. Therapeutic conversations are distinctly politicized processes because of their ability to leave dominant social processes and practices in place or to interrupt them by bringing them into discussion. Critical clinical approaches integrate the internal, personal experience within a structural, sys-temic, socio-political analysis, recognizing that there is no self outside the social. Brown articulates specific approaches to working with the impacts and effects of experiencing sexualized violence, while simultaneously locating the experi-ence within collective cultural practices that excuse, perpetuate, and normalize a social context of sexualized violence. Case examples with excerpts of therapeutic conversations illustrate the principles and practices of critical clinical approaches and provide practical options for practitioner use.

In chapter 5, Tod Augusta-Scott explores the ways in which a history of trauma and violence is often present among men who use violence. For men to take responsibility to stop their violence against female partners and repair the effects of what they have done, their experiences of both trauma and dominant masculinity need to be addressed. The aftermath of trauma and dominant mas-culinity serve to reinforce each other. To engage in these conversations, this approach moves beyond the victim/perpetrator binary. Augusta-Scott explores ways to acknowledge the pain, suffering, and vulnerability of men who have themselves been victimized, while also holding them accountable and responsible for their unhelpful choices in using violence against others. This approach embraces the importance of attending to men's experiences of being harmed and harming others, experiences of being oppressed and oppressing others, in a manner that helps men deal with their trauma history, which may not only lead to them taking greater responsibility for their choices, but also to understanding their impact. Through exploring their own trauma histories, men may therefore develop a stronger empathy for those they have hurt. In addition, this chapter illustrates work with men's voluntary responses to the involuntary effects of past trauma in the present.

Drawing on the authors' backgrounds in social work and anthropology, in chapter 6 Catherine Bryan and Tessa Barrett explore the potential of critical clinical social work practice informed by ethnographic inquiry in working with veterans. Together, these two fields highlight the possibilities for social work's engagement with marginalized populations and its ongoing commitment to social justice. The ethnographic project of this chapter is to offer insight into the social through an in-depth exploration of the individual, read through and against theory. In a manner of speaking, this is also the project of social work, be it in the context of teaching, research, front-line work, or clinical practice. Bryan and Barrett explore alternative ways of working with the trauma that veterans experience.

In chapter 7, Nancy Ross and Jean Morrison challenge the neoliberal interpretation of substance use problems experienced by girls and women from an individualistic, shame-based perspective. Stigma and shame have crafted the gendered experience, as girls and women are too often silenced by the discourse of individualized blame. Alcohol and pharmaceutical corporations, supported within a capitalist system, target girls and women with the aim of exploiting vulnerability and marginalization. In a counter-response, Ross and Morrison highlight the ways in which a critical clinical practitioner can work alongside this population to create a sense of "safety," "belonging," and "voice." These three metaphors signify processes of healing from oppression, trauma, and substance use problems. The authors share the experiences of women who participated in an educational film on substance use problems entitled *Women of Substance*, where space was created for the women's stories to come forward. Through this experience, the women found their voices and were able to contribute to a societal shift in how substance use problems are understood through a gendered lens. The medicalized and pharmaceutical lens crafted in the image of a young adult male was disrupted, creating space for the distinct experiences of girls and women. Ross and Morrison illustrate how a feminist critical perspective influences a critical clinical approach to assisting girls and women in reauthoring their identity.

Cassandra Hanrahan and Darlene Chalmers write in chapter 8 about the value of incorporating animals into social work, particularly in the areas of mental health and trauma. They offer a unique and important examination of the critical clinical dimensions of incorporating animals into social work, ranging from the application of specialized animal-assisted interventions to the minimum preparedness of knowing about useful community resources. Given all the ways in which companion animals in particular figure into the lives of so many— within client populations and among practitioners—Hanrahan and Chalmers address the absence of animals in mainstream social work theory and practice. For many, companion animals are members of family systems, and for some, they are significant others. They argue that the multi-faceted benefits of positive human-animal interactions to mental and physiological health—whether as a result of therapeutic interventions with specified goals and guided by a health or para-health professional or simply companionship—and the link between animal abuse and other forms of violence (including domestic, child, and elder abuse) are increasingly scientifically documented and supported. Hanrahan and Chalmers suggest social work must refocus its vision and broaden its mission to include non-human animals not as a special interest add-on, but as a structural imperative involving the pivotal concepts of human privilege, interspecies relationality, environmental sustainability, peaceful coexistence, and compassionate conservation.

Taken together, the chapters in part II elaborate on the effects of trauma on people's lives without pathologizing or labelling the creative ways that people cope. A critical clinical approach recognizes the many ways in which trauma is experienced, and how ways of coping may be both creative and helpful, while sometimes also having harmful effects. The use of violence is seen as political and discursive in a patriarchal, heterosexist, classed, and racialized world. Trauma work must move beyond being "informed" to deliberate approaches to providing critical clinical trauma practice that are not only collaborative, but also emphasize the client's power, safety, and control throughout the process.

Part III of the book centres on critical social welfare and institutional practices. It focuses on social welfare practices, including work with immigrant and refugee families and child welfare workers, mother and child welfare assessment, and the impact of regression state policy on those living with HIV/AIDS.

In chapter 9, Ifeyinwa Mbakogu argues that social work is a contested profession with positive and negative connotations for marginalized populations. Critical social workers are aware of the "power" social workers have in determining the nature and extent of social services for potential clients. Service users are also aware of the inherent "power" of social workers in improving their situations; however, marginalized persons are often reluctant to access social services or seek the services of social workers. Mbakogu notes that while community workers in marginalized communities emphasize the high need for social services within their communities, there is an unmatched low number of people accessing these services. She posits that this may be related to service users' perception of the manner in which care is provided, the absence of culturally appropriate approaches, and the likely stigma (for users and family members) attached to accessing care in some social service agencies. Rooted in postcolonial theorizing about the unmasking of the voices and experiential knowledge of the client, this chapter builds from a case study that recognizes the conflict between social work interventions and the client's perspective. The chapter advocates a balance within the client and social worker relationship that fosters a respectful engagement with the client to unmask the voiced and unvoiced within a judicious and holistic approach that includes rather than excludes, respects rather than undermines, the client and their family network.

Chapter 10, by Sara Torres, Monique Nutter, Donna-Mae Ford, Yvonne Chiu, and Kathi Campbell, illustrates the role of cultural brokers as intermediaries between immigrant and refugee families and child welfare workers in Edmonton, Canada. The authors emphasize the importance of critical intercultural communication and awareness to preventing entry and/or re-entry of children and youth into state care. Children from socially marginalized and oppressed groups have historically been overrepresented in child welfare settings and among children and youth in care. Racism and systemic discrimination have been shown to be factors in this overrepresentation. Many immigrant and refugee families experience high levels of stress and vulnerability, often resulting from pre-migration factors and post-migration conditions such as poverty, and challenges in navigating new social and cultural contexts, potentially heightening the risk of child welfare involvement. Through a practice-based and theory-informed culturally responsive collaborative family intervention program, they explore how cultural brokers negotiate the relationship between immigrant and refugee families and child welfare workers. Cultural brokers share evolving knowledge and skills by facilitating critical intercultural communication between child welfare staff and immigrant and refugee families. The skills involved include cultural assessment, cultural mediation, and conflict resolution, as well as matching of care and community resources. Cultural brokers engage the broader community and mobilize family and community strengths and resilience factors, as well as foster critical interculturally aware, people-centred (and less intrusive) child intervention practice.

Using a case example, in chapter 11, Marjorie Johnstone explores through the lens of epistemic injustice the risk assessment process used by Family Youth and Child Services of Muskoka when it removed Tammy Whiteman's daughters from her home (Fricker, 2007). In 2008, Whiteman's daughters were removed because of serious concerns about mental health and child rearing. Hair-strand drug testing performed by the Motherisk lab at Toronto's SickKids Hospital had produced results indicating that Tammy was using large amounts of alcohol. Her protestations that this was incorrect went unheard and she was told that she was in denial and must attend counselling. Several years later, she and her lawyer set up a house-arrest monitor with technology that could measure alcohol use and after 90 days she had the hair-strand drug test repeated. This again resulted in a finding of heavy alcohol use. It was then discovered that the test was actually measuring the alcohol content in her hairspray. In this chapter, Johnstone contributes useful concepts for considering power, inequity, and injustice in human interactions. She postulates that epistemic injustice is a fundamental wrong done to someone specifically in their capacity as a knower/subject of knowledge. Johnstone builds on Fricker's (2007) concepts of testimonial injustice and epistemic objectification to analyze the child protection assessment process used in this case example and explores how we can enrich and enhance our practice by incorporating the clinical implications of Fricker's work into our practice.

In chapter 12, Eli Manning and MT O'Shaughnessy reflect on the legislative history of AIDS quarantine in British Columbia. British Columbia is the only Canadian province that mandates treatment as prevention, calling for "universal" HIV testing, immediate treatment initiation for those who test positive, and lifelong treatment adherence to prevent HIV transmission. The authors explore the implications in protecting the public from HIV infection and how critical clinical social work can intervene. They approach these questions from different angles—one as a person living with HIV, the other as an activist and researcher. They share similar concerns regarding the ethical, political, and material consequences for people living with HIV in British Columbia under the rule of treatment as prevention. Archival research highlights not only the debates of Bill 34, but also exposes the present-day legislative and regulatory possibilities that could be mobilized under treatment as prevention. Based on lived experience, a first-hand account of treatment as prevention reveals the historical similarities between today's promotion of this HIV intervention and the 1987 calls for AIDS quarantine. Manning and O'Shaughnessy discuss how the lives of people living with HIV are impacted by the hyper-medicalization and neoliberalization of HIV prevention, the rollback of patient privacy rights, extensive and mandatory viral surveillance, intensified criminalization of HIV tied to viral load, the use of directly observed therapy for those with less than optimal adherence, and the deregulation of public health interventions. They question the ethics and politics invested in coercive HIV interventions used for the betterment of public health and propose how critical clinical social work can mediate the negative aspects of treatment as prevention throughout Canada.

Part IV, "Working in the Context of Marginalization, Oppression, and Diversity," explores critical clinical approaches related to culturally appropriate practice. In chapter 13, Wanda Thomas Bernard, Josephine Etowa, and Barbara Clow present the findings of a three-year study relating to spirituality and its implications for social work practice. They explored the strategies African Canadian women in rural Nova Scotia use to manage their health, given the challenges they face with regard to the accessibility of health care. The study revealed how an Africentric conception of spirituality is a fundamental component of Black women's lived experience. There are many examples in the literature of the role that spirituality plays as a resource for the health and well-being of African Canadian people (Este & Bernard, 2006; Beagan, Etowa, & Bernard, 2012). In this chapter, the women's narratives reveal that Black women often turn to a spiritual being for guidance, healing, and support. The women's descriptions highlight that spirituality can be considered a lifestyle or attitude. They view prayer as an action that is an outcome of a spiritual attitude. For some, spirituality is a strategy for dealing with their grief, while for others it is a way of coping with everyday stress, including the stress of racism. The strong association between spiritual care, health, and well-being is examined in the context of ways in which spirituality, as an aspect of critical clinical practice, can be used as a vital resource for social work practice in African Canadian communities. This chapter draws on case examples to illustrate Africentric critical clinical social work.

In chapter 14, Gail Baikie examines Indigenous social work praxis in between worldviews and its significance for critical clinical social work practice. Through her research, which explores how Indigenous social work praxes emerge at the interstices—or borderlands—of Indigenous and Euro-Western worldviews, the author challenges epistemic power of dominant knowledge systems and its impact on Indigenous clients and social workers. It is argued that because of the colonization process, many Indigenous people no longer see the strength of their Indigenous knowledge, suggesting minds have also been colonized. Gail Baikie developed the decolonizing critical reflection research method to enable participants to sort through the Indigenous and colonizing worldview influences on their professional praxis. This method can be adapted for direct critical clinical practice with clients. Critical reflection can enable mindful actions that interrupt and disrupt colonizing social relations and structures. She explores an Indigenist and decolonizing methodology for investigating the borderlands between Indigenous and Euro-Western worldviews, and suggests that this understanding of the borderland can inform critical clinical practice.

Judy MacDonald in chapter 15 writes about counterbalancing life with chronic pain through storying women's experiences of (dis)Ability. She argues that living with chronic pain leaves one struggling for "normalcy," trying to make sense of the fundamental operations of one's body and the meaning of suffering, while at the same time navigating the social construction of wellness (Jackson, 2002; MacDonald, 2008; Wendell, 1996). The medical model of (dis)Ability has overshadowed pain interventions to the point that sufferers are being negatively impacted (Greenhalgh, 2001). MacDonald argues that women sufferers' pain stories are often not believed or minimized and are pathologized by health professionals who question what they gain through their pain experience. Social workers and other health professionals need to listen to sufferers' stories and find ways to learn from them, deriving insight from sufferer knowledges in order to more effectively attend to their health care needs. MacDonald draws upon her postmodern narrative research study, which invited women in the helping professions who were living with chronic pain to share their stories. Within these storylines, richness of the human spirit is revealed as women find ways to negotiate ableist social structures and barriers. Living with chronic pain is emotionally exhausting, as the sufferer draws on the depth of their strength to get through an ordinary day. Yet within their struggle, balance is found as they creatively manoeuvre their impairments and find a negotiated space of coping. The focus of this chapter is assisting pain sufferers to find ways to counterbalance impacts of impairment with living life.

The starting point for chapter 16, by Joan Harbison and Donna Pettipas, is an examination of how older people's voices are constrained and their well-being endangered by the many manifestations of an embedded, profound, and increasingly complicated societal ageism present within many cultural contexts. The stage designated as old age includes the greatest diversity of all age groups. The culture, education, interests, political views, and financial situations of those at this stage vary widely, as do their physical and mental abilities. Notwithstanding these diverse characteristics, for the most part the dominant discourse on aging focuses on a narrow biomedical decline and decay model, one in which aging is seen as a "problem to be treated," by medical or other means. Older individuals' contributions in whatever form and context are rarely sought and when made remain unacknowledged and hence invisible. This is increasingly true even within many cultural groups where older people have traditionally been revered. Thus, it has become possible to view older people as a burden at every level of society including the political-economic, socio-medical, and the familial (Phillipson, 2013). Further, they have become not just objects of a medical gaze focused on decline and decay, but have been exhorted to address this decline in particular ways, notably through tenets that constitute "successful aging." Within this societal and institutional context those in later life have internalized messages that lay siege to their opportunities for meaningful lives and to their individual sense of positive self-worth. Harbison and Pettipas suggest that the challenge to clinicians working with older people is to join with them in overcoming their internalized ageism and their wariness of the motivations of the helper as "other" and "othering," and hence to support the use of their own voices to express and validate their needs and wants. In this chapter, they use case examples and materials to illustrate how critical clinical interventions can be crafted in various contexts to not only support the (re)emergence of older people's voices, but also to provide them with tools and strategies to meet the challenges of being old in today's society.

In part V, the concluding section of the book, Jeff Karabanow, Sarah Oulton, Meagen Bowers, and Cyndi Hall describe in chapter 17 the history and practices of the Social Work Community Clinic, which opened its doors in June 2014, in a donated space in a local parish hall. The Community Clinic provides case management and supportive counselling for marginalized community members, simultaneously supplementing existing resources in Halifax while acting as a site for community development and student skill-building. With very few resources initially, the clinic now has its own rented space, serves a caseload of over 300 marginalized community members, and has provided field placement experiences for social work, pharmacy, and occupational therapy students. The clinic is an original project addressing service provision gaps, while responding to employment trends calling for increases in university-level theory/practice experiential education. The chapter highlights the steps taken to create and develop the clinic with a social justice/anti-oppressive foundation, and the practice teaching approaches used with students. Experiential education at the clinic is focused on supporting students to make connections between theory and practice while embracing interdisciplinary learning and collaboration. This chapter describes how the community clinical practitioners integrate an interprofessional and community-university partnership culture in their day-to-day work with marginalized populations. Through case vignettes, this chapter demonstrates social justice through the politicization of individual and societal problems through critical clinical practice when working with some of the most vulnerable groups in the community.

In the book's conclusion, Catrina Brown and Judy MacDonald synthesize the authors' approaches and argue how critical clinical therapeutic conversations can be forms of social resistance and transformation, contributing to social justice through counterstorying the influence of unhelpful and oppressive social discourses. We review how, taken together, the contributors address the impact of dominant discourses on people's lives and demonstrate practices that resist them through the creation of counterstories. In these concluding remarks, we illustrate how dominant discourses limit speech and often make voicing experiences dangerous. While recognizing the oppressive aspects of constrained speech, the authors collectively resist these practices of power by speaking beyond master narratives. In critical clinical social work practices, critical theories such as anti-oppressive, feminist, postcolonialist, postmodern, and social justice are integrated with direct critical clinical practice. Historical and theoretical anchors of anti-oppressive social work theory and practice extend across social movements, community organizing, welfare rights, organizational change, unionization, and decolonization (Baines, 2017). Critical clinical practice is committed to social activism and change through resisting and challenging colonial and neoliberal practices and their oppressive impact.

ACKNOWLEDGEMENTS

We would like to acknowledge and thank the many people the authors of this volume have worked with over the years for sharing their experiences, knowledge, and insights with us.

REFERENCES

Baines, D. (2017). *Doing anti-oppressive practice: Building transformative, politicized social work* (3rd ed.). Toronto: Fernwood.

Banks, S. (2011). Ethics in an age of austerity: Social work and the evolving new public management. *Journal of Social Intervention, 20*(2), 5–23.

Beagan, B., Etowa, J., & Bernard, W. T. (2012). "With God in our lives he gives us the strength to carry on." African Nova Scotian women, spirituality, and racism-related stress. *Mental Health, Religion, and Culture, 15*(2), 103–120.

Brown, C. (2016). The constraints of neo-liberal new managerialism in social work education. *Canadian Review of Social Work, 33*(1), 115–123.

Clarke, J. (2004). *Changing welfare, changing states: New directions in social policy.* London: Sage.

Este, D., & Bernard, W. T. (2006). Spirituality among African Nova Scotians: A key to survival in Canadian society. *Critical Social Work, 7*(1).

Fricker, M. (2007). *Epistemic injustice power and ethics of knowing.* Oxford: Oxford University Press.

Greenhalgh, S. (2001). *Under the medical gaze: Facts and fictions of chronic pain.* Berkeley: University of California Press.

Jackson, M. (2002). *Pain: The fifth vital sign.* Toronto: Random House Canada.

MacDonald, J. (2008). Anti-oppressive practices with chronic pain sufferers. *Social Work in Health Care, 47*(2), 135–156.

Mudge, S. L. (2008). The state of the art: What is neo-liberalism? *Socio-Economic Review, 6*, 703–731.

Phillipson, C. (2013). *Ageing.* Cambridge, UK: Polity Press.

Rogowski, S. (2011). Managers, managerialism and social work with children and families: The deformation of a profession? *Practice: Social Work in Action, 23*(3), 157–167.

Walker, M. U. (1998). *Moral understandings. A feminist study of ethics.* New York: Routledge.

Weinberg, M. (2016). *Paradoxes in social work practice: Mitigating ethical trespass.* New York: Routledge.

Wendell, S. (1996). *The rejected body: Feminist philosophical reflections on disability.* New York: Routledge.

CHAPTER 1

Critical Clinical Social Work: Theoretical and Practical Considerations

Catrina Brown

INTRODUCTION

In this chapter I will elaborate on a critical clinical social work approach that involves the interpretation and integration of anti-oppressive and social justice paradigms of social work into direct practice. Critical clinical practice involves a reflexive integration of critical theory and critical approaches to practice that interrupt dominant epistemology and discourses that currently shape therapeutic interventions and reinforce dominant social relations of power (Audet & Pare, 2018; C. Brown, 2003; C. Brown & Augusta-Scott, 2007; Chambon, Irving, & Epstein, 1999; Epstein, 1994; Foucault, 1988; Strong & Pare, 2003; Tseris, 2013). This is reflected in postmodern critiques of central concepts related to practice such as power, knowledge, experience, self, emotion, and ethics, while recognizing the oppressive discursive and structural influences that shape people's lives. For Jerome Bruner (1986, p. 144), narratives are "not only structures of meaning but structures of power as well." Within a critical clinical approach, a positioned counterviewing of problem-saturated stories makes possible a contextualized exploration of how these stories developed (C. Brown, 2017, 2018, 2019; Madigan, 2003). Through this counterviewing, counter-discourses and resistance can emerge that challenge these structures of meaning and power (Butler, 1993; Foucault, 1991). Critical clinical conversations can purposively disrupt the discursive mechanisms of power that often shape people's stories and negative identity conclusions.

CRITICAL CLINICAL

This is a social justice approach to social work practice that intentionally ensures that critical theory and understandings of problems or struggles people experience are reflected in the approach to therapeutic conversations. Feminist and narrative approaches are two well-developed examples of this approach. It is an approach that critiques labelling, diagnosis, and pathologization. Instead, the meaning of the problem is explored and the creativity of strategies people use to cope is acknowledged. Practitioners using a critical clinical approach explore how these problems emerged in a social context, how they make sense, and avoid an individualizing approach that places blame and emphasizes deficits and failures. A critical clinical approach is collaborative, recognizing that both clients and practitioners bring partial knowledge and agency to the conversation. The social work practitioner is aware that they have more institutional power and that the client is the one who is vulnerable; therefore, the client's power, control, and safety are central. All efforts are made to avoid retraumatizing and revictimizing clients (L. Brown, 1994; Burstow, 2003; Herman, 1992, 2015; Shaffer, 1987). Critical clinical practice is aware of the discursive aspect of people's lives and experiences and this is unpacked in therapeutic conversations. Through unpacking the discursive aspects of people's stories, practitioners explore the connections between power and knowledge (C. Brown, 2014a, 2014b, 2018). The social diversity of people's lives and oppressive experience are a focal point of the contextualization of the work.

COUNTER-DISCOURSES

In critical clinical social work practice, counter-discourses, counter-narratives or counterstories challenge dominant, hegemonic, and often oppressive constructions of social realities (McKenzie-Mohr & Lafrance, 2014). These counter-discourses can produce a different and preferred account or story. For Foucault (1973), discourses are social "practices that systematically form the objects of which they speak" (p. 49). White and Epston (1990, p. 19) state, "We are subject to power through the normalizing 'truths' that shape our lives and relationships." Thus, knowledge and power are joined through discourse (Foucault, 1980a). Critical clinical social work practice explores the way that dominant discourses shape the stories that people bring to therapeutic conversations, and by doing so, we are also unpacking power: "As stories are discursive, the living and telling of them are inseparable. We form or constitute our experiences as we speak of them, and as we speak of them, we experience them" (C. Brown & Augusta-Scott, 2007, p. xxi). We are therefore involved in a process of exploring how these discursive stories are put together, what they mean to the person, and if there is a counterstory or counter-discourse they would prefer.

COUNTERVIEWING

Counterviewing involves bringing a different perspective, lens, or interpretation to exploring a story. It takes into account the performances of self-surveillance where one is always aware of a potential audience. In this process, people's problems, which reflect self-criticisms and cultural expectations about who one "should" be, are explored. People have internalized conversations that often result in internalized negative storylines about how they measure up (Madigan, 2003, 2007). According to Madigan (2007) internalized conversations are a focal point for "pathways to change" in therapeutic conversations. Counterviewing questions unpack these internalized storylines by looking at what they mean, the history of their development, and alternative ways to interpret the problem. Counterviewing can unmask mechanisms of power at play often seen through efforts at self-management and self-discipline (C. Brown, 2014a). Counterviewing questions help to deconstruct the history and meaning of the problem story and explore possible preferred alternative stories.

Drawing significantly on feminist and narrative approaches within this chapter, I will explore how "experiences" as social narratives can be analyzed through discourse analysis. This approach unpacks how stories are historically, socially, and politically constructed and contextualized, rather than individualized. I adopt a non-pathologizing, anti-disease model approach that views people's stories, and ways of coping and surviving, as making sense even when they may be unhelpful to them in other ways. The chapter unpacks and challenges dominant discourses of, for instance, mental health, substance use, violence, trauma, and well-being. By unpacking and counterviewing negative identity conclusion and the dominant unhelpful discourses that sustain it, we can replace these with preferred alternative stories.

Many academics, social work educators, and researchers committed to social justice and social change have strong theoretical understandings of human suffering and oppression. The integration of critical theory and critical clinical practice, however, involves a deliberate process that is thoughtful and disciplined. While social work's theoretical and political strength often translates well into policy, research, and community development social work practice, it does not automatically translate into critically based clinical practice. Critical clinical practice in social work is reflected in Baines's statement, "Social work is not just a neutral caring profession, but an active political process" (2017, p. 7).

Indeed, as Baines (2017, p. 13) states, "There is never a one-to-one direct translation of theory into practice in any situation, and the rapidly changing, multi-level world of AOP [anti-oppressive practice] is no different." Critical clinical practice does require a strong theoretical foundation. Yet, social work often needs to clearly articulate what the integration of critical thinking and critical practice looks like, especially if we are to educate people to do this work. Many social justice critically based social workers and schools of social work have heard feedback from neoliberal social work agencies and government that our students need more clinical skills. While we are committed to offering critical clinical skills through a social justice lens, we are simultaneously committed to resisting the demands of neoliberalism on social work practice. We need to offer integrated critical theory and critical clinical practice to our students with a clear sense of neoliberalism's impact on the policies and institutional structures within which social workers practice. Indeed, this means critiquing the neoliberal, managerialized approaches of agencies, hospitals, and government, which increasingly emphasize biomedical, decontextualized, depoliticized, diagnostic, pathologizing, one-size-fits-all, standardized, "evidence-based," short-term quick strategies. While these practices pose as objective and neutral, they do not address inequity and oppression. As Baines and Waugh (2019, p. 250) argue, "One of the main victims of this rationalisation of practice has been the hallmark trust-based, dignity-enhancing, time-intensive relationships generally thought to form the impetus and means for change within social work endeavour." Arguably, accepting the neoliberal hegemonic discourses and larger political economy that shapes and demands them does not and cannot produce the best social work practice for our clients or society at large (Baines & Waugh, 2019; C. Brown, 2016). We need to be reflexive about which theoretical frameworks we rely on and what epistemologies our ideas reflect. We need to ask ourselves: Is my clinical practice consistent with anti-oppression and contributing to social justice? Critical clinical practice does not emerge simply because one is grounded in anti-oppressive, decolonizing, and social justice theory. We need to think about how these ideas are translated into intentional alternative practices.

Arguably, the most well-established and elaborated forms of critical clinical practice rooted in critical theory are empowerment/harm reduction–based feminist and narrative therapies. These approaches are rooted in social constructionism and understand that social work practice/therapy is always political. They are purposively on the side of social change and social justice. Rooted in radical critique and analysis, they offer alternative critical approaches to practice. Critical clinical practice can draw on these collaborative approaches, which emphasize clients' strengths and agency alongside their vulnerability, marginalization, and pain often related to trauma, oppression, and marginalization. The emphasis and ethical stance in critical clinical practice involves minimizing power differences in the social work practice context by stressing client safety, power, and control over their own choices, and transparency throughout the work. This chapter outlines an approach to addressing issues of power in therapeutic conversations, exploring how power and resistance play out in day-to-day life and in the internalized problem stories people tell about themselves. I begin with an overview of what feminist and narrative practice can offer critical clinical practice in social work. I then provide an elaboration of concepts central to critical clinical practice followed by a critique of dominant biomedical discourse. The chapter concludes with a brief illustration of counterviewing "body talk" (C. Brown, 2007b, 2007d, 2014a), followed by two appendices that list the epistemological positions and assumptions present in critical clinical practice.

SOCIAL CONSTRUCTIONISM

Social constructionism reflects the belief that human beings create their realities, and that these realities act back upon them. We are created by social life, and we create social life (Marx, 1978; Mead, 1977; Smith, 1999). We are not simply products, yet these socially created realities typically become taken for granted in day-to-day life and become part of what is seen to be normative. Indeed, dominant socially constructed reality becomes so taken for granted, we lose sight of its social creation, treating it as if it were natural. According to Berger and Luckmann (1967), what is defined as real, is real in its consequences. As social meaning and social life become normative and sedimented, they become naturalized, dehistoricized, and depoliticized. While some critics see social constructionism as a new form of determinism, we are reminded that there is always space to resist social realities, in part through contradictions and paradoxes (Baines & Waugh, 2019; Butler, 1993; Foucault, 1991; Pease, Goldingay, Hosken, & Nipperess, 2016). Similarly, in narrative therapy, the story metaphor suggests we create our stories and our stories create us. We do not create our stories by ourselves—they emerge within the context of the meaning available to us. The context of meaning is always social and does not exist separate from social life (C. Brown & Augusta-Scott, 2007). This is consistent with Butler's position (1993) that social life is not all "free play," as choice is always constrained. Foucault (1980a, 1980b) and White (1997) also observe that power is both constraining and constitutive or productive. Even the production of alternative knowledges and subjectivities does not escape power (White, 1997). Power is always present in its constraining and productive effects (Flaskas & Humphreys, 1993). The writing of new stories allows us to live by new preferred stories. The meaning-making process is social, and this is central to critical clinical practice. Here we can contest, challenge, and recreate alternative stories that allow for greater possibilities.

As you read this chapter, ask yourself the following questions:

1. What are the central concepts unpacked in this chapter and how does a counterviewing of them inform what critical clinical practice looks like?
2. How does counterviewing stories challenge oppression?
3. How are power and knowledge joined in dominant social discourses?
4. How does critical clinical social work approach the disease model and pathologization of people's struggles?
5. Why are collaborative conversations important to critical clinical practice?
6. Why is it important for a critical clinical practitioner to be positioned rather than trying to be neutral?
7. How is clinical work political?

INTEGRATING CRITICAL THEORY AND CRITICAL PRACTICE

Feminist Practice

In the early 1980s, I developed a feminist approach to working with a continuum of weight preoccupation and eating "disorders" at a community-based women's health clinic (see C. Brown, 1993a, 1993b; C. Brown & Jasper, 1993;

C. Brown & Zimberg, 1993). When I attended feminist workshops that had a strong feminist analysis, I was surprised to see that this analysis was often not translated directly into critical practice. While they often focused on the media and the pressure on women to be thin, the analysis did not extend to the suffering women were experiencing and the unhelpful, often coercive practices within the primarily hospital-dominated approach to service delivery. Nor did they typically acknowledge women's agency and efforts at resourcing their bodies as a way to establish a sense of control and power over their lives (C. Brown & Jasper, 1993; Gremillion, 2003). While as feminist therapists they adopted an empowerment and collaborative approach, they had not yet critiqued the dominant practices of weighing women and policing their eating behaviour and, in general, the medical surveillance and control of girls and women in eating disorder treatment centres. A feminist approach to working with women and their bodies begins with the idea that women must be in control of their own bodies; they need to be able to feel safe and in control, and to have choice (C. Brown, 1993b). This was an enormous gap and many years later, it still is in most biomedically based treatment centres. This story is illustrative of the idea that radical critique or analysis in and of itself is not enough when we are engaged in critical clinical practice with clients. We also need intentional practices that reflect radical critiques and that provide consistent alternative approaches.

Beginning in the late 1970s, feminist approaches to therapy began to avoid the medicalization of women's experiences and struggles and to situate these struggles within the context of their lives (C. Brown, 2019). The "personal is political" is a phrase associated with the women's movement of that time, as feminists asserted that women's personal lives and experiences were always political in patriarchal society (Burstow, 2003; Carrington, 2016; Levine, 1982). Approaches to practice were centred on the meaning of women's experiences in the context of their lives. Women's voices were emphasized and encouraged, and dominant "expert" pathologizing approaches were typically rejected (Burstow, 1992). Therapeutic approaches emphasized women's safety, power, and control in the work (C. Brown, 1993b). Coping strategies such as substance use were seen to make sense and harm-reduction strategies were often used (C. Brown, 2011; C. Brown & Stewart, 2005, 2007, 2008; Burstow, 2003). In addition to critiques of the medicalization of women's lives through, for instance, psychiatrization, was the recognition and politicization of sexualized violence and trauma against women including interpersonal violence, rape, incest, and sexual abuse (C. Brown, 2018). Feminist approaches to practice emerged as ways to acknowledge violence against women and to avoid retraumatizing or revictimizing women. What is now referred to popularly as "trauma-informed practice," due, in no short measure, to the early trauma work of feminist therapy, has been largely depoliticized. Indeed, to this day, feminist approaches to working with trauma remain the most politicized theoretical and practice approaches.

Alongside fighting for the right to control our own bodies through reproductive choice, access to birth control and abortion, and the right to control birthing practices, the women's movement fought for changes in law, creating the rape shield law, equal property rights, and marriage and family law changes around divorce and child custody. Feminist approaches challenged dominant social discourses, and over time had some impact on producing counter-discourses that could be seen at least in part through changes in law. These political actions drew from both feminist and Marxist social critique and visions for a more just society.

Importantly, while these issues impacted all women, women who lived in poverty, and/or were racialized, living with a (dis)Ability, and/or queer identified began to insist that their voices and experiences must be more central to the conversation. While all of these issues were women's issues, the focus shifted away from common and overlapping interests to acknowledging, valuing, and centring differences among women. Intersectionality, now emphasized in feminist work, stresses overlapping oppressive identities in women's experiences (Bowles, 2012; Marecek, 2016; Morrow & Weisser, 2012), at least in part as an important challenge to the false universalizing of women and in recognition of women's diversity. Feminist writing on working with those who experienced incest and abuse continues to be the foundation of the trauma work done today and was importantly extended to address the complexity of difference and diversity among women (see L. Brown, 1994; Brown & Root, 1990; Comas-Diaz & Green, 1994; Goodman et al., 2004).

INTERSECTIONALITY

Intersectionality theory was developed by Crenshaw (1989) and Hill Collins (1990, 2019), highlighting the fluidity and complexity of social categories of inequality, exclusion, and oppression. Crenshaw focused our attention on the "crossroads of multiple oppressions" (Marecek, 2016, p. 177). Marecek emphasizes that "intersectionality theory focuses on the intersecting categories upon which such systems are built. In short, people are not intersectional, social categorizations are" (2016, p. 177). According to Marecek, structural social categories "mark people's position in hierarchical social structures. People inhabit such social categories, which together constitute the matrix of privilege and oppression that structures social life" (p. 178). Intersectional theory then centres on exploring and challenging overlapping social categories and hierarchical structures that serve to maintain relations of oppression and domination. Drawing on McCall (2005), I am adopting a deconstructive and critical approach to complex intersectionality and social categories (anti-categorical) at the same time that I am strategically taking up the interrelatedness of the social impact of categories such as race, gender, age, sexual orientation, poverty, and (dis)Ability (intercategorical).

POSTMODERNISM

Postmodernism offers a critique of modernism, abandoning its notion that we can attain "pure" or "absolute truth" through science or inquiry. It rejects modernism's belief in objectivity, or the idea of one knowable universal truth. It further critiques assumptions about how it is we know what we know, exposing objectivity as a fiction (Flax, 1990). Postmodernism challenges the "totalization" of dominant truth claims. Postmodernism, or poststructuralism, calls into question dominant taken-for-granted truth claims or master narratives, often arguing that knowledge and power are co-implicated (C. Brown, 2007a; Nicholson, 1990; Butler & Scott, 1992). Normative day-to-day assumptions, or taken-for-granted realities, operate as practices of power. In Foucault's (1995, p. 45) view, "truth is no doubt a form of power." What is taken up as knowledge is partial, multiple, perspectival, and fluid. As Bordo (1993) states, we cannot be in all places at all times, or speak from all vantage points. Haraway (1988) notes that in an effort to avoid absolutism, we can fall into a relativist stance, one that is not positioned. Both totalization and relativism, she argues, are a way of "being nowhere while claiming to be everywhere" (p. 584). Social justice work is, however, positioned on the side of social critique and transformation (C. Brown, 2012). All knowledge is interpretive and there are always alternative competing accounts. Therefore, "knowledge is never point-of-viewless" (J. Bruner, 1991, p. 3). Postmodernism takes apart a number of central concepts relevant to social work, including the self, experience, knowledge, and power, exploring ways that these concepts can reify power. It suggests that the reliance on either/or binary constructions of power is very limiting and tends to organize dominant truth claims (e.g., body/mind, individual/social, emotion/thinking, man/woman, Black/White). A both/and position allows for more complexity and nuance in our interpretation of social life. It further critiques the reliance on socially constructed and essentialist social categories that tend to reflect and reinforce dominant social relations of power. Essentialist practices presume that the creation of social categories is a reflection of truth and is natural, pregiven, and relatively unchangeable (C. Brown, 2012). Critical clinical approaches to social work practice are likely to adopt the position that there is no stable, fixed, or essential self or identity, as these are seen to emerge within cultural and relational practices.

With the influence of postmodernism, all social categories faced ongoing interrogation, and were seen to be sites for social change and social action as well as reflections of dominant social relations of power (Nicholson, 1990). We see this today in the shift in gender non-conforming, non-binary, trans, and queer focused theory, which translates into practices that move away from heteronormativity and binary constructions of gender and sexuality (Duong, 2012; Singh, 2016). Although categories may have been unpacked, they are still needed for political purposes. The social categories of race and gender, for instance, have been foundational for organizing social change, as places from which to speak and take action. Yet, most marginalized groups have been variously involved in both rejecting and accepting aspects of social categories (Alcoff, 1988; C. Brown, 1994, 2012; hooks, 1990). Over time, critiques have become more nuanced and are constantly changing. All this said, very specific practice strategies developed within feminist therapy or feminist practice with a growing attention to diversity.

Narrative Practice

Narrative therapy emerged in the 1980s through the work of Michael White and David Epston (1990), which in many ways was a brilliant clinical integration and application of Michel Foucault's work. Drawing on the metaphor of the story or narrative, they emphasized that we live storied lives, and that these stories are socially constructed and political. People make sense of their lives through stories: this is a meaning-making process. In this process, stories do not simply reflect our lives, they constitute our lives (White & Epston, 1990).

Stories are transmitted largely through socially mediated language and social interaction within specific cultural and historical contexts. The meanings that we attach to these events are thus never singular, individual, or simply subjective, never outside the social, but have shared intersubjective meaning within the cultural nexus of power and knowledge. (C. Brown & Augusta-Scott, 2007, p. ix)

The stories that people tell about themselves and their lives usually invoke socially available, but often inadequate and limited social discourses. Critical social theorists have argued that knowledge and power are inseparable (Baines, 2017; Foucault, 1980a, 1980b; Haraway, 1988; Hick, Fook, & Pozzuto, 2005; Marx, 1978; Smith, 1990). Discourse is thus both social and political, and often reflects a joining of knowledge and power. As interpretations, stories often reflect thin or incomplete descriptions of experiences. Critical clinical practice is interested in the development of thicker descriptions, ones that explore disqualified aspects not told in dominant stories of the self. Drawing on Foucault, we can see how normalizing processes of self-surveillance regulate and manage who we think we should be and shape our thoughts and preferences (C. Brown, 2007b, 2007d, 2014b). As such, self-stories are flawed; they are not perfect accounts. Importantly, for Foucault, these normalizing processes of self are "techniques of power." Jerome Bruner (2002, p. 78) says,

A self-making narrative is something of a balancing act. It must, on the one hand, create a conviction of autonomy, that one has a will of one's own, a certain freedom of choice, a degree of possibility. But it also must relate the self to a world of others.... But the commitment to others that is implicit in relating oneself to others of course limits our autonomy. We seem virtually unable to live without both autonomy and commitment.

We are reminded that while knowledge and power are co-implicated, they are not simply reducible to each other. According to Tanesini (1999), knowledge is more than simply an instrument of power; they are said to "imply one another" (Redekop, 1995, p. 314). Discourse is described by Foucault (1973, p. 49) as putting into social circulation the conflation of knowledge and power; discourses are social "practices that systematically form the objects of which they speak." From the perspective that power and knowledge are co-implicated, my therapeutic stance is that "knowledge is never innocent and power is never simply constraining" (C. Brown, 2007b). Departing from modernist views of power,

Foucault (1980a, 1980b) maintains that power is both constraining/repressive and constitutive/productive. He states, "discourse can be both an instrument and effect of power, but also a hindrance, a stumbling-block, a point of resistance and a starting point for opposing strategy" (1980a, p. 101). Social life leaves space for counter-discourse and resistance (Butler, 1993; Foucault, 1991; Pease & Nipperess, 2016). In therapeutic conversations, this is helpful in challenging binary notions of "expert" knowledge or "truth," and the idea that one either has knowledge or does not, or one either has power or does not. This allows us to construct a collaborative approach where both the client and practitioner are partial knowers and neither is simply a product of power. As social beings we are both created by social life and creators of social life (Durkheim, 1966; Marx, 1978; Mead, 1977; Smith, 1990, 1999). The narrative process then centres clients as active subjects and agents in their own lives who can create counter-discourses or counter-narratives.

Yet, dominant social discourses and normalizing truths are often significant in shaping the stories that clients bring to therapeutic conversations. In this approach to clinical practice, one is, then, always unpacking or deconstructing how people's stories are put together or organized throughout their lives, and exploring the impact of their stories on their identities and well-being. Very often people squeeze their stories into discursive frameworks that do not offer a useful or helpful fit. From a narrative framework, people do not create their stories by themselves—there is no single author. Stories are always multiple, always social constructions, influenced by the surrounding culture, and have an enormous impact or influence on the constitution of people's identities. We can see this among women who are raped within the context of a rape culture. By this I mean that rape is in many ways simultaneously ignored, minimized, and normalized (Gavey, 2005; Gay, 2018; Keyser, 2019; Wunke, 2016). Within rape culture, rape is treated as "just sex" and often women are blamed by others and blame themselves when they are raped. The discursive context of rape makes it difficult for women to story their experiences of sexualized violence (C. Brown, 2013; McKenzie-Mohr & Lafrance, 2011); indeed, as Butler (1997) suggests, this discourse produces injurious speech.

When one's stories are forced into discursive structures that are sexist or racist, for instance, the subsequent story of oneself is, at least in part, likely to be injurious. So, storytelling is not straightforward, and it is not neutral. Narrative therapy draws on anthropology for its approach to stories of experience (E. Bruner, 1986a, 1986b; J. Bruner, 1986; Geertz, 1973, 1986). Taken together, a number of central approaches emerge that become key to critical clinical practice.

Both feminist and narrative approaches are examples of critical clinical practice. These politicized approaches are congruent, both acknowledging social constructionism, the politics of daily life and experience, the need for social change and offering ways to practice that advance social critique and change. While feminism can offer an intersectional gender critique, narrative approaches offer the metaphor of the story and how stories operate to organize people's lives and their experience of reality. Today, decolonization (Baikie, 2019; Baskin, 2011), (dis)Ability (Carter, Hanes, & MacDonald, 2012; MacDonald, 2000, 2008), and queer theory (Butler, 1993, 2000; Duong, 2012) have much to offer critical clinical practice. Like feminist and narrative theory, critical theory—including Marxist/feminist political economy, postcolonial, and queer theory—is invested in resisting harmful dominant discourse and the way that this discourse silences other accounts, shaping and maintaining marginalization, oppression, and unequal social power relations. These approaches, separately and together, recognize that people often internalize unhelpful dominant discourses or narratives as if they were inherently real or true and/or struggle to live within frameworks that do not fit. The story metaphor is very useful to critical clinical social work as we so often see our clients feeling hopeless and oppressed under the influence of these dominant discourses (e.g., gender, race, sexuality, ability, self-blame, health, addiction, mental illness, resiliency) and structural relations of power within neoliberal capitalism, patriarchy, and institutionalized racism.

The social categories of mental health and well-being need to be unpacked, as they significantly shape therapeutic discourse. As Audre Lorde (1984, p. 115) famously states, "we can never dismantle the master's house with the master's tools." We need to be aware that leaving intact dominant social discourses that reify social relations of power and oppression is not helpful if the intention is to address the social context of the problems people experience and if we really do want to resist and challenge the dominant and oppressive social relations that shape society.

CONCEPTUAL ENTRY POINTS

Key conceptual entry points to explore in critical clinical social work practice include sharing knowledge and power in collaborative practice; unpacking and re-storying experience and emotion; depathologization and social and historical contextualization of individuals' struggles; non-essentialized approaches to diverse and intersectional identities and the concept of self; challenging dominant and oppressive social discourses that reinforce negative identity conclusions;

counterviewing unhelpful stories; and creating counterstories that resist taken-for-granted, hegemonic, and unhelpful assumptions and marginalization and that reflect preferred identities, alongside the integration of analyses of how discursive and institutional practices and structural systems of power and oppression are often co-implicated in people's struggles. These ideas will be discussed as I move through this discussion. Thus, concurring with Smith's (1990) notion of conceptual practices of power and Lorde's (1984) argument that we must dismantle the masters' tools, if we wish to incite change, we must unpack central concepts like self, knowledge, experience, power, and difference (C. Brown, 2012).

Critical clinical social work critiques naturalistic or essentialist ideas of the self. This means critical clinical work is not looking for the discovery of the "real" or undiscovered self (C. Brown, 1994, 2012; Fuss, 1989; White, 2001). Instead, it views the self as socially constructed, political, and fluid, and correspondingly explores notions of a *preferred* self rather than "real self." Social processes of participating in normalizing practices in the ongoing construction of the self are seen to reflect modern mechanisms of social power (C. Brown, 2007b, 2007c; Foucault, 1980a). These normalizing practices are political, ensuring both constraint and conformity while appearing to solely reflect individuality and self-expression. We explore how subjects (identities) are socially constituted and deconstructed in our work. We are interested in avoiding reinscribing dominant discourses of "normalcy" in our practice and exploring resistance and alternative ways of being. We need to challenge and resist the essentialism and totalization of harmful dominant discourse with critical clinical conversations. These discursive practices often reinscribe ageism, racism, colonization, anti-Semitism, anti-Islamism, sexism, ableism, social class, heterosexism, transphobia, and xenophobia. People often essentialize and totalize themselves, as well as internalize dominant unhelpful stories, which often leads to profoundly painful, harmful, and constraining accounts of themselves and their lives.

Experience

Following postmodern thinking on experience, critical clinical work unpacks experience and emotions as central to people's stories. While respecting and centring clients' stories of experiences, these stories are externalized with the intention of understanding the effects of internalized problem stories and creating counterstories (Morgan, 2000). In this process of externalization, the individual's identity is separated from the problem. The disqualified aspects of people's lives that have been rendered invisible by dominant stories are also explored. Baikie (2019, this volume) describes this in her approach to decolonizing methods of critical reflexivity, which encourages making visible the valued aspects of experience that may be rendered invisible in the borderlands of practice. Similarly, in narrative therapy the known and familiar is unpacked, and the *absent but implicit* is made visible (White, 2000, 2007). Along with Scott (1992), I argue that experience "is at once an interpretation and in need of interpretation" (p. 38). We cannot take experience at face value or treat experience stories as simply individual as if they are outside the social (C. Brown, 2007d; Smith, 1990, 1999; White, 1989). Stories of experience often reflect and reify dominant social relations of power (C. Brown, 2012; Morgan, 2000; White, 1994).

Experience is a significant and valued concept for social workers and as such it needs to be interrogated. Taking from narrative approaches, critical clinical practice can explore how experiences are historically shaped and socially organized. Experiences are not neutral and never simply individual, as they emerge fully within social and political contexts (Smith, 1990). Our accounts or stories of experience draw on the social discourses available to us. This means we make meaning of our experiences, at least in part, through the meanings available to us. We often internalize meanings and ideas that may be injurious. And, given the constraining discourses available to story experience, people often struggle in telling their stories. Thus, in critical clinical work, like narrative work, we need to unpack stories and help to resist parts that are not helpful and explore what parts a person experiences as meaningful and helpful. We often need to create alternative *preferred stories* to live life by, rather than those of internalized dominant discourses (e.g., fatphobia, failure, gender, mental illness, addiction, racism, sexism, ableism, heteronormativity) and the limiting binary constructions these discourses often depend on (e.g., fat/thin, man/woman, gay/straight, Black/White, able/dis(Abled), powerful/powerless, healthy/unhealthy, strong/weak).

Knowledge

Post-positivist knowledge is seen as socially constructed, political, perspectival, and as only ever partial (Haraway, 1988). Critical clinical work is positioned on the side of social justice and social transformation and recognizes there is no one universal truth, no objective truth. Knowledge and power are reflected and reified in the production and performance of dominant social discourses. A central element of critical clinical practice is the deconstruction of oppressive dominant social discourses, including those associated with pathologizing and medical-izing daily life and individual struggle arising from social contexts of oppression and marginalization. According to Foucault (1980b, p. 93), "We are subjected to the production of truth through power and we cannot exercise power except through the production of truth."

The Self or Subject

Chambon (1999) reminds us that while Foucault's analysis of power and knowl-edge is very useful to social work, his work on the idea of *the subject* also of-fers a very significant contribution. She notes that the relationship between the self, power, and social work practices must be examined. Social mechanisms of power shape individuals and communities of people and, therefore, Foucault's analysis of power is not separate from his analysis of the person. Too often, the self is taken up as natural and pregiven, as something we individually create, improve, and celebrate in consumer society. The essentialized self is then taken up as outside of power. Yet, in our work with individuals and communities we can see the ways power and knowledge shape our sense of identity and self. The negative stories people tell about themselves invariably constrain them and dis-qualify alternative accounts.

Foucault recognizes that his intention to produce transformative knowledge *disturbs* and that this work is intended to disrupt what we assume to be true in an absolute sense, including notions of the self. Within critical clinical social work practice, like social justice–based theory, we need to "redefine and reorient what we do and what we know" (Chambon, 1999, p. 53). Therefore, this reflexivity is at the heart of critical clinical practice, shifting certainties, practices, and habits present in the stories people tell about themselves as they live their lives (Fook, 2016). According to Foucault (1995), it is important to see power as more than repressive, to acknowledge how it is also productive. It is thought that people do not want to see the ways that power enters our sense of self because it "requires humans to confront how power is implicit in our very subjectivity, that which people wish to honour and privilege as individual, private and outside the social" (C. Brown & Augusta-Scott, 2007, p. xxi). Practices of power are often centred in our self-surveillance and self-correction to norms and expectations. Indeed, the construction of self within culture necessarily involves self-regulation and self-discipline, especially within the neoliberal era of constraint, regulation, and control (C. Brown, 2007b, 2014a, 2016).

Collaborative Practice and Therapeutic Alliance

Collaborative practice recognizes that both the practitioner and client bring *partial* knowledge to the therapeutic conversation (C. Brown, 2007c, 2012; Brown & Augusta-Scott, 2018; Haraway, 1988). This approach avoids binary notions of the "expert," which arise from either authorizing and essentializing experience as if it were outside social construction and power, or seeing either the client or therapist as an expert knower. Each brings partial knowledge and is an active subject who contributes to the conversation. The therapist is understood to have more power by way of their institutional and professional roles and because the client is the one who is vulnerable in this context. However, the emphasis and ethical stance in critical clinical practice involves increasing shared power in the therapeutic context by stressing safety, client power, and control over their own choices, and transparency throughout the work. Within this collaborative approach, clients' stories are contextualized and their strengths and agency, alongside their vulnerability, marginalization, and pain, are emphasized. Taken together, the approach is one that encourages rather than shuts down possibilities for living a preferred life and identity.

CRITICAL NARRATIVES AND RESTORYING PROBLEM STORIES

Overall, "experience" narratives can be analyzed through discourse analysis. I explore both dominant and alternative narratives that reflect social critique and a commitment to social justice. Stories are, therefore, historically, socially, and politically contextualized, rather than individualized. A non-pathologizing, anti-disease model approach is adopted that sees people's stories and ways of coping as surviving, as making sense, even when they may also be unhelpful to them (C. Brown & Stewart, 2008).

McKenzie-Mohr and Lafrance (2011) describe the problem of telling stories without words as a form of "tightrope talk." Dominant stories often individualize and depoliticize. People often find there is a lack of language or frameworks to use to tell their stories within dominant cultures of meaning (Hare-Mustin, 1994). Fricker (2003) refers to this as epistemic injustice. People negotiate the telling of their stories, yet the stories often fail them. We need to unpack negative identity conclusion, rather than treating these conclusions as truth, and generate more positive identity conclusions through re-authoring conversations (White, 2001, 2004). Dominant discourse can be described as *injurious speech*.

Butler (1997, p. 137) suggests that "conversations involve injurious speech acts that reproduce horrible, paralyzing, and long-lasting negative effects on how individuals view themselves." It is, therefore, according to Madigan (2003), important to counterview injurious speech acts, to unpack and challenge unhelpful discourses such as self-surveillance/audience, illegitimacy, escalating fear, negative imagination, invidious comparison, internalized bickering, hopelessness, perfection, and paralyzing guilt.

Epistemological shifts in how we understand pain and suffering are needed. A move from only positivist/scientific or constructionist approaches (Ussher, 2005, 2010) to a material discursive approach allows for pain and suffering to be situated within the dual and necessarily intertwined context of people's lives and bodies. The material discursive "involves experiences grounded in the materiality of the body which continually, and reciprocally, feed back into people's experiences in the social context of their everyday lives" (Stoppard, 2000, p. 21).

NEOLIBERALISM

Neoliberalism reflects a small government approach, reducing the welfare state and its responsibilities. Instead, the individual is responsibilized, rather than the state, for social risks such as illness, unemployment, and poverty. This mechanism of power works by encouraging individual participation in their responsibility through focusing on self-care, self-improvement, and misleading notions of choice and resilience. Neoliberalism holds no responsibility for individuals while deploying these indirect techniques to control them. The technology of responsibilization overlaps with healthism, where individuals are held responsible for their health and well-being (Lemke, 2001).

The infiltration of neoliberalism into mental health and well-being discourses, policies, and practices emphasizes the notion of responsibilization (Lemke, 2001; Marecek, 2006). Individual choice, determination, strength, and resilience—concepts important to empowerment- and strengths-based social work—have been co-opted to focus on individuals' responsibility for their mental health and well-being in general. Dominant mental health discourses individualize, decontextualize, and emphasize personal responsibilization for the causes and treatment of their problems. Under neoliberalism, where the principles of a market-based economy become central to all social life, the focus is on the individual's ability to be self-managed and self-regulated and, ultimately, to be responsible for their own recovery (C. Brown, 2007b, 2019; Morrow & Weisser, 2012).

The focus on "recovery" involves a self-management expectation that one will comply with the biomedical expertise and the best practices of healthism advocated (i.e., regulating eating, substance use, and exercise). The imperative to recovery coexists with the imperative of self-management and responsibilization. Overall, the reinvigoration of recovery focuses on the individual and is inadequate in addressing social and structural inequities with its lack of attention to race and gender and other forms of oppression (C. Brown, 2019; Weisser, Morrow, & Jamer, 2011). Morrow and Weisser (2012, p. 28) problematize this reinvigorated focus on recovery in mental health and well-being and argue that we must address the social and structural impediments to recovery:

> These social and structural aspects are articulated and enacted through a number of dimensions of power such as biomedicalism, racialization, sanism, sexism, ageism, heterosexism, etc., calling out for an intersectional social justice analysis of recovery. That is, an analysis that foregrounds an understanding of power as it is distributed in the mental health care system, and the accompanying interlocking forms of oppression through which it operates.

Further, the cultural imperative of self-management reflects a normative expectation that individuals' discipline and control themselves (Bordo, 1993; C. Brown, 2007b, 2007d, 2014a). People's focus on disciplining themselves reflects the dominant self-management discourse central in normalization processes of self (C. Brown, 2014a; Foucault, 1980a; Gremillion, 2003). Self-management and self-surveillance are structured by dichotomized either/or assumptions in policing the self, including good/bad, in control/out of control, good enough/not good enough, powerful/powerless, being productive/unproductive, active/lazy, and successful/failure. Neoliberalism also requires "emotional regimes" that ensure a tightly controlled subjectivity (C. Brown, 2019):

> The dominant culture of self-management shapes the expectations and performance of emotion management. Within a postmodern informed social constructionist lens rather than an essentialist one, we can acknowledge rather than avoid the emotional or feeling life that people often experience as driving the narrative thread in their problem stories or struggles. The experience of emotion cannot be separated from the meaning we associate with lived events.... Emotion is not innocently or privately subjective. (C. Brown, 2019, p. 158)

Critiques of neoliberalism and neoliberal perspectives often focus on the impact of market principles on the economic and social distribution of goods, which correspondingly reinscribes and intensifies social power differences based on gender, race, and class. Braedley and Luxton (2010, p. 6) also acknowledge the effects of neoliberalism on everyday life and the specific ways that we learn to "understand who we are and how we live our lives." In this way, neoliberal thought penetrates all aspects of social life, including how we construct ourselves. For Braedley and Luxton, this is a significant difference between classical liberalism and neoliberalism. Morrow and Malcoe (2017) explore the specific impact of neoliberalism on social justice in mental health. The dominant approach to mental health reinforces and reflects social injustice through its decontextualized, individualized biomedical emphasis on disorders and mental illness:

> Absent from this official story are perspectives and forms of evidence that start with an analysis of power and consider the social, political, cultural, and economic production of mental health problems and solutions. Absent too are the diverse voices of experience—psychiatric survivors and those who have lived with various forms of social marginalization and (not unrelated) emotional suffering and thus have important knowledge regarding the utility of mental health reforms, supports, treatment and care. (p. 6)

Morrow and Malcoe (2017) define social injustice in mental health in terms of structural injustice and suggest that no matter how well intended we are as social workers, we contribute to social oppression and injustice when we simply invoke the dominant and normative mental health and well-being practices centred on biomedicine and pathologization of the individual. This includes not just the way we interpret people's struggles, but how we have conversations about them as well. Within a neoliberal context, there are often fewer social workers who are required to see more and more clients for shorter periods of time. Many of the struggles people live with, including co-occurring mental health and substance use issues and the aftermath of trauma, cannot generally be dealt with effectively in short durations of time. Yet, social workers are advised that the short-term approaches are evidence based and these claims are expected to be accepted at face value. Arguably, it is not so much their questionable claim of clinical effectiveness that determines the approaches advocated, but their cost-effectiveness (C. Brown, 2016). The "burnout" that social workers experience, as a result of work environments that increasingly demand larger caseloads, decreased control over their work, increased paperwork, and pressure to see people for short periods of time, is framed as an individual problem of the social worker rather the effect of institutional practices (see Walker, 1986). Weinberg (2010) raises the ethical issue of how social workers are seen as individually responsible rather than part of a much larger process over which they have little control.

DEPATHOLOGIZATION AND CONTEXTUALIZATION

The world of mental health, substance use, and well-being is not a neutral one. There are competing paradigms, yet these paradigms do not exist on equal playing fields. Most notably, the medical or disease model prevails and is given significant social legitimacy, authority, and power. Although it is socially constructed, it is framed as scientific and neutral. There is a systemic expectation that absorbs social workers into these dominant practices. As social workers, it is important that we engage critically with the dominant discourse of psychiatric categories, labelling, diagnoses, and pathologization. Our thinking and professional training emphasizes the idea that people's lives and experiences exist in a social context and are shaped by access to power.

Not all people experience mental health and substance use issues in the same way. We need to be careful not to overgeneralize or totalize descriptions. For example, men and women often have quite different experiences in relation to mental health and well-being (Augusta-Scott & Maerz, 2017; Ussher, 2011). Not all women have the same experiences as each other, as they are influenced by intersectional matrixes of privilege and oppression (Marecek, 2016; Morrow & Weisser, 2012). Moreover, Black women and White women often experience mental health and substance use issues in different ways (Beauboeuf-Lafontant, 2007; Cain, 2009; Nicholaidis et al., 2010). Trans, non-gender conforming, and queer-identified individuals experience significant rates of depression (Davy, 2015; Duong, 2012; Hoffman, 2014; Lehavot & Simmoni, 2011; Singh, 2016), as do Indigenous women living in First Nations communities (Baskin, 2011, p. 194). It is important that we do not totalize people to a diagnosis where this becomes the defining aspect of their identity; for example, instead of seeing individuals as experiencing a problem with alcohol use, they are problematically totalized as an "addict" or "alcoholic."

CRITICAL FRAMEWORK: RESISTING THE MEDICALIZATION OF SOCIAL LIFE

There is a strong history of challenging psychiatry and the medicalization of social life by feminists, medical sociologists, and anti-sanism/anti-psychiatry and

MAD scholars and activists (see Burstow, 1992, 2003; Burstow & Weitz, 1988; Foucault, 1988; Lefrancoise, Beresford, & Russo, 2016; Penfold & Walker, 1983; Smith & David, 1975). Within these critiques, psychological suffering is linked to broad social, economic, and political contexts. From Burstow's (2003) perspective, psychiatry is a "regime of ruling."

Thomas Szasz (1961, 1974) in his classic work argues that the whole idea of mental illness is a myth. He describes the notion as socially constructed and political. Instead, he uses the term *problems in living*. Similarly, Caplan (1995) asks the following questions: How do we determine what is normal? What is "crazy"? Where do the normative standards of normal/abnormal or health/unhealthy come from? What are they based on? This is supported by Phil Brown (1995), who critiques the naming and framing process in diagnosing social life. Caplan opposed the masochistic personality disorder diagnosis when the American Psychiatric Association wanted to include it in the *Diagnostic and Statistical Manual of Mental Disorders* (DSM) in 1985, as it was predicated on the assumption that women should be considered abnormal when they put others' needs before their own. In 1987, she fought against inclusion of the diagnosis premenstrual dysphoric syndrome, which pathologized women's bodies. Similarly, Laura Brown (1992) and Herman, Perry, and van der Kolk (1989) note the commonality of complex trauma among women who are diagnosed as having borderline personality disorder. Feminist researchers have also questioned the medicalization of women's depression and explored the social contexts related to their experiences of depression (Lafrance & Stoppard, 2006, 2007; Stoppard, 1997; Stoppard & Gammell, 2003).

Caplan was involved in a DSM consultation in 1994 regarding gender and was able to observe how the process works. She concluded that there was a "false aura of scientific precision," which is very misleading (1995, p. 15). She observes that despite their common use, very little is known about how drugs work and if they are effective and, if so, how they are effective. Importantly, she highlights that research shows that therapeutic relationships are the most important factor in providing care; this typically suggests a different therapeutic focus, one that is not rushed by institutional time and fiscal constraints. Caplan asks ethical questions about what a therapist can or cannot do, what they can realistically accomplish, and whether they are honest about this with themselves and their clients.

Lafrance and McKenzie-Mohr (2013) argue that the master status of the DSM offers a "lure of legitimacy" and that critiques of it are largely ignored. This "biomedical construction of distress offers the lure, or promise, of validating persons' pain and legitimizing their identities" (p. 119). Yet, this biomedical approach often delegitimizes other forms of knowing or interpretations of people's struggles, such as those that situate the problems in the context of people's lives. Strong (2012) and Ussher (2010) argue that the DSM serves to "medicalize misery." Strong suggests that narrative therapy helps clients recognize, resist, and overcome forms of "discursive capture" and that "'discursive capture' occurs when a single prescribed discourse affords linguistic poverty" (p. 60). This creates a "poverty" of possibility for telling one's story.

Despite the power of the DSM, Frances and Widiger (2012) suggest that it is simply a guide to psychiatric diagnosis—nothing more, nothing less. They suggest that it is imprecise, fallible and limited, elastic, imperfect, and uses nonspecific markers, but is inescapable. Their critique also demonstrates the social construction of the DSM, challenging its efforts to appear scientific and objective while remaining largely descriptive. They reject its biological reductionism, noting that it is constantly changing: of the original diagnoses, only six are left in the now over three hundred included in the manual. Like Caplan (1987a, 1987b), Frances and Widiger (2012) suggest that it fails to meet its own standards of being objective, unbiased, scientific, and evidence based. This, they argue, is evident in the gender and race bias of the interpretation and application of the DSM (see Becker & Lamb, 1994; Caplan, 1987a, 1987b, 1995; Marecek & Gavey, 2013). Cermele, Daniels, and Anderson (2001) illustrate the social construction of notions of mental illness through dominant definitions of what is normal and evidence of stereotypical notions of gender and race.

CRITICAL CLINICAL COUNTERVIEWING OF BODY TALK

When we move beyond dominant biomedical interpretations, we can see that eating "disorders" are embodied performances of gender that provide women a way to simultaneously *speak and hide*. "Body talk refers to culturally specific ways women speak or communicate through their bodies" (C. Brown, 2014a, p. 174; see C. Brown, 2007d; Ussher, 2010). As a site for struggle, the body can tell stories of undeniable anguish. Women's "body talk" may also convey the *"yet to be spoken,"* while both reproducing and resisting dominant social scripts (C. Brown, 2014b). "Through the body, women may speak the unspoken struggles and resistance they may have yet to fully acknowledge to themselves or others" (C. Brown, 2014a, p. 174). Body talk also conveys the many ways people tell their stories. Resisting dominant discourses, "speaking out and beyond these hegemonic discourses" (McKenzie-Mohr & Lafrance, 2014, p. 191), is dangerous and people often attempt to negotiate this telling by being partial or indirect.

We can resist a pathologizing and medicalizing approach to body talk if we listen beyond the words, especially as women and other marginalized groups find that the dominant scripts often do not fit their life experiences. Not only does resisting master narratives challenge taken for granted and oppressive constructions of truth, they also disrupt discursive power.

Thinness as a social metaphor represents the "docile body," the regulated individual within a regulated social body. We turn ourselves into subjects absorbed by improvement, management, and performance of self (Foucault, 1980a). Individual practices of self-management are normalization processes of self. Emotional feeling speech is entangled in self-regulation as a mechanism of social power (C. Brown, 2014a). Since the 1970s, when thinness became tied to self-mastery and value in Western society, the language *feeling fat* and *feeling thin* has become known and familiar. While the expressions of *feeling thin* and *feeling fat* are not actually feelings, they are encoded feeling speech that reveals women's embodied and socially located distress. Control of the body has come to be equated with the highly desired sense of control or mastery of the self, which is emphasized in neoliberal society.

We cannot separate the experience of women who struggle with anorexia (self-starvation) and bulimia (bingeing and purging) from the mainstream experience women often have of their bodies (Bordo, 1993; C. Brown, 2007b; 2007d; 2014a). Most women have difficulties accepting their bodies, believing they do not measure up to ideas of a more "ideal self" (Lawrence, 1984). Most women think they are too fat and strive to be thinner: "Anorexia and bulimia are extensions of most women's experiences with weight, whereby weight preoccupation is seen to exist on a continuum that includes fear of fatness, denial of appetite, exaggeration of body size, and rigid dieting" (C. Brown, 2014a, p. 178). Women with anorexia often desire to achieve total control in one area of their lives, while feeling out of control in other respects. While this "control paradox" can often be seen in everyday weight preoccupation, it is often rendered invisible. Gauging one's "good enoughness" is tied to constraint, surveillance, discipline, and compliance to dominant gendered and racialized expectations, which includes both control over excess and constraint of expression.

When we combine the idea of the control paradox (Lawrence, 1979; C. Brown, 1993b, 2014a) with the work of resourcing the body as an expression of the cultural imperative of self-management (Gremillion, 2003), we can tie together the feeling world with the discursive. We too often see, among those struggling with this control paradox, a rigid approach, harsh self-judgment, lack of self-compassion, and a kind of emotional totalitarianism (C. Brown, 2014a).

With anorexia, the perceived absolute sense of control through intense self-surveillance and deprivation is the ultimate prize—so valuable one will risk dying for it. The fear of losing control is, in contrast, devastating and terrifying. The more out of control one feels, the more one comes to rely on control established through the rigid emotional regime and control of the body required by anorexia, or extreme self-starvation. This struggle reflects negative consequences in the social creation of the neoliberal subject.

Counterviewing Body Talk

A commitment to an eating "disorder" can be counterviewed as a "unique outcome" or as a time of living outside the problem-saturated story, a time when women try to defend and privilege their own immediate emotional needs before those of others. In part, the caring labour women are still expected to perform can be seen in a minimizing of their own needs. This commitment to an eating "disorder" is therefore a powerful form of resistance to socially constructed expectations of gender performance for women. It is common to hear women say "this is the only thing I have for me" as they hold even tighter to it. Restorying can build on such unique outcomes, strengthening a woman's willingness to express herself with conviction even if someone else does not like it. Rather than pathologize the control paradox, we need to hear how women are standing up for themselves, their needs, and their desire to feel more control over their lives. Arguably, all marginalized groups take a risk in expressing their distress, which is already in itself often a form of protest or resistance. Through counterviewing body talk, direct and deliberate communication may begin to replace indirect and partial speaking through the body. Scaffolding conversations take apart the known and familiar, allowing for other possibilities to emerge. As an example of critical clinical practice, feminist narrative therapists develop a scaffolding or structured mapping of questions (White, 2007) that can move women from these taken-for-granted assumptions that infuse the entanglement of feelings and thoughts.

Counterviewing Conversations

I have organized a sample counterviewing conversation of body talk into three sets of questions.

Exploring the Meaning of Fatness and Thinness
The first set of questions provides an example of beginning to unpack the meaning of fatness and thinness in a woman's life.

- Could you tell me what it feels like to you when you feel fat?
- When are you most likely to feel fat?
- When did you first feel fat?
- When you feel fat, what do you feel this says about you?
- Do you ever feel thin?
- What does this feel like to you?
- When you feel thin, what do you feel this says about you? What does it take to feel thin?
- What does this feel like? (adapted from C. Brown, 2014a, p. 187)

Feeling Thin, in Control, and Good

The next set of questions explores the connection between the issues of feeling thin and in control, and feeling good about oneself.

- How does feeling thin make you feel more in control?
- What do you feel you have to do to get to that thin feeling?
- What happens when that thin feeling goes away?
- Why do you think you feel out of control when you don't feel thin?
- Tell me more about what feeling out of control feels like?
- What does it take to control your eating? (adapted from C. Brown, 2014a, p. 187)

Control Paradox

The third set of questions explores the control paradox and the difficult struggle of letting go of coping through controlling the body. In doing so, the counterviewing questions asked of the client help deconstruct the self-management discourse and the unhelpful dominant story that being thin and in control make her feel good about herself and her life.

- How hard would it be to give up controlling your body and eating?
- If people were to see you bingeing and purging, what would they learn about you that they are not usually aware of?
- How do you feel about people knowing these things?
- How is your control over your body important to you?
- How does it feel when people ask you to give up something important to you?
- What does it feel like they are really asking you to do?
- What makes it really hard to give up?
- What don't people get about why you want this in your life right now? (adapted from C. Brown, 2014a, p. 187)

These questions explore how body talk is meaningful and useful to women and is therefore difficult to give up. A progression of questions can allow the client to explore how to negotiate *what others want for her* and *what she wants for herself.* This approach also moves away from the idea that she is a "resistant client" and instead acknowledges how her self-management efforts may make sense while also causing her some harm. It is important to recognize that in conforming to the demands of a neoliberal world, the gendered resourcing of the body seeks power through the display of self-management and mastery, while offering an enticing personal sense of power and control.

Externalization

I argue that externalization of women's body talk needs to explore how their feelings are tied to dominant discourses of thinness and self-management and unhelpful identity conclusions. When the social construction of emotion and experience remain intact and unquestioned, their privileging can result in an inadequate externalization of problem stories and subsequently limit the capacity of therapy to help create counterstories that allow for alternative and preferred identity conclusions. This counterviewing may help create a counterstory that resists the allure of the control paradox, a mechanism of power that demands an intensified self-management while promising self-value and satisfaction through this neoliberal performance of self.

EXTERNALIZATION

This approach was developed by Michael White (White & Epston, 1990). The problem is externalized, rather than seen as an expression of individual deficit or failure. It is consistent with social work's belief that we need to contextualize people's problems and the adoption of a depathologizing approach. It is central to the deconstruction of the problem and reduces the effects of labelling, pathologizing, and guilt, shame, and blaming. Stories such as "I am worthless," "I am unlovable," "It is all my fault," "I am bad," or "I am stupid" are unpacked. Externalizing conversations "unpack the dominant story or narrative about events or themes in people's lives and the meaning given to them. They, therefore, involve externalizing the internalized conversation. Externalization helps people separate from "truth" discourses and the notion of one universal or unitary knowledge. The problem is constructed as the performance of oppressive and dominant knowledge" (C. Brown & Augusta-Scott, 2007, p. xxxi). Through externalization, we explore the history and effects of these truths and disqualified aspects of experience. We deconstruct the influence of these discourses and move toward people having more influence on the effects of the discourse or the story of their lives.

CONCLUSION

Critical clinical practice is an intentional social justice–based direct intervention that integrates critical theory and critical practice. It contends with not only the dominant discourses that shape therapeutic conversations, but also mental health, substance use, violence, trauma, and well-being discourses that together often pathologize, individualize, and decontextualize people's struggles in life. I have argued that dominant social discourses often shape people's stories of experience and can contribute to unhelpful and oppressive identity conclusions. Critical clinical approaches see people's stories as socially constructed within existing social relations and available social discourses. There is little doubt that people's stories are constrained by the limited discourses available to them. They try to find a way to make sense of their experiences within dominant social narratives, which provide inadequate accounts of their experiences and tend to reify oppressive dominant discourse. Counterviewing these discourses raises the possibility for the creation of counterstories of resistance to unhelpful discourses and unequal social relations of power. The co-occurrence of biomedicalization and neoliberalism serve to hold people individually responsible for their own health and well-being, regardless of the oppressive and marginalizing circumstances of their lives. This is accomplished in large measure through the mechanisms of power that operate through normalizing processes of self that emphasize self-management. Dominant discourses of self, experience, power, and knowledge are unpacked within critical clinical approaches. This enables practitioners and clients to work collaboratively to challenge stories that are not working for them in their lives.

Externalizing problem stories shifts the process of responsibilization, where individuals are held responsible for their own suffering and inequities. The problem is the problem and the individual is not pathologized. As such, critical clinical work does not rely on diagnostic categories and labelling. Individuals are encouraged to explore their problems in the context in which they occurred and how they are influencing their lives. Through therapeutic conversations, they can begin to establish influence over the problem and counterstories that allow them to live by preferred identities and lives. The epistemology of critical clinical social work intersects with congruent practice strategies emphasizing the client's power, choice, and control in a collaborative relationship. I have demonstrated in this chapter critiques of neoliberalism, responsibilization, biomedicalization, and dominant mental health, well-being, and trauma discourses that, taken together, do not work well for most people. As we live storied lives, I have encouraged the creation of counterstories that reflect a social justice approach to mental health and well-being.

REFERENCES

Alcoff, L. (1988). Cultural feminism versus post-structuralism: The identity crisis in feminist theory. *Signs: Journal of Women in Culture and Society, 13*(3), 405–436.

Audet, C., & Pare, D. (2018). *Social justice and counseling: Discourse in practice.* New York: Routledge.

Augusta-Scott, T., & Maerz, L. (2017). Complex trauma and dominant masculinity: A trauma-informed, narrative therapy approach with men who abuse their female partners. In T. Augusta-Scott, K. Scott, & L. Tutty (Eds.), *Innovations in interventions to address intimate partner violence: Research and practice* (pp. 75–92). New York: Routledge.

Baikie, G. (2019, March 15). Indigenous social work praxis in-between worldviews. Speaker Series, School of Social Work, Dalhousie University, Halifax, Nova Scotia.

Baines, D. (2017). *Doing anti-oppressive practice: Building transformative, politicized social work* (3rd ed.). Toronto: Fernwood.

Baines, D., & Waugh, F. (2019). Afterword: Resistance, White fragility and late neo-liberalism. In D. Baines, B. Bennett, S. Goodwin, & M. Rawsthorne (Eds.), *Working across difference: Social work, social policy, and social justice* (pp. 247–260). Australia: Red Globe Press.

Baskin, C. (2011). *Strong helpers' teachings: The value of Indigenous knowledges in the helping professions.* Toronto: Canadian Scholars' Press.

Beauboeuf-Lafontant, T. (2007). "You have to show strength": An exploration of gender, race, and depression. *Gender and Society, 21*(1), 28–51.

Becker, D., & Lamb, S. (1994). Sex bias in the diagnosis of borderline personality disorder and posttraumatic stress disorder. *Professional Psychology: Research and Practice, 25*(1), 55–61.

Berger, P., & Luckmann, T. (1967). *The social construction of reality: A treatise in the sociology of knowledge.* New York: Anchor Books.

Bordo, S. (1993). Reading the slender body. In *Unbearable weight: Feminism, Western culture, and the body* (pp. 185–214). Berkeley: University of California Press.

Bowles, L. (2012). The problem with the phrase *women and minorities*: Intersectionality— an important theoretical framework for public health. *American Journal of Mental Health, 102*(7), 1267–1273.

Braedley, S., & Luxton, M. (2010). Competing philosophies: Neo-liberalism and challenges of everyday life. In S. Braedley & M. Luxton (Eds.), *Neo-liberalism and everyday life* (pp. 3–21). Montreal & Kingston: McGill-Queen's University Press.

Brown, C. (1993a). The continuum: Anorexia, bulimia and weight preoccupation. In C. Brown & K. Jasper (Eds.), *Consuming passions: Feminist approaches to weight preoccupation and eating disorders* (pp. 53–68). Toronto: Second Story.

Brown, C. (1993b). Feminist therapy: Power, ethics, and control. In C. Brown & K. Jasper (Eds.), *Consuming passions: Feminist approaches to weight preoccupation and eating disorders* (pp. 120–136). Toronto: Second Story.

Brown, C. (1994). Feminist postmodernism and the challenges of diversity. In A. Chambon & A. Irving (Eds.), *Essays on postmodernism and social work* (pp. 33–46). Toronto: Canadian Scholars' Press.

Brown, C. (2003). Narrative therapy: Reifying or challenging dominant discourse. In W. Shera (Ed.), *Emerging perspectives on anti-oppressive practice* (pp. 223–246). Toronto: Canadian Scholars' Press.

Brown, C. (2007a). Dethroning the suppressed voice: Unpacking experience as story. In C. Brown & T. Augusta-Scott (Eds.), *Narrative therapy: Making meaning, making lives* (pp. 177–196). Thousand Oaks, CA: Sage.

Brown, C. (2007b). Discipline and desire: Regulating the body/self. In C. Brown & T. Augusta-Scott (Eds.), *Narrative therapy: Making meaning, making lives* (pp. 105–131). Thousand Oaks, CA: Sage.

Brown, C. (2007c). Situating knowledge and power in the therapeutic alliance. In C. Brown & T. Augusta-Scott (Eds.), *Narrative therapy: Making meaning, making lives* (pp. 3–22). Thousand Oaks, CA: Sage.

Brown, C. (2007d). Talking body talk: Blending feminist and narrative approaches to practice. In C. Brown & T. Augusta-Scott (Eds.), *Narrative therapy: Making meaning, making lives* (pp. 269–302). Thousand Oaks, CA: Sage.

Brown, C. (2011). Reconceptualizing feminist therapy: Violence, problem drinking and re-storying women's lives. In D. Baines (Ed.), *Doing anti-oppressive practice: Building transformative, politicized social work* (2nd ed., pp. 95–115). Toronto: Fernwood.

Brown, C. (2012). Anti-oppression through a postmodern lens: Dismantling the master's tools. *Critical Social Work, 3*(1), 34–65.

Brown, C. (2013). Women's narratives of trauma: (Re)storying uncertainty, minimization and self-blame. *Narrative Works: Issues, Investigations and Interventions, 3*(1), 1–30.

Brown, C. (2014a). Untangling emotional threads, self-management discourse and women's body talk. In S. McKenzie-Mohr & M. Lafrance (Eds.), *Women voicing resistance: Discursive and narrative explorations* (pp. 174–190). New York: Routledge.

Brown, C. (2014b, May). *Women's body talk and the incitement of the "Yet to be Spoken": Narrative matters*. Paper presented at the International Conference on Narrative Research, Practices, and Issues: Storying the World, American University at Paris, France.

Brown, C. (2016). The constraints of neo-liberal new managerialism in social work education. *Canadian Review of Social Work, 33*(1), 115–123.

Brown, C. (2017). Creating counterstories: Critical clinical practice and feminist narrative therapy. In D. Baines (Ed.), *Doing anti-oppressive practice: Building transformative, politicized social work* (3rd ed., pp. 212–232). Toronto: Fernwood.

Brown, C. (2018). The dangers of trauma talk: Counterstorying co-occurring strategies for coping with trauma. *Journal of Systemic Therapies, 37*(3), 38–55.

Brown, C. (2019). Speaking of women's depression and the politics of emotion. *Affilia: Journal of Women and Social Work, 34*(2), 151–169.

Brown, C., & Augusta-Scott, T. (Eds.). (2007). *Narrative therapy: Making meaning, making lives.* Thousand Oaks, CA: Sage.

Brown, C., & Augusta-Scott, T. (2018). Reimagining the intersection of gender, knowledge and power in collaborative therapeutic conversations with women and eating disorders and men who use violence. In D. Pare & C. Audet (Eds.), *Social justice and narrative therapy* (pp. 143–158). New York: Routledge.

Brown, C., & Jasper, K. (1993). Why women, why weight, why now. In C. Brown & K. Jasper (Eds.), *Consuming passions: Feminist approaches to weight preoccupation and eating disorders* (pp. 16–35). Toronto: Second Story.

Brown, C., & Stewart, S. (2005). Experiences of harm reduction among women with alcohol use problems. *Canadian Journal of Community Mental Health, 24*(1), 95–113.

Brown, C., & Stewart, S. (2007). Making harm reduction work for women: Restorying dominant addiction discourse. In N. Poole & L. Greaves (Eds.), *Highs and lows: Canadian perspectives on women and substance use* (pp. 431–440). Centre for Addiction and Mental Health and the British Columbia Centre for Excellence in Women's Health.

Brown, C., & Stewart, S. H. (2008). Exploring women's use of alcohol as self-medication for depression. *Journal of Prevention and Intervention in the Community, 35*(2), 33–47.

Brown, C., & Zimberg, R. (1993). "Getting beyond weight": Women's health clinic weight preoccupation program. In C. Brown & K. Jasper (Eds.), *Consuming passions: Feminist approaches to weight preoccupation and eating disorders* (pp. 400–408). Toronto: Second Story.

Brown, L. (1992). A feminist critique of personality disorders. In L. S. Brown &
M. Ballou (Eds.), *Personality and psychopathology: Feminist reappraisals* (pp. 206–228).
New York: Guilford Press.

Brown, L. (1994). *Subversive dialogues: Theory in feminist therapy*. New York: Basic Books.

Brown, L. (2004). Feminist paradigms of trauma treatment. *Psychotherapy: Theory, research,
practice, training, 41*(4), 464–471.

Brown, L., & Root, M. (Eds.). (1990). *Diversity and complexity in feminist therapy*.
New York: Harrington Park Press.

Brown, P. (1995). Naming and framing: The social construction of diagnosis and illness.
Journal of Health and Social Behavior, 35(Extra issue: Forty years of medical sociology:
The state of the art and directions for the future), 34–52.

Bruner, E. (1986a). Ethnography as narrative. In V. Turner & E. Bruner (Eds.), *The
anthropology of experience* (pp. 139–155). Chicago: University of Illinois Press.

Bruner, E. (1986b). Experience and its expressions. In V. Turner & E. Bruner (Eds.), *The
anthropology of experience* (pp. 3–50). Chicago: University of Illinois Press.

Bruner, J. (1986). *Actual minds, possible worlds*. Cambridge, MA: Harvard University
Press.

Bruner, J. (1991). The narrative construction of reality. *Critical Inquiry* (Fall), 1–21.

Bruner, J. (2002). *Making stories: Law, literature, life*. Cambridge, MA: Harvard
University.

Burstow, B. (1992). *Radical feminist therapy: Working in the context of violence*. Thousand
Oaks, CA: Sage.

Burstow, B. (2003). Toward a radical understanding of trauma and trauma work. *Violence
Against Women, 9*(11), 1293–1317.

Burstow, B., & Weitz, D. (Eds.). (1988). *Shrink resistant: The struggles against psychiatry in
Canada*. Vancouver: New Star Books.

Butler, J. (1993). *Bodies that matter: On the discursive limits of "sex."* New York: Routledge.

Butler, J. (1997). *Excitable speech: A politics of the performative*. New York: Routledge.

Butler, J. (2000). *Gender trouble: Feminism and the subversion of identity*. London:
Routledge.

Butler, J., & Scott, J. (Eds.). (1992). *Feminists theorize the political*. New York: Routledge.

Cain, R. (2009). "A view you won't get anywhere else"? Depressed mothers, public
regulation and "private" narrative. *Feminist Legal Studies, 17*, 123–143.

Caplan, P. (1987a). The name game: Psychiatry, misogyny and taxonomy. *Women and
Therapy, 6*(1/2), 187–202.

Caplan, P. (1987b). The psychiatric association's failure to meet its own standards: The
dangers of self-defeating personality disorder as a category. *Journal of Personality
Disorders, 1*(2), 178–182.

Caplan, P. (1995). How do they decide who is normal? In *They say you're crazy: How the world's most powerful psychiatrists decide who's normal* (pp. 1–32). New York: Addison-Wesley.

Carrington, H. (2016). Feminism under siege: Critical reflections on the impact of neoliberalism and managerialism on feminist practice. In B. Pease, S. Goldingay, N. Hosken, & S. Nipperess (Eds.), *Doing critical social work: Transformative practices for social justice* (pp. 226–240). Crows Nest, Australia: Allen and Unwin.

Carter, I., Hanes, R., & MacDonald, J. (2012). The inaccessible road not taken: The trials, tribulations and successes of disability inclusion within social work post-secondary education. *The Canadian Journal of Disability Studies, 1*(1). doi:10.15353/cjds.v1i1.23

Cermele, J., Daniels, S., & Anderson, K. (2001). Defining normal: Constructions of race and gender in the DSM-IV Casebook. *Feminism and Psychology, 11*(2), 229–247.

Chambon, A. (1999). Foucault's approach: Making the familiar visible. In A. Chambon, A. Irving, & L. Epstein (Eds.), *Reading Foucault for social work* (pp. 51–82). New York: Columbia University Press.

Chambon, A., Irving, A., & Epstein, L. (Eds.). (1999). *Reading Foucault for social work.* New York: Columbia University Press.

Comas-Diaz, L., & Green, B. (1994). *Women of color: Integrating ethnic and gender identities in psychotherapy.* New York: Guilford Press.

Crenshaw, K. (1989). Demarginalizing the intersection of race and sex: A Black feminist critique of antidiscrimination doctrine, feminist theory and antiracist politics. *University of Chicago Legal Forum, 1*(8), 139–167.

Davy, Z. (2015). The DSM-5 and the politics of diagnosing transpeople. *Archives of Sexual Behaviour, 44*(5), 1165–1176.

Duong, K. (2012). What does queer theory teach us about intersectionality? *Politics and Gender, 8*(3), 370–386.

Durkheim, E. (1966). *The rules of sociological method.* New York: Free Press.

Epstein, L. (1994). *The therapeutic idea in contemporary society.* Paper presented at School of Social Work Postmodernism Workshop, University of Toronto.

Flaskas, C., & Humphreys, C. (1993). Theorizing about power: Intersecting the ideas of Foucault with the "problem" in family therapy. *Family Process, 32*, 35–47.

Flax, J. (1990). Postmodernism and gender relations in feminist theory. In L. Nicholson (Ed.), *Feminism/postmodernism* (pp. 39–62). New York: Routledge.

Fook, J. (2016). *Social work: A critical approach to practice* (3rd ed.). Thousand Oaks, CA: Sage.

Foucault, M. (1973). *The birth of the clinic: An archeology of medical perception.* London: Tavistock.

Foucault, M. (1980a). *The history of sexuality: Vol 1. An introduction.* New York: Vintage.

Foucault, M. (1980b). *Power/knowledge: Selected interviews and other writings 1972–1977.* New York: Pantheon.

Foucault, M. (1988). *Madness and civilization: A history of insanity in the age of reason.* New York: Vintage.

Foucault, M. (1991). Politics and the study of discourse. In G. Burchell, C. Gorden, & P. Miller (Eds.), *The Foucault effect: Studies in governmentality* (pp. 53–72). London: Harvester.

Foucault, M. (1995). Strategies of power. In W. Anderson (Ed.), *The truth about the truth: De- and re-confusing the postmodern world* (pp. 40–45). New York: Tarcher/Putnam.

Frances, A., & Widiger, T. (2012). Psychiatric diagnosis: Lessons from the DSM-IV past and cautions for the DSM-5 future. *Annual Review of Clinical Psychology, 8,* 109–130.

Fricker, M. (2003). Epistemic injustice and a role for virtue in the politics of knowing. *Metaphilosophy, 34*(1/2), 154–173.

Fuss, D. (1989). *Essentially speaking: Feminism, nature and difference.* New York: Routledge.

Gavey, N. (2005). *Just sex? The cultural scaffolding of rape.* New York: Psychology Press.

Gay, R. (2018). *Not that bad: Dispatches from rape culture.* New York: HarperCollins.

Geertz, C. (1973). *Thick descriptions: Toward an interpretative theory of cult*ure. New York: Basic Books.

Geertz, C. (1986). Making experiences, authoring selves. In V. Turner & E. Bruner (Eds.), *The anthropology of experience* (pp. 373–338). Chicago: University of Illinois Press.

Goodman, L., Liang, B., Helms, J., Latta, R., Sparks, E., & Weintraub, S. (2004). Training counseling psychologists as social justice agents: Feminist and multicultural principles in action. *The Counseling Psychologist, 32*(6), 793–837.

Gremillion, H. (2003). *Feeding anorexia: Gender and power at a treatment center.* Durham, NC: Duke University Press.

Haraway, D. (1988). Situated knowledges: The science question in feminism and the privilege of partial perspective. *Feminist Studies, 14*(3), 575–599.

Hare-Mustin, D. (1994). Discourses in the mirrored room: A postmodern analysis of therapy. *Family Processes, 33,* 19–35.

Herman, J. (1992). *Trauma and recovery: The aftermath of violence—From domestic abuse to political terror* (1st ed.). New York: Basic Books.

Herman, J. (2015). *Trauma and recovery: The aftermath of violence—From domestic abuse to political terror* (2nd ed.). New York: Basic Books.

Herman, J., Perry, C., & van der Kolk, B. (1989). Childhood trauma in borderline personality disorder. *American Journal of Psychiatry, 146,* 490–495.

Hick, S., Fook, J., & Pozzuto, R. (2005). *Social work: A critical turn.* Toronto: Thompson Educational Publishing.

Hill Collins, P. (1990). *Black feminist thought: Knowledge, consciousness, and the politics of empowerment*. New York: Routledge.

Hill Collins, P. (2019). *Intersectionality as critical social theory*. Durham, NC: Duke University Press.

Hoffman, B. (2014). An overview of depression among transgender women. *Depression Research and Treatment*, 1–9. doi:10.1155/2014/394283

hooks, b. (1990). Postmodern Blackness. *Postmodern Culture*, *1*(1). Baltimore, MD: Johns Hopkins University Press.

Keyser, A. (2019). *No more excuses: Dismantling rape culture*. Minneapolis, MN: Twenty-First Century Books.

Lafrance, M. (2007). A bitter pill: A discursive analysis of women's medicalized account of depression. *Journal of Health Psychology*, *12*(1), 127–140.

Lafrance, M., & McKenzie-Mohr, S. (2013). The DSM and its lure of legitimacy. *Feminism and Psychology*, *23*(1), 119–140.

Lafrance, M., & Stoppard, J. (2006). Constructing a non-depressed self: Women's accounts of recovery from depression. *Feminism and Psychology*, *16*(3): 307–325.

Lafrance, M., & Stoppard, J. M. (2007). Re-storying women's depression: A material-discursive approach. In C. Brown & T. Augusta-Scott (Eds.), *Narrative therapy: Making meaning, making lives* (pp. 23–38). Thousand Oaks, CA: Sage.

Lawrence, M. (1979). Anorexia nervosa: The control paradox. *Women's Studies International*, *2*, 93–101.

Lawrence, M. (1984). *The anorexic experience*. London: The Women's Press.

Lefrancoise, B., Beresford, P., & Russo, J. (2016). Editorial: Destination Mad studies. *Intersectionalities*, *5*(3), 1–10.

Lehavot, K., & Simmoni, J. (2011). The impact of minority stress on mental health and substance use among sexual minority women. *Journal of Consulting and Clinical Psychology*, *79*(2), 159–170.

Lemke, T. (2001). The "birth of bio-politics": Michel Foucault's lecture at the Collège de France on neo-liberal governmentality. *Economy and Society*, *30*(2), 190–207.

Levine, H. (1982). The personal is political: Feminism and the helping professions. In G. Finn & A. Miles (Eds.), *Feminism in Canada: From pressure to politics* (pp. 175–210). Montreal: Black Rose Books.

Lorde, A. (1984). Age, race, class, and sex: Women redefining difference. In *Essays and speeches* (pp. 114–123). Freedom, CA: The Crossing Press.

MacDonald, J. (2000). A deconstructive turn in chronic pain treatment: A redefined role for social work. *Health and Social Work*, *25*(1), 51–58.

MacDonald, J. (2008). Anti-oppressive practices with chronic pain sufferers. *Social Work in Health Care*, *47*(2), 135–156.

Madigan, S. (2003). Counterviewing injurious speech acts: Destabilizing eight conversational habits of highly effective problems. *International Journal of Narrative Therapy and Community Work, 1*, 43–59.

Madigan, S. (2007). Watching the other watch: A social location of problems. In C. Brown & T. Augusta-Scott (Eds.), *Narrative therapy: Making meaning, making lives* (pp. 133–150). Thousand Oaks, CA: Sage.

Marecek, J. (2006). Social suffering, gender, and women's depression. In C. L. Keyes & S. H. Goodman (Eds.), *Women and depression: A handbook for the social, behavioral, and biomedical sciences* (pp. 283–308). Cambridge, UK: Cambridge University Press.

Marecek, J. (2016). Invited reflection: Intersectionality theory and feminist psychology. *Psychology of Women Quarterly, 40*(2), 177–181.

Marecek, J., & Gavey, N. (2013). DSM-5 and beyond: A critical feminist engagement with psychodiagnosis. *Feminism and Psychology, 23*(1), 3–9.

Marx, K. (1978). *The German ideology.* In R. Tucker (Ed.), *The Marx-Engels reader* (pp. 146–200). New York: Norton.

McCall, L. (2005). The complexity of intersectionality. *Signs: Journal of Women in Culture and Society, 30*(3), 1771–1800.

McKenzie-Mohr, S., & Lafrance, M. (2011). Telling stories without the words: Tightrope talk in women's accounts of coming to live well after rape or depression. *Feminism and Psychology, 21*(1), 49–73.

McKenzie-Mohr, S., & Lafrance, M. (2014a). Women's discursive resistance: Attuning to counter-stories and collectivizing for change. In S. McKenzie-Mohr & M. Lafrance (Eds.), *Creating counterstories: Women resisting dominant discourses in speaking their lives* (pp. 191–205). New York: Routledge.

McKenzie-Mohr, S., & Lafrance, M. (Eds.). (2014). *Women voicing resistance: Discursive and narrative explorations.* New York: Routledge.

McWade, B. (2016). Recovery-as-policy as a form of neoliberal state making. *Intersectionalities: A Global Journal of Social Work Analysis, Research, Polity, and Practice, 5*(3), 62–81.

Mead, G. (1977). *On social psychology.* Chicago: University of Chicago Press.

Morgan, A. (2000). *What is narrative therapy?* Adelaide, Australia: Dulwich Centre Publications.

Morrow, M., & Malcoe, L. H. (Eds.). (2017). Introduction: Science, social injustice, and mental health. In M. Morrow & L. H. Malcoe (Eds.), *Critical inquiries for social justice in mental health* (pp. 3–30). Toronto: University of Toronto Press.

Morrow, M., & Weisser, J. (2012). Toward a social justice framework of mental health recovery. *Studies in Social Justice, 6*(1), 27–43.

Nicholaidis, C., Timmons, V., Thomas, M., Waters, A., Wahab, S., Mejia, A., & Mitchell, S. (2010). "You don't go tell White people nothing": African American women's perspectives on the influence of violence and race on depression and depression care. *American Journal of Public Health, 100*(8), 1470–1476.

Nicholson, L. (Ed.). (1990). *Feminism/postmodernism*. New York: Routledge.

Pease, B., & Nipperess, S. (2016). Doing critical social work in the neoliberal context: Working on the contradictions. In B. Pease, S. Goldingay, N. Hosken, & S. Nipperess (Eds.), *Doing critical social work: Transformative practices for social justice* (pp. 3–24). Crows Nest, Australia: Allen and Unwin.

Pease, B., Goldingay, S., Hosken, N., & Nipperess S. (2016). *Doing critical social work. Transformative practices for social justice.* Crows Nest, Australia: Allen and Unwin.

Penfold, P., & Walker, G. (1983). *Women and the psychiatric paradox*. Montreal: Eden Press.

Redekop, F. (1995). The "problem" of Michael White and Michel Foucault. *Journal of Marital and Family Therapy, 21*(3), 309–318.

Scott, J. (1992). Experience. In J. Butler & J. Scott (Eds.), *Feminists theorize the political* (pp. 22–40). New York: Routledge.

Shaffer, B. (1987). *To a safer place* [film]. National Film Board, Canada.

Singh, A. (2016). Moving from affirmation to liberation in psychological practice with transgender and gender nonconforming clients. *American Psychologist, 71*(8), 755–762.

Smith, D. (1990). *The conceptual practices of power: A feminist sociology of knowledge.* Toronto: University of Toronto Press.

Smith, D. (1999). *Writing the social: Critique, theory, and investigations.* Toronto: University of Toronto Press.

Smith, D., & David, S. (Eds.). (1975). *Women look at psychiatry: I'm not mad, I'm angry.* Vancouver: Press Gang Publishing.

Stoppard, J. (1997). Women's bodies, women's lives and depression: Towards a reconciliation of material and discursive accounts. In J. Ussher (Ed.), *Body talk: The material and discursive regulation of sexuality, madness and reproduction* (pp. 10–32). New York: Routledge.

Stoppard, J. (2000). *Understanding depression: Feminist social constructionist approaches.* New York: Routledge.

Stoppard, J., & Gammell, D. (2003). Depressed women's treatment experiences: Exploring themes of medicalization and empowerment. In J. Stoppard & L. McMullen (Eds.), *Situating sadness: Women and depression in social context* (pp. 39–61). New York: New York University Press.

Strong, T. (2012). Talking about the DSM-V. *International Journal of Narrative Therapy and Community Work, 2,* 54–64.

Strong, T., & Pare, D. (2003). *Furthering talk: Advances in the discursive therapies.* Boston: Kluwer.

Szasz, T. (1961). The myth of mental illness. *The American Psychologist, 15*(2), 113.

Szasz, T. (1974). *The myth of mental illness: Foundations of a theory of personal conduct.* New York: Harper and Row.

Tanesini, A. (1999). *An introduction to feminist epistemologies*. Malden, MA: Blackwell.

Tseris, E. (2013). Trauma theory without feminism? Evaluating contemporary understandings of traumatized women. *Affilia: Journal of Women and Social Work, 28*(2), 153–164.

Ussher, J. (2005). Unravelling women's madness: Beyond positivism and constructivism and towards a material-discursive-intrapsychic approach. In R. Menzies, D. Chunn, & W. Chan (Eds.), *Women, madness and the law: A feminist reader* (pp. 19–41). London: Glasshouse.

Ussher, J. (2010). Are we medicalizing women's misery? A critical review of women's higher rates of reported depression. *Feminism and Psychology, 20*(1), 9–35.

Ussher, J. (2011). Gender matters: Differences in depression between women and men. In D. Pilgrim, A. Rogers, & B. Pescosolido (Eds.), *The Sage handbook of mental health and illness* (pp. 103–126). London: Sage.

Walker, G. (1986). Burnout: From metaphor to ideology. *Canadian Journal of Sociology, 11*(1), 35–55.

Weinberg, M. (2010). The social construction of social work ethics: Politicizing and broadening the lens. *Journal of Progressive Human Services, 21*(1), 32–44.

Weisser, J., Morrow, M., & Jamer, B. (2011). *A critical exploration of social inequities in mental health recovery literature*. Vancouver: Centre for the Study of Gender, Social Inequities and Mental Health.

White, M. (1989). Experience: Therapy in the world of experience. *Dulwich Centre Newsletter, 1*, 4–6.

White, M. (1994). The politics of therapy: Putting to rest the illusion of neutrality. *Dulwich Centre Newsletter, 1*, 1–4.

White, M. (1997). *Narrative of therapists' lives*. Adelaide, Australia: Dulwich Centre.

White, M. (2000). Re-engaging with history: The absent but implicit. In *Reflections on narrative practice: Essays and interviews* (pp. 35–58). Adelaide, Australia: Dulwich Centre.

White, M. (2001). Narrative practice and the unpacking of identity conclusions. *Gecko: A Journal of Deconstruction and Narrative Ideas in Therapeutic Practice, 1*, 28–55.

White, M. (2002). Addressing personal failure. *International Journal of Narrative Therapy and Community Work, 3*, 33–76.

White, M. (2004). Working with people who are suffering the consequences of multiple trauma: A narrative perspective. *International Journal of Narrative Therapy and Community Work, 1*, 45–76.

White, M. (2007). *Maps of narrative practice*. New York: Norton.

White, M., & Epston, D. (1990). *Narrative means to therapeutic ends*. New York: Norton.

Wunke, E. (2016). Notes on rape culture. In *Notes from a feminist killjoy: Essays on everyday life* (pp. 47–108). Toronto: Book Thug.

APPENDIX A

Principles for Critical Clinical Practice

This list reflects an epistemological stance toward counselling practices centred on well-being and coping, mental health, addiction, and trauma. In critical clinical practice, the relationships between the self, society, story, and social justice are key.

- Start from a place of respect, being affirming and non-judgmental, and double listening. Be present and focused.
- Understand that in the therapeutic conversation both the social worker and client bring knowledge.
- Recognize that practitioners are not neutral or bias-free. This is not possible.
- Recognize that what is presumed to be truth or factual is very often contestable.
- Place experience in social context and acknowledge intersectionality of identity experiences.
- Recognize that experience stories do not reflect truth, but are socially constructed accounts.
- Understand that experience is not neutral or apolitical.
- Understand that there is no one story or one experience.
- As human experience is always social, the meanings associated with the experience must be explored and unpacked.
- The self is socially constructed, so avoid essentializing or treating as pre-given, natural, and unchangeable "traits" or "characteristics" assigned to people.
- Avoid essentializing or totalizing people by reducing them to one aspect of their identity or life experience (e.g., "You are bad," "You are good," "You are violent," "You are a victim," "You are a schizophrenic," "You are an addict," "You are an anorexic").
- Acknowledge that there are similarities and differences in people between and among social groups (i.e., do not essentialize or totalize difference or sameness).
- From a social justice lens, question simply adopting expert-based labels and diagnoses that reflect the dominant social discourse of the DSM. Instead, try to make sense of people's experiences and what they mean from their perspective.

- Avoid medicalizing people's lives and adopting one-dimensional approaches to understanding the embodied self.
- Understand that the growth of biomedicine in mental health care, particularly brain science, often has appeal, but it is never enough. The brain and mind are not the same thing. Avoid offering totalizing explanations of people's suffering based on brain science.
- Be aware of the limitation of binary either/or constructions, including oppressed/oppressor, powerful/powerless, man/woman, gay/straight, mind/body, healthy/unhealthy, expert/non-expert, subjective/objective, and social/individual.
- Understand that people are both social and embodied. Expressions of the body, including pain, fatigue, and lack of concentration, also tell stories. For instance, we see the embodied experience of self in people's experiences of pain, depression, anxiety, trauma, addiction, or eating "disorders." The body is always in the grip of culture.
- Challenge the subordinated position of social work in the helping profession. There is a need for social workers to interrogate dominant paradigms and reposition our own, rather than just adopting those of other professions.
- Unpack major concepts and assumptions, including recovery, resilience, health, strength, addiction, stigma, and restorative justice.
- Unpack important concepts, such as experience, knowledge, power, self, and the relationship between these concepts.
- Do not just encourage clients to tell and retell stories. We also often need to work together to re-author or counterstory them.
- Emphasize individual action and agency.
- Understand that social work practitioners are positioned on the side of social justice and social change. Reflecting a social justice position, our epistemological positions resist and challenge sexism, racism, colonialism, ageism, homophobia, heteronormativity, fat prejudice, sanism, biomedicalism, and the injustices of class disparity and poverty in society. The dominant discourses that reify these oppressive social relations are unpacked for their impact on people's lives within critical clinical work.
- Recognize that the unhelpful dominant discourses of personal failure and being not deserving need to be unpacked (see Madigan, 2003; White, 2001, 2002).

APPENDIX B

Principles in Critical Clinical Practice

The following practice principles reflect critical epistemological assumptions:

- Begin with an empathetic, gentle, warm, caring, compassionate stance that is focused and present.
- Demonstrate active listening, listening beyond the words, and double listening.
- Work from a place of what is viable, include harm reduction and contracting as needed.
- Demystify the process of working together. Be transparent and use straightforward communication (avoid professional jargon).
- Emphasize clients' choice, control, power, and safety.
- Minimize power differences where possible.
- Recognize that a focus on a strong therapeutic alliance is necessary for effective work.
- Repeat back to clients what things mean to them; how they interpret their experiences.
- Stress empowerment and emphasize strengths while also exploring where people feel vulnerable.
- Allow the client to control the pacing.
- Emphasize that people are more than victims, and encourage agency. Explore what is possible.
- Use self-disclosure thoughtfully, but only to assist the conversation. Adopt a position of non-neutrality as an ally and advocate.
- Strive for the work to be collaborative, but for the focus to be the needs of the client and not the social worker.
- Demonstrate trustworthiness, that you can tolerate difficult stories, and that you have something to contribute to the conversation.
- Share knowledge, advocate, and provide resources.
- Appreciate and respect people's distrust of you as a practitioner.
- Remember that both client and practitioner have partial knowledge, and both contribute to collaborative conversation.
- Explore the history and influence of the problem on the person's life.

- Adopt practices of counterviewing the problem story; explore dominant discourses and assumptions.
- Gently challenge unhelpful conclusions through counterviewing.
- Explore the client's influence over the problem: When has it not existed?
- Externalize the problem. The person is not the problem. How did the problem develop and in what context?
- Collectivize the problem as part of a process of exploring how the person's responses make sense and are often common. Explore how others may share a similar reaction or experience and how it is social. For example, many women who experience sexualized violence blame themselves. Counterviewing and counterstorying the story involves collectivizing this reaction. (Collectivizing can sometimes be done in group work.)
- Examine the overall context of the problem (how, where, what, when, and why) and context of the person's life (e.g., gender, race, poverty, sexual orientation).
- Explore how people often feel they have power in some ways and not in others.
- Acknowledge the person's strengths and do not focus on their internalized story of deficits without unpacking the development and meaning of this story.
- Practice double listening through listening beyond the words to the silence and the yet to be spoken. Listen to body language and the many ways people speak—often through their coping strategies.
- Listen even when it is difficult to do so. Do not shut down people's pain, vulnerability, and anger.
- Notice gaps and contradictions in stories and explore these.
- Explore how stories may involve oppression, resistance, and agency.
- Appreciate how difficult/dangerous it is to tell stories, especially those that are painful or shameful.
- Appreciate how the constraints and limitations of dominant discourse can create a poor fit for people's experiences and, therefore, how people may struggle to tell their story.
- Appreciate people's understandable ambivalence toward change and the difficulty of even small changes.

- Recognize the importance of harm-reduction strategies and baby steps.
- Recognize the creativity of coping strategies that are often both adaptive/helpful and unhelpful. For instance, explore how binge drinking is helpful in dealing with pain or anxiety and how it may get in the person's way.
- Avoid labelling and diagnosis. Instead, focus compassionately on the meaning and context of the experience.
- Look for what makes sense about people's stories instead of pathologizing them.
- Recognize and acknowledge the self-care and self-compassion often used in coping strategies.
- Encourage the importance of and need for self-care and self-compassion. This is an issue for many women who are often very good at taking care of others and less adept at taking care of themselves. Recognize that many people do not feel they deserve self-care and self-compassion.
- Work with clients to develop alternative, more helpful counter-stories that resist dominant and oppressive discourse and support their preferred self and their values.
- Ensure that you explore whether trauma has occurred in a person's life and be prepared to see how it connects to other issues or struggles that are present (i.e., relational injury).
- Be aware of the coexistence of many types of issues; for instance, depression, anxiety, substance use, eating-related and body-image issues and trauma.
- Avoid retraumatizing and revictimizing people.
- "Normalize" reactions to trauma and violence.
- Take responsibility for learning and gaining knowledge and awareness of available resources where needed.
- Be reflexive about practice.
- Be aware of an anti-oppressive and decolonizing practice position.

CHAPTER 2

Critical Clinical Ethics

Merlinda Weinberg

INTRODUCTION

In the profession of social work in Canada, *ethics* is a key concern for ensuring sound practice and for the protection of the public. Over time, this emphasis on ethics in the profession has increased, resulting in the expansion of books on the topic, and more inclusive and elaborate codes of ethics (Banks, 2011). Licensing for practitioners and continued registration often require ongoing professional education in ethics (see, for example, Nova Scotia College of Social Workers, 2018). Yet practitioners, particularly those concerned with the enduring inequalities in society and the need for social transformation in Euro-Western societies, often perceive that the traditional approach to ethics does not adequately address their concerns. As a means to counter these inadequacies, this chapter goes beyond a dominant approach to ethics, tying together a *critical theoretical* orientation toward ethics and outlining the implications for critical clinical practice.

In this chapter, I outline two dimensions of complexity that contribute to ethical struggles and the difficulty of practising as a critical clinician. The first element is that all social workers must navigate and resolve underlying fundamental structural paradoxes in the field. One paradox is the societal mandate to be agents of care for service users, but also responsible for the protection of the most vulnerable in society. This latter authorized duty can lead to the need to control service users who might cause harm (for example, in child welfare). There are other fundamental paradoxes (such as having multiple service users in a case with differing needs), which create ethical dilemmas and contribute to the difficulty of acting from a critical perspective. These paradoxes are explored in the chapter through a child welfare case.

The second dimension that creates barriers for critical clinical practice is that the current environment is one of austerity, where the ideals of the profession are largely not supported. The context of neoliberalism and managerialism, with the primary values of economies and efficiency, will be outlined. In order to work toward a more equitable society, workers need time and support to ensure a social safety net, which is difficult to accomplish in the present context. The work in child welfare again illustrates significant pressures and strictures in working critically.

Given these impediments, what workers are able to actively "do" may be limited. In child welfare, where control issues figure heavily and constraints in terms of time and resources are significant, this is especially the situation. But changes in workers' attitudes and language, for instance, are always available, even in the most restrictive environments. This chapter outlines some approaches for bringing a critical clinical ethical perspective to bear, regardless of the pressures and limitations in one's agency.

CRITICAL THEORY

Critical theory is an overarching term that encompasses a number of theoretical frameworks, including, but not limited to, feminist, post-structural, queer, and anti-racist theories. What unites these divergent approaches is a critique of the status quo and a political commitment to transforming society to one that is more equitable. There is an underlying assumption that those who are marginalized labour under structural disadvantage. Emphasis is put on power dynamics in the society. How language shapes what is taken as truth and the connection between language and knowledge are examined. The advantages of being a professional are also questioned, recognizing the risk of supporting the existing societal conditions in order to maintain the privileges of being a professional.

As you read this chapter, ask yourself the following questions:

1. How useful do I find the codes of ethics in helping me resolve ethical struggles?
2. How does the current environment affect my ability to act ethically and critically?
3. Does the notion of ethical trespass change how I understand ethical practice and, if so, how?

4. How do language/discourse and culture complicate acting ethically and critically?

5. In an era of fiscal restraint, what new strategies do I now have for practising ethically and critically that could have been applied to this case?

CASE OF AN APPREHENSION OF A CHILD

The following case was taken from a research project on ethics in social work. It involves a child welfare worker's struggle regarding the apprehension of a child. I have tried to maintain the actual words of the practitioner, including her use of the term *scam*. But, no matter how "true" to a situation one aims to be, a case takes a snapshot that includes neither the process element nor the fact that the discussion is influenced by the relationship with the interviewer and the need by a participant to be seen as competent and ethical. In addition, what people say they do and what actually occurs are not one and the same. Furthermore, I have abbreviated a six-page transcription, making selections about what is "relevant," which by default omits nuances, reducing the "messiness" of practice. Thus, some suggest that case studies for ethics are inadequate devices and should be eliminated completely (Kean, 2018). Despite these critiques, case scenarios continue to be useful for examining practice. All names are pseudonyms. The quotation marks represent the actual words of the participant in the research study. Here is the case:

A mother, Laila, contacted the child welfare worker, Jen, asking for her three-year-old son, Musa, to be taken into foster care because Laila was depressed and could not look after him. Laila had "seen her family doctor for depression." At first, Jen did not remove Musa but instead "organized with [Laila's] friends for her to spend the night," thinking this would "let her have a break." However, Jen kept "the file open."

After this episode, Jen had "been calling her" but Laila was "not answering her phone." Finally, Musa answered the phone and Jen was able to connect with Laila. Jen made a visit and "things had significantly deteriorated," so Jen "questioned" her earlier judgment and wondered if she had "left [Musa] at risk." She stated, "you start to question whether you've done the right thing in terms of your comfort level." Laila was "non-responsive." "The state of her house had deteriorated" and the "boy was a little more dishevelled." At the same time, Musa was "obviously very bright" and Jen thought, "mom's done a lot of great things with him." Jen felt, "You try not to be so intrusive. I think it's a horrible thing to take kids away from their families.... It's horrible for ... the kids."

Nonetheless, Jen decided to apprehend. She wanted the removal to be "voluntarily so we wouldn't have to go to court." Jen believed, "court is necessary but it's not always the best option if you can work with the family." Jen thought Laila "would be lucid enough to sign a voluntary agreement for him to come into care" and was "explaining to her the repercussions of going to court." However, Laila was, again, "non-responsive." Jen acknowledged that she was "getting somewhat frustrated, saying … 'This isn't a game. You know we can't sit here all night.'" Jen realized that she "couldn't have [Laila] sign … and expect that it would be acceptable." Jen said, "there's no way I could ethically or morally have her sign this document. Even though I know I could probably ask her to sign it and she would sign it."

Jen said it was "not good for [Laila's] son to see this and clearly he knows something weird is going on cause he … [said] 'I need to go with you.' And I was just shocked that a little boy would say that to me." Jen continued, "we're walking out the door, he's … dressed and ready to go, holding my hand. And mom starts crying and said something in their language, my guess [is] it was something like 'don't go' … so he started crying and then he wouldn't leave." Jen "ended up having to call police and it was helpful" … because … the crisis unit came." Jen continued, "that's such a horrible thing to say that I'm calling the police." Nonetheless, Jen discussed the advantages of involving the crisis team since it meant that the "crisis nurse … was able to relay that information to the hospital." Otherwise, Jen found it "hard [be]cause … you cannot get a consistent nurse or physician or psychiatrist."

Laila went to the hospital and Musa was taken into care. However, "they discharged [Laila]… and then … the following day [Laila] called the hospital again." Laila was "calling 911 non-stop." Finally, they "admitted her … on the fourth or fifth time." Ultimately, Laila was admitted for "about three weeks" then "discharged with medications," but Musa was "still in care."

Jen continued, "at the same time her friends were telling [Jen] that [Laila's] husband, [Faisal], who was back in their home country, had told mom to do this … it was an immigration scam… so [if]…she was not fit to care for her son … [then Faisal] would get immigration faster to Canada." Jen elaborated: the friends "said … he's been telling her to do this, to call 911 as often as possible. So here I am with that information, thinking is that true or is it really mental health? And not knowing…. And then to see her, to be able to kind of come out of that unresponsive state and kinda hug [Musa] and [say] 'don't go.'… I started to question what's really going on here." Ultimately Jen decided, "I think it ended up being more mental health. My guess is that her husband's demands of her probably added to it."

There are a number of ethical clinical issues for the practitioner to consider in this case:

1. Was Laila's parenting adequate and was Musa at risk? Does Jen need to apprehend?
2. Was Laila competent to sign a voluntary agreement?
3. Could Jen reduce the power differential and avoid court?
4. Was this a mental health crisis or an immigration "scam"?

We will address elements of these ethical dilemmas for the practitioner throughout the chapter.

THE INADEQUACY OF THE DOMINANT APPROACH TO ETHICS IN SOCIAL WORK

The dominant or privileged approach to ethics in the profession has focused on codes of ethics, with discourses centring on workers' conduct to ensure the right way of behaving toward service users. Discourse refers to "any regulated system of statements" (Henriques, Hollway, Urwin, Venn, & Walkerdine, 1984). Some discourses are more dominant or privileged than others, representing the political interests of certain segments of society. Built into these systems of statements are both a thesis and its opposite, which create norms and express moral judgments (Billig et al., 1988). Any discourse is part of a whole complex of discourses and practices that have material effects and can lead to consequences. For instance, a familiar privileged discourse is that child welfare is in place for the protection of vulnerable children. Using it to get a spouse into the country can be viewed as fraudulent, rendering a client morally reprehensible and a caseworker as incompetent if she does not spot this unauthorized use of services.

Contributing to what is taken as dominant are codes of ethics that outline a series of principles. It is assumed that by identifying the principles in a situation and using a good decision-making model (see, for example, Hepworth, Rooney, Rooney, & Strom-Gottfried, 2017, p. 81), one can sort out the right action to take in a dilemma, thus ensuring professional accountability. Codes are also designed to be inspirational and contribute to professional credibility and status. This latter fact has both pros and cons from a critical perspective, given the critique that professionals' power and privilege maintain a one-up, one-down relationship with service users.

There are numerous inadequacies with the privileged approach (Walker, 1998; Weinberg & Campbell, 2014). One difficulty is that often more than one principle applies. Which should take precedence? Had Jen used principles from the codes to guide her practice, two relevant ones would have been: (1) the right to impose limits on self-determination to protect others (Canadian Association of Social Workers [CASW], 2005, p. 5) and (2) the importance of serving the needs of clients and social justice (p. 6). Laila's or Faisal's needs may conflict with those of Musa. You could assume Musa's needs take priority over Laila's, but what are his needs? Do Musa's needs include having his dad in Canada, for instance? And the need for social justice raises the question of how culture and language complicate what is taken as "good enough" mothering. It may also be a factor in the mental health diagnosis of depression. How do you ethically deal with the potential harm inflicted when you are both an agent of discipline (toward Laila), but also of care? We will come back to this question later.

There are other shortcomings of the traditional approach (Weinberg & Campbell, 2014). It is based on a model that emphasizes the *universal* character of principles, assuming they can be utilized regardless of context. But we shall now explore how the context is central to what should be part of ethical critical deliberations.

ETHICS

There are many definitions of ethics. Some emphasize characteristics one should have, such as courage or honesty, while others highlight behaviour and determining the right or wrong way to act. Others accentuate one's moral obligations in relationships. In social work, this encompasses both the responsibilities of service users (such as a mother toward her child) and also professionals' accountability for their actions (Banks, 2011). Philosophers have tended to use a broader lens, asking, "how should we live?" (Addelson, 1994), which requires focusing on what kind of society we need to construct that will support human flourishing. Yet another approach is to question the kind of relationship you should have with yourself (Foucault, 1984). In this chapter, we will incorporate some of these ways of understanding ethics.

THE CURRENT ENVIRONMENT

Social work is currently being practised in an era of neoliberalism (Mudge, 2008) and managerialism (Clarke, 2004; Rogowski, 2011). Neoliberalism refers to both a philosophy and processes whereby the values of the for-profit world have been adopted in social services. These values include the importance of the bottom line and efficiencies over a commitment to meeting the needs of the most vulnerable. Since the 1990s, Canada has moved to what is referred to as a "residual" model of welfare (Chappell, 2014) in which rather than the state taking the major responsibility for the needs of citizens, the emphasis is on providing only what is absolutely essential. Furthermore, the neoliberal perspective is that individuals are responsible for their own well-being and morally reprehensible if they fail. These discourses contribute to attitudes of victim-blaming rampant in society and impact service users and practitioners. There are many consequences to the residual model, with a reduction in services and benefits being a major one (Aronson & Sammon, 2000).

Alongside this philosophy of neoliberalism has been an emphasis on managerialism, which suggests that management strategies from the for-profit sector should be applied to non-profit agencies. This trend has resulted in prioritizing evidence-based practice, working to targets, extensive documentation, reduced time for direct practice, bigger caseloads, an increase in rules and regulations (Dominelli, 2004; Weinberg & Taylor, 2014), frequent reorganizations, and diminished autonomy for practitioners (Banks, 2011; Clarke, 2004).

In the child welfare case described here, there were hints of the effects of these trends. Workers report feeling very stressed by time constraints and large caseloads (Weinberg, 2016) and this is apparent in Jen's frustration with how long it was taking to get Laila to respond to her. In addition, Jen spoke about the lack of consistency with hospital personnel and the negative effects in communication. For her part, Laila was not admitted to hospital for depression until at least her fourth request. Could this be related to limited resources and not just assessment of Laila's needs? Might there be any connection between Faisal's difficulty being admitted to the country and neoliberalism? How much do all these factors affect ethical practice and ensuring that social justice goals are achieved? I believe that these are important structural elements that a universalistic approach to ethics fails to encompass.

PARADOX AND ETHICAL TRESPASS

Compounding present-day socio-political influences is the reality that social work professionals are always straddling unresolvable paradoxes in society (Weinberg, 2016). One is the contradictory need to be both agents of discipline and of care. Discipline refers to both "acts of punishment and correction and to fields of knowledge that diagnose deviance from the norm and intervene to remove it" (Chambon, Irving, & Epstein, 1999, p. 271). In this case, the disciplinary act was apprehension of Musa, since Jen evaluated Laila as being an "inadequate" mother and Musa as "in need of protection." At the same time, Jen is expected to care for this family and meet the principle of "respecting the unique worth and dignity of all people" and upholding "human rights" (CASW, 2005, p. 4). This is a fundamental paradox (one of a number) at the heart of the profession (Weinberg, 2016), leaving social workers in a conundrum about how to ensure ethical practice.

While critical clinical practice strives to be non-judgmental toward service users, recognizing the pervasive structural barriers they may face, judgment is an unavoidable but necessary component of social work, such as evaluating the adequacy of parenting or determining who receives services or resources and how much they should get. Jen did not want to apprehend, recognizing that this was "horrible," but she also understood the necessity of determining if Musa was "at risk." The contradiction of judgment versus being non-judgmental is yet another intrinsic paradox in practice that complicates acting ethically and critically.

The third paradox is that Jen is responsible to Musa, but also to Laila. The priority of doing the least harm and protecting the defenceless may point to Jen's primary responsibility being for Musa; nonetheless, because in social work a case may involve obligations to more than one person, others may be injured by social work action. This is another fundamental paradox in the field—namely, workers' responsibilities to more than one service user with conflicting needs in a case. In this scenario, while removing Musa might protect him from harm, it might also be devastating for Laila. This is perhaps implied in Jen's description of Laila's response of crying at his removal. And one can anticipate that there is injury to Laila by having her child taken from her care, even if she requested it at the time.

The traditional approach of using codes and decision-making tools does not adequately address the inextricability of these paradoxes, implying that it is possible to "get it right," a problematic discourse. It has been suggested that *ethical trespass* is an unavoidable component of critical practice. We cannot eliminate uncertainty and harm in ethics (Kendall & Hugman, 2013); we can only attempt to make the best, if imperfect, choice. When Jen chooses to remove Musa, while it may protect him from a mother who is unable to ensure his care, it may also result in unanticipated harms. For one, we know that there can be trauma for children when separated from their parents. How therapeutic the placement is for Musa is an open question. Furthermore, the norm of "acceptable" parenting is reinforced and may be an inaccurate assessment for some future parent.

ETHICAL TRESPASS

Melissa Orlie (1997, p. 5), taking a term first identified by the philosopher Hannah Arendt, refers to ethical trespass as the "harmful effects ... that inevitably follow not from our intentions and malevolence but from our participation in social processes and identities." She elaborates that it is especially people such as practitioners who set the norms of what is perceived as acceptable and healthy behaviour that are likely to trespass. This means that there may be unintended ill consequences from the intervention of a practitioner due to the rendering of judgments. It is not out of evil intention, but because social workers are required to be those agents of discipline. In addition, because workers' decisions always impact others (albeit sometimes indirectly), what may be good for one person may not be for another, resulting in inadvertent harms for the latter person. These conundrums make operating critically and seeking social justice goals very complex.

SELF-REFLEXIVITY

In thinking about how she handled the situation with Laila, Jen stated, *"you start to question whether you've done the right thing."* This is an example of her being self-reflexive. Reflexivity has been defined in multiple ways (Fook, 2002; Kondrat, 1999). Critical reflexivity according to Kondrat (1999, p. 459) has four elements: (1) simple conscious awareness, (2) critiquing that awareness, (3) understanding how one's history and personhood have impacted the therapeutic process, and (4) one's consciousness of the processes by which meaning, identities, and structures are created. The key to this last component is an understanding that one inevitably contributes to the construction of societal structures (Kondrat, 1999, p. 465) and therefore one must always be reflecting on one's stance in either supporting or altering society. (This is one reason that ethical trespass is unavoidable.) D'Cruz, Gillingham, and Melendez (2007, p. 77) also identify this last component in their definition of self-reflexivity as "a critical approach to professional practice that questions how knowledge is generated and, further, how relations of power influence the processes of knowledge generation."

They added another component to their definition of self-reflexivity, namely, the importance that emotions play in knowledge creation and in power. We will explore this element later in the chapter.

Self-reflexivity is especially important around ethical issues. It involves reflecting on the discrepancy between our intentions and the outcomes of our work. It requires examining the consistency between our values and the effects of our behaviour. It involves asking questions such as "do I want to be the sort of person who does X?" (Meyers, 1994). These questions illustrate Foucault's (1984) notion of ethics as the relationship we have with ourselves. Self-reflexivity is an essential skill for critical clinical ethical practice.

Jen's self-reflexivity about the implications of apprehension for the family was revealed when she expressed that she tried *"not to be so intrusive"* since *"it's a horrible thing to take kids away from their families."* What is missing from her analysis is to ask why she behaved as she did and, further, to ask how this scenario is impacted by structural constraints that Laila is facing. Jen's process would have been enhanced had she asked questions, suggested by Kondrat (1999, p. 466), such as what are my assumptions, beliefs, and values in thinking of Laila as potentially "dishonest or fraudulent"? And "are there contradictions between my avowed intentions or values and the structural outcome of my activities?" Focusing on the question "how should we live?" is a useful adjunct to the dominant spotlight of "what should I do?" In asking how we should live, the current state of society can be highlighted, bringing in societal injustice and inequalities that maintain marginality. All these questions, but particularly the last, are pertinent for critical practitioners who are concerned about acting ethically and dismantling unequal structures and working toward social transformation.

POWER AND A RELATIONAL APPROACH

The implications of ethical trespass are that social workers must consistently and consciously examine their use of power, an essential dimension of critical clinical ethical practice. Michel Foucault, a post-structural theorist, referred to power not as an essence a person does or does not have, but as a quality that flows and is exercised in relationships between people. He discussed power as productive (Chambon et al., 1999), by which he meant two things. First, through the use of power, individuals can act in positive ways, such as protection of vulnerable children. This is an important theoretical contribution since we sometimes see power as solely a negative force that subjugates people. Second, power "produces" identities, such as creating a category of "a child in need of protection" or an "inadequate mother." This is also noteworthy since practitioners are key architects in the construction of identities through their judgments about what constitutes "normalcy" and through their ability to secure those constructions as "truth."

Jen demonstrated a critical clinical approach as she grappled with her use of power. She recognized that calling the police for the family was "*horrible*," perhaps because of the repressive element of power toward Laila. Additionally, Jen wanted to equalize the dynamics of power by obtaining a voluntary agreement that would have avoided court proceedings. While it is not ever possible to make the relationship between practitioner and service user entirely egalitarian (Brown, 1994), it is possible to reduce the power differential. A critical clinical ethical approach involves attempts to ease, as much as possible, the power hierarchy in relationships. Jen did employ her power by making the agreement non-voluntary and used a rationale of ethics, namely a lack of competence on the part of the mother to sign a truly voluntary agreement.

Notice how institutional framings are also part of that decision. While not stated overtly, Jen outlined that she "*couldn't have her [Laila] sign ... and expect that it would be acceptable.*" Acceptable to whom? You could speculate that she is referring to people who would potentially be evaluating her practice: the courts, her professional association, and her superiors. Institutional policies and procedures and laws are part of a diffuse network in the operation of power even when they are not present, shaping actions and knowledge, as they were in this instance for Jen. They are also part of the context, making the current dominant ethics approach, which emphasizes universal principles that are applicable across contexts, insufficient as an instrument for ethics. In critical clinical ethical work, it is important to treat the context as your client (Fook, 2002), which we will explore more fully later in the chapter. Jen did this when she looked beyond the family to consider respite for Laila. Jen also viewed bringing in the crisis team as a way of gaining more consistency for Laila's treatment for depression.

Despite the recurrent belief that workers lack power, in relation to clients they wield significant power. Recognition of privilege and power can work to reduce the power imbalance through tactics available to critical clinical ethical social work. Social workers can choose *not* to employ their power. Jen wanted to avoid exercising her power by giving Laila a break, involving friends to help her. Another example of a tactic would be to eschew scrutinizing a client's use of resources. Or a practitioner could decide to wait to review a file on a client until she has made her own evaluation. Of course, workers need to assess the risk of not having that prior information, but the record stands in for the real-life human being, "speaking" for that individual in someone else's voice, taking on a weight that is difficult for the flesh-and-blood client to negate (De Montigny, 1995).

Using one's power to work toward a relational approach is also a tool in critical clinical ethical practice. A relational approach takes into account multiple perspectives, such as attempting to understand the situation as Laila might view it. I suspect more compassion and empathy in the relationship is likely when a more nuanced approach is taken, even if the decision is the same. Those intangible qualities may be difficult to measure in the evidence-based orientations of neo-liberalism and managerialism, but could have important benefits and represent critical ethical practice. The significance of a therapeutic alliance is foundational in clinical work (CASW, 2005) and has been the source of an enormous amount of research to substantiate that, regardless of approach, the alliance is a crucial factor for the outcome of treatment (Goldfried & Davila, 2005; Horvath, Del Re, Fluckiger, & Symonds, 2011). Collaboration and consensus are key to therapeutic success and ethical critical practice (Drisko, 2017). At times, this means altering the worker's agenda to negotiate a fit with that of the service user. Shared goals and objectives for achieving those aims are important dimensions (Goldfried & Davila, 2005). But with the rise in caseloads, more emphasis on documentation, and fewer resources (all of which are part of neoliberalism and managerialism), a relational approach is difficult to actualize, despite the best of intentions on the part of workers. This is particularly the case in mandated settings such as child welfare. Furthermore, the paradox of being responsible for discipline, not just care, contributes to the difficulty of attaining such a relational bond.

UTILIZING EMOTIONS

In dominant approaches to ethics, as we have seen, the emphasis is on rational cognitive processes to ensure good decision-making. Objectivity is the goal, as if somehow the knower and what is known can be separated, an epistemological position that has been widely disputed (Haraway, 1988). The privileged position is that emotions are non-rational and outside of an individual's control, making them poor vehicles through which to determine an ethical course of action (Bagnoli, 2011; Monin, Pizarro, & Beer, 2007). Emotions influence clinicians in many ways, sometimes positively and sometimes negatively. Affect is more likely aroused for people to whom we are closely connected. Loyalty, anxiety about conflict, or a wish to lessen regret can influence decision-making, for example (Rogerson, Gottlieb, Handelsman, Knapp, & Younggren, 2011). All of these motivations can be problematic.

However, there is research suggesting that emotions are not necessarily involuntary. For instance, emotions can be utilized to provide an account of one's actions (Edwards, 2001). This might be the case when Jen talked about being *"shocked"* when Musa said he needed to go with her. While Jen states that she did not want to apprehend, her shock at Musa's statement gives her justification for taking him away from Laila. Since Jen would want to be seen as competent for the interviewer (and herself), this emotional reaction provides a rationale that, while not necessarily conscious, presents her in a positive light as doing the "right" thing as a clinician.

Furthermore, it is practitioners' very embodied perspectives, including their emotional reactions, that allow them to engage and develop empathy, essential first steps in creating a therapeutic alliance necessary to making sound judgments (Hardesty, 2015). There is research that substantiates that in ethical decision-making emotions are a key factor, with some theorists asserting that the rational cognitive processes occur *afterward* to justify the choices enacted (Haidt, 2001). Others suggest that both emotions and cognition enhance ethical processes (Craigie, 2011).

Emotions can also be regulated and can function as a red flag that something is not right. Emotions can vicariously evoke your empathy toward others, focusing attention on the need for moral judgments. This is one meaning of reflexivity, namely, the utilization of emotions to help understand power dynamics. Affect can help us to reflect on our values and moral concerns (Pizarro, 2000), offering the possibility of ethical self-transformation (Zembylas, 2003) and political resistance to problematic systemic oppression.

Notice the expression of emotions for Jen when she spoke about it being "*horrible*" to "*take away a child*" and that it was also "*horrible*" to "*say you are calling the police.*" These empathetic responses did not ultimately change the actions that Jen took, demonstrating that they were under her control and used in concert with her rational judgments. Additionally, in terms of her decision-making process, she used her "*comfort level*" to question her earlier assessment. Thus, emotions, in conjunction with cognitive processes, can strengthen moral judgments and need to be brought more firmly into the arsenal of techniques clinicians use for ethical critical processes.

INCORPORATING AN UNDERSTANDING OF DIFFERENCE

There has been an under-theorization of difference in the examination of ethics in the helping professions. Although the CASW code (2005) does identify discrimination, respect for diversity, and "the right of individuals to their unique beliefs" (p. 8), there is little recognition of structural disadvantage, institutional inequalities, or discrimination and prejudice as these factors play out in social work practice and in ethics. Critical clinical ethics requires highlighting inequity, bias, and racism for subordinated groups.

Structural disadvantages are impediments to advancement and inequality that result from a society and its institutions reinforcing the advantage of some groups through laws, policies, and organizational procedures that are taken for granted and seen as normative, but maintain the disadvantage of other groups. For instance, the normative age at which a child is "allowed" to watch over a younger sibling (and this is viewed as an appropriate expectation) may differ for families of limited income or for families from other cultural heritages and for child welfare authorities. Nonetheless, child welfare may deem this behaviour as "neglect" when it varies from the established institutional standard, potentially leading to serious consequences for families whose values diverge.

Under neoliberalism, those who are already marginalized are often blamed for their own troubles, contributing to continuing oppression and exclusion from the benefits of society. There is not sufficient emphasis on the fact that evaluations about people's functioning and access to resources are based on middle-class, white, Euro-Western norms. Therefore, it should come as no surprise that there is a significant overrepresentation of racialized and poor clients in social services and corrections in Canada (CASW, 2018; Hennessy, 2013; Livingstone & Weinfeld, 2015; Truth and Reconciliation Commission of Canada, 2015). An ethical perspective in critical clinical work puts these issues front and centre.

Jen was aware of the structural disadvantage for Laila as a mother without a partner. Jen wondered about the possible need for respite and believed that by calling in a wider circle of supports to *"give her a break,"* Laila might be able to function and keep Musa. However, she failed to go a step further in working cross-culturally and critically. How might any mother of a different culture experience a white Western worker coming into her home and evaluating her functioning? What did Jen know about Laila's values or beliefs? How might this situation have changed had Jen brought in an interpreter? Social work is built on relationship, but that is fundamentally hampered when language and cultural barriers exist and are not recognized and ameliorated. By only mentioning that Laila said *"something in her language"* and making a guess about what she was saying, Jen continued a process of othering, where Laila is objectified and treated as inferior and as the "other."

Critical clinical ethical work requires practitioners to utilize a number of strategies to work across difference. The first is employing an ongoing self-reflexive stance about possible blinders since we all have been socialized in systems that support discrimination. It also requires recognizing the structural barriers that differentially impact ethno-racial populations and seeking to re-move them.

AVOIDING BINARIES AND USE OF DISSIDENT SPEECH

Power is exercised in the use of language. Awareness of how language constructs particular ways of understanding the world through the acceptance of privileged discourses is necessary for critical clinical ethical practice. Statements such as "dishonesty of clients is wrong and should not be supported by social workers" represent a dominant discourse. Seeing the link between knowledge and power is essential. Therefore, critical clinical ethical strategies must include a constant attentiveness to the processes by which those who are marginalized are "othered."

In thought, a key component is to avoid either/or thinking, namely the formulation of binaries. Constructing subjects as "worthy" or "unworthy" is an illustration of that cognitive process in clinical practice. Problematizing the taken-for-granted discourses involves trying to think outside the box and examining the possibility of other than the usual explanations. This is an important component of critical clinical ethical practice. Jen wondered if Laila was truly depressed or if she was using the removal of Musa as an immigration "scam." She suspected it was both. Her final assessment included a more nuanced approach that avoided a binary. Generally, how might that approach change things clinically and/or ethically, if at all?

One must take a stand with regard to the dominant discourses, and the policies, laws, and practices that operate in the field, either supporting, or resisting and potentially disrupting taken-for-granted ways of operating (Krumer-Nevo, 2017).

RESISTANCE

Resistance refers to "an act that counters coercive practices of social control and oppressive ways in which power relations are exerted" (Strier & Breshtling, 2016, p. 112). Power is exercised between individuals and is never total; therefore, as Foucault asserts, wherever there is power there is also resistance (1976/1978, p. 95). The internal contradictions and paradoxes in the profession make any action a potential source of resistance. Discomfort around the contradiction between your personal or professional values and what is happening organizationally can be a trigger. Resistance involves both thought and action, opposing the status quo and creating alternate discourses and practices, which are important elements of an ethical critical clinical approach. Actions can be overt or covert (Fine & Teram, 2013; Weinberg & Taylor, 2014). Those that are covert may benefit an individual service user, but those that are overt have the potential to transform society to one that is more socially just.

Social work has always been in the liminal space between the ruling elite and the underclass, with the potential for practitioners to act as champions for the marginalized (Hyslop, 2018). In critical ethical clinical practice, it is easy to see oneself as taking the moral high ground. We need to try to avoid this, both for ourselves and for the clients that we are serving. It is equally important to resist always viewing service users as victims in a hostile uncaring system and critical clinicians as their saviours. These are binaries to be shunned. Clients have some capacity to direct their lives (within the constraints we have been discussing), using their agency and strengths despite the structural barriers. Furthermore, they are not always "in the right." They can act dishonestly, for instance, and could in fact be involved in scams. Fook states, "We should not assume that the people we are advocating for are necessarily blameless" (2002, p. 151).

Simultaneously, for ethical and critical practice it is necessary to broaden the lens of practice, bringing in an analysis of the structural barriers in clients' lives. What needs to be considered is what obstacles they encountered and if their actions were a consequence of trying to overcome those. Dominant discourses can become taken-for-granted ways of thinking about an issue. In the case of social work practice, those discourses can often reinforce stereotypes of what constitutes the "unworthy" client. Laila could be seen as a problematic service user because she asked Musa to be taken into care as a means of getting Faisal into Canada. In clinical ethical practice, reframes can help highlight social inequities and reduce moral judgment about behaviours that traditionally are viewed as reprehensible. These forms of resistance are processes by which workers can adapt, subvert, and reconstruct alternative discourses (Thomas & Davies, 2005). Use of "dissident speech" (Meyers, 1994) can reshape how "problematic" behaviour is understood. Dissident speech provides an alternate understanding of an issue, bringing out views that are often not part of conscious awareness (Meyers, 1994). Thus, dissident speech can be recuperative to the ethical view of a morally damaged individual and act as a form of healing by creating new storylines that are more positive (Nelson, 2001). It is a useful tactic for critical clinical ethical practice. For example, Jen could have stated that for Laila an immigration "scam" was a clever strategy for overcoming the difficulties of getting Faisal into Canada when structural disadvantage is high, even if she could not support Laila's tactic (Weinberg, 2006). In assessment it is important to always see "symptoms" as strategies for coping and to reframe the possible "advantages" or strengths in those symptoms. This approach to assessment enhances one's ethical critical clinical practice.

APPROACHES

Critical clinicians need to recognize that there is no neutral, value-free, objective way of functioning as a clinician. Social work ethics and practice are political activities infused with power relations (Weinberg, 2018). All practice is political and all ethical decisions either support the status quo or move toward a more equitable society. By political, I am referring to all the strategies that practitioners use to pursue power, to utilize power to influence actions, and to gain acceptance of certain ways of operating in a society (Payne, 2005). Social workers are architects of what gets taken as truth, health, and normalcy. Practices that take into account social justice, power dynamics, and inequities in society are required for sound critical clinical ethical practice.

In addition, it is necessary to see organizations as part of the scope of your practice (Fook, 2002). This may include critiquing organizational policies and procedures. Since it is much more difficult to outflank a group than an individual, finding allies who perceive issues in similar ways improves your chances of challenging structural problems. Discovering common values and motivations between the needs of service users and management and employing language to frame those commonalities can be methods for critical clinical ethical practice. Use of data and documentation (bedrocks of neoliberalism and managerialism) can provide the necessary evidence to make your case for institutional and societal change. In this way, you can act as a translator between client and organizational needs and critical clinical ethical strategies.

Going beyond your organization to build coalitions amongst like-minded practitioners whose politics and ethics include a social justice lens will increase the chance of real social transformation. A component of critical clinical ethical practice is to view your responsibility as including political action. In the United States, a study revealed that fewer than half of practitioners were politically active (Pritzker & Lane, 2017). One wonders what the statistics would reveal in Canada. Having time to implement strategies is a crucial, albeit scarce, factor in neoliberal times (Hoefer, 2016). However, advocacy and activism continue to be important strategies to undo the effects of neoliberalism and operate as ethical critical clinicians. Could Jen have advocated for immigration services to explore getting Faisal into the country? Being educated in the value of social justice can influence political involvement. Reflecting on power dynamics that continue to perpetuate social inequality is a first step in critical clinical ethical practice, but that awareness must move from recognition to action and developing the required skill set. Crucial tactics include policy analysis that identifies the fundamental inequality of current broad structures, moving beyond piecemeal policy tinkering (Mulally, 2010). For instance, could Jen have found allies in her agency to negotiate for policy changes that would have required the child welfare department to provide interpreters when working with families whose first language is not English?

CONCLUSION

In this chapter, I explored several components that contribute to the challenge of ethical practice for critical social workers: neoliberalism, ethical trespass, and the paradoxical nature of social work practice. I also addressed the insufficiency of the traditional approach to ethics. Despite the challenges, it is possible to practice critically and ethically. Even in the most repressive settings, where the responsibility to discipline is high (such as in child welfare), there are strategies practitioners can use. The use of self-reflexivity is key. Going beyond the question of "what is the right thing to do?" to ask "how should we live?" can bring into focus social inequalities. Between workers and service users, the strategic use of one's power and the orientation toward a more collaborative relationship are important techniques. Relying on one's emotions is a tool to identify ethical issues. Critical clinical work requires sensitivity to difference and the likelihood that those who are marginalized in some category such as race are likely unfairly disadvantaged in our society, thus requiring steps to ameliorate the obstacles they face. Avoiding binaries and reframing dominant discourses through dissident speech is available to critical practitioners regardless of their setting. Seeing one's responsibility as changing society at a mezzo level, such as one's organization, and at a macro level, through activism, is an imperative step for critical clinicians. Ultimately, making the link between personal troubles and structural barriers underpins a critical clinical approach to ethical practice.

REFERENCES

Addelson, K. P. (1994). *Moral passages: Toward a collectivist moral theory*. London: Routledge.

Aronson, J., & Sammon, S. (2000). Practice and social service cuts and restructuring: Working with the contradictions of "small victories." *Canadian Social Work Review*, *17*(2), 167–187.

Bagnoli, C. (Ed.). (2011). *Morality and the emotions*. New York: Oxford University Press.

Banks, S. (2011). Ethics in an age of austerity: Social work and the evolving new public management. *Journal of Social Intervention, 20*(2), 5–23.

Billig, M., Condor, S., Edwards, D., Gane, M., Middleton, D., & Radley, A. (1988). *Ideological dilemmas.* London: Sage.

Brown, L. S. (1994). *Subversive dialogues.* New York: Basic Books.

Canadian Association of Social Workers. (2005). *Code of ethics.* Retrieved from http://www.casw-acts.ca/sites/default/files/attachements/CASW_Code%20of%20 Ethics_0.pdf

Canadian Association of Social Workers. (2018). *Understanding social work and social welfare: Canadian survey and interviews with child welfare experts.* Retrieved from https://www.casw-acts.ca/en/social-work-and-child-welfare-new-report

Chambon, A. S., Irving, A., & Epstein, L. (Eds.). (1999). *Reading Foucault for social work.* New York: Columbia University Press.

Chappell, R. (2014). *Social welfare in Canada* (5th ed.). Toronto: Nelson Education.

Clarke, J. (2004). *Changing welfare, changing states: New directions in social policy.* London: Sage.

Craigie, J. (2011). Thinking and feeling: Moral deliberation in a dual-process framework. *Philosophical Psychology, 24*(1), 53–71.

D'Cruz, H., Gillingham, P., & Melendez, S. (2007). Reflexivity, its meanings and relevance for social work: A critical review of the literature. *British Journal of Social Work, 37,* 73–90.

De Montigny, G. (1995). *Social working.* Toronto: University of Toronto Press.

Dominelli, L. (2004). *Social work: Theory and practice for a changing profession.* Cambridge, UK: Polity Press.

Drisko, J. (2017). Active collaboration with clients: An underemphasized but vital part of evidence-based practice. *Social Work, 62*(6), 114–121.

Edwards, D. (2001). Emotion. In M. Wetherell, S. Taylor, & S. J. Yates (Eds.), *Discourse theory and practice: A reader* (pp. 236–246). London: Sage, in association with the Open University.

Fine, M., & Teram, E. (2013). Overt and covert ways of responding to moral injustice in social work practice: Heroes and mild-mannered social work bipeds. *British Journal of Social Work, 43*(7), 1312–1329.

Fook, J. (2002). *Social work: Critical theory and practice.* London: Sage.

Foucault, M. (1978). *The history of sexuality: Vol. 1. An introduction.* R. Hurley (Trans.). New York: Vintage Books. (Original work published in 1976)

Foucault, M. (1984). On the genealogy of ethics: An overview of work in progress. In P. Rabinow (Ed.), *The Foucault reader* (pp. 340–372). New York: Pantheon Books.

Goldfried, M. R., & Davila, J. (2005). The role of relationship and technique in therapeutic change. *Psychotherapy, 42*(4), 421–430.

Haidt, J. (2001). The emotional dog and its rational tale: A social intuition approach to moral judgment. *Psychological Review, 108*(4), 814–834.

Haraway, D. (1988). Situated knowledges: The science question in feminism and the privilege of partial perspective. *Feminist Studies, 14*(3), 575–599.

Hardesty, M. (2015). Epistemological binds and ethical dilemmas in frontline child welfare practice. *Social Services Review, 89*(3), 455–489.

Hennessy, T. (2013). First Nations: The long shadow of assimilation. Retrieved from http://www.policyalternatives.ca/publications/facts-infographics/ first-nations-long-shadow-assimilation

Henriques, J., Hollway, W., Urwin, C., Venn, C., & Walkerdine, V. (1984). *Changing the subject: Psychology, social regulation and subjectivity.* New York: Routledge.

Hepworth, D. H., Rooney, R. H., Rooney, G. D., & Strom-Gottfried, K. (2017). *Direct social work practice: Theory and skills* (10th ed.). Toronto: Thomson, Brooks/Cole.

Hoefer, R. (2016). *Advocacy practice for social justice* (3rd ed.). Chicago: Lyceum Books.

Horvath, A. O., Del Re, A. C., Fluckiger, C., & Symonds, D. (2011). Alliance in individual psychotherapy. *Psychotherapy, 48*(1), 9–16.

Hyslop, I. (2018). Neoliberalism and social work identity. *European Journal of Social Work, 21*(1), 20–31.

Kean, S. (2018, July 30). Why doctors should read fiction. *The Atlantic.* Retrieved from https://www.theatlantic.com/health/archive/2018/07/ medicine-doctors-fiction/566342/

Kendall, S., & Hugman, R. (2013). Social work and the ethics of involuntary treatment for anorexia nervosa: A postmodern approach. *Ethics and Social Welfare, 7*(4), 310–325.

Kondrat, M. E. (1999). Who is the "self" in self-aware: Professional self-awareness from a critical perspective. *Social Service Review, 73*(4), 451–477.

Krumer-Nevo, M. (2017). Poverty and the political: Wrestling the political out of and into social work theory, research and practice. *European Journal of Social Work, 20*(6), 811–822.

Livingstone, A.-M., & Weinfeld, M. (2015). Black families and socio-economic inequality in Canada. *Canadian Ethnic Studies, 47*(3), 1–23.

Meyers, D. T. (1994). *Subjection and subjectivity: Psychoanalytic feminism and moral philosophy.* New York: Routledge.

Monin, B., Pizarro, D. A., & Beer, J. S. (2007). Deciding versus reacting: Conceptions of moral judgment and the reason-affect debate. *Review of General Psychology, 11*(2), 99–111.

Mudge, S. L. (2008). The state of the art: What is neo-liberalism? *Socio-Economic Review, 6,* 703–731.

Mullaly, B. (2010). *Challenging oppression and confronting privilege* (2nd ed.). Toronto: Oxford University Press.

Nelson, H. L. (2001). Identity and free agency. In P. DesAutels & J. Waugh (Eds.), *Feminists doing ethics* (pp. 45–62). New York: Rowman and Littlefield.

Nova Scotia College of Social Workers. (2018). Guiding social work practice. Retrieved from http://nscsw.org/practice/

Orlie, M. A. (1997). *Living ethically, acting politically.* Ithaca, NY: Cornell University Press.

Payne, M. (2005). *Modern social work theory* (3rd ed.). Chicago: Lyceum.

Pizarro, D. (2000). Nothing more than feelings? The role of emotions in moral judgment. *Journal for the Theory of Social Behavior, 30*(4), 355–375.

Pritzker, S., & Lane, S. R. (2017). Political social work: History, forms, and opportunities for innovation. *Social Work, 62*(1), 80–82.

Rogerson, M. D., Gottlieb, M. C., Handelsman, M. M., Knapp, S., & Younggren, J. (2011). Nonrational processes in ethical decision making. *American Psychologist, 66*(7), 614–623.

Rogowski, S. (2011). Managers, managerialism and social work with children and families: The deformation of the profession? *Practice: Social Work in Action, 23*(3), 157–167.

Strier, R., & Breshtling, O. (2016). Professional resistance in social work: Counterpractice assemblages. *Social Work, 61*(2), 111–118.

Thomas, R., & Davies, A. (2005). Theorizing the micro-politics of resistance: New public management and managerial identities in the UK public service. *Organizational Studies, 26*(5), 683–706.

Truth and Reconciliation Commission of Canada. (2015). *Honouring the truth, reconciling for the future: Summary of the final report of the Truth and Reconciliation Commission.* Retrieved from http://www.trc.ca/assets/pdf/Honouring_the_Truth_Reconciling_for_the_Future_July_23_2015.pdf

Walker, M. U. (1998). *Moral understandings: A feminist study of ethics.* New York: Routledge.

Weinberg, M. (2016). *Paradoxes in social work practice: Mitigating ethical trespass.* New York: Routledge.

Weinberg, M. (2018). The politics of ethics in human services: Duelling discourses. *Ethics and Behavior, 28*(6), 497–509.

Weinberg, M., & Campbell, C. (2014). From codes to contextual collaborations: Shifting the thinking about ethics in social work. *Journal of Progressive Human Services, 25*, 37–49.

Weinberg, M., & Taylor, S. (2014). "Rogue" social workers: The problem with rules for ethical behaviour. *Critical Social Work, 15*(1), 74–86.

Zembylas, M. (2003). Emotions and teacher identity: A poststructural perspective. *Teachers and Teaching: Theory and Practice, 9*(3), 213–238.

PART II

CRITICAL CLINICAL PRACTICE: MENTAL HEALTH, TRAUMA, AND SOCIAL JUSTICE

CHAPTER 3

Feminist Narrative Therapy and Complex Trauma: Critical Clinical Work with Women Diagnosed as "Borderline"

Catrina Brown

INTRODUCTION

Feminist narrative practice shaped by feminist post-structural critique offers a clearly articulated integration of theory and direct practice. In this chapter, I will outline the significant contribution that intersectional feminist post-structural epistemology and critique can offer the direct critical clinical practice of social work. Through adopting a feminist narrative lens, I will illustrate critically based direct practice with a focus on gender and mental health counselling, drawing on examples from the substantive overlapping practice areas of trauma, depression, eating "disorders," and alcohol use.

I will focus on the story of Violet and her struggles with the effects of significant childhood trauma, including relationship difficulties, depression, suicidality, body image, bulimia, depression, and alcohol use.[1] This case example illustrates how difficult it often is to tell one's story and the centrality of the therapeutic relationship between the client and therapist when working with chronic multiple childhood traumas that have a significant and ongoing effect on living one's life as an adult. Within mainstream clinical approaches to practice, this kind of story is often presented as uncommon, and in psychiatric terms, as "co-morbid" or as "co-occurring disorders." Like so many women with trauma histories, Violet was also "diagnosed" by her psychiatrist as "borderline" and was strongly discouraged from addressing her experiences of abuse. In this chapter, I will argue that these co-occurring struggles are intricately linked, not as individual deficit or pathology, but as ways of coping and responding to sexual, physical, and emotional childhood abuse (L. Brown, 1992, 2004; Burstow, 1992, 2003; Courtoise, 2004; Haskell, 2012; Herman, 1992, 2015; Lafrance &

McKenzie-Mohr, 2013; Maracek, 2006; Ussher, 2010; Webster & Dunn, 2005). In Violet's case she experienced chronic lifelong multiple forms of abuse and violence. Despite her psychiatrist's admonitions, Violet insisted on working through her traumatic experiences and its sequelae. He threatened to stop working with her if she proceeded in her efforts to address her experiences of trauma and sexualized violence as he believed she did not have sufficient "ego strength" to do so. Violet was certain she needed to tackle the effect of the trauma history on her life. While this work proved to be very difficult, it was also essential to Violet's well-being, as is often the case.

From a critical clinical approach to practising social work, and through discussing working with Violet, I will address several important considerations in the context of trauma work: the constraints and dangers of telling a trauma story; the importance of double listening—for the absent but implicit—to hear what is difficult to speak; how Violet's story is socially constructed; what dominant social discourses are reflected in her story; and how difficult processes of change are. It is often assumed that storytelling is straightforward, unencumbered, apolitical, and a mirror reflection of "real" events. Within these therapeutic conversations, I will emphasize how building a strong therapeutic alliance is a necessary aspect of shaping positive outcomes. Deliberate attention to the therapeutic relationship is at the centre in trauma work, especially for those women labelled "borderline," who very often, and understandably, struggle with trusting anyone and fearing abandonment. These struggles and fears make perfect sense as consequences of trauma. The lived experience of the therapeutic relationship provides important entry points for working with these fears and struggles.

COUNTERVIEWING

Counterviewing is a practice in narrative therapy that critically questions taken-for-granted and normative aspects of the stories people live, which tend to disqualify other interpretations and often limit how people live their lives.

COUNTERSTORY

In narrative therapy, a counterstory is a new preferred story that emerges through collaborative therapeutic conversations. This new story develops through questioning the limitations of the dominant story (or stories) negatively influencing a person's life. This dominant story is often influenced by negative life experiences and dominant social discourses. Dominant stories are often a thin description: "I am stupid," "I am weak," "I am a failure," "I am unlovable." By exploring times people have lived outside of and challenged the dominant story, new stories start to emerge. Over time, these new stories are thickened. These new, more helpful preferred stories are called counterstories.

As you read this chapter, ask yourself the following questions:

1. How can we create a counterstory of the borderline diagnosis?
2. What does listening beyond labelling and diagnosis tell you about the effects of trauma?
3. How does counterviewing the borderline diagnosis result in potentially alternative stories?
4. Why are collaborative conversations important to critical clinical practice?
5. Why is the relationship between the therapist and client important to people who have experienced trauma?

THE DANGEROUS SINGLE STORY OF THE BORDERLINE DIAGNOSIS

It is important to acknowledge at the onset how common it is for women who have dealt with complex and often lifelong experiences of abuse to be labelled and pathologized as having borderline personality disorder (Herman, 1992; Herman, Perry, & van der Kolk, 1989).

For many years, research has shown that this diagnosis is primarily given to women who almost invariably have a trauma and abuse history (Becker & Lamb, 1994; L. Brown, 1992, 2004; Cermele, Daniels, & Anderson, 2001; Marecek & Gavey, 2013; Tseris, 2013). Feminists have critiqued the psychiatrization of women for decades as can be seen in Smith and David's (1975) book, *Women Look at Psychiatry: I'm Not Mad, I'm Angry.* Women who live with a "borderline" diagnosis are often seen as angry, non-compliant, resistant, and attention seeking, experience ongoing suicidality, and as such, are too often written off as being beyond help. This behaviour is disapproved of as it does not conform to dominant gender discourse. Little effort is made to see why they struggle so hard to be in the world. While they have often been psychiatrized, diagnosed, and prescribed medication, these women have typically received very little psychotherapy; therefore, their experiences have often not been heard and, importantly, many if not most relationships have let them down. Because of a failure to establish positive therapeutic relationships, most professional interventions have served to reinforce their learned expectations of people: they can't be trusted or depended on, they don't really care, they don't understand them, and they will eventually let them down, and betray, violate, or abandon them. Consequently, it is precisely for this reason that I will emphasize that the therapeutic alliance is at the heart of doing trauma work with women, especially those labelled "borderline."

STORIES AND THE CREATION OF COUNTERSTORIES

Stories are not neutral. They are not simply individual constructions. Stories emerge in social, cultural, political, and historical contexts (Brown & Augusta-Scott, 2007; Morgan, 2007; White, 2001, 2002, 2007). They can challenge or reify harmful and unhelpful ideas. The work of therapy very often involves unpacking the meaning and construction of people's stories over time, the influence of the stories on their lives, and the creation of more helpful counterstories.

Storytelling and listening are very often messy, nuanced, and political. The narrative therapy tradition has shown that most stories are full of gaps and contradictions, and that what is left out is often as important as what is not. It is often assumed that people "know" how to solve the struggles they are experiencing, and that they just need to tell their story. While this idea is rooted in an effort to adopt an empowerment approach where people's experiences are valued and important, it renders invisible just how seriously people struggle, and just how lost, stuck, and even incapacitated they can become in that struggle. In contrast, the biomedical/disease model, particularly in the context of neoliberal social service delivery, often discourages clients from being "too dependent" and encourages them to avoid anything that sounds like an "excuse," which has the effect of practitioners not listening deeply enough, compassionately enough, or with enough nuance to what clients' stories mean (C. Brown, 2016; Esposito & Perez, 2014; Horton, 2007; McWade, 2016; Morrow & Weisser, 2012; Sakellarion & Rotarou, 2017; Weisser, Morrow, & Jamer, 2011).

Stories very often emerge from dominant social discourse, subsequently reflecting and reinforcing dominant social relations. Feminist narrative therapy emphasizes that in trauma work, collaborative therapeutic relationships are needed and that dominant discourses (including those of sexism, racism, class, sexual orientation, age, and ability) that shape women's trauma stories are unpacked. This therapeutic approach is seen as political and as on the side of social justice and social change. It is important in trauma work to reject a deficit model, which presumes responses to trauma are disordered (Burstow, 2003). A narrative framework instead explores what trauma has meant to women and how it has shaped their lives. Within feminist narrative practice, we explore together ways to create counterstories that resist dominant discourse and how coping responses to trauma make sense. At the same time, we also acknowledge strategies that were meant for survival and protection that may no longer work well for the individual. In particular, a feminist narrative collaborative approach that centres on the therapeutic relationship will tease out the impact of trauma on the woman's experience of relationships and how this may interrupt her preference for stronger social connections, care, and support.

FEMINIST NARRATIVE COLLABORATIVE APPROACH

A feminist narrative approach to critical clinical social work acknowledges that there are two subjects in the room—the client and the therapist (Brown & Augusta-Scott, 2018). They are involved in an ongoing conversation that unpacks people's stories by looking at how they were put together over time, what social discourse helped shaped the story, how the story has influenced their lives, and how the story may work for and against them (White, 2001, 2004). These collaborative conversations further explore how the person may also have been able to have influence over and resist the problem story and begin to develop possible new stories about identity that the person prefers (Morgan, 2007). The collaborative therapeutic conversation explores the meaning of lived events and stories of experiences. For example, what does it mean to a child to be repeatedly abused, how do they make sense of this, how does it shape how they see themselves and others in the world, how does it shape what they learn to expect for themselves and others in the world, and how does it shape how they view life? Herman (1992, p. 96) observes that "the child trapped in an abusive environment is faced with formidable tasks of adaption."

Abused children are especially vulnerable, often experiencing themselves as hostages in their own homes, with nowhere to go and no one to tell. Herman (1992, 2015) emphasizes the importance of acknowledging the disrupted caretaking relationships, where children often continue to protect and love the ones assaulting them. They often live with a sense of overwhelming chaos and anxiety and a lack of predictability or logic for the physical and psychological assaults they experience. Many abused children live in a climate of domination, terror, and shame. Little attention is given to their needs or feelings, contributing to a story that they are not of value. As such, all abuse involves a critical lack of respect for and neglect of the emotional well-being of a child. According to Herman, traumatized children often develop difficulty with regulation of emotional states. The child must make sense of their situation in order to survive, to preserve hope and meaning in the face of despair. In order to preserve their attachment to their parent(s) or caretaker(s), children often blame themselves. This *doublethink* is critical, as it allows children to preserve attachments to their parent(s) in the face of the abuse. In cases of severe abuse, children may alter their minds to keep the abuse a secret from themselves and may adopt "dissociative" states where they alter their consciousness to convince themselves that their parent is not to blame, that there is nothing wrong with them (Herman, 1992, 2015). According to Herman (1992, p. 96):

> [The child] must find a way to preserve a sense of trust in people who are untrustworthy, safety in a situation that is unsafe, control in a situation that is terrifyingly unpredictable, power in a situation of helplessness. Unable to care for or protect herself, she must compensate for the failures of adult care and protection with the only means at her disposal, an immature system of psychological defenses.

Despite efforts at coping, trauma experiences are rarely without consequences. Themes of experiences around coping, trust, safety, control, fear, power, helplessness, and identity are critical in doing trauma work. Herman goes on to describe the impact of a traumatic environment producing the coexistence of creative means of adapting or coping that may be simultaneously harmful or helpful in the long term. Ways of coping with the effects of trauma can be seen in a host of "symptoms" both physical and psychological, such as depression, anxiety, eating disorders, substance use, and "dissociation." She states that "these symptoms simultaneously conceal and reveal their origins; they speak in disguised language of secrets too terrible for words" (1992, p. 96).

When we put trauma experience itself and adaptive trauma responses together with a lack of adequate discursive and social frameworks to speak of them, the danger of speaking often means speaking indirectly or partially. I appreciate Herman's significant contribution to trauma work, particularly her deeply understood grasp of the pain and wounds that we see in the aftermath of trauma. Yet, along with Burstow (2003), I shift away from Herman's diagnostic approach. I agree that "trauma is a not a disorder, but a reaction to a kind of wound. It is a reaction to profoundly injurious events and situations in the real world and, indeed, to a world in which people are routinely wounded" (Burstow, 2003, p. 1302).

Beginning in the 1980s, feminists led the way to making it known how common violence toward women and children is in patriarchal society, and how significantly violence impacts their lives. The "personal is political" (Levine, 1982) approach seeks to make sense of, rather than pathologize, women's responses to trauma and violence by listening to and hearing women's stories and by having an impact on policy and law. An intersectional feminist lens allows for a gender analysis of why most perpetrators are male and most victims are female. A feminist analysis of power and subjugation is essential to understanding the trauma of sexual abuse, female sexual victimization, and physical abuse. Feminist groundbreakers influenced the current trauma-informed thinking, but differed in that they remained fully political. Rather than simply being informed, they informed others and did trauma work in a systematic way consistent with feminist politics, acknowledging issues of power and social context (see, for example, Armstrong, 1978; Brownmiller, 1975; Butler, 1978; Courtoise, 1988; Forward & Buck, 1988; Herman, 1981, 1992; Pizzey, 1974; Russell, 1986; Shaffer, 1987; Terr, 1990).

Today we talk about "trauma-informed" work as if it was a new discovery, detached from the historical work of the women's movement. The goal of trauma-informed work is to minimize harm, not to treat trauma (Poole, 2013). Feminist work continues to lead the way for women to tell their trauma stories and for them to be heard. Women's struggles to articulate their experiences and be heard has been an ongoing focus within feminism. Despite all this groundbreaking work, women still find themselves struggling to tell their stories, to find a framework for their stories in the context of master narratives that often prevail. Talking of trauma is often experienced as dangerous (C. Brown, 2013, 2019). Feminist narrative practice makes space for women's trauma stories and appreciates the constraints that often limit their speech (DeVault, 1990; McKenzie-Mohr & Lafrance, 2011, 2014a, 2014b).

The neurological impact of trauma on the body/brain has become a significant focal point of trauma-informed work today, particularly in hospitals and government agencies. In 1992, Herman wrote that the body response to trauma may involve brain chemistry, but therapeutically, she argued, there is much to do that involves thoughts, behaviours, meanings, and relationships. This is where critical clinical approaches to trauma are centred—in helping people to rewrite unhelpful stories about themselves and their ways of coping, while also championing their ability to cope, and to help co-create meaningful and preferred counterstories. Some choose medication for anxiety and depression, for example, and that can be helpful, too. Learning about intrusive symptoms such as flashbacks, memories, and nightmares is important. However, typically critical trauma work cannot be reduced to a biomedical framework or "brain science." A critical clinical feminist approach to trauma needs to avoid totalizing trauma responses to neurology as this shuts down conversations about what trauma has meant to women and the effects it has had on their lives. The conversation is a different one when we talk about trauma experiences and what they mean, when we situate these experiences within the oppressive social relationships and structures of power in patriarchal, capitalist, neoliberal, racist, ableist, and homophobic society. Within these structures and relations of power, the individual subject is often naturalized and essentialized. As such, people's experiences and emotional responses are seen as individual and internal, as though they exist outside social construction and social realities. The more recent sharp biomedical turn, legitimized by the lure of neuroscience, centres much of women's trauma stories in the brain, producing a depoliticized, decontextualized, and arguably dehumanized understanding of women's experiences of abuse and trauma (C. Brown, 2018; Morrow & Weisser, 2012; Tseris, 2013). Consistent with groundbreaking feminist trauma work beginning in the 1970s, a critical clinical feminist lens offers a focus on women's experiences of trauma and how they make meaning of the trauma within the discursive meaning-making context of society. This approach emphasizes women's agency and the need for them to feel safe and in control in the therapeutic conversation.

Thus, as critical feminist narrative therapists we "double listen" to stories for the "absent but implicit" (C. Brown, 2018; White, 2002, 2007). Therapy needs to begin with allowing the story to be told with all its imperfections and messiness, however the person wishes to tell it—through pictures, drawings, even multiple ways of speaking (sometimes called *symptoms*) such as the "body talk" of eating "disorders," or through substance use as a way of coping with pain (C. Brown, 2014). It is common for women with histories of trauma, whose bodies have been exploited and abused, to struggle with and through their bodies. Therapists must communicate that they can both hear the trauma stories and handle them. Otherwise they will interrupt the healing relationship, especially if the woman determines she can't risk talking to the therapist. At the same time, we must begin by assuming that the therapist will not get the "whole" story, as there is no one whole story to get. There are many reasons for this, some of which are simply the qualities of storytelling. However, more importantly, telling stories of trauma is difficult and dangerous, both psychologically and socially. Moreover, not only is talking of trauma dangerous, there is often also a lack of social discourse and language that fits with trauma experiences.

Prevailing dominant discourses often fail women when they attempt to tell their stories, as the constituting discourse and language is often inadequate. Dominant discourse not only fails to provide a framework to tell trauma stories, but it has also been part of the social world that creates sexualized violence and the negative identity stories women are often left with. As such, critical clinical work involves both double listening to the experiences and unpacking dominant discourses within and around the story. Within a "rape culture," rape is too often normalized as everyday sex; this is elaborated in Gavey's (2005) book *Just Sex? The Cultural Scaffolding of Rape* and Gay's (2018) *Not That Bad: Dispatches from Rape Culture.* McKenzie-Mohr and Lafrance (2011, 2014a, 2014b) suggest women are confronted with a deeply limited cultural context and available frameworks in which to speak of their experiences within rape culture. DeVault's (1990) notion of "linguistic incongruence" is reflected in women's attempt to negotiate agency and blame in ways that dominant social narratives do not allow. McKenzie-Mohr and Lafrance (2011, pp. 64–65) describe this as "tightrope talk":

> Any attempts at "both/and" talk that include elements of dominant assumptions can be missed or mis-heard because of the power of the dominant narratives to overtake more subtle shadings of meaning. The speakers are faced with the formidable challenges of "tightrope talk" when they attempt to construct themselves as both agents and patients; responsible and not responsible.

There are dangers associated with this tightrope talk. Fear of being seen as making too big a deal, complaining, and causing other people trouble reflect gendered scripts for performing the "good woman," which reward women for minimizing their experiences of conflict and not upsetting others. When explored, uncertainty may fade or slip away, allowing a more determined, entitled, and confident voice to emerge. If both the women telling trauma stories and those listening to trauma stories are uncertain, ambivalent, and afraid, that which is pushed underground and rendered invisible can remain silenced or disqualified, and uncertainty is reinforced (C. Brown, 2014, 2018). In the end, it can result in "writing out" these aspects of women's stories when they often need to be included as integral and meaningful. It is important to be aware of the negative effects of leaving uncertainty intact, especially as it offers valuable possibilities if explored. We can wade in the ambivalence and uncertainty without being driven to resolve them in absolute terms. Instead, we can explore what produces ambivalence and uncertainty—and what stories ambivalence and uncertainty tell. Cautious fledgling accounts are often present in uncertainty. We need to enter the uncertainty field, not avoid or deny it. These seeds of alternative or disqualified stories needed gentle encouragement, as disqualified stories can quickly retreat again into invisibility, minimization, and often self-blame. Similarly, McKenzie-Mohr and Lafrance (2011) argue that helpful counterstories reside within the disqualified story.

When listening with compassion and gentleness, we "listen beyond the words" (DeVault, 1990, p. 101). This allows us to listen to the dominant story as well as other interpretations and experiences that live outside dominant unhelpful stories, which are often self-blaming and pathologizing. These "unique outcomes" or "sparkling moments" are often an entry point for new preferred stories (White, 2007).

People often do not express or tell their stories directly. This is particularly true of trauma stories. If not compassionately encouraged to speak in a climate of safety, people will often shut their stories down and even recant them. My research has shown that uncertainty is not just a product of trauma, but also reflects the influence of the dominant discourse on women and trauma that creates fragmented memory of the events and supports blaming women for the violence and minimizing the seriousness of the violence; uncertainty often reveals the dangers of speaking and a struggle with speaking and hiding simultaneously (C. Brown, 2007c, 2013, 2014, 2018). Therapy conversations need to counterview (Madigan, 2003) dominant discourse, which will bring forward the prevalence and impact of the violence.

I argue that critical practice begins by intentionally not reifying or reinscribing mainstream clinical discursive practices. This involves critical attention to the social construction of mental health discourse itself, the social context in which mental health issues emerge, and the internalization and effects of dominant discourse within trauma stories. Critical direct practice can benefit from the earlier contributions of feminist therapy and critical medical sociology, which rejected the disease model of mental health, its pathologization of daily life, the use of stigmatizing labelling and diagnosis, and the decontextualization and depoliticization of people's struggles. A post-structural approach such as the feminist narrative approach I adopt here is not just a theoretical approach, but an integrated critical direct practice (C. Brown, 2018; Drauker, 1998; Duvall & Beres, 2007).

My approach to critical practice maintains that the theoretical approach and direct practice itself need to be reconceptualized in relation to each other. For instance, if we abandon disease-based notions of eating "disorders" and addiction, we can collaboratively counterview these issues in clinical settings and help individuals create counterstories that produce greater possibilities for living beyond these struggles. A feminist narrative strategy, for example, can allow for an understanding of women's resourcing of their bodies through eating "disorders" as a way to talk or voice their struggles (C. Brown, 2007c, 2014, 2017). Similarly, this approach can allow for an understanding of the problem use of alcohol among women, not as a disease, but as a way of coping. As trauma is often an overlapping story in many of women's mental health issues, including eating "disorders" and addictions, it will be acknowledged in the counterviewing of these issues. Women's trauma experiences often show up in ongoing depression and anxiety (Cusack, Morrissey, & Ellis, 2008).

Rather than pathologizing these experiences and focusing on deficits, counterviewing allows the conversation to unpack how depression and anxiety make sense. In this way, counterviewing sets up different strategies for practice grounded in what mental health issues mean to those experiencing them. In both instances, I explore how we collaboratively deconstruct the mainstream approach, develop a counterviewing of problem stories, and create more helpful counterstories through feminist narrative therapeutic conversations. Throughout, I emphasize the way that women's struggles and ways of coping make sense. By moving beyond dominant discursive practices we can allow for a counterviewing that enables collaborative therapeutic conversations in which women are active subjects in their own lives.

The neoliberal context of practice increasingly demands compliance with short-term directed therapeutic practices in, most notably, solution-focused brief therapy and cognitive behavioural therapy (C. Brown, 2018, 2019; McWade, 2016; Morrow & Weisser, 2012; Pease & Nipperess, 2016). Many women experience multiple coexisting problems related to histories of trauma and are too often dismissed by the mental health system. Critical clinical social work practice needs to create diverse programming that can allow the complexity of these issues to be addressed. Historically, the women's movement brought these issues into the public sphere and created women-centred approaches to the work. The work we need to do is not new and we can look to women-centred community-based programming in Canada as the sites of the most effective approach to this work. We have to find ways to hold on to a social justice approach when confronted with the limitations of neoliberalism and biomedicine. I will discuss the importance of taking the time needed to develop a strong therapeutic alliance with women who have experienced complex trauma.

In Violet's case, as in the cases of many women who have experienced significant trauma and abuse, therapy and supports often take long periods of time, particularly as developing bonded, collaborative therapeutic relationships takes time and is arguably critical to this work.

As a child, Violet was abused by her father, grandfather, two uncles, and two brothers from the age of 5 to the age of 18. She described herself as the "house prostitute" and said that her bedroom was a "revolving door." Her mother was emotionally and physically abusive to her. At the same time, the family was well-respected in the rural community. When I first met Violet, she was 26 years old, timid, very quiet, and afraid to speak. She seemed wounded and very vulnerable. This is not necessarily a common presentation of self, but it was notable in her case. Violet had been diagnosed as "borderline," as so many women who have experienced tremendous childhood trauma and abuse are. She often thought of suicide. She had few friends and as she was estranged from her family, she had no family support. She did have a few key support people in the social service system. I am deeply grateful for having the opportunity to work with women with experiences like Violet's.

This case example illustrates how difficult it often is to tell one's story, and the centrality of the therapeutic relationship between client and therapist when working with chronic multiple childhood traumas that have a significant and ongoing effect on living one's life as an adult. In Violet's case, she is absolutely certain of the abuse—there is little minimization, but talking about it as it affected her life and relationships was more uncertain. Although Violet did not minimize the violence, it had become completely normalized in her life. She did believe there had to be something about her, something wrong with her, for the abuse in all its forms to continue to occur. Violet's struggles have arisen from a complex and long-term experience with childhood trauma. Research clearly demonstrates that trauma, particularly childhood trauma, is associated with mental health and health problems. The development of binge eating, body-image issues, use of alcohol, depression, and suicidality in Violet's adult life appeared to be a direct result of trying to cope with the consequences of the trauma.

HEALING RELATIONSHIPS IN THE CONTEXT OF RELATIONAL INJURY

Relational injury is a common effect of trauma that occurs within relationships. In this section, I offer several examples of working with Violet that emphasize the importance of carefully attending to conflict between the therapist and client to avoid thickening the relational injury that results from experiences of abuse (Herman, 2015). Through the therapeutic relationship, I illustrate a counterstory to the expectations that Violet may have of relationships. Violet was referred to me by a feminist sexual assault and abuse organization. Violet reported to me that she had been diagnosed as "borderline" and that her psychiatrist had said that she did not have the ego strength to take part in a sexual abuse support group. I supported her choice to be in the group and communicated that I thought it would be helpful. Following a strong first session where rapport was developed and Violet shared an initial brief account of her life, we agreed to meet again. At the end of the appointment, as we were approaching the door, Violet asked me if she could have a hug. I understood this would be meaningful to her and may further establish our budding connection. Despite this, something held me back. I was uncomfortable as I felt I had to hug her so she wouldn't get upset. It hit me that if I felt this way, I could not hug her as it was the worst message to send to a woman whose whole life had involved invasions of her physical boundaries. Further, she may have not developed a strong sense of having the right to her own physical boundaries. My intention was to be as honest and transparent in our work as I could be to help establish trust and a strong therapeutic alliance. As I had observed in the session that she was very vulnerable and easily hurt, I suspected that she might experience me not hugging her as rejection and abandonment and feel hurt by my decision. I also suspected that this would be a central theme in our work together. On the surface, not hugging her seemed like a bad way to start; however, I paid attention to my "countertransference." I said gently and calmly, "I have a policy of not hugging my clients because so many have had their boundaries violated and I want to ensure that physical boundaries are really clear in our work." Violet was fighting back tears. I then said, "Violet, I have really enjoyed meeting you today and I think we can do some really good work together. I agree with you about the importance of addressing your history of abuse. I really hope that you understand me not hugging you is not about you. I really want to see you again." She smiled, a small brief smile. At this early stage in our work, which took place over a three-year period, we were to meet twice a week. I waited to see if she would come again and she did. After checking in with her, I went back to the hug and debriefed it again. I didn't avoid it. I took the opportunity to say to her that sometimes in our work together things like this might come up and that even though it is hard, it is important that we can talk about it. I tried to communicate in a respectful manner that although some of these conversations are very difficult, it is important for us to be honest and straightforward with each other. As Violet's relationships had been problematically affected by her traumatic abuse experiences, unpacking the hug request allowed us to set up some expectation around communication in our therapeutic relationship at its onset. At the same time, not avoiding the difficulty of this conversation allowed me to communicate that I was competent and trustworthy, and that I wouldn't shy away from difficult material.

Not too much further along in our work, Violet was hitting my cat with a rolled-up piece of paper during the session. I said to Violet, "I am wondering what is going on with you right now. I know you aren't actually hurting my cat, but I don't think it's a good idea to hit her. What do you think might be happening for you right now?" She was upset that I raised this because it was about our relationship. She said, "Well, your cat gets more love than I have ever had." I acknowledged how painful that must be and we moved on to focus on this very important area of Violet not feeling loved. The dual process of expressing an expectation that she not hit my cat, and acknowledging her resentment toward my cat and her pain because she was aware she had not been cared for or loved as much, engaged the relationship dynamic of having different experiences in the same moment and tolerating this. Further, she was sorting out her relationship with me, and figuring out what she expected. She wanted to feel like she mattered to me. Ultimately, she wanted connection and to feel cared for and was expressing this following my disapproval of her actions toward my cat. These were not easy things for Violet to want or express and they were powerful unique outcomes—times when Violet was living outside her dominant story of relationships. It was important to be able to explore these tensions in a gentle way, but not to avoid them (C. Brown, 2007a).

These kinds of moments in therapy are easy for therapists to avoid because they seem like they may produce conflict. I have found that each time something like this happens in the context of other similar conversations and a safe, respectful relationship, it is a valuable entry point into not only how one negotiates conflict, difference, and power in relationships, but also other areas; for example, in this case, to Violet expressing how she had never felt very loved or cared for. Indeed, we spent a lot of time talking about how this felt.

On another occasion, I was five minutes late for our session. Violet interpreted this as evidence I did not want to see her. She was angry at me and expressed herself fairly aggressively; it was the most angry and aggressive she had been to that point. I said to her, "I understand that you are angry at me. I should not have kept you waiting and I should have planned my transportation better. I need you to know, though, I am not late because I don't want to see you." I explained that my lateness was due to transportation delays and that I was sorry for keeping her waiting. We went into the counselling room and continued to focus on her right to be angry, and then moved to a place of understanding that I did not mean it as a slight. Key to this was Violet learning she could work out these feelings of being let down, rejected, or abandoned. It was important that I not shut those feelings down; however, instead of allowing these thoughts and feelings to firmly take root, they were explored and unpacked. She was also able to explore her expectation and fear that I would let her down and possibly abandon her. Through our conversation she had an opportunity to explore what this means to her.

She resisted her own desire to give up on me, to abandon our relationship because she felt I was rejecting and abandoning her. I had to be ever vigilant in addressing this issue in our work. I needed to be genuine and express myself even if it might cause conflict or difficult feelings. But I also had to realize that this was likely to trigger feelings of expected anger, rejection, abandonment, and hurt. Avoiding this would be a critical mistake. Each time an issue like this came up, it was an entry point into tackling these issues in the moment as the feelings were occurring. As Violet was fearing abandonment and being hurt and was angry about having been abandoned in her life, we would explore these feelings. Each time we dealt with one of these issues in a helpful, meaningful, and non-pathologizing way, it strengthened our relationship. Importantly, it also strengthened her sense of what she might expect for herself and from others in relationships. The initial response of therapists might be to avoid these relational issues, missing the opportunity to collaboratively construct a counterstory about relationships. The difficulty and diligence of this kind of work is, it seems, why women diagnosed as "borderline" often feel abandoned and even retraumatized by their therapists. This relationship healing work itself was at the heart of our work together. According to Herman (1992, p. 133),

> The core experiences of psychological trauma are disempowerment and disconnection from others. Recovery, therefore, is based upon the empowerment of the survivor and the creation of new connections.... No intervention that takes power away from the survivor can possibly foster her recovery, no matter how much it appears to be in her immediate best interest.

Power and Control

Issues of power and control are critical throughout the work of therapy (C. Brown, 2007b). Herman (1992) elaborates on the therapeutic alliance, stressing that it must be "painstakingly built" by the collaborative efforts of the client and therapist. She states:

> Therapy requires a collaborative therapeutic working relationship in which both partners act on their basis of their implicit confidence in the value and efficacy of persuasion rather than coercion, ideas rather than force, mutuality rather than authoritarian control. These are precisely the beliefs that have been shattered by the traumatic experience. Trauma damages the [patient's] ability to enter into a trusting relationship; it also has an indirect but powerful impact on the therapist. As a result, both patient and therapist will have predictable difficulties coming to a working alliance. These difficulties must be understood and anticipated from the outset. (p. 136)

While this may not be a central issue for all women who have experienced trauma, it makes sense that it is often an issue for those who have experienced severe childhood and lifelong abuse and trauma. Experiences of helplessness and terror often shape what women who have experienced complex trauma expect will happen in relationships. This is too often how they have experienced relationships. It is therefore central to critical trauma work that we seek to develop a collaborative relationship that centres and collectivizes the woman's experience, that seeks to ensure that she has power, control, and a sense of safety while exploring what is often painful. Central aspects of trauma experiences often include a sense of powerlessness, lack of control and safety, and fear and anger.

It is almost surely the case that therapists will not always meet their clients' simultaneously hopeful and doubtful expectations of them and when they inevitability do not, the anger and hurt experienced and often expressed is not just against the therapist, but also everyone else who has failed her. This often includes previous therapists. Therapists cannot personalize this response and be defensive. They also cannot assume there is no validity to the anger expressed against them. This is why it has to be talked about and explored. I cannot emphasize enough how important this emotional terrain is. If we wish to avoid re-traumatizing traumatized women, we cannot communicate to them they should not be wounded, hurt, or angry. They need to be able to express these feelings without censure and they also need to be unpacked. We need to explore how it makes sense that women who have experienced complex trauma often feel they have been repeatedly and painfully let down and that they cannot count on people. And while it makes sense that women often subsequently live with the story that everyone will painfully let them down and hurt them, we must also work at co-creating an alternative story that resists this expectation in order to limit its influence in shaping the rest of their lives.

From a feminist narrative approach, the dominant unhelpful story might be, "People will always exploit and abuse me so I cannot trust or depend on anyone" and the corollary, "I don't deserve to get the love and care I want." Often part of this story is, "I am not good enough, I deserve what happened to me." In critical clinical therapy, women who have experienced lifelong trauma need to be encouraged to voice their anger and hurt, not have it shut down because it makes the therapist uncomfortable or feel wounded. Instead, we need to double listen, be supportive and empathetic, and invite exploration of what underlying assumptions may not be helpful in this instance (White, 2000, 2004). For example, when I was five minutes late I most certainty did not intend to reject or abandon Violet, yet I understand why she would feel this way given her life experiences. I needed to present back to her both of these parts of the conversation so we could explore them. I thought it would be helpful for Violet to distinguish between what is "now" and what was "then," as they seemed blurred together. The alternative story or counterstory that might be developed is, "People are not perfect and will sometimes let me down or hurt me, but I can still expect to be treated fairly, with respect, and non-abusively," and "I do deserve love and care."

Unpacking Emotion

Through a feminist post-structural lens, emotions are not simply subjective. Emotions are in the grip of culture and neither innocently nor privately subjective (C. Brown, 2014, 2018). They exist with a discursive field that shapes their meaning. Informed by social constructionism, rather than an essentialist understanding, we can acknowledge rather than avoid the emotional or feeling life that people often experience as driving the narrative thread in their problem stories or struggles. The experience of emotion cannot be separated from the meaning we associate with lived events (C. Brown, 2007a). Once we enter the realm of meaning making, we are in the social realm. As we seek to make sense or meaning of our life experiences, we necessarily move beyond a one-dimensional notion of emotional embodiment that results in the essentialism of emotion (C. Brown, 2019).

While extra-discursive or outside discourse in its ability to produce material observable effects, and experienced as embodied, internal subjective reality, emotion is inextricably entwined in the social meaning-making processes of experience and life itself. As we begin to shift away from binary constructions of emotion as either essentialist, pregiven, asocial, and internal or socially and politically constructed, there is a need to both recognize and understand how simultaneously we are emotionally embodied subjects and emotions are always social things (Turner, 2009). The embodied experience is at once physical and embedded in social meaning and possibility. The social management and performance of emotions is shaped by "feeling rules" and cultural norms (Hochschild, 1983; Turner, 2009). Differences in the management of emotions for social co-operation and control of conflict are impacted by status and power (Turner, 2009). According to Ahmed (2004), we need to ask what emotions do. As cultural practices, "emotions matter" for politics. Emotions are gendered, as we can see by the discouragement of expression of anger, strong opinions, conflict, or "being selfish" or "difficult," as well as the social expectations of emotional labour among women and girls, and fear, humiliation, and vulnerability among men and boys (C. Brown, 2019). Indeed, it is emotions such as these that often result in a "borderline" diagnosis among women. When we engage in therapeutic conversation, we often focus on emotion as a central part of experience. Doing so allows for an entry into the deconstruction of the social and political discursive field.

DANGERS OF TRAUMA STORIES: FINDING VOICE

Telling one's story of trauma is often experienced as dangerous (C. Brown, 2013, 2018). There is so much at risk. In the process of remaining silent, women's voices are often rendered invisible. Arguably, a strong and safe therapeutic alliance may help facilitate the finding of one's voice.

One day early in our work together, Violet asked me to retrieve a book of her drawings that I had been asked to keep safe. These were drawings of her sexual abuse. They all had one thing in common—Violet did not have a mouth in any of the drawings. Violet wanted the book because she wanted to draw a mouth on the pictures. I was struck by how powerful and meaningful this was and how certain she was of this. I was deeply moved.

She did not want me to alter the original pictures in any way, so I suggested I photocopy the images. I gave her pencil crayons and crayons to pick from. She sat on the floor and examined the pictures. She said she wanted to draw a mouth that was not too sexual. We spent some time talking about what color the mouths should be so they would not seem to be too sexual. After some thought she told me she was going to draw mouths on her pictures that were open, but only a little, and that were purple, not red. She purposely went about reimaging—indeed, restorying these images—drawing semi-open, purple mouths on every drawing. She was taking charge of how she was going to continue trying to voice her story of abuse and trauma and of their effects on her life.

As she finished drawing the mouths, she looked up at me with tear-filled eyes and tears fell down my cheeks. I was aware of how powerfully connected we were in that moment. I wanted to genuinely show her how moved I was so I did not hide that I was crying. I gently said to her, "This is an incredible thing you have just done." She was nodding her head. "You have given yourself a voice."

Often, women who have trauma histories like Violet's do not trust that the therapist can tolerate hearing the full story and the horror that sometimes goes with it. They need to discover that the therapist can tolerate the story and won't shut it down, avoid it, or shift the subject. The drawing of mouths on her pictures was a turning point in our work together. She also never sat on the floor again.

Violet's story demonstrates much of what I have tried to write about since: women finding their voice, restorying their experiences, learning to tolerate their own needs and feelings, to take up space, to acknowledge their pain, and to learn how to trust relationships without fear of abandonment, betrayal, and abuse. In all of this, Herman's (1992) work *Trauma and Recovery* has had a significant influence. Herman emphasizes the need for women to feel safe and in control as we do the therapeutic work, to not be pathologized but understood, and to learn to build a strong healing relationship that models how relationships are not about one person knowing or having all the power.

Much of our work together on trauma and its effects on her was put on the backburner when Violet got into a deep state of despair and would feel suicidal—when the pain was too much to bear. We had a well-established approach to this, as it came up often enough. She would talk through her distress in the session and I would listen and provide crisis-based counselling—present focused, problem solving, assessment based, and minimizing harm. This included assessing suicidality by asking if she had a method and means. We would agree at the end of each session like this that she would not harm herself or kill herself before we met and talked again in the counselling room. The session would continue until she could make this agreement. We would determine a time for checking in and set up a specific appointment for soon after. Then we would contract or negotiate around what would happen if she felt like this agreement would be too difficult to keep. She could call me or a crisis centre she was comfortable with. She never did call me in the middle of the crisis. Instead, she went to a community crisis centre that had beds that Violet and I had liaised with. Over several years of working together, she made one actual attempt with pills, and ended up in the emergency room. After waiting most of the night and being assessed by a psychiatric resident, she went home. She communicated to me that this experience was so horrible that she didn't ever want to have to relive it, and that she would contact me or the crisis centre in the future.

While we worked together on her experiences of trauma, on relationships, on her emotional needs, regulation, and coping, and depression, we would focus on the despair, loneliness, and hopelessness that would escalate when she was suicidal. Trauma work is not straightforward: there are always a lot of balls in the air. The work is not linear and there is not a straight line between struggling and being "recovered." Using a feminist narrative approach, we want the problem (trauma and its effects) to have less influence on Violet and for Violet to begin to have more influence on the problem. This means significant shifts in meaning.

CONVERSATIONS ON COPING WITH TRAUMA AND ITS EFFECTS

I have focused on the importance of the therapeutic relationship in addressing and eventually beginning to counterstory relational injury. In the context of a safe and strong therapeutic alliance, it is possible to make sense of the effects of trauma and the creative ways that people cope, rather than pathologizing and labelling them. Like many women who experienced childhood sexual, physical, and emotional abuse, Violet struggled with feeling depressed. In order to comfort and numb herself from her pain, she would rely on either binge eating or drinking. It is possible to ask questions that allow for a counterviewing of common pathologizing approaches to women's experiences of trauma.

Exploring Depression

At the beginning of our work, Violet was chronically sad and depressed. Counterviewing questions I asked Violet in our conversations include the following:

> How did the abuse make you feel sad?
> How did the abuse make you feel hopeless?

How did the abuse make you feel about yourself?

What did the abuse tell you about what you can expect from people?

What influence has feeling depressed had on your life?

Are there times you feel less depressed?

What is different about those times?

How can you have more of those times?

What would your life be like without depression?

Violet used food as a way to comfort herself and take care of herself. We explored what she was feeling or not feeling when she wanted to emotionally eat. She would use food to deal with feeling depressed. Her history of abuse and trauma left her often feeling empty, that her needs were not important, and that what she felt did not matter. She had never felt cared for or loved and had learned few ways to comfort or soothe herself. She would feel warm, comforted, and soothed when she ate emotionally. She would sometimes binge eat and purge. This was more often associated with feeling anxious, rejected, abandoned, angry, and hurt. She also struggled with her body image because she wanted to lose weight and be what she thought of as more attractive, while at the same time she did not want to be thinner and attract more sexual attention.

She was concerned about her emotional eating as it felt out of control. We would explore her eating as an entry point into acknowledging and making space for her emotional needs and for self-compassion. We would talk about how important these needs were and having ways to comfort herself. Here are some questions we explored:

What is going on for you, Violet, when you turn to emotional eating?

Does eating give you a feeling of comfort?

What does this feel like?

What are other ways you have comfort in your life?

Do you feel it makes sense that you use food to give you comfort?

Is that important to you?

When you feel depressed are you more likely to eat?

What other feelings are going on?

Is it okay to give yourself permission to take care of yourself when you are
    feeling depressed?

Is eating one way you can do this?

As a child were you able to soothe yourself?

What other ways do you soothe yourself now?

Similarly, Violet sometimes used alcohol as a way to numb the pain and deal with depression. We know that with trauma people often experience a "dialectic of trauma" (Herman, 1992), oscillating between intrusiveness of memories and painful feelings to numbing or "dissociating" from them. Numbing from pain is a protective response. It is critical that we acknowledge how women cope with trauma histories and their effects, such as depression. Food and alcohol are commonly used to provide comfort and protection (Brown & Stewart, 2008; Stewart, Brown, Devoulyte, Theakston, & Larsen, 2006). These coping strategies need to be explored and not pathologized. Women's creativity and agency can be seen through these coping strategies. They need to be reframed as ways women are trying to take care of themselves, and the need to take care of themselves should be seen as important and valuable. It is helpful, at least in part, to see these methods as forms of harm reduction as people struggle with the effects of trauma. We also need to appreciate that these methods of taking care of themselves may be the best they know. We might ask Violet the following questions:

> Do you see your drinking as related to the abuse?
> How does drinking help you deal with the pain?
> Are there ways in which it does not help you?
> Is it similar to eating in any way?
> Is the comfort and numbing that eating and drinking give you important to you?

The counterviewing questions (provided below) about trauma effects and trauma allow for the possibility for more helpful counterstories to emerge. By the time we stopped working together, Violet had started to form a few friendships and express interest in other women. She was speaking much more directly and assertively about her needs and feelings. We had a very strong therapeutic relationship, which allowed her to do some serious relationship healing. At this point in the work, Violet had begun to embrace a more helpful alternative story about relationships. Together, we could see the future of a counterstory for Violet's life that is not deficit based and could see hope for relationships. Her story of relational injury had been at least partially shifted toward one where positive meaningful relationships are more possible.

> What are your expectations in the new friendships you have formed?
> Do you expect these friends to let you down?

What will you do if they let you down?

Who knows how much work you have done on relationships?

If you continue to develop and build these relationships, what do you hope your future will look like?

Women diagnosed as "borderline" are very often misunderstood. Therapists often find them difficult to work with, angry, lashing out, unpredictable, combative, and unpleasant. It is so important not to abandon and reject these women, as they have already had too much of this in their lives. They need compassion and patience, not judgment. They have reasons to be angry and hurt. They need to be encouraged to speak about what has happened and its effects, and to work to develop more helpful coping strategies than, for example, binge eating or drinking or self-harm. Yet, when women use these strategies as ways to cope, a harm reduction approach needs to be taken. As we can see from Violet's case, it makes sense that she would comfort and soothe herself with food, and sometimes bingeing and purging to cope with feelings of rejection, abandonment, anger, and hurt, and at other times use alcohol as a way of numbing pain. She was learning to regulate her emotions and coping the best way she could. We would unpack what was going on when she ate for comfort or binged/purged and try to understand and acknowledge these efforts at coping. It made no sense to suggest she simply stop these methods of coping. It was pretty clear she needed that comfort and soothing, needed ways of regulating feeling out of control and overwhelmed. In critical trauma work, exploring coping and emotional regulation is a central part of the work and often takes time within a strong therapeutic alliance. This is a valuable step in the work of addressing the aftermath of trauma, as better forms of coping and regulating may emerge over time when women are ready alongside new identity stories that shift blame and responsibility for trauma experiences, expectations of relationships, and for themselves in the world.

CONCLUSION

In this chapter, I have illustrated how difficult it often is to tell one's story and the centrality of the therapeutic relationship between the client and therapist when working with chronic multiple childhood traumas that have a significant and ongoing effect on living one's life as an adult through exploring Violet's story. It is difficult to imagine being dispassionate or bias-free about child sexual abuse, incest, battery, neglect, or violence against women. People's stories of trauma often reveal the creative efforts humans make to survive. Trauma has a profound impact on the developing child, who may produce some adaptive/functional coping methods or others that result in deleterious effects. Usually there is a bit of both. When humans face horror or terror, they often use all their resources to cope and survive: they often survive what seems impossible to survive. Yet, the trauma is not without its effects. As humans, our coping can be undeniably creative; for example, the ability to escape in our minds even just momentarily by pretending to be someone else or going somewhere else in our minds to escape. I have argued that we need to adopt a non-pathologizing approach to trauma work. I find it is important to take the stance that the ways women cope with complex trauma make sense. Through the establishment of a strong collaborative therapeutic alliance, a foundation can be created to do the often emotionally risky trauma work, to counterview relational injury, and to create subsequent counterstories of relationships.

NOTE

1. The case I am discussing is a composite case based on multiple women I have worked with who were diagnosed within the biomedical system as "borderline" and who have struggled with both the label and the effects of childhood abuse and trauma.

REFERENCES

Ahmed, S. (2004). *The cultural politics of emotion*. Edinburgh: Edinburgh University Press.

Armstrong, L. (1978). *Kiss daddy goodnight*. New York: Hawthorn.

Bass, E., & Davis, L. (1988). *The courage to heal. A guide for women survivors of child sexual abuse*. New York: Harper and Row.

Becker, D., & Lamb, S. (1994). Sex bias in the diagnosis of borderline personality disorder and posttraumatic stress disorder. *Professional Psychology: Research and Practice*, *25*(1), 55–61.

Brown, C. (2007a). Dethroning the suppressed voice: Unpacking experience as story. In C. Brown & T. Augusta-Scott (Eds.), *Narrative therapy: Making meaning, making lives* (pp. 177–196). Thousand Oaks, CA: Sage.

Brown, C. (2007b). Situating knowledge and power in the therapeutic alliance. In C. Brown & T. Augusta-Scott (Eds.), *Narrative therapy: Making meaning, making lives* (pp. 3–22). Thousand Oaks, CA: Sage.

Brown, C. (2007c). Talking body talk: Blending feminist and narrative approaches to practice. In C. Brown & T. Augusta-Scott (Eds.), *Narrative therapy: Making meaning, making lives* (pp. 269–302). Thousand Oaks, CA: Sage.

Brown, C. (2013). Women's narratives of trauma: (Re)storying uncertainty, minimization and self-blame. *Narrative Works: Issues, Investigations and Interventions, 3*(1), 1–30.

Brown, C. (2014). Untangling emotional threads, self-management discourse and women's body talk. In S. McKenzie-Mohr & M. Lafrance (Eds.), *Women voicing resistance: Discursive and narrative explorations* (pp. 174–190). New York: Routledge.

Brown, C. (2016). The constraints of neo-liberal new managerialism in social work education. *Canadian Review of Social Work, 33*(1), 115–123.

Brown, C. (2017). Creating counterstories: Critical clinical practice and feminist narrative therapy. In D. Baines (Ed.), *Doing anti-oppressive practice: Building transformative, politicized social work* (3rd ed., pp. 212–232). Toronto: Fernwood.

Brown, C. (2018). The dangers of trauma talk: Counterstorying co-occurring strategies for coping with trauma. *Journal of Systemic Therapies, 37*(3), 38–55.

Brown, C. (2019). Speaking of women's depression and the politics of emotion. *Affilia: Journal of Women and Social Work, 34*(2), 151–169.

Brown, C., & Augusta-Scott, T. (2007) (Eds.). *Narrative therapy: Making meaning, making lives.* Thousand Oaks, CA: Sage.

Brown, C., & Augusta-Scott, T. (2018). Reimagining the intersection of gender, knowledge and power in collaborative therapeutic conversations with women and eating disorders and men who use violence. In D. Pare & C. Audet (Eds.), *Social justice and narrative therapy* (pp. 143–158). New York: Routledge.

Brown, C., & Stewart, S. H. (2008). Exploring women's use of alcohol as self-medication for depression. *Journal of Prevention and Intervention in the Community* (Special Issue on Depression), *35*(2), 33–47.

Brown, L. (1992). A feminist critique of personality disorders. In L. S. Brown & M. Ballou (Eds.), *Personality and psychopathology: Feminist reappraisals* (pp. 206–228). New York: Guilford Press.

Brown, L. (2004). Feminist paradigms of trauma treatment. *Psychotherapy: Theory, Research, Practice, Training, 41*(4), 464–471.

Brownmiller, S. (1975). *Against our will: Men, women, and rape.* New York: Simon and Schuster.

Burstow, B. (1992). *Radical feminist therapy: Working in the context of violence.* Thousand Oaks, CA: Sage.

Burstow, B. (2003). Toward a radical understanding of trauma and trauma work. *Violence Against Women, 9*(11), 1293–1317.

Butler, S. (1978). *The conspiracy of silence: The trauma of incest.* Volcano, CA: Volcano Press.

Cermele, J., Daniels, S., & Anderson, K. (2001). Defining normal: Constructions of race and gender in the DSM-IV casebook. *Feminism and Psychology, 11*(2), 229–247.

Courtoise, C. (1988). *Healing the incest wound.* New York: Norton.

Courtoise, C. (2004). Complex trauma, complex reactions: Assessment and treatment. *Psychotherapy: Theory, Research, Practice, Training, 41*(4), 412–425.

Cusack, K. J., Morrissey, J. P., & Ellis, A. R. (2008). Targeting trauma-related interventions and improving outcomes for women with co-occurring disorders. *Administration and Policy in Mental Health and Mental Health Services Research, 35*(3), 147–158.

DeVault, M. (1990). Talking and listening from women's standpoint: Feminist strategies for interviewing and analysis. *Social Problems, 37*(1), 96–116.

Drauker, C. B. (1998). Narrative therapy for women who have lived with violence. *Archives of Psychiatric Nursing, 12*(3), 162–168.

Duvall, J., & Beres, L. (2007). Movement of identities: A map for therapeutic conversations about trauma. In C. Brown & T. Augusta-Scott (Eds.), *Narrative therapy: Making meaning, making lives* (pp. 229–250). Thousand Oaks, CA: Sage.

Esposito, L., & Perez, F. M. (2014). Neoliberalism and the commodification of mental health. *Humanity and Society, 38*(4), 414–442.

Forward, S., & Buck, C. (1988). *Betrayal of innocence: Incest and its devastation.* New York: Penguin Books.

Gavey, N. (2005). *Just sex? The cultural scaffolding of rape.* New York: Psychology Press.

Gay, R. (2018). *Not that bad: Dispatches from rape culture.* New York: Harper Collins.

Haskell, L. (2012) A developmental understanding of complex trauma. In N. Poole & L. Greaves (Eds.), *Becoming trauma informed* (pp. 9–28). Toronto: Centre for Addiction and Mental Health.

Herman, J. (1981). *Father-daughter incest.* Cambridge, MA: Harvard University Press.

Herman, J. (1992). *Trauma and recovery: The aftermath of violence—From domestic abuse to political terror* (1st ed.). New York: Basic Books.

Herman, J. (2015). *Trauma and recovery: The aftermath of violence—From domestic abuse to political terror* (2nd ed.). New York: Basic Books.

Herman, J., Perry, C., & van der Kolk, B. (1989). Childhood trauma in borderline personality disorder. *American Journal of Psychiatry, 146*, 490–495.

Hochschild, A. (1983). *The managed heart: The commercialization of human feeling.* Berkeley, CA: The University of California Press.

Horton, E. (2007, December). Neoliberalism and the Australian healthcare system. Paper presented at the 2007 Conference of the Philosophy of Education Society of Australasia, Wellington, New Zealand.

Lafrance, M., & McKenzie-Mohr, S. (2013). The DSM and its lure of legitimacy. *Feminism and Psychology, 23*(1), 119–140.

Levine, H. (1982). The personal is political: Feminism and the helping professions. In G. Finn & A. Miles (Eds.), *Feminism in Canada: From pressure to politics* (pp. 175–210). Montreal: Black Rose Books.

Madigan, S. (2003). Counterviewing injurious speech acts: Destabilizing eight conversational habits of highly effective problems. *International Journal of Narrative Therapy and Community Work, 1*, 43–59.

Marecek, J. (2006). Social suffering, gender, and women's depression. In C. L. Keyes & S. H. Goodman (Eds.), *Women and depression: A handbook for the social, behavioral, and biomedical sciences* (pp. 283–308). Cambridge, UK: Cambridge University Press.

Marecek, J., & Gavey, N. (2013). DSM-5 and beyond: A critical feminist engagement with psychodiagnosis. *Feminism and Psychology, 23*(1), 3–9.

McKenzie-Mohr, S., & Lafrance, M. (2011). Telling stories without the words: Tightrope talk in women's accounts of coming to live well after rape or depression. *Feminism and Psychology, 21*(1), 49–73.

McKenzie-Mohr, S., & Lafrance, M. (2014a). *Women voicing resistance: Discursive and narrative explorations.* New York: Routledge.

McKenzie-Mohr, S., & Lafrance, M. (2014b). Women's discursive resistance: Attuning to counter-stories and collectivizing for change. In S. McKenzie-Mohr & M. Lafrance (Eds.), *Creating counterstories: Women resisting dominant discourses in speaking their lives* (pp. 191–205). New York: Routledge.

McWade, B. (2016). Recovery-as-policy as a form of neoliberal state making. *Intersectionalities: A Global Journal of Social Work Analysis, Research, Polity, and Practice, 5*(3), 62–81.

Morgan, A. (2007). *What is narrative therapy?* Adelaide, Australia: Dulwich Centre Publications.

Morrow, M., & Weisser, J. (2012). Toward a social justice framework of mental health recovery. *Studies in Social Justice, 6*(1), 27–43.

Pease, B., & Nipperess, S. (2016). Doing critical social work in the neoliberal context: Working on the contradictions. In B. Pease, S. Goldingay, N. Hosken, & S. Nipperess (Eds.), *Doing critical social work: Transformative practices for social justice* (pp. 3–24). Crows Nest, Australia: Allen and Unwin.

Pizzey, E. (1974). *Scream quietly or the neighbours will hear.* New York: Penguin Books.

Poole, N. (2013). *Trauma informed practice.* British Columbia Centre of Excellence for Women's Health and Ministry of Health, Government of British Columbia.

Russell, D. (1986). *The secret trauma: Incest in the lives of girls and women.* New York: Basic Books.

Sakellarion, D., & Rotarou, E. (2017). The effects of neoliberal policies on access to healthcare for people with disabilities. *International Journal for Equity in Health, 16*, 199.

Shaffer, B. (Director). (1987). *To a safer place* [Film]. Canada: National Film Board.

Smith, D., & David, S. (Eds.). (1975). *Women look at psychiatry: I'm not mad, I'm angry.* Vancouver: Press Gang Publishing.

Stewart, S., Brown, C., Devoulyte, K., Theakston, J., & Larsen, S. (2006). Why women with alcohol problems binge eat? Exploring connections between binge eating and binge drinking among Nova Scotia women. *Journal of Health Psychology, 11*(3), 409–425.

Terr, L. (1990). *Too scared to cry: Psychic trauma in childhood.* New York: Harper and Row.

Tseris, E. (2013). Trauma theory without feminism? Evaluating contemporary understandings of traumatized women. *Affilia: Journal of Women and Social Work, 28*(2), 153–164.

Turner, J. (2009). The sociology of emotions: Basic theoretical arguments. *Emotion Review, 1*(4), 340–354.

Ussher, J. (2010). Are we medicalizing women's misery? A critical review of women's higher rates of reported depression. *Feminism and Psychology, 20*(1), 9–35.

Webster, D., & Dunn, E. (2005). Feminist perspectives on trauma. *Women and Therapy, 28*(3/4), 111–142.

Weisser, J., Morrow, M., & Jamer, B. (2011). A critical exploration of social inequities in mental health recovery literature. Vancouver: Centre for the Study of Gender, Social Inequities and Mental Health.

White, M. (2000). Re-engaging with history: The absent but implicit. In M. White, *Reflections on narrative practice: Essays and interviews* (pp. 35–58). Adelaide, Australia: Dulwich Centre Publications.

White, M. (2001). Narrative practice and the unpacking of identity conclusions. *Gecko: A Journal of Deconstruction and Narrative Ideas in Therapeutic Practice, 1*, 28–55.

White, M. (2002). Addressing personal failure. *International Journal of Narrative Therapy and Community Work, 3*, 33–76.

White, M. (2003). Narrative practice and community assignments. *International Journal of Narrative Therapy and Community Work, 2*, 17–55.

White, M. (2004). Working with people who are suffering the consequences of multiple trauma: A narrative perspective. *International Journal of Narrative Therapy and Community Work, 1*, 45–76.

White, M. (2007). *Maps of narrative practice.* New York: Norton.

CHAPTER 4

Critical Clinical Approaches with Girls and Their Experiences of Sexualized Violence

Marion Brown

INTRODUCTION

Sexualized violence is a central organizing experience of teenaged girls, on the level of a public health concern in Canada and beyond. Prevailing therapeutic approaches tend to focus on the internalized effects of the violence, with emphasis on individualized coping strategies. While attention to the subjective experience is, of course, required, such approaches are typically depoliticized and decontextualized, thus reinscribing conventional scripts of binary gender power dynamics and leaving intact the cultural practices that normalize sexualized violence from males to females. This is an injustice to all girls, both current and future, and dismisses a clear opportunity to disrupt the discourses that perpetuate rape culture. Therapeutic conversations are distinctly politicized processes because of their potential to interrupt dominant social processes and practices through reflection, dialogue, analysis, and action. Critical clinical approaches integrate personal experiences within a structural, systemic, socio-political analysis, recognizing that there is no self outside this social context. This chapter articulates three principles of critical clinical approaches and their relevance for working with the impact and effect of experiencing sexualized violence: bridging binaries, parsing power, and connecting with the collective. Each principle is applied to a case example, providing practical options for practitioner use.

As you read this chapter, ask yourself the following questions:

1. What are my fundamental assumptions about how sexualized violence is perpetuated? What do I consider to be the contributing factors?
2. What are the binaries to which social work often contributes? What would it take to reorient to a framework of multiple perspectives in the field of sexualized violence?

3. What are the examples of material and discursive operations of power in my field of practice? What are their effects on the people with whom we work?

4. What are examples of collective action strategies that hold promise for the field of sexualized violence?

Two young fish are swimming along when an elder fish swims by and says, "How's the water today?" Mystified, one young fish turns to the other and says "Water? What's water?" Sexualized violence is our water. It is a feature of social life so ubiquitous that it is rarely questioned, as prevalent and routine as the water: ever present yet barely visible.

Sexualized violence is aggression that has been made sexual, a particular construction of violence that imprints hurt and harm upon the physical, emotional, mental, and spiritual dimensions of our embodied selves. It is experienced primarily by women, people who identify as non-binary or trans, and children, and is equally likely to affect any age, class, and race, however, racialized people are differentially targeted (Black et al., 2011). The pervasive normalization and trivialization of sexualized violence abounds, and represents a health, social, and public safety issue (DeGue et al., 2014).

SEXUALIZED VIOLENCE

Sexualized violence is a range of behaviours and actions, and words written and spoken, that are rooted in sexual aspects of the body and that reflect imbalances in concrete manifestations of power, as well as intangible expressions of power. It is a contextually relevant, societally constructed phenomenon of expression that includes street-calling, groping, harassment, stalking, genital exposure, exploitation, date rape, sexual assault, and victim blaming/shaming.

Critical clinical approaches mobilize critical social theory into therapeutic practice. They are particularly suited to working with those who have experienced sexualized violence because they contextualize individual and collective experiences and make direct connections to organized systems of power relations and how they manifest in people's lives. Contextualizing action and accounts of action finds theoretical grounding within intersectional analyses, which understand people as multi-dimensional beings with each facet of our personal, social, and political identity inextricably intertwined with all the others (Crenshaw, 1995).

Critical clinical approaches uphold multiple and complex identities, histories, circumstances, and politics. Individual experience is situated in historical, social, and political context, which helps us examine social processes and structures, their implications and effects (Fook, 2016). Together, these levels of action hold promise for changes on the levels of individual and collective experiences, civil rights, and economic, social, sexual, and cultural rights. Upholding both individual experience and context demands us to uphold complexity, and not reduce or simplify cause and effect.

CRITICAL CLINICAL WORK

Critical clinical work balances a socio-political analysis of the systemic forces on people's lives with a personally contextualized analysis of the meanings made of life within those systems. Critical clinical approaches aim to unhook us from stuck self-identities by exploring and expanding a range of possible interpretations of what is happening in our worlds.

Further, in critical clinical work we do not just hear stories and leave them intact. We interact with the stories we hear: we question, probe for detail, follow hunches, speculate about what else could be happening, and suggest alternative explanations (C. Brown, 2017). This is a particularly poignant perspective when working with people who have experienced sexualized violence, for while disrupting the notion that there is inherent truth to stories told *about us* can feel vindicating, disrupting the notion that there is inherent truth in *our own* stories and experiences can feel destabilizing. Critical clinical approaches acknowledge that our deeply valued, personally experienced self-stories are not inherently true or truer than other accounts; indeed, no single story can capture all meanings and implications. Critical clinical approaches seek additional and alternative interpretations, drawing out multiple perspectives, thinking, talking, and working through dialogue, and questioning, probing, and supposing, led by the question "what are the possibilities here?" more than "what is the right/true answer here?" These analytic features mean that we don't focus on sexualized violence in isolation from the context in which it occurs. Rather, we challenge systemic factors and social conditions that reinforce the culture of sexualized violence through advocacy for federal and provincial law reform, activism through Take Back the Night marches, and therapeutic approaches with individuals and groups.

In this chapter, I isolate three principles of critical clinical approaches—bridging binaries, parsing power, and connecting with the collective—and detail how each maps onto therapeutic work with three teenaged girls with whom I have worked around their experiences of sexualized violence.

PRINCIPLE ONE: BRIDGING BINARIES

The notion that for most situations there are two distinct ways to categorize action, belief, or identity, with little attention to shared middle ground, is a cornerstone of Western thought, to the degree that, as with all social constructions, binaries are taken as exhaustive and thus as "given." Dualistic thinking suggests that such classifications are mutually exclusive and categorically conclusive: never the two shall meet. This bifurcation has become deeply engrained in Western patterns of thought and action such that we regularly constitute choices based on either "this" or "that." Examples of dualistic or dichotomous thought that we use in popular speech include thinking a person is good or bad, that there is a right or wrong way to approach something, that there is a winner and a loser in a challenge, that if it is not my fault it must be your fault, and so on. Dichotomous categories order phenomena into polar, independent opposites that are hierarchialized according to preference and worth, thus they carry a normative component to the choices we make in relation to them (Fook, 2016). In the uneven weighting of bifurcated options, there is an embedded hierarchy where one position is valued as preferable to the other. As a result, people, decisions, circumstances, and positions are assigned a worth and a ranking that accords dominance/power/privilege to those that are preferred and subjugation to those on the underbelly. Binaries encourage thinking along a one-dimensional, easily classified plane, simplifying the complexities of thoughts, feelings, and experiences that exist within each of us. Given that we live in a societal context wherein efficiency and precision are highly valued, dualistic thought is often prioritized and regarded as the hallmark standard (Fook, 2016).

In social work, we invoke binaries when we separate "us," the social workers, from "them," the clients, and when we organize around constructs such as healthy/unhealthy, right/wrong, good/bad, private/public, true/untrue, weak/strong, male/female, and victim/perpetrator. These separations are steadfast in social work practice. And yet, on a deeply intuitive level, most of us know that our choices, motivations, thoughts, and feelings and their implications are not cut and dried, are not so definitively one thing or another. Most of us live in the grey area between polar opposites, traversing along various continua and living with the tensions and contradictions that exist in such fluid motion. Still, the persistent construction that funnels the shape of our thoughts and actions remains stubbornly intact: we either like or don't like the new kid at school, we are either at fault or to be vindicated in a dispute, or we are weak when we cry and strong when we don't.

Critical social work's manner of analysis, which aims to join rather than divide, respects the complications and contradictions of social lives and aims to uphold all of them, recognizing they are operating at all times. It accepts that we both shape and are shaped by structures and means of interaction; we are active agents as well as passive recipients. As we engage in our lives, we impose meanings, expressions, and expectations that further shape that with which we are engaged. Critical social work identifies incongruous performances of the social, such as those reflected in magazines that simultaneously headline concern over the startling rates of depression among girls, critique the sovereignty of rebellious angry girls, and sound the moral alarm over girls who refuse to conform to conventional scripts of femininity, displaying the tension among the concurrent narratives of girls as sad, mad, or bad (M. Brown, 2011).

Principle into Practice

The constructs of victim and survivor communicate a binary in the field of sexualized violence. We do not currently have a single term that adequately connotes that one is and/or can be both a victim and a survivor, an example of how language creates confines into which we pour our experiences, leading us to think that the words adequately capture who we are. Each individual term infers particular qualifiers: typically associated with *victim* are ideas of helplessness, powerlessness, weakness, and vulnerability—contributing to a construction of the passive and the failure; typically associated with *survivor* are resilience, strength, toughness, and overcoming obstacles—contributing to a construction of the active and the successful. As with most, there is a fiction to this binary: most people experience and express both vulnerability and strength.

In critical clinical practice, we take time to explore the nuances of the stories and the languages used within them that clients feel meaningfully reflect their lives. We listen to the words, often writing them down to both externalize the issues and provide a focus for our detailed examination. We know the stories and the words are those available to us through cultural and social means.

Jaylyn was a 15-year-old girl of African descent whose White, adult male neighbour had been sexually abusing her for the past two years. He had been friendly when she was younger, a friend of the family through living nearby, and she was used to his greetings and brief conversations. The progression of his actions began with prolonged looks and gestures, which left Jaylyn confused and uncertain about how to interact with him. She didn't mention anything to her parents because she didn't want to be seen to be overreacting or judgmental of a man she considered to be old and lonely. He began to ask her for assistance with retrieving items from the garage and bringing them into the house. He was then hugging her to thank her, then holding onto her beyond her comfort, and thereafter intermittently constructing a series of reasons for touching her and rationales for her to touch him, with increasing invasion of her boundaries to the point of physical sexual assault. Jaylyn was confused and fearful. She was conflicted about the "helpless older neighbour" construction he enacted, which she'd grown up with and was upheld by her parents and older brothers, and which continued to have her thinking she should be helpful when he asked. She didn't understand why sometimes he would "try something" and other times he would not. She said she felt like she was a "sucker" and an "idiot" because she couldn't foresee what he would do in any given interaction. Those were the terms that suited her more than the ones she had heard in many presentations at school: victim and survivor.

One of my foci with Jaylyn was to flesh out what the terms *victim* and *survivor* meant to her, and how, if at all, one or both had ever fit her sense of herself. On hearing her first responses, I probed the story back to early messages about victim and survivor, and how she may have applied them to herself or others across a range of situations. I asked about meaningful people in her life, and how they use the terms, if at all. I was listening for multiple definitions and multiple applications of their use, noting each of them, and reinforcing that these words can have many meanings across many contexts: each one on their own is partial, only one slice of a story. I was also seeking to understand if there is a pattern of her understanding or use of the terms. At the same time, I was listening for exceptions to that pattern, and times that she dismissed their use in favour of her own, or familial- or community-patterned uses and definitions of the terms. I also asked about societal messaging she has heard with these terms attached, not only related to sexualized violence but anywhere and everywhere. I asked her if she thought victims can be strong and if survivors feel challenged. Together, we explored if there are other words that lay between victim and survivor that might capture her experience differently or better. This was a delicate exploration, as I took care neither to police nor judge her choice of words, rather wondering aloud, creating a genealogy of the words, and breathing life into alternate possible meanings of the relevant words and their cohabitation within one person.

Breaking the framework of binaries allows for the possibility that Jaylyn can be both victim and survivor, that she is not always at risk of exploitation, and that she can access a full range of possibilities through the process of collapsing the dualistic divide. She can fill these socially constructed terms with refreshed meanings, a technology of power that she can carry with her to resist categorization and its inherent simplification of her life.

The reconciliation that she could simultaneously hold identities of both victim and survivor did not sit easily for Jaylyn. It felt chaotic, unsettled, an identity that was not cohesive. Prevailing societal and cultural messaging had been effective: she had internalized that to be a survivor was better than to be a victim, and to resolve a feeling or issue was better than to be in flux. Yet she also acknowledged that some days she accepted her weepiness and other days she was frustrated with herself for it. Some days she wrote streams of anger-fuelled journal entries, other days they were full of fear and shame, and still other days they were about her soccer team, her friends, and the school dance. She wanted a linear progression to being "better" and putting this portion of her past behind her. Operating here are internalized disciplinary practices of the self—the self-surveillance that is the ultimate aim of self-/social regulation within the binary structure of either victim or survivor (C. Brown & Augusta-Scott, 2007). We explored how this approach was limiting for her and normalized the seemingly contradictory responses and meanings given to experiences of trauma and violence. The socially constructed rhetoric of binary thinking obscures that everyone engages in contradictory performances and interferes with allowing people to live with coexisting vulnerability and strength.

This meaning making was necessarily nested within the multi-dimensional facets of Jaylyn's life, thus we contextualized according to personal, family, neighbourhood, and societal messaging about what it means to be racialized, a daughter and younger sister, currently able-bodied, and a 15-year-old young woman navigating adult relationships in her community, school, and town. Societal structures and social processes ascribe social power differentially based on our sex, gender, sexual orientation, racialization, class, age, and ability (Crenshaw, 1995). Thus our exploration was unique to Jaylyn's identity markers, individual and collective history, and current material life situation.

PRINCIPLE TWO: PARSING POWER

Critical clinical work is committed to identifying, deconstructing, and transforming operations of power, both material and discursive. Critical social work grew out of a modernist framework that centred on materialist analyses of static structures of power—institutions, laws, policies, and governing bodies—that create social practices that mirror particular prevailing beliefs and values about how things should be (Fook, 2016; Mullaly & West, 2017). These concrete, normative foundations are not value-neutral or objective. These terms obscure that social structures and systems are socially constructed, typically by those who have powerful means for influencing thought and action. And, as social beings within those social structures, we are all participating in operations of power every day.

Material refers to that which is materialized in the external social world, a manifestation that can be seen and touched. Material analyses recognize that structural settings in the social sphere (organizations, agencies, institutions, laws, policies) get organized according to priorities. Societal structures are rooted in historicized arrangements and expressions of power and governed by the interests of the dominant, with concrete effects on the rest, for example through judicial bodies and health policies (Mullaly & West, 2017). Drawing from modernism's conceptualization of power as a concrete commodity, material analyses study the ways in which social structures ascribe power and allocate resources according to gender, race, ethnicity, age, ability, and sexual orientation. These analyses detail the injustices meted out through systems and social structures and swing the locus of responsibility away from individuals and toward social arrangements. Individual lives are scaffolded by social, economic, and political arrangements that play out within the social structures of family, school, religion, health, and work. Structural, materialist analyses critique individualized explanations and provide a systemic analysis of factors affecting individual lives.

Growing from these important roots, critical clinical work has been influenced by postmodern and post-structuralist thought and incorporates a discursive analysis, the intangible gestures of power—the ways customs are codified, the manner of speaking that varies among audiences—that also create social practices that mirror prevailing beliefs and values about how things should be. It's a shift to include not only the overt, but the covert—the interactional dynamics and meaning making that continue to reify dominant beliefs and expectations. Therapists and educators working in the field of sexualized violence, for example, bring forward the position that how we talk about sexuality both liberates and constrains individuals as well as communities. Both the content and our means of communicating send important messages about sexuality that are explicitly and implicitly performed and consumed by audiences. We both shape and are shaped by these discourses; we both reproduce and resist them.

If material or structure is the "what"—the content of power—discourse is the "how"—the *process* of power; discourse is constructed ways of thinking that constitute power. The content is always influenced by the how: how we consume it, how we produce it, and how we communicate it. The how is the means by which the content comes to life. Discourse is the idea that things do not exist outside of our doing or naming them; it is the act of doing or naming that creates them (Chambon, 1999). Words and gestures, inclusion and exclusion, not only reflect meanings; they actively shape meanings as we use them.

Critical clinical approaches, in bridging binaries and parsing operations of power, examine both external structures and constructed, internally held ways of thinking. Critical clinical approaches recognize that power operates through structures that dominate and oppress, yet it also operates through constructed and changing social relations. In practice, then, critical clinical approaches expose structures and social relations as constructed in time and space, and as therefore transformable (Fook, 2016). We identify and question, critique, explore, and disrupt the external structures, the social relations, and the personal constructions, recognizing that these are interconnected and always operating. In practice with girls regarding sexualized violence we directly challenge the construction of the passive subject and discuss ways to be engaged in and closer to taking up power to act in and on our lives. What is presented as fact and truth—about ourselves, about justice, about the meaning of these experiences—is therefore contested, and agency becomes a central organizing concept. Practice methods focus on interaction, dialogue, self-reflection, analysis, and collective, politicized action.

Principle into Practice

One example of engaging with the both/and of material and discursive operations of power in therapeutic conversations about sexualized violence is to ask what the "rules" are regarding sexuality, gender, unwanted and desired sexual contact, body, and scripts of masculinity and femininity within family, neighbourhood, school, community, social media, and the world beyond. I took this approach in working with Maris, a 17-year-old Jewish girl whose image, naked and under the influence of alcohol, was circulated on social media. Maris had been with people she considered friends at a house party. This group regularly drank alcohol around each other, and while frequently documenting these occasions with Snapchat and Instagram, she had never been aware of any compromising photos being taken of any member of the group. She was devastated by what she considered betrayal by her friends, stunned numb in her shame and embarrassment. She moved between what felt like the impossibility of returning to school and any sort of social connection there and her grief at facing her parents' simultaneous disappointment in her behaviour and concern for her well-being. All possibilities and expectations felt overwhelming to her, caught as she was in a quagmire of guilt, shame, and horror. I began our conversations by externalizing this overwhelm and framing it as a series of rules: what she feels she can and cannot, should or should not say, do, think, ask, and be, as well as *where* she feels she can and/or wants to say, do, think, ask, and be. I wondered aloud about where and how these rules are connected to social expectations and how they have come to be that way, both generally, and specifically in relation to her, a 17-year-old Jewish girl with her family's particular access to resources and expressions of class. This work was to unearth all the options, particularly the ones that felt most at the fringes of what she considered possible. We drew a wide account of all the ways in which she is impacted by conceptions of rules and all the ways in which she makes sense of the impacts on her sense of herself as an embodied being.

Throughout these conversations I probed for, as well as suggested, a fine detailing of these rules as a mechanism of power, differentiating the methods. For example, I talked and asked about how some rules are written down and others are spoken and still others are implied by body language and intonation. Some are reflected in programs and specific supports, and some are reflected in positions people hold or in the wearing of a uniform. Some are specific to Jewish high-school girls living in mid-sized towns on the east coast of Canada in the 2000s. Other rules are captured in phrases such as "it's just the way things are" or "you just don't do that." Maris identified examples from across her life that fell into each of these dimensions.

I asked about the rules that we have for ourselves that may have begun as normative social practices, yet now feel like they have a life of their own inside of us—normative practices of self. Maris's example of this was family messaging about never getting into trouble. As a Jewish person, her mother had raised her with the consciousness that she will be more scrutinized, more surveilled, and therefore more at risk of the institutional gaze. Not only had Maris taken heed of her mother's concerns, she also did not want to worry her mother. Over the years, her mother's messaging became her own, resonating deeply, for example, when she learned of anti-Semitic graffiti on the synagogue.

In our work together, I probed and speculated about the manner of talk about the rules: Where is the talk bold and directive? Where is the talk subtle and suggestive? I asked about the delivery of the rules: Who is/are the communicator(s)? Where and when are the rules promoted? I asked what the dominant themes are and talked about rhetoric: Where and when does the talk seem genuine? Forced? Contrived? Personally meaningful? We were drawing out that how we talk about sexuality, gender, unwanted and wanted sexual contact, body, and scripts both liberate and constrain us individually as well as in communities. Expanding the rules in these ways reveals the many expressions of power that exist in our lives. Some feel big, fixed, and external to us—perhaps too big for us to feel we can take on, such as how teenaged girls are allowed to be sexual. Yet exploring a breadth and depth of expressions of power can also illuminate instances where we can see possibility for a reconstruction of how to engage, how to ascribe new meanings, and where decision points might open.

DISCURSIVELY HELPFUL/HARMFUL

I use the term *discursively helpful* to capture the experience of interactions and exchanges, words and actions, that exist in the sphere of interpretation and are taken up as affirming and validating. I use the term *discursively harmful* for those dynamics, which again live in the interpretive domain, that are experienced as threatening, undermining, and/or hurtful.

MATERIALLY HELPFUL/HARMFUL

I use the term *materially helpful* to denote the supports that come in concrete forms, through people enacting their positions, through content, and through other substantive representations of affirmation and validation. I use the term *materially harmful* for the concrete artifacts and tangible articles and positions taken that contribute to feelings of pain and/or vulnerability.

In my work with Maris, this archaeology of the rules led to discussion about the following: the teen health centre at the school, and its role/efforts in educating students about the connection between alcohol consumption and sexualized violence (experienced as materially helpful); the guidance counsellor's response to Maris when she learned of Maris's experience (experienced as discursively helpful); the photograph that circulated on social media of Maris undressed and passed out (experienced as materially harmful); the stares, whispers, and exclusion in the hallways at school (experienced as discursively harmful); Maris's parents' response when they learned of the incident (experienced as materially helpful and discursively unhelpful); learning of the law regarding sharing of explicit images online (experienced as materially helpful); and the police officer's skepticism that charges would be laid (experienced as discursively harmful). I asked about the messaging Maris was taking inside herself through all these experiences, and what rules she was applying to herself. In each instance, we were talking along a continuum of what felt weighty and difficult to shift and what felt even slightly malleable to her in thought and action. I return to Maris's story later in the next section, given that connecting with the collective became a means through which to negotiate the rules.

PRINCIPLE THREE: CONNECTING WITH THE COLLECTIVE

Sexualized violence occurs within intra-personal, interpersonal, and extra-personal spaces. While often distilled to a unilateral interpersonal interaction—a communication from one or more to another/others—it also lives within the people involved (intra-personal) and beyond any people involved (extra-personal). Another framework for understanding its scope is to consider the individual, institutional, and societal contexts of sexualized violence. Individual contexts include narratives about experiences; decisions regarding reporting; disclosure to family, friends, and legal bodies; testimonials; emotions; and internalized constructions. Institutional contexts include educational spaces, law enforcement, the justice system, social policies, and media. The societal domain includes the social and economic conditions that make women, non-binary and trans people, and children vulnerable to violence through the tools of sexism, racism, ableism, homophobia, transphobia, neoliberalism, imperialism, and late capitalism (Baker & Bevacqua, 2018). Music, television, movies, magazines, social media, and video games are expressions of this extra-personal, societal plane, from which we all make meaning, take notice, and derive personally held, intrapersonal meanings that we live out with others. Indeed, sexualized violence is a form of "social conduct" (Coates & Wade, 2007, p. 513) that exists on a superseding plane around and across all of us. A central site of analysis and action is therefore the macro social space, a focus that again finds congruence with critical clinical social work.

Critical clinical work is grounded in the structural conditions of people's lives and how these are taken up by the subject. It contextualizes individual experiences within societal structures and systems, linking personal, private happenings with public conditions and social relations. Moreover, it *politicizes* personal, private happenings by examining the economic and cultural conditions and social relations for operations of power.

The individual unit is very often the point of therapeutic intervention; it is frequently our point of entry. Yet a consciousness of the collective balances the experiences of the individual and the implications for the collective. It's another expression of bridging a binary, this one of me/we, and it bears mention again here because there has long been a tension in feminist anti-rape work surrounding a perceived shift away from collective efforts for social change and toward individualized efforts to improve the lives of those who have experienced sexualized violence. In critical clinical work, individual experiences are situated within the collective experience. Feminists have long referred to this principle as the "personal is political." This central tenet holds strong in critical clinical work, as well it needs to. For, in social work as well as other disciplines, from individualizing often comes pathologizing and being solely responsible for amelioration. Critical clinical work is committed to co-locating the self and the social.

Principle into Practice

When working with girls who experience sexualized violence, I put myself in the conversation by using the language of "we"—a collective social body that experiences sexualized violence. I frame this collective by talking about being fish in the water together, all of us schooled in the requirements and regulations of the social. It's an environment to which we all contribute: we both shape and are shaped by the social world, and we all can only know ourselves in and through the social world. Naming the shared context is more than a method of therapeutic joining. It stems from the critical clinical commitment to situate individual experiences *within* the social, and, in so doing, to locate responsibility *beyond* the individual, connecting the individual with a cohort of others who have shared conditions of living.

Bea was 17 years old, White, and identified as genderqueer, using the pronouns she/her. Bea's closest friend had noticed bruises on her body and after much probing learned that Bea's boyfriend, Mitch, slapped and pushed her, and squeezed his hands around her arms, waist, and neck when he was angry. He would regularly behave in these ways prior to or following their being intimate.

Bea's friend immediately told a teacher at school, who called Bea's parents. Her parents were shocked and fearful that their daughter would be/could be in such a relationship. They forbade her to see the boy and required that she attend counselling; they accompanied Bea to her first appointment with me. They were distraught, twisted with worry, and feeling futile in having an influence in the situation. Bea was not resistant to talking with me, and after her parents left, she made it clear that she would not be ending the relationship with Mitch. She was articulate and forthcoming in her reasons for staying with him: being abused as a boy led to him conflating physical aggression with love and he was working on controlling the physical manifestations of his anger. She felt proud of herself for believing in him and being committed to their relationship, and she felt the violence was what she could physically and emotionally handle. She understood, in an externalized and logical way, the concerns of her parents, friend, and teacher. Yet she dismissed them because she was sure she could handle Mitch and believed he would change, so she had no intention of not seeing him anymore.

Bea's experiences, beliefs, and values were thriving within the contemporary rhetoric of young love. Unpacking ideas and practices of the broader culture was where we started, exploring how they were serving the problematics of Bea's situation; they are the fertile ground within which Bea's relationship with Mitch had taken root. I drew on Bea's understanding of the concerns as the entry point to consider the constructs of gender, power, fear, love, pleasure, safety, threat, and sexual embodiment. We stayed with an externalizing approach; when talking about these things in a distanced way, abstracted from her own life, she was interested and engaged. However, when distilling them down into her choices and circumstances, she clouded over and was reluctant. The work was to merge this binary of budding politicized understanding of social relations with Bea's own story, to situate her experiences within the material and discursive cultural operations of sexualized violence in an effort to mobilize questions, ideas, and possibilities that could lead her to consider different choices.

Bea had grown up singing in choirs and had a younger sister. She was regularly in the company of girls and felt a deep identity kinship there, apparent in her transitioning as a young child from her male biological sex to her female gender. Our externalizing conversations expanded talk about the culture of girlhood today: the pressures, the contradictory messages, the consistency of fixed expectations. We parsed these into the dominant storylines and those less weighted, detailing how they affected her uniquely as a genderqueer person, and how they affected her sister, mother, aunts, female cousins, and friends. Moving across and between accounts of individualized and collectivized girlhood, we retained her thoughts, feelings, and experiences as both distinct from and embedded in a broader, communal sisterhood. We each brought in personal and public examples of experiences where we saw girls' efforts to both reconcile with and rupture regulation of their sexuality and where we consider girls' possibilities as both fixed and fluid. For example, media reports and opinion pieces routinely detail what a girl was wearing when she was sexually assaulted, speculate on how much she had been drinking when she was harassed, and propose that she should avoid walking alone in the dark. Yet girls disrupt daily the imposition of clothing regimes, devise strategies for drinking alcohol with friends with whom they establish safety rules, and talk on their cellphones when navigating the section of their route home that requires walking alone.

Girls and women have taken to the Internet to develop unique platforms to address sexualized violence through community building, knowledge mobilization, and collective resistance. Social media offer an accessible platform for "do it yourself activist media-making" (Rentschler, 2014, p. 66), which includes blogs, video logs, videos, and zines that post testimonials, share advice, generate tactics for resistance, encourage advocacy, and, importantly, build networks of affective, collective response via real-time, mobile means. I introduced Bea to ihollaback. org (dedicated to ending harassment) and she found stfurapeculture.tumblr.com (dedicated to exposing rape culture), in the context of our sharing examples of regulation and resistance. She learned through the exchanges, felt validated by the testimonials, was energized by the fearlessness, and felt drawn into a sense of virtual and localized communities. She came to see herself as part of something bigger than one life, one set of experiences, and as having access to a variety of tools to navigate the love and the harms she felt in her relationship with Mitch. She was especially drawn to the imagery of carrying the sisterhood in her back pocket, and she began talking to Mitch through her conceptualization of the sisterhood, situating her fears, needs, and desires within the collective, feeling its strength to mobilize her words and action. It was through her commitment to all girls that she exercised this voice. Ultimately, identifying with the collective led her away from an intimate relationship with Mitch. She now takes gender and women's studies at university and edits an online zine for girls.

Similarly, as Maris and I unpacked the rules and regulations of female sexuality, our quest for examples took us to those available online. It was here that Maris learned about SlutWalks, the grassroots, worldwide activism wherein the objectification of women is seized back from the holds of sexualized violence. SlutWalks flout patriarchy's rules and regulations of female sexuality and renounce its control over defining what is appropriate dress, behaviour, expression, and choices. It is an innovative and energetic antidote to slut-shaming, which, like the social media sites, is bolstered by the participation of a massive community of women worldwide (Carr, 2013). For Maris, to be singled out as a slut at her high school felt a lonely, vulnerable place to be, weighty and difficult to shift. Yet when she was reading, posting, watching online, and then marching with a throng of "sluts" who bridged the binary of virgin and whore, who manifested material power in their walk and deployed discursive power with their talk, Maris began to remodel her own rules.

CONCLUSION

Critical clinical work foregrounds the self and the social as interwoven and intersectional, requiring that we contextualize personal experiences within the historical-social-political fabric of our lives. This approach is acutely relevant for working with those who have experienced sexualized violence because of the willingness to work with this complexity, continually moving among and across the multiple dimensions of people's lives, refusing to distill them to any one dimension. Further, critical clinical approaches make explicit the multiple expressions and versions of power and deconstruct how they operate in people's lives. Thus, no story can be individualized nor isolated from historical, social, and political context, and social processes and structures, their implications and effects, are meticulously unpacked. This is the work required, when accompanying experiences of sexualized violence: we need to nest individual experience within context, interact with the stories we hear to broaden alternative interpretations, and challenge systemic factors and social conditions that reinforce the culture of sexualized violence. These are promising and progressive tools for disrupting the cultural practices that perpetuate sexualized violence. By bridging binaries, parsing power, and connecting with the collective, therapeutic conversations regarding sexualized violence are politicized and contextualized. Exemplified through Jaylyn navigating layers and expressions of her identity, Maris testing an expanded set of rules for herself, and Bea, who took up blogging to reestablish her agency in her sexual embodiment, each case illustrated a principle of critical clinical practice in action; each case disrupts a developmental, linear transition through experiences of sexualized violence. I posit that they provide ways of living that are another normative subjectivity where contradictions can be managed. This is promising conceptual space for thinking about what lies between the fixed and the transient in identity and experience. While ambiguous and complicated to do so, "if we do not walk in dangerous places and different types of terrain, nothing new will be found, no explorations are possible, and things remain the same" (Grosz, 1994, p. 173). Critical clinical work enters such dangerous places to disrupt binaries, deconstruct operations of power, and collectivize for resistance in the field of sexualized violence.

REFERENCES

Baker, C. N., & Bevacqua, M. (2018). Challenging narratives of the anti-rape movement's decline. *Violence Against Women, 24*(3), 350–376.

Black, M. C., Basile, K. C., Breiding, M. J., Smith, S. G., Walters, M. L., Merrick, M. T., ... Stevens, M. R. (2011). *The National Intimate Partner and Sexual Violence Survey summary report*. Atlanta: Centers for Disease Control and Prevention.

Brown, C. (2017). Creating counter-stories: Critical clinical practice and feminist narrative therapy. In D. Baines (Ed.), *Doing anti-oppressive practice: Building transformative, politicized social work* (3rd ed., pp. 212–232). Toronto: Fernwood.

Brown, C., & Augusta-Scott, T. (2007). Introduction. In C. Brown & T. Augusta-Scott (Eds.), *Narrative therapy: Making meaning, making lives* (pp. ix–xliii). Thousand Oaks, CA: Sage.

Brown, M. (2011). The sad, the mad, and the bad: Co-existing discourses of girlhood. *Child and Youth Care Forum, 40*, 107–120.

Carr, J. L. (2013). The SlutWalk movement: A study in transnational feminist activism. *Journal of Feminist Scholarship, 4*, 24–38.

Chambon, A. (1999). Foucault's approach: Making the familiar visible. In A. Chambon, A. Irving, & L. Epstein (Eds.), *Reading Foucault for social work* (pp. 51–82). New York: Columbia University Press.

Coates, L., & Wade, A. (2007). Language and violence: Analysis of four discursive operations. *Journal of Family Violence, 22*, 511–522.

Crenshaw, K. (1995). *Critical race theory: The key writings that formed the movement*. New York: Norton.

DeGue, S. A., Valle, L. A., Holt, M., Massetti, G., Matjasko, J., & Tharp, A. T. (2014). A systematic review of primary prevention strategies for sexual violence perpetration. *Aggression and Violent Behavior, 19*(4), 346–362.

Fook, J. (2016). *Social work: A critical approach to practice* (3rd ed.). Thousand Oaks, CA: Sage.

Grosz, E. (1994). *Volatile bodies: Toward a corporeal feminism*. Bloomington: Indiana University Press.

Mullaly, B., & West, J. (2017). *Challenging oppression and confronting privilege: A critical approach to anti-oppressive and anti-privilege theory and practice* (3rd ed.). Toronto: Oxford University Press.

Rentschler, C. A. (2014). Rape culture and the feminist politics of social media. *Girlhood Studies, 7*(1), 65–82.

CHAPTER 5

Exploring Trauma and Masculinity among Men Who Perpetrate Intimate Partner Violence

Tod Augusta-Scott[1]

INTRODUCTION

Many men who are high risk for severe intimate partner violence have been traumatized through experiences of childhood abuse and neglect (Capaldi, Knoble, Shortt, & Kim, 2012; Cuartas, 2002; Rosenbaum & Leisring, 2003; Simoneti, Scott, & Murphy, 2000; Webermann & Murphy, 2019). These experiences of trauma can negatively influence men's understandings of masculinity, which then supports habitually unhelpful ways of thinking, feeling, and acting. Working with men who use violence involves both addressing the effects of trauma and learning to take responsibility for their use of violence. Moving men toward taking responsibility involves exploring trauma's impact on their understanding of relationships and emotions. Under the influence of trauma, men often become detached from their values and conflate anger and conflict with abuse. When men are initially invited to look at their actions, they often do not see abuse—they see only expressions related to anger and conflict. Men's sense of agency and choice about how they respond to anger and conflict is also often outside their awareness. To support men to take responsibility for their choices to abuse, men need to address the impact of trauma experiences on them, recognize their agency, and clearly learn to differentiate abuse from anger and conflict.

As a result of childhood trauma, these habitual ways of thinking, feeling, and acting can stem from states of dissociation. The trauma literature shows that dissociation is an adaptive response among abused and traumatized children as a way to escape the abuse and protect themselves (Herman, 2015). Among those perpetrating intimate partner violence, it is estimated that about one-fifth to one-third report dissociative experiences when they are violent (Cuartas, 2002; Daisy & Hien, 2014; Dutton, Fehr, & McEwen, 1982; LaMotte & Murphy, 2016; Simoneti et al., 2000; Webermann & Murphy, 2019). This means that while as a child dissociating was largely an adaptive response, in adulthood dissociating while erupting with rage can become quite dangerous. Judith Lewis Herman (2015) describes a dialectic of trauma that involves an oscillation between constriction (numbing out or dissociating) and intrusion (nightmares, flashbacks, powerful/overwhelming emotion) and a semi-constant state of hyperarousal (a state of watching for danger). The state of intrusion is exhausting and as such is often replaced with constriction. Difficulties regulating emotions such as anxiety and anger are also part of the negative effects of trauma. Additionally, those who have experienced complex and ongoing abuse and trauma often learn not to trust people and to expect that they will be mistreated and betrayed, alongside ongoing vulnerability, and feelings of shame, lack of control, and powerlessness. (Augusta-Scott & Maerz, 2017; Simoneti et al., 2000; Taft, Murphy, & Creech, 2016). Taken together, feelings of distrust in relationships, expecting betrayal, difficulties with anger, and a sense of powerlessness that arise from trauma play a significant role in interpersonal violence and must be addressed. Men need to address and deal with the sequelae of trauma and how that becomes part of their own use of violence. They need to deal with their own pain if they are to successfully address the pain they are causing others.

Those adopting a trauma approach to interpersonal violence intervention are not suggesting that this makes the use of violence acceptable. They are attentive to the possible danger of men attributing blame to childhood trauma and not accepting responsibility for their own behaviour (Kilgore, Lehmann, & Schrag, 2019). In the past, I resisted adopting a trauma-based approach to working with men because I was concerned that validating men's experiences of childhood trauma and, further, current experiences of dissociation when they were perpetrating violence would suggest that men were not responsible for their violence and may encourage more violence. I now recognize that men are often both perpetrators and victims and, as adults, fully responsible for their choices at the same time. I also assumed men were initially *aware* of their agency when often they were not. As I accepted men's accounts of their violence over time, I could see one of the effects of trauma on men was to render their agency and responsibility invisible. Men may be unaware of their agency, but this does not mean they do not have agency. I found ways of validating experiences of dissociation, while at the same time inviting men to notice how they have agency and responsibility to interrupt these habitual thoughts, feelings, and actions. Men need to be invited to notice habitual thinking, feelings, and actions related to previous trauma, so their agency becomes visible to them. Men who dissociate while perpetrating abuse are described as participating in dissociative interpersonal violence (Taft et al., 2016).

The negative effects of trauma leave men without a definition for taking responsibility for the harm they have done to others. Instead, experiences of trauma can teach men that admitting to bad behaviour and being responsible is dangerous. Most men were beaten and invalidated as children if they made poor choices. As a result, intervention needs to redefine poor choices and build pathways to taking responsibility. Intervention also needs to challenge notions of masculinity that normalize avoiding responsibility in relationships and encourage men to do so. All ideas and practices associated with masculinity need to be redefined in terms that support men taking responsibility and acknowledging their experiences of trauma and vulnerability.

Repairing the harm of trauma can be very difficult, and men are often unsure how to do so. As abused children, they felt unsafe, and as men, they often do not feel safe enough to identify how they were harmed by abuse. The ideas they developed about themselves under the influence of trauma often still shape how they see themselves as adults. Men often learn to hide their victimization and protect themselves through a self-defensive stance, that is, retaliation, which protects them from being harmed again. In this process, the notion of self-defence is complex. The dialectic of trauma sets up a self-defensive position that often obscures men's retaliation. Trauma-based intervention needs to explore ways that men defend themselves and make clear distinctions between what is helpful and not helpful to both themselves and others. For instance, while use of violence may feel defensive, retaliation is ultimately not an effective response. Indeed, it is harmful. A process needs to be established to give men the opportunity to identify the harm done to them and to explore and repair the effects of the harm. Intervention also needs to challenge how trauma-influenced masculinity often normalizes and encourages men to avoid focusing on their victimization, yet, ironically, keeps them acting like they are being victimized or could be victimized; therefore, they are always protecting themselves from others. Ideas and practices typically associated with masculinity need to support men finding ways to repair the harm they have experienced while caring and respecting others at the same time.

When redefining masculinity, I am not creating an essentialist idea about men or masculinity (Augusta-Scott, 2006, 2007a, 2009). I resist, for example, essentializing men as powerful and in control. Further, I resist essentializing masculinity or men as a problem. The ideas about masculinity do not define men or determine who men are. At the same time, ideas of masculinity can have a powerful influence on men's choices. I recognize that some notions of masculinity support men's irresponsible choices, while other ideas of masculinity support men's responsible choices. Unhelpful notions of masculinity, such as that men need to have power and control over their female partners, are reinforced by men's experiences of trauma. To stop men's violence, intervention must address the negative effects of trauma, including the negative influence trauma has on men's understandings of masculinity, which leads them to perpetrate abuse and make irresponsible choices.

When I am redefining masculinity with men, I am not re-essentializing masculinity in a universal, timeless, absolute manner. Instead, I am helping a man define masculinity, in a particular situation or moment, in a manner that supports taking responsibility to stop violence and repair harm. Sometimes, this process involves defining masculinity as making responsible choices and defining such practices as being strong or brave. At other times, masculinity is defined as strong and brave in a manner that supports a man being vulnerable and open. I use the idea of femininity in a similar manner. Again, I am not invoking masculinity in a manner that suggests that it is the "opposite" of femininity, or that the ideas are mutually exclusive.

For many years, I only defined masculinity as a problem and believed it was the only reason men chose to abuse. I dismissed trauma as an explanation because most men who have been victimized in childhood do not perpetrate abuse in their adulthood. At the same time, I never dismissed masculinity as an explanation, despite the fact that most boys do not eventually rape and beat women. This reality suggests that most men have experiences of masculinity that support making responsible choices, as evidenced by most men's positive relationships with their female partners.

While many men who experienced childhood trauma do not abuse others, most men I work with who perpetrate severe abuse have experiences of childhood trauma. I had never considered that perhaps both experiences—trauma and masculinity—were interacting with each other to lead men to choose violence (Augusta-Scott & Maerz, 2017). Perhaps it was not only experiencing trauma that was the problem, but the meaning made of the trauma. Perhaps the problem was not all ideas associated with masculinity, but trauma *influencing* men's ideas about masculinity that, in turn, support men's violence against their partners. Under the influence of trauma, masculinity is defined as the "opposite" of femininity, mutually exclusive, and valuing masculinity over femininity.

As you read this chapter, ask yourself the following questions:

1. How do the negative effects of trauma influence men's ideas about masculinity and contribute to their lack of understanding of taking responsibility to repair harm done to themselves?
2. How do the negative effects of trauma influence men's ideas about masculinity and contribute to their lack of understanding about abuse?
3. How do the negative effects of trauma influence men's ideas about masculinity and contribute to their lack of understanding of taking responsibility to stop the abuse and repair harm to others?
4. In stopping men's severe violence against their female partners, how can a social worker attend to dissociative interpersonal violence and men's agency and responsibility at the same time?
5. Why is it important to resist gender essentialism in our efforts to stop men's perpetration of intimate partner violence, while still investigating ideas associated with masculinity that lead them either to take responsibility or to avoid responsibility?

DIFFERENTIATING ABUSE FROM ANGER AND CONFLICT

To have men take responsibility to stop their abuse, they need a clear definition of abuse (Pence & Paymar, 1993) that distinguishes it from anger and conflict (Jenkins, 1990, 2009). The negative effects of trauma render abuse invisible to them by conflating it with anger and conflict. By creating a clear definition of abuse, the process pushes back on the negative effects of trauma. Before I ask men about abuse, I ask them a series of questions about what is important to them in relationships, what they value in relationships, and what they would prefer their relationships to be like. Most men talk about wanting fair, respectful, and safe relationships. Although men may indicate that they value respectful, caring, safe relationships, this does not mean they have been successful in living up to these values, nor does it mean that their sense of masculinity hasn't been influenced to lead them to also want unnegotiated power and control in the relationship. Asking men questions about wanting loving, caring relationships helps to emphasize factors that inhibit abuse. In contrast, much theory and research in the intimate partner field focuses primarily on factors that motivate abuse (e.g., wanting power and control), rather than inhibit it (e.g., wanting respectful and caring relationships) (Bartholomew, Cobb, & Dutton, 2015).

As part of these questions, I also begin to ask them what they do not want in their relationships. This line of inquiry begins the process of men defining abuse for themselves. I avoid asking them for examples of their own behaviour. By asking men for their definition of abuse without asking them about their behaviour, they can respond to the question in a more reflective manner without feeling that they need to defend themselves against implicit or explicit accusations that they are abusive. I start the conversation by asking, "What are the effects of abuse?" Men proceed to say that abuse leads people to be frightened, controlled, threatened, hurt, disrespected, and so forth. Starting with an exploration of the effects of abuse helps prevent debates about whether yelling or emotional abuse are actually abuse. Once men determine that abuse makes people feel threatened or scared, the fact that threats and emotional abuse are examples of abuse is self-evident (Augusta-Scott, 2008; Jenkins, 2009).

As in the process of defining abuse, the therapeutic posture that I adopt in conversations with men is very important (Rosenbaum & Leisring, 2003; Taft et al., 2016). If I adopt an expert posture in which I educate men early in our conversations about the negative influence of trauma on them, I risk contributing to the negative effects of trauma. One of the negative effects of trauma is men not trusting themselves and assuming they are unknowledgeable. When I adopt a didactic, expert posture with men, as I would, for example, when telling them what abuse means, I reinforce these negative effects of trauma. Further, if I offer solutions, as represented by giving men "homework," they are less invested in the solutions. They may even blame me when my imposed solutions do not work. Rather than adopt an expert posture, I engage in a posture of curiosity and collaboration (Brown & Augusta-Scott, 2018). I invite men's own values, knowledge, and skills forward. I ask them about the effects of trauma on their own lives and what is important to them. Through this process the negative effects of trauma on their identity are challenged and they experience themselves as knowledgeable and capable. Further, to educate men about the effects of trauma, before they have a definition of abuse or know what taking responsibility means, risks giving them more justifications and excuses for perpetrating abuse.

In the process of defining abuse, there are often important distinctions to make between anger and abuse, as well as conflict and abuse (Jenkins, 2009). One of the ways abuse is made invisible through the effects of trauma is that yelling and screaming are often conflated with anger and conflict. Many men

describe themselves as simply having a "bad temper" or having an "anger problem." They often presume that I am going to offer them an anger-avoidance or
conflict-avoidance course. To make visible what men have learned about anger
and conflict, I ask, "What did you learn growing up about expressing anger and
how to resolve conflict?" Men often say they learned that both anger and conflict
were synonymous with violence, screaming, and yelling. I then ask, "What was
the effect of the yelling and violence on you?" They report feeling terrorized,
afraid, and so forth. Having already explored their definition of abuse, I then
ask, "I wonder if some of these ways of expressing anger or dealing with conflict
were actually abusive?"

DEFINING ABUSE

Childhood trauma contributes to men's abuse of their female partners because the effect of trauma over time leaves men with no definition of abuse to
identify the problem. Instead, men confuse abuse with expressing anger and
conflict. To stop men's abuse, men need to create a clear definition of abuse,
distinct from their definitions of conflict and anger.

Men are asked to consider their agency, choices, and decisions in relation
to anger and conflict. These questions are often dumbfounding for men because
this line of questioning challenges their habitual (abusive) ways of expressing
anger and engaging in conflict. I challenge the idea that they have no agency
over how they handle conflict and express anger. I ask, "Conflict is just a part
of life for every relationship. Given that respect is important to you, how would
you prefer to handle conflict? Anger is just a part of life for everyone. There are
important injustices to be angry about. Given that you value respect, how would
you prefer to express anger and resolve conflict?" I then ask, "Is there a difference between anger and abuse?" In this way, this explanation clarifies that the
problem is abuse—not anger or conflict.

Finally, in their efforts to be respectful in their relationships, I ask them to
consider how defining abuse clearly is helpful to them. I ask, "How is it helpful
to use the term *abuse* rather than confusing it with anger or conflict?" (Jenkins,
2009). Men often say that when they can see their behaviours as abuse it allows
them to understand the serious effects of the behaviour. One man said, "It is
painful for me to think about my behaviour as abuse but it helps me be clear
about what I don't want to be doing." Further, they can see that they do not

need to choose abuse in their relationships. Using the term *abuse* actually gives them a better hold on standing up to these behaviours and making choices more aligned with how they would prefer to be in their relationships. Through this process, men challenge the negative involuntary effects of trauma by creating for themselves a clear definition of abuse.

Previously, I assumed men thought that anger and conflict were excuses for abuse. I presumed men were aware that yelling, screaming, and threats were abuse and that they were justifying their abuse. As a result, I confronted them on this assumption by insisting, "there is no excuse for abuse." In retrospect, I realize I was creating an unnecessary and unhelpful opposition in the conversations. What I didn't realize is that men were not trying to justify abuse, they were simply saying that they felt angry and experienced conflict. The problem was that the negative effects of trauma often left men without a definition of abuse. Given the opportunity to define abuse, men don't justify it or conclude that participating in it is a good idea for building healthy families. When given the opportunity to consider the effects of abuse and define abuse for themselves, men clearly state that it is wrong. They then proceed to explore how they might express anger and conflict in a non-abusive way.

Much of the research identifies that men conflate abuse with conflict. Such research posits that men are "recoding" violent acts only to reduce the seriousness of the episode (Boria, del Castillo, Carbajosa, & Maruello, 2013; Harris, Palazzolo, & Savage, 2012; Kilgore et al., 2019; Lamb, 1991). While some men are recoding to minimize the seriousness of the abuse, other men in fact are not recoding their violent acts. They are actually just using the code they have always lived with. Many men do not already have a definition of abuse to recode; instead, they are seeing abuse the same way they did in childhood, as conflict and anger.

Masculinity and Anger

Trauma influences ideas about masculinity for these men with regard to anger and conflict. From experiences of trauma, men are conditioned to think that the only way to remain safe is to feel angry and avoid any vulnerable emotions (Augusta-Scott & Maerz, 2017). Men are often abused for showing fear, sadness, or pain. Trauma, in turn, influences masculinity by normalizing men's avoidance of pain, fear, and sadness, while encouraging men to express only anger. To address masculinity influenced by trauma, I often invite men to consider how they learned to avoid sharing emotions other than anger. Men often state that if they showed pain or fear, they were beaten and told that they were weak. I ask, "If a child is influenced by the idea that he has to avoid vulnerable feelings and can only show anger, how does this affect a person over time?" Men are clear about the negative effects these ideas can have on a person over time: when anger is not enough to avoid the pain, men rely on alcohol, work, extreme sport, and so forth. Of course, trauma-influenced masculinity often encourages excessive drinking, working, and sports, rendering normal and invisible these effects of trauma.

I then begin the process of redefining masculinity in a manner consistent with facing vulnerable feelings rather than avoiding them through becoming angry. I ask men questions about the father they would prefer to be. I may ask, "What do you want your children to learn from you about how to express their anger? About how to resolve conflict?" Many men respond with the phrase, "I don't want them to do what I've been doing." I ask, "Do you want your children to learn how to experience all of their feelings or to avoid most of their feelings through becoming angry?" Trauma-influenced masculinity often encourages men to deal with conflict through aggression and violence rather than talking through issues, negotiating, and finding win-win possibilities. It is unsurprising given how trauma-influenced masculinity affects men's habitual, assumed ways of being that men readily confuse anger and conflict with abuse.

Trauma also leads men to conflate their experiences of vulnerability and weakness with their identity: because they experience weakness, they are weak. Trauma-influenced masculinity colludes with the idea that an experience of vulnerability and weakness means a person is weak. I invite the men to separate identity from experiences of being vulnerable and weak: "When your child experiences weakness or vulnerability, do you want them to think of themselves as being a weak person as a result?" I continue to redefine masculinity by stating, "Men often learn that sharing their vulnerable feelings makes them weak. But what does it take to actually face fear and pain rather than avoid it with anger or drinking?" Men often say, "It takes a lot." I ask, "Does it take more strength and courage to face your fears or to avoid them by becoming angry?" Men are clear that it often takes much more to face their fears and share their pain. In this manner, I continue to redefine masculinity: "Do you think a person facing their fears would make them stronger or weaker over time? Would they feel more able or less able to deal with their problems if they were facing them over time rather than avoiding them? Would you respect yourself more for facing your vulnerable feelings and problems over time or respect yourself less?" This process is not about simply replacing one essentialist notion of the self (e.g., the men are weak) with another essentialist notion of the self (e.g., the men are strong). The men are neither essentially weak nor strong. The questions are attaching strength and courage to the men's practices to live up to their values. Associating living their values with strength and courage is often helpful for men. This inquiry does not preclude men's experiences of weakness and vulnerability or suggest that there is anything essentially wrong with a person when they have these experiences.

Taking Responsibility

To have men take responsibility to stop their abuse, they need a clear under-standing of taking responsibility and the meaning of making bad choices. The negative effects of trauma conflate men's identities with their bad behaviour, giving men the idea that bad behaviour means they are bad (Taft et al., 2016). Further, the effects of trauma often leave men unaware of how to take respon-sibility to both stop violence and repair the harm they have done to others and their relationships. By separating men's identities from their bad behaviour and by creating a clear definition of taking responsibility, the process pushes back on the negative effects of trauma (Taft et al., 2016).

DEFINING TAKING RESPONSIBILITY

Childhood trauma contributes to men's abuse of their female partners be-cause it leaves these men unaware of what taking responsibility means or even that it is possible. Instead, men learn to conflate people's identities with their bad behaviour (e.g., I made a bad choice, therefore I am bad) and to mini-mize their responsibility by denying bad behaviour and blaming it on others. To stop men's violence, men need to separate bad behaviour from their identities and create a definition of "taking responsibility" for their violence.

To support men to take responsibility for their abuse, that is, their bad be-haviour, I invite men to create a definition of bad behaviour that separates it from a person's identity. I ask, "What do you want your children to learn about making poor choices? What do you want them to learn about what it says about them? Do you want them to learn that a bad choice means they are bad or just that they made a bad choice?" Men often say that they want their children to learn that "everyone makes a bad choice sometimes." They want their children to learn that their bad behaviour does not define them. They are aware that they may not always live up to their values. The objective is to get back on track with how a person prefers to be. In this manner, men separate bad behaviour from a person's identity. I then ask, "What difference would it make for your children to have bad choices separated from their identity?" The men indicate that creating the separation would make it easier to face bad choices, because they don't have to feel the pain of conflating their bad behaviour with their identity. I then ask men if this is the same meaning that they want to make of their own bad choices, particularly as it relates to their abuse. The men often affirm that this is the same meaning of bad choices that would be helpful for them as they work to take responsibility.

Over time the negative effects of trauma leave men with no experience of taking responsibility. Many men were simply beaten and invalidated when they made bad choices. They were simply condemned as being bad. They never learned that taking responsibility was even a possibility. They never learned how to take responsibility for the harm they caused and they never experienced anyone taking responsibility for the harm done to them. Consequently, these men never learned that taking responsibility could lead toward repairing the harm done to others and respecting themselves for doing so at the same time. To counter these negative effects of trauma, I invite men to define taking responsibility for their adult selves.

Masculinity and Responsibility

Trauma also influences masculinity for these men regarding their ideas about taking responsibility. From the influence of trauma over time, men learn that having problems or acknowledging bad choices means they are weak. A negative effect of trauma on men is that they protect themselves from the threat of feeling worthless by avoiding ever appearing as if they have made bad choices or have problems. Trauma-influenced masculinity, in turn, normalizes men's avoidance of problems and bad choices, encouraging them to pretend they "know everything" and "never need to ask for help." Men's constant state of pretending they have no problems or don't make poor choices is supported by trauma-influenced ideas about masculinity. Further, this masculinity often leaves men bereft of how to take responsibility because they are not encouraged to even acknowledge poor choices or problems for which they might take responsibility. It is unsurprising, given how trauma influences masculinity and men's habitual, assumed ways of being, that men do not initially take responsibility for harming others.

To address how trauma-influenced masculinity impacts men's ideas about taking responsibility for harming others, I begin the process of redefining masculinity in a manner consistent with taking responsibility rather than blaming others or making excuses for one's choices. To build men's definition of taking responsibility and to redefine masculinity, I ask about the father they would prefer to be: "What do you want your children to learn about how to respond to their poor choices?" Men talk about wanting their children to admit their poor choices and to learn from them so they don't repeat them. Further, they want them to acknowledge the effects of their poor choices on others so that they can repair the harm they have done. After exploring the importance of taking responsibility to them, I ask, "What type of role model do you want to be for your children regarding taking responsibility?" Men indicate that they want children to learn from their example how to take responsibility. I also invite men to consider ways in which people avoid taking responsibility for their choices. I ask, "Why is it important to you that your children take responsibility for their choices rather than simply making excuses for their choices and avoiding the consequences?"

Finally, I also want men to associate taking responsibility for harming others with building self-respect, rather than leading them toward self-defeat. I state, "I can see you feel ashamed about what you have done to your partner and children. What does your shame tell me about your values?" (Jenkins, 2009). Men often indicate that they do not know. I respond with, "What would it say about your values if you could think about the effects of what you did and not feel ashamed?" Men are often clear that if they didn't feel shame, it would mean that they didn't care, value respect, love, and so forth. Then I repeat, "So what does it say about you that you do feel ashamed?" Men identify that their shame tells them that they do care, they are not okay with the violence, and they do want fairness in their relationships. I then ask, "What's the difference between helpful shame and unhelpful shame when a person makes a poor choice or acts in a manner they are not proud of?" Often men indicate that unhelpful shame is when they conflate a bad choice with their identity, meaning, "I made a bad choice, therefore, I am bad." Men report that helpful shame is simply a signal that they have acted against their values and how they prefer to be as husbands, fathers, and men.

Differentiating Self-Defence from Retaliation

To have men take responsibility to stop their violence and repair the harm they have done to others, men also need to take responsibility to address the harm done to themselves through childhood trauma. Many men have not had the opportunity to feel safe enough to identify the influence childhood trauma has on their ideas and assumptions about life. Instead, trauma influences masculinity for these men so that they simply work to both deny any experiences of victimization and ensure they are never hurt again (Ellis, Winlow, & Hall, 2017). Before adopting a trauma-based approach, my intervention had limited effectiveness because I was trying to have men take responsibility to stop their violence against others without simultaneously getting men to take responsibility to repair the harm done to themselves. To stop men's violence against women, men also need to focus on repairing the harm done to them through violence at the same time. Research indicates that the neglect of men's mental health needs, that is, men attending to the effects of trauma on themselves, is common in the field (Klostermann, Kelley, Mignone, Pusateri, & Fals-Stewart, 2010; Lipsky, Caetano, & Roy-Byrne, 2011).

The negative effects of trauma leave men feeling constantly under threat and, therefore, always seeking to protect themselves through self-defence (Taft et al., 2016). As children, men learn that to defend themselves they have to harm the person harming them. Many men learn "if someone hurts you, you hurt them" or "if someone disrespects you, you disrespect them." Initially, they say, "If she didn't yell at me then I wouldn't have yelled at her. She started it. She provoked me." One negative effect of trauma is that it leaves men thinking that *all* of their responses to people harming them are simply negative expressions of self-protection. They perceive that their partners are to blame for their actions because retaliation is always justified. Distinctions are not made between self-protection and retaliation. As a result, men often are left assuming that self-protection includes retaliation. Further, men's retaliation is assumed and habitual and often their agency is outside of their awareness (Winslow & Hall, 2009).

To address men's habitual retaliation or getting even, I ask men to consider their agency and responsibility in the face of feeling threatened. I begin by inviting men to look at their partners' agency and responsibility. I ask, "Who is responsible for your partner's choices?" Men are clear that their partner is responsible for their own choices. I then ask, "Who is responsible for your choices?" Men are clear that they are responsible for their own choices. I then ask, "Given the assumption that people are responsible for their own choices, who is responsible for your partner choosing to yell?" Men are clear that, if their partner chooses to yell, she is responsible for her choices. Similarly, I ask, "Who is responsible when you choose to yell?" Not surprisingly, men initially find responding to this question more difficult because their agency has been outside of their awareness and they have been habitually blaming others for their yelling for a long time. At the same time, when asked these questions, men do not create an explicit double-standard and build an argument in which their partner needs to take responsibility for her choices while they do not.[2]

ADDRESSING HARM

Childhood trauma contributes to men's abuse of their female partners because it leaves men unaware of how to take responsibility for the harm that was done to them in childhood. Instead, men deny their victimization and proceed to retaliate against others, intending to protect themselves from ever being hurt again. Men need to take responsibility to address how they have been harmed, while attending to the harm they have done to others at the same time.

I then continue to interrupt men's habitual retaliation or counterattack by drawing on their value for respect: "I understand that for you being respectful is important. Does that include when your partner is being disrespectful? When your partner goes down the disrespect path by starting to yell, do you want to hold on to your own value for respect or would you be prepared to follow her down the disrespect path? What happens if you follow her down the disrespect path? What effect does going down the disrespect path have on you?" Men are clear that they feel much worse after they go down the disrespect path and then begin to consider the damage they have done as a result. They are also clear that it has significant costs for the relationship.

Often men become dumbfounded by questions that hold them to their own definition of respect, while at the same time highlighting their agency. When confronted with what decisions they want to make in response to their partner's yelling, many men never thought there was any possibility other than yelling back at her, retaliating in self-defence. For example, I ask, "What could happen if you didn't follow her down the disrespect path? How would you prefer to respond to her yelling at you?" I then highlight men's agency further and interrupt the retaliation justification by asking, "So it sounds like her disrespect is a real 'warning sign' for you, telling you to take a 'timeout' to prevent yourself from escalating toward choosing disrespect?" The men often agree and are now aware of their agency and their responsibility.

I continue to interrupt the habitual retaliation by asking, "Some men get influenced by the idea 'you hurt me, so I hurt you,' 'you disrespect me, so

I disrespect you.' Where do these ideas lead a relationship over time?" Men are often clear that they simply lead to more disrespect and hurt, especially if both parties are influenced by the idea. Then I ask, "If you could spot these ideas influencing you, what would you have to remind yourself of to stay on the respect path?" Men often say they would have to remind themselves, "I don't have a right to disrespect her just because she is disrespecting me. Two wrongs don't make a right. If I retaliate, I harm myself, her, and our relationship more over time."

To help define retaliation as a problem, I then invite men to make distinctions between retaliation and self-defence. I ask, "What is the difference between retaliation and self-defence?" Men often say that self-defence is not about trying to harm the other but just trying to protect oneself from being harmed. Men often conclude that their retaliation is about trying to harm the other person, that is, abusing them. Upon making these distinctions, men often conclude that there is no excuse for abuse, even if someone else is abusing them.

While men need to separate self-defence from retaliation with partners who threaten them, many men are retaliating against partners who are actually not threatening them. The negative effects of trauma leave men perceiving threats even when none are present (Taft et al., 2016). One of the negative effects of childhood trauma is that men learn that close relationships are dangerous. They often have difficulty separating past abusers from their partners. In addition, sometimes men who have also been betrayed in past adult relationships have a hard time separating past partners from their present partner when they are angry or in conflict. Men often mistrust and feel threatened by their current partner even though she could be honest and committed to the relationship. To help men separate these past experiences from their present, I invite them to speak of their current partner's values. When men are outside of the moment of anger or conflict, they are often clear that their partner is trustworthy, loving, caring, and respectful. I ask, "Does the threat you feel from your current partner feel similar to any situations you have experienced in the past?" Men usually affirm that it does. I then ask, "When do you first remember feeling this way?" Men inevitably talk about feeling under threat when they were younger or in a past relationship with a partner. I invite men to describe these experiences and then ask, "Given how you've described your partner, do you think in the moment you might be confusing the past and the present?" Helping men distinguish between past experiences of threat and their present experiences can help them recognize they are safe in their current relationship. As a result, they may be more willing to engage in the vulnerability that long-term intimate relationships require.

They can allow their partner to ask them to change and point out a poor choice without thinking their partner is attacking them.

There is research that suggests that in some relationships women and men both feed the escalation to yelling, screaming, and violence (Cordova, Jacobson, Gottman, Rushe, & Cox, 1993; Gondolf & Beeman, 2003; Kelley et al., 1983; O'Leary & Slep, 2003; Reis, Capobianco, & Tsai, 2002; White, Merrill, & Koss, 2001; Winstock, 2007; Winstock & Eisikovits, 2008). While both partners are often aware of the other person's contribution to the escalation, their own contribution to the escalation is often outside of their awareness. Men often say, "I can't change if she doesn't change." As a man develops a definition of taking responsibility, he comes to realize that to make a relationship work "it takes two," but it only takes him to remove himself from the escalation, regardless of if his partner continues to escalate or not. A similar strategy can be used with the woman: she can learn to take responsibility to stop her participation in the escalation, regardless of if her partner does or not. Regrettably, such research that identifies this mutual escalation can lead to interventions that blur the issue of people taking responsibility for their choices by suggesting that the de-escalation for both must also be mutual, which is not the case.

Masculinity and Retaliation

For men to attend productively to the harm done to themselves, I also need to address how trauma influences ideas about masculinity that lead men to be ashamed of being victimized. An effect of childhood trauma is that men assume they should be ashamed of being victimized (Taft et al., 2016). Men are ashamed of their victimization because they were often told implicitly and explicitly that they were to blame for their own victimization: if they had not made a bad choice, if they were not bad, then they would not have been abused. Men's victimization is conflated with their identity. The negative effects of trauma influence masculinity by encouraging men to deny their victimization. Being a victim is a sign of being weak. Men are encouraged never to ask for help for fear this will make them appear weak.

To address the conflation of men's identities with their victimization, that is, with the idea that being abused means there is something wrong with them, I ask, "Who is responsible when a child is harmed?" Men often insist the person who did the harm was responsible—not the child. I ask, "Does being victimized mean they are weak? Does being harmed say anything about their identity or does it just mean they were hurt?" They also affirm that being victimized doesn't say anything about a child's identity, it just means they were hurt by someone. This process helps separate men's identities from the experience of being victimized. I ask, "If a child was harmed, would you want them to ask for help or to keep it to themselves?" Men are clear that they would want the child to ask for help. I then ask, "So they shouldn't feel ashamed or embarrassed to ask for help—why not? Does it mean they are weak?" Men often affirm that being victimized doesn't mean there is something wrong with them or that they are weak. Then I ask, "I wonder if this message is the same or different from the messages you received as a child? Who was responsible for the harm done to you as a child? What should you have learned about what being harmed says about you? Did you learn that you could ask for help?"[3]

DEFINING MASCULINITY

Childhood trauma can influence men's ideas about masculinity. Trauma-influenced masculinity may support men: to be angry and avoid other emotions, to avoid taking responsibility, to be self-absorbed, and to confuse retaliation with self-defence. To stop men's violence, men must define masculinity in a manner that supports taking responsibility to repair both the harm they have done to others and the harm that has been done to them.

Trauma influences masculinity so that men do not consider repair for themselves and believe that the only thing they can do is retaliate, sometimes even pre-emptively, so they protect themselves from being harmed again. Trauma-influenced masculinity normalizes and encourages men always to be hypervigilant about retaliating. Men learn that walking away when someone is harming them means they are weak and that a man should never "let other people walk over you." Of course, if backing down makes one weak, one would never back down or show weakness if they were intent on defending and protecting themself. Trauma-influenced masculinity leaves men feeling like they should not back down over any provocation, lest they be vulnerable to being hurt. They are to protect their honour and their identity.

To counter these effects of trauma-influenced masculinity and interrupt men's habitual retaliation, I invite men to consider what other values are important to them that might lead them to walk away in the face of being threatened. I ask, "What values would you be standing up for in your relationship by walking away?" Men often state they would be standing up for respect in the relationship, a caring relationship. I ask, "How much strength is required to take a stand for your values by walking away when someone is disrespecting you? Would choosing to walk away and not retaliate make you stronger or weaker over time?"

Trauma-influenced masculinity gives men the path of retaliation but does not give men a safe pathway from which to thoughtfully consider and effectively address the harm they have experienced. Men are not given the opportunity to study their victimization, to consider the habitual ideas and feelings that were created by the effects of trauma on them over time. Most men assume that repair for themselves is not an option. As a result, I support men to identify how they have been harmed and recognize their own agency to take responsibility to repair these harms. Men can find ways of creating safety for themselves in a manner that is respectful toward themselves and others. Through this process, they can study their previously (misguided) efforts at denying their victimization and simply working to prevent future harm through retaliation.

In an effort to redefine masculinity, I invite them to reconsider ideas of weakness: "Does it take more strength and courage to face how one is harmed or to avoid it? Would facing these harms make a person weaker or stronger over time?" I continue, "Do you think a person acknowledging how they have been hurt and working to heal this hurt would make them stronger or weaker over time? Would they feel more able or less able to deal effectively with their own hurt feelings over time? Would you respect yourself more for repairing your hurts over time or for avoiding them by simply trying to protect yourself from perceived threats?"

Ironically, by not acknowledging their victimization to resolve it, the process of trying to perpetually prove they are not victims and protecting themselves from ever being hurt again keeps their victimization unresolved and consuming most of their focus. Trauma often leads men to assume they are constantly under threat and therefore they become hypervigilant and self-absorbed in their own protection and self-defence. Again, trauma-influenced masculinity encourages this singular, self-absorbed focus: "each man for himself," "you have to look out for number one," and so forth.

To address this self-focus, I invite men to explore how they can attend to both themselves and others at the same time. I ask, "I'm wondering if there is a way in which you could both respect yourself and your partner at the same time? I'm wondering if there is a way of saying what you want and don't want that could leave both people feeling respected?" Further, men can find ways of creating safety for themselves in a manner that is respectful toward themselves and others. Through this inquiry, men learn how to take responsibility to repair the harm done to themselves at the same time as they repair the harm they have done to others.

An effect of trauma is that it often leaves men with a profound experience of being powerless and their lives being out of their control. They grow up with the uncertainty of not being in control and never knowing when they were going to be violated or neglected. As a result, to create safety and protection for themselves, men seek to have unnegotiated power and control over others, including their partners. Rather than acknowledging this experience of powerlessness and being out of control, trauma-influenced masculinity normalizes and encourages men to want unnegotiated power and control over others, particularly their female partners. I colluded with trauma-influenced masculinity: I presumed men simply wanted power and control for the sake of power and control (Augusta-Scott, 2001). I thought men would be reluctant to give up unnegotiated power and control in their relationships because it worked to get them what they wanted. What I did not recognize is that unnegotiated power and control in a relationship does not result in the power and control over their lives that the men seek. Unnegotiated power and control often results in power and control that is temporary and does not contribute to a sustainable, intimate, long-term relationship, which most men desperately want. Unnegotiated power and control erodes relationships over time and ultimately leaves men feeling more powerless and out of control (Rosenbaum & Leisring, 2003; Taft et al., 2016).

CONCLUSION

For men to take responsibility to stop abuse and repair harm done to their female partners and their relationships, intervention needs to attend to the negative effects of childhood trauma. To address the effects of childhood trauma and take responsibility in the present, men need to clarify conflict and anger as distinct from abuse. They also need to develop a definition of taking responsibility, while learning to separate their identities from their bad behaviour. This process involves challenging trauma-influenced masculinity, which encourages men to avoid facing bad choices and taking responsibility for harm against others. Finally, to take responsibility to stop abuse, men also need to take responsibility to repair the negative effects of childhood trauma, which often leave them hypervigilant about needing to defend and protect themselves. In this process, they need to be able to differentiate between self-defence and when self-defence becomes harmful retaliation.

NOTES

1. I want to acknowledge the contribution of Leland Maerz of the Bridges Institute, who was an important dialogue partner during the development of this chapter and gave generously of his time to offer valuable feedback on various drafts.

2. I outline elsewhere my initial concerns about addressing women's abuse in conversations with men about their own abuse (Augusta-Scott, 2007b). I was concerned that talking about women's abusive behaviour might mitigate men's responsibility and implicate their partners in being responsible for their choices to use violence. I now realize that victimization is not an excuse for abuse: men can be both perpetrator and victim, powerful and powerless, and fully responsible for their choices at the same time. Another concern was that acknowledging men's victimization might redirect funding from services for women to services for men. I now think those who are abused, regardless of gender, deserve to have access to services. Undoubtedly, more women would access services for victimization. Similarly, those who (also) have perpetrated abuse, regardless of their gender, deserve to have access to services. Undoubtedly more men would access these services.

3. Of course, some men do acknowledge their victimization when they were younger, and trauma-influenced masculinity leaves them ashamed of themselves for being victimized. These men continue to conflate their identity with their experience of victimization. As a result, concluding that they are *only* a victim, they also feel like they have no agency from which to repair the harm done to them or the harm they have done to others.

REFERENCES

Augusta-Scott, T. (2001). Dichotomies in the power and control story: Exploring multiple stories about men who choose abuse in intimate relationships. *Gecko, 2*, 31–68.

Augusta-Scott, T. (2006). Talking with men who have used violence in intimate relationships: An interview with Tod Augusta-Scott. *International Journal of Narrative Therapy and Community Work, 4*, 23–30.

Augusta-Scott, T. (2007a). Challenging anti-oppressive discourse: Uniting against racism and sexism. In C. Brown & T. Augusta-Scott (Eds.), *Narrative therapy: Making meaning, making lives* (pp. 211–228). Thousand Oaks, CA: Sage.

Augusta-Scott, T. (2007b). Conversations with men about women's violence: Ending men's violence by challenging gender essentialism. In C. Brown & T. Augusta-Scott (Eds.), *Narrative therapy: Making meaning, making lives* (pp. 197–210). Thousand Oaks, CA: Sage.

Augusta-Scott, T. (2008). *Narrative therapy: A group manual for men who have perpetrated abuse; Facilitator's manual, participant's manual.* Truro, NS: Bridges Institute Publishing.

Augusta-Scott, T. (2009). A narrative therapy approach to conversations with men about perpetrating abuse. In P. Lehmann & C. Simmons (Eds.), *Strengths based batterers intervention: A new paradigm in ending family violence*. New York: Springer.

Augusta-Scott, T., & Maerz, L. (2017). Complex trauma and dominant masculinity: A narrative therapy approach with men who choose to abuse their female partners. In T. Augusta-Scott, K. Scott, & L. Tutty (Eds.), *Innovations in interventions to address intimate partner violence: Research and practice*. New York: Routledge.

Bartholomew, K., Cobb, R. J., & Dutton, D. G. (2015). Established and emerging perspectives on violence in intimate relationships. In M. Mikulincer, P. R. Shaver, J. A. Simpson, & J. F. Dovidio (Eds.), *APA handbook of personality and social psychology: Vol. 3. Interpersonal relations* (pp. 605–630). Washington, DC: American Psychological Association.

Boria, S., del Castillo, M., Carbajosa, P., & Maruello, C. (2013). Context of treatment and therapeutic alliance: Critical factors in court-mandated batterer intervention programs. *Spanish Journal of Psychology, 16*(4). doi:10.1017/sjp.2013.43

Brown, C., & Augusta-Scott, T. (2018). Reimagining the intersection of gender, knowledge and power in collaborative therapeutic conversations with women and eating disorders and men who use violence. In D. Pare & C. Audet (Eds.), *Social justice and narrative therapy* (pp. 143–158). New York: Routledge.

Capaldi, D. M., Knoble, N. B., Shortt, J. W., & Kim, H. K. (2012). A systematic review of risk factors for intimate partner violence. *Partner Abuse, 3*, 231–280.

Cordova, J. V., Jacobson, N. S., Gottman, J. M., Rushe, R., & Cox, G. (1993). Negative reciprocity and communication in couples with a violent husband. *Journal of Abnormal Psychology, 102*, 559–564.

Cuartas, A. S. (2002). Dissociation in male batterers. *Dissertation Abstracts International: Section A, 62*, 1–171.

Daisy, N. V. & Hien, D. A. (2014). The role of dissociation in the cycle of violence. *Journal of Family Violence, 29*, 99–107.

Dutton, D. G., Fehr, B., & McEwen, H. (1982). Severe wife battering as deindividuated violence. *Victimology, 7*(1/4), 13–23.

Ellis, A., Winlow, S., & Hall, S. (2017). "Throughout my life I've had people walk all over me": Trauma in the lives of violent men. *The Sociological Review, 65*(4), 699–713.

Gondolf, E. W., & Beeman, A. K. (2003). Women's accounts of domestic violence versus tactics-based outcome categories. *Violence Against Women, 9*, 278–301.

Harris, K. L., Palazzolo, K. E., & Savage, M. W. (2012). "I'm not sexist, but …": How ideological dilemmas reinforce sexism in talk about intimate partner violence. *Discourse and Society, 23*, 643–565.

Herman, J. L. (2015). *Trauma and recovery: The aftermath of violence—From domestic abuse to political terror* (2nd ed.). New York: Basic Books.

Jenkins, A. (1990). *Invitations to responsibility: The therapeutic engagement of men who are violent and abusive.* Adelaide, Australia: Dulwich Centre Publications.

Jenkins, A. (2009). *Becoming ethical: A parallel, political journey with men who have abused.* Dorset, UK: Russell House Publishing.

Kelley, H. H., Berscheid, E., Christensen, A., Harvey, J., Huston, T., Levinger, G., ... & Peterson, D. (1983). Analyzing close relationships. In H. H. Kelley et al., *Close relationships* (pp. 20–64). New York: Freeman.

Kilgore, C. D., Lehmann, P., & Schrag, R. V. (2019). Discourse after a batterer intervention program: A qualitative analysis of "letters from the future." *Violence Against Women, 25*(5), 593–613.

Klostermann, K., Kelley, M. L., Mignone, T., Pusateri, L., & Fals-Stewart, W. (2010). Partner violence and substance abuse: Treatment interventions. *Aggression and Violent Behavior, 15,* 162–166.

Lamb, S. (1991). Acts without agents: An analysis of linguistic avoidance in journal articles on men who batter women. *American Journal of Orthopsychiatry, 61,* 250–257.

LaMotte, A. D., & Murphy, C. M. (2016). Trauma, posttraumatic stress disorder symptoms, and dissociative experiences during men's intimate partner violence perpetration. *Psychological Trauma: Theory, Research, Practice, and Policy, 9,* 567–574.

Lipsky, S., Caetano, R., & Roy-Byrne, P. (2011). Triple jeopardy: Impact of partner violence perpetration, mental health and substance use on perceived unmet need for mental health care among men. *Social Psychiatry and Psychiatric Epidemiology, 46*(9), 843–852.

O'Leary, K. D., & Slep, A. M. (2003). A dyadic longitudinal model of adolescent dating aggression. *Journal of Clinical Child and Adolescent Psychology, 32,* 314–327.

Pence, E., & Paymar, M. (1993). Education groups for men who batter: The Duluth model. New York: Springer.

Reis, H. T., Capobianco, A., & Tsai, F. (2002). Finding the person in personal relationships. *Journal of Personality, 70,* 813–850.

Rosenbaum, A., & Leisring, P. A. (2003). Beyond power and control: Towards an understanding of partner abusive men. *Journal of Comparative Family Studies, 34,* 7–22.

Simoneti, S., Scott, E. C., & Murphy, C. M. (2000). Dissociative experiences in partner-assaultive men. *Journal of Interpersonal Violence, 15,* 1262–1283.

Taft, C. T., Murphy, C. M., & Creech, S. K. (2016). *Trauma-informed treatment and prevention of intimate partner violence.* Washington, DC: American Psychological Association.

Webermann, A. R., & Murphy, C. M. (2019). Childhood trauma and dissociative intimate partner violence. *Violence Against Women, 25*(2), 148–166.

White, J. W., Merrill, L. L., & Koss, M. P. (2001). Predictors of premilitary courtship violence in a Navy recruit sample. *Journal of Interpersonal Violence, 16*, 910–927.

Winslow, S., & Hall, S. (2009). Retaliate first: Memory, humiliation and male violence. *Crime, Media, Culture, 5*, 285–304.

Winstock, Z. (2007). Toward an interactional perspective on intimate partner violence. *Aggression and Violent Behavior, 12*, 348–363.

Winstock, Z., & Eisikovits, Z. (2008). Motives and control in escalatory conflicts in intimate relationships. *Children and Youth Services Review, 30*, 287–296.

CHAPTER 6

Strategies for Critical Clinical Practice in Veterans' Mental Health

Catherine Bryan and Tessa Barrett

INTRODUCTION

This chapter draws on insights formulated at the intersection of two modes of inquiry, analysis, and practice, to parse out the constraints of practising critical social work in the bureaucratic and clinical context of veterans' mental health. Despite their more pragmatic methodological differences, the ontological objectives of social work and anthropology can be very similar. Anthropology offers insight into large-scale social, cultural, and economic structures through in-depth exploration of the small-scale practices and relationships that are simultaneously generated by and generative of those structures. At the same time, through its analysis it challenges those structures insofar as through them power, fairness, and access to resources are unequally distributed. This is also the aim of critical social work, which transforms those insights and contestations into intervention. Our contribution, then, follows from the integration of our different, yet kindred, perspectives and professional experiences. More precisely, we approach our case study in the spirit of anthropology's ethnographic method, reading it through and against theory (in this instance, political economy) to generate a foundation for clinical practice firmly rooted in an understanding and critique of capitalism.

An amalgamation of multiple cases and presenting issues, our case study illustrates the challenges of authentically client-centred, critically guided work within large, bureaucratic clinical settings. Read through the theoretical contributions of political economy, these challenges present even more strongly, and the possibility of their resolution through one-to-one therapeutic relationships seems all the less likely. At the same time, those contributions prompt us to reposition ourselves vis-à-vis our clients in these types of settings. While not a complete reversal of the conservative and individualistic impulses of mainstream intervention, this chapter offers three strategies to counter these impulses in a particular moment in historical time informed by the logics of advanced, neoliberal capitalism. Broadly stated, these are: (1) countering historic trespass, (2) adaptation of protocol, and (3) navigating and negotiating institutional appeasement.

In these ways, rather than offering a novel approach (or rehearsing existing critical modalities), this chapter seeks to resolve one of the principle challenges faced by social workers—that is, the reconciliation of mainstream practice with critical, progressive politics in therapeutic settings that often reinforce social inequality through their adherence to dominant forms of intervention. The intervention at the centre of our discussion, cognitive behavioural therapy (CBT), is not, then, at its inception or in its standard delivery, critical.

COGNITIVE BEHAVIOURAL THERAPY

Cognitive behavioural therapy represents a wide array of generally present-focused clinical strategies and techniques, all of which are guided by underlying principles of cognitive theory and behaviourism. The specific interventions aim to target "unhelpful" thoughts, beliefs, and assumptions about self, others, and the world or behaviour.

Moreover, as revealed in the critical scholarship of social work and adjacent disciplines, CBT offers no analysis of power or of social location and context (Brown & Ballou, 1992). And yet, as an intervention, it is ubiquitous. If we take seriously our own critiques of the contemporary neoliberal state and its expanding mandate of welfare retrenchment (Ferguson & Lavalette, 2013; Garrett, 2009; Pollack & Rossiter, 2010; Rossiter & Heron, 2011)—not to mention the growing threat of the alt-right and its infiltration of Canadian politics (Mirrlees, 2018; Perry & Scrivens, 2016; Scrivens & Perry, 2017)—critical intervention may be increasingly relegated to the spaces and opportunities we create, rather than offered as the blueprint for practice.

As you read this chapter, ask yourself the following questions:

1. In what ways does the bureaucratic organization and functioning of organizations dictate the terms and possibilities of the interventions you work with?

2. How do the ideologies underpinning organizations manifest themselves in and through your interventions, and to what effect?

3. How might a client's proximity to and integration in labour markets inform their material and psychosocial well-being?

4. How might the contributions of political economy facilitate a more client-centred practice in a context largely informed by mainstream clinical approaches?

5. What are the limits of critical practice within these settings? And what covert and overt actions can critical clinical practitioners take to expand those limits, if not circumvent them altogether?

POLITICAL ECONOMY AND CRITICAL SOCIAL WORK

As a theoretical framework, political economy focuses our attention on the ways in which state and capital intersect and are mutually constitutive.

POLITICAL ECONOMY

Political economy is at once "a thing" and the "study of that thing." It refers to the intersection, interaction, and/or convergence of economics and politics in a society, *and* it refers to an area of study that takes as its subject those intersections, interactions, and convergences. When referring to, for example, the political economy of Canada or the "West" in the 21st century, we are typically referencing capitalist political economy, and more precisely, neoliberal capitalist political economy.

For social work, political economy has long been a central and important consideration (Corrigan & Leonard, 1978). Even when researchers and practitioners do not name it as such, our scholarship and interventions necessarily rub up against the priorities of and barriers established by capitalist political economy. In the contemporary moment, we can identify, at minimum, three overarching ways social workers in their professional capacity, as both researchers and practitioners, are likely to encounter capitalism. First, as scholars engaged in research, we often explore political economy through our analytical engagements with policy—both social and economic—and its impact on the material conditions of people's lives. Second, as practitioners and front-line workers, we contend with the uneven consequences of capitalism, reinforced by the state, and the inequalities it generates and relies on (Jones, 1983; Powell, 2001). These include inequalities rooted in economic status or class, and gender, but also—drawing on the contributions of Cedric J. Robinson (1983/2000)—those connected to processes of racialization.

RACE CAPITALISM

Conceptualized by Robinson, race capitalism draws our attention to the ways in which capitalism relies on socially constructed, yet taken-for granted, ideas of race and racial hierarchy to justify and naturalize unequal power relations, distribution of resources, and access to wealth.

Third, social workers work in systems that, since the 1980s, have been routinely subjected to the logics of the neoliberal state (Ferguson & Lavalette, 2006).

NEOLIBERALISM

Neoliberalism is an ideological framework and a set of practices. As David Harvey argues, neoliberalism is "a theory of political economic practices that proposes that human well-being can best be advanced by liberating individual entrepreneurial freedoms and skills within an institutional framework characterized by strong private property rights, free markets, and free trade. The role of the state is to create and preserve an institutional framework appropriate to such practices" (Harvey, 2005, p. 2).

Diverging from the purported ideals of the welfare state, which sought to mediate the relationship between labour and capital through redistribution, neoliberalism prioritizes capital and, as such, offers solutions in line with market-based principles. Though economic in its framing, this realignment has required a reimagining and re-institutionalization of what constitutes entitlement, as well as the conditions under which entitlement is established (Gazso, 2012; Sassen, 1996; Shamir, 2008). Encapsulated in the language and practices of welfare retrenchment, the resources we have at our disposal are increasingly fewer, such that, as the consequences of advanced capitalism reveal themselves (precarity and poverty following from unemployment and underemployment), the ability to provide meaningful assistance has waned. In the absence of a robust safety net, social workers are limited in their ability to mediate and redress the consequences of capitalism, a system that does not, through the course of its operations, provide for people beyond the wage-labour nexus.

THE WAGE-LABOUR NEXUS

Premised on the notion of a free transactional relationship between those who sell their labour (workers) and those to whom they sell it (the owners of the means of production), the wage-labour nexus refers to one of capitalism's key methods of generating and accumulating profit. Through it, in exchange for wages, the worker's labour and its outcome become the property of their employer. What is critical for this discussion is the dependency that the wage-labour nexus has generated. Indeed, in the absence of wages or money more broadly, survival becomes nearly impossible.

In each instance, social work practitioners work for and against this system, simultaneously reinforcing (Newman, 2007; Raeymaeckers & Dierckx, 2012; van Berkel, Caswell, Kupka, & Larsen, 2017) and contesting (Ferguson & Lavalette, 2006; Hyslop, 2012) its conditions and injustices.

The capitalist mode of production bears down directly on the lives of our clients, fostering dependency on money, but concurrently limiting access to wages through the mobilization of inequality (Maynard, 2017; Melamed, 2015; Robinson, 1983/2000). Somewhat counterintuitively, then, but reflective of the broader paradigm of neoliberal governance, a growing number of countries—including Canada—have tended toward investing in the employability of their citizens, rather than the provision of direct transfer payments and the funding of supportive social services (Gazso & McDaniel, 2010; Peck, 2002; Wacquant, 2010). And yet, evident in rates of minimum wage read against the cost of living, such employment does little to redress poverty (Gazso, 2012; Herring, 2019; Rose, 1995; Wacquant, 2017); it does, however, direct dependency away from the state and, moreover, it serves as an important mechanism of capital accumulation (Fudge, 2005; Peck, 2001). Under this regime, social workers are often called upon to facilitate the integration of "unproductive" subjects into stratified labour markets (Egdell & McQuaid, 2016; van Berkel et al., 2017).

In other words, in this context, the profession functions to the direct benefit of capitalism. Here, we might elaborate on what Weinberg (2016) refers to as the fundamental structural paradox of social work practice. Weinberg identifies this paradox as an outcome of social work's proximity to the state, and the extent to which this generates a dual role of care and discipline. This paradox is exacerbated by the state's proximity to capital. It is not then, the state in and of itself that demands social work's disciplinary function. Rather, it is the collaboration of state and capital that requires this work. Such a purpose offers a puzzle for social workers, who must hold in balance the task of producing and reproducing workers for capital, with the profession's core values of dignity for the person, social justice, and equity.

THE CASE OF DANIEL

Our case study focuses on a unique clinical setting that offers mental health support to veterans of the Canadian Armed Forces. The therapeutic work undertaken in this setting is highly coordinated and prescriptive. As detailed here, it is reflective of models of care that are individualistic, pathologizing, and reinforcing of systemically produced inequalities—notably, in this regard, where class inequity and processes of racialization are concerned. As such, our case study reveals the limitations of critical clinical practice while simultaneously demonstrating the need for it. The critical social worker is present, but her capacity to fully intervene in and shape the outcome of Daniel's presenting issues is constrained. She is, in this setting, charged with the task of implementing a predetermined course of action, which she does, though strategically. In what follows, we describe Daniel's life leading up to his diagnosis, the clinical setting in which that diagnosis was determined, and the trajectory of care that followed. From there, we offer three key strategies, inspired by our reading of critical political economy, that allow practitioners to attune themselves to the harms inflicted by the capitalist mode of production, and to reorient their therapeutic engagements, making them more responsive to the presence of those harms in their clients' lives.

Daniel is a 57-year-old African Nova Scotian, with a 25-year history of service with the Royal Canadian Navy. Daniel ended his service over a decade ago when he was medically released for a physical condition. Finding work proved difficult due to Daniel's physical injuries and repeated experiences of racial discrimination. After hearing a story in the news about services available to veterans with diagnosed operational stress injuries, Daniel contacted

Veterans Affairs Canada (VAC). Soon after, Daniel was assigned a VAC case manager who completed a referral to a local mental health clinic, where Daniel was scheduled for a comprehensive psychiatric assessment for a VAC disability claim. The assessment undertaken at this meeting included a two-hour interview with a psychiatrist and the collection of brief psychometrics. Typical of the neoliberal assessment emphasis on measurement and metrics, the psychiatrist applied screening tools for depression, general anxiety, post-traumatic stress disorder, overall well-being and distress, and substance use (i.e., GAD-7, PHQ-9, OQ-45, PCL-5, AUDIT), and relied on collateral information from Daniel's spouse. Reflecting the biomedical model, the assessment concluded with a diagnosis of post-traumatic stress disorder (PTSD; chronic) and major depressive disorder with anxious distress (MDD; mild, recurrent), the physical and mental health symptoms of which severely restricted his functioning in all areas (occupational, social, leisure).

As Daniel had never participated in psychotherapy, a short-term intervention was recommended. He was referred for cognitive behavioural therapy (CBT) to target his mood, to be followed by a trauma-focused therapy to address his PTSD symptoms. These were to be delivered by a clinical social worker. Daniel was on a waitlist for psychotherapy for three months. During this time, the psychiatrist's report was submitted to VAC in support of new disability claims for PTSD and MDD. Several months later, Daniel learned that the claim for PTSD was adjudicated favourably, but the claim for MDD was not. He was also informed that in 18 to 24 months, VAC would request a reassessment for the PTSD claim, at which time, Daniel would have to again meet with the psychiatrist, who would determine the severity and persistence of his diagnosis. In the intervening time, Daniel was expected to complete the recommended treatments to address his diagnosis and enroll in the VAC Rehabilitation Services and Vocational Assistance Program (RSVAP). Again, responsive to the system's neoliberal tendencies, the timeline for these interventions was predetermined and relatively tight.

STRATEGIES FOR CRITICAL CLINICAL INTERVENTION

Despite the social origins of his mental health condition, the course of action described above corresponds not only to the standard course of action embarked upon in a mainstream clinical context, but also to dominant medical models of assessment and treatment. In contrast to critical clinical approaches, the biomedical model offers individualized understandings of and treatments for a range of health concerns. Corresponding to dominant ideologies rooted in the capitalist mode of production, such an approach has the tendency to obscure the social and environmental causes of disease or ill health, focusing instead on identifying and treating individual pathology. With the social and material hidden from view, systems rooted in the biomedical model tend to be highly dependent on experts who provide care to clients. This hierarchy is further cemented both in the context of neoliberal service provision broadly, and in veteran's mental health more specifically. In the case of Daniel, therapy was facilitated, but also complicated, by the partnership between the federal government (VAC) and the provincial health authority. And even as the status afforded to veterans in terms of public mental health provision exceeds that of civilians, neoliberal modes of governance and service delivery shape the experience of accessing treatment. For example, as in many public mental health systems, the expectation is that clinicians adhere to "evidence-based" biomedicalized therapies, minimize risk, and reduce systems, but that they do so within as brief a time frame as possible. This corresponds to many neoliberal trends, including reductions in public spending on services and supports (Teghtsoonian, 2009) and increasingly restrictive eligibility criteria (Ramon, 2008), coupled with a heightened focus on labour-market participation. For Daniel, the context of neoliberal service provisioning was, in some ways, tempered by the highly bureaucratic structures of veterans' affairs, which are designed to facilitate access to mental health care.

Despite its specificity, Daniel's experience exemplifies the neoliberal model of work-oriented welfare, but it does so in a unique way. Under the workfare model, eligibility for benefits is determined through a person's demonstrated willingness to work. This is communicated to caseworkers in a variety of ways, including but not limited to documenting contact with potential employers and attending labour-market readiness workshops. Where veterans are concerned, eligibility is determined on a sliding scale. That said, rather than corresponding to one's willingness to work, eligibility is established when an absolute inability to work is demonstrated, such that the more severe and persistent a person's condition is, the less likely they are to work, and the greater the monetary support they're likely to receive. For Daniel, returning to work was not an option. Even with a reduction in his symptoms, structural constraints limited his capacity to earn sufficiently and subjected him to various forms of discrimination. For a clinical social worker, trained in or motivated by the tenets of critical social work practice, balancing the needs of the client and the agency is challenging. In what follows, we outline three strategies that might facilitate a critical practice in an otherwise conservative clinical setting. These are (1) countering historic trespass, (2) modifying protocol, and (3) negotiating institutional appeasement. Each offers insight into how one might exercise critical perspectives in a therapeutic setting located at the intersection of conventional clinical practice and a complicated bureaucratic system. Steeped in the ideologies of neoliberalism, this system holds clients in close proximity to precarious labour markets throughout the course of therapeutic treatment. As a result, critical social workers must contend not only with client distrust (of both the clinician and the system), but also with the reality that benefits may be denied if the treatment is successful.

Strategy One: Countering Historic Trespass

HISTORIC TRESPASS

The term *historic trespass* signals the involvement of social workers, historically and in the contemporary moment, in state-initiated and -supported projects of dispossession, displacement, and oppression in the service of Canadian colonialism and the expansion of capitalism.

The context of veteran's mental health is one in which individual clients often feel very little autonomy. For Daniel, his status as a racialized person in a place (Nova Scotia) where anti-black racism is prevalent and racism-related stress is increasingly well-documented (Beagan, Etowa, & Bernard, 2012; Este & Bernard, 2006; McCurdy, 1995) left him even more vulnerable. Added to this is the problematic involvement and interference of the state vis-à-vis black communities in the province. Here, we can look to a multitude of examples: the dispossession of Africville residents and their forced relocation to Halifax's inner city (Nelson, 2000), the overrepresentation of black children in state "care" (Maynard, 2017), and the overt criminalization of black people by the criminal "justice" system (Archibald, 1989; Khenti, 2014; Palacios, 2016). How can trust be established in a context characterized and experienced as racist? And how can trauma work be successful when the individual's stress reactions are—following from their experiences as a racialized person—reasonable? Phrased differently, given how social workers are aligned with state power, our presence, regardless of who we are, might trigger reactions in our clients. In turn, this might trigger a reaction in a clinician who may be unaccustomed to problematizing their proximity to and participation in systems and structures that are racist.

To do the work of acknowledgement, validation, and space-making effectively, clinical social workers must critically and authentically situate themselves, their power, and the power of the profession in the social and economic structures that have given rise to the race-based trauma and ill health they encounter in their clients. Indeed, to contend with capitalism in our practices requires that we can (1) identify and articulate the ways in which capitalism generates and sustains racialized inequalities in the service of capital accumulation, (2) acknowledge the extent to which those inequalities often benefit some while disadvantaging others, and (3) recognize the extent to which social work has, through historic and contemporary forms of trespass within communities of colour, reinforced and reproduced this system, safeguarding white dominance. Such an engagement with the self is a longstanding practice of critical social work (Fook & Gardner, 2012; Knott & Scragg, 2016; Heron, 2005; Mandell, 2008). Kondrat (1999) offers an early framework for this practice, arguing that professional self-awareness must be constituted in more than the individual psychology of the practitioner or their interactions with specific clients. Rather, and drawing on Giddens's "structuration theory," she explores the potential of professional self-awareness as grounded in the transaction between the "self" and larger social structures and systems. Such an approach is now, nearly 20 years later, widely celebrated and deployed; moreover, it has been expanded by scholars of critical social theory to include more rigorous accounts of power (Heron, 2005) and an integration of intersectionality theory (Mattsson, 2014). An important addition to critical reflexivity, for the purposes of acknowledging and countering historic trespass rooted in the twin processes of capitalism and racism (Robinson, 1983/2000), can be found in Robin DiAngelo's formulation of white fragility (2011).

WHITE FRAGILITY

White fragility, DiAngelo writes, "is a state in which even a minimum amount of racial stress becomes intolerable, triggering a range of defensive moves. These moves include the outward display of emotions such as anger, fear and guilt, and behaviors such as argumentation, silence, and leaving the stress-inducing situation" (2011, p. 57).

DiAngelo's analysis offers insight into encounters that, experienced as interruptions to the norm by white people, provoke adverse reactions in them.

Challenges to the social worker's authority may provoke similar kinds of re-actions. Given the largely voluntary nature of veterans' mental health, such a provocation may seem unlikely; presumably, the client is there because they wish to be and, moreover, they are supported financially (if tenuously) for their ef-forts. And yet, as the example of Daniel illustrates, frustration and anger, often directed at the clinician, are not uncommon. The strategies deployed to under-mine white fragility offer important insight into how social workers might better contextualize and, following from that, undermine the imbalances of power that characterize the client-worker relationship, particularly when the client is a per-son of colour and the social worker is white. Relinquishing power begins with understanding the fallacy of that power, and more precisely, the ways in which power is deliberately distributed and unevenly allocated. Critical clinical prac-titioners, then, situate their assessment in the social and material, as opposed to assigning individualist or pathologizing meaning to their client's experience. At the same time, the critical clinical practitioner validates the client's own under-standing of their situation by drawing insight from (rather than shutting down) client expressions of anger and frustration. With Daniel, this meant exploring experiences of racism both inside and outside the military and acknowledging the role of social work in perpetuating racism and inequality.

Understanding that our profession as empowered by the state and, by exten-sion, capital helps us to do that work. Described in the preceding section, politi-cal economy offers us a framework through which to identify not only inequality and its consequences, but also its root causes. Again, if race—a purposeful social construct—is organized in the service of capital accumulation, and if capital-ism is ubiquitous, dictating the terms of our own participation and inclusion in social, economic, and cultural life, then we cannot disentangle our power or our privileges from the system that produces and reproduces racism. From that vantage point, we can situate adverse reactions (to contestations of our power; client anger and frustration) within the system that imbues our profession with power, and we can begin to temper those reactions. This entails acknowledging past wrongs—historic forms of trespass by the profession vis-à-vis the racialized communities to which many of our clients may belong. It also means that we accept and make space for our clients' (or our colleagues') anger and frustration because we assume responsibility for the system—not as something we control, but as something we benefit from.

In Daniel's case, the first step was to acknowledge structural racism and to situate his experience, trauma, and resilience within those structures, their history, and their legacy. In the context of Daniel's therapy, this meant gradual imaginal exposure to and processing of what it meant to be in the military, but more precisely, what it meant to be the only black sailor on the ship; what it meant to constantly be on alert; and what it meant to have to defend himself against harm from fellow sailors—the very people who were meant to have his back. Sidestepping these realities would likely result in additional harm. Naming them, while insufficient as a remedy, aided in the establishment of trust and allowed Daniel to feel and express a full range of emotion. This included negative thoughts and expressions of anger directed at the social work clinician, who, regardless of her mandate to provide care, represented the very systems that Daniel had experienced as discriminatory and oppressive. The critical social worker, despite her obligation to implement the treatment protocol, was responsive to Daniel, validating his perceptions and understandings, grounding them in the reality of racism and inequality; she also created space for Daniel to simply communicate those perceptions and understandings, and to do so in an uncensored and unfiltered manner.

Strategy Two: Modifying Protocol

Given histories of unwelcome and harmful intervention by those working in the service of the state, the prescriptive nature of VAC-mediated mental health services may serve as a barrier to the development of a positive and productive therapeutic relationship with racialized veterans. Read against structural forms of violence meted out by the state through the interventions of social workers, there is no reason to anticipate that such service—tailored to the schedule of the state—would be perceived of and experienced as less violent. Critical intervention in this space requires that the clinician not only be aware of the ways in which power is unevenly distributed, but also that they take steps to introduce balance to that distribution. Modifying protocol is key in this regard. The approach to working with Daniel was designed to first target his depression through basic CBT, to be followed by trauma-focused therapy.

The mainstream approach for the treatment of depression in CBT is behavioural activation. Through this treatment, the client monitors activity and corresponding mood, and from there—with the clinician—sets goals (e.g., activities of daily living, activities once enjoyed, or new behaviours that the client would like to try). For Daniel, these included grocery shopping and eating a meal in a restaurant. In each instance, however, his capacity to gain mastery over the activity was limited by the persistent worry that something negative would happen. Additionally, given the compounding influence of repeated experiences of racial discrimination over his lifetime, Daniel would enter social situations and public places with his guard up. Hypervigilance and an increased startle response, coupled with his expectation of racist encounters, made these activities intolerable. What became quickly evident to both Daniel and the critical clinical social worker was that in the absence of trauma-based treatment that focused on the persistence of racism and racialization in his life and their effects, in addition to his military exposure to violence and risk, the CBT would have nominal effect. Adapting the protocol in such a way to acknowledge the impact of racism in Daniel's life and those experiences as central to his trauma was, as such, a requirement of effective intervention, and furthermore, to establishing a relationship that did not duplicate or reproduce historic encounters with social work. In changing course, the clinician communicated to Daniel her willingness to work with him, as opposed to simply conceding to the structures of the agency. That said, the tools available to the clinician remained in line with the mandate and standard procedures of the agency.

Prolonged exposure was borne out of emotional processing theory, developed by Foa and Kozak (1985), as a framework to understand anxiety struggles and the effective mechanisms of exposure therapy. The most basic idea of emotion processing theory is that fear, as a cognitive structure, is a "program" for escaping danger. When fear is present in response to an actual threat, the structure provides adaptive action in response to that threat. If the fear response is a false alarm, that is, there is no actual threat to one's life, health, or well-being, the fear structure becomes problematic. Prolonged exposure therapy is typically delivered in approximately 10 weekly 90-minute sessions. Prolonged exposure sessions follow a manualized structure and are audio-recorded for the client to listen to between sessions and include in vivo (situational) exposure. The rationale for in vivo (situational) exposure is presented, and client and therapist co-construct a hierarchy of avoided situations. Together, client and therapist also generate anchor points for the client's subjective units of distress to enhance the therapist's understanding of the relative difficulty of hierarchy items. Over the course of the first two sessions, the client and therapist identify exposures that the client will practise between sessions, while also practising breathing retraining and listening to audio recordings of the sessions. In session three, the therapist presents the rationale for imaginal exposure, followed by the client's first imaginal re-experiencing of the trauma memory. Following this, the therapist and client discuss and process the feelings that arose during the exposure. The client is asked to listen to the recording of the exposure session daily, and to continue to practise in vivo exposures. Subsequent sessions follow this structure, with the option to explore the most distressing aspects of the trauma between sessions six and nine. As the client's sense of distress is reduced over time, the duration of imaginal exposures decreases. Session ten includes a last retelling of the trauma memory with a focus on what has changed over the course of the treatment and consulting with the client to determine their sense of their own progress. This model has also faced critiques of potentially retraumatizing people.

Again, we are confronted with a highly prescriptive model within prevailing dominant models of service delivery that fails to account for pre-existing socially meted out traumas, or the uneven positioning of people of colour within economic systems or structures. In Daniel's case, while the threats associated with life in the military were no longer present, racism and the threat of racist encounters remained constant. The social worker's decision to pursue prolonged exposure therapy, then, required a caveat that acknowledged the persistence of racism in Daniel's life. Moreover, while prolonged exposure therapy was eventually useful for Daniel, allowing him to gain control over his symptoms, very quickly it became clear that its delivery as conventionally organized and described above, did not meet his needs; more precisely, because he was expected to enter social spaces where he had, historically, not felt welcome, he required specific socially and culturally relevant support. This was compounded by the rapidity of gentrification in the neighbourhoods of his childhood and youth, and the extent to which formerly comfortable spaces were no longer. Modifying protocol in this instance, then, required the social worker to recognize the limits of her own effectiveness. A white, middle-class woman, she had no historic or contemporary ill-ease with the spaces, new or old, of white, middle-class Halifax, nor did she have direct experience with racism.

Though not officially part of Daniel's intervention plan, the critical clinical social worker—responding to Daniel's expressed interest—referred him to an occupational therapist who would accompany Daniel on planned outings (corresponding to his objective). The occupational therapist, unlike the social worker, shared a similar cultural background with Daniel and had the capacity to speak directly to racism and its effects. This therapist accompanied Daniel through the in vivo exercises, and in so doing, provided him with a more experiential learning opportunity, as she and Daniel, coming from similar (though not identical) social locations, were able to more effectively identify and debrief both subtle and overt encounters with racism when and as they occurred. At the same time, in collaboration with the social worker and in conversation about those encounters, Daniel identified an interest in supporting his community as a means of redressing the prevalence and consequences of racism. For Daniel, this meant volunteering at his local church and community centre, working with young people and older adults. Shortly after the work with the occupational therapist, Daniel was increasingly able to tolerate the difficulty of these repeated exposures such that he was eventually completing them independently. Daniel expressed feelings of renewed confidence and competence and could complete tasks and activities that he had previously been unable to: going to church, attending a concert, and grocery shopping. Moreover, through these activities, he was re-building his social network and re-establishing connections to his cultural community. Despite the treatment's success, these modifications were controversial amongst the members of the treatment team. In the first instance, the intervention diverged from the initial formulation of the treatment plan. And, in the second, the use of the occupational therapist required additional resources and extended the length of the treatment beyond its original parameters.

Strategy Three: Navigating and Negotiating Institutional Appeasement

Much like in other health care systems, the challenge of engaging in a critical social work practice in veterans' mental health is compounded by the interdisciplinarity that characterized the clinical team, and in the specific context where Daniel was receiving treatment, the presence of researchers and data analysts. The social worker charged with Daniel's care, then, was accountable not only to Daniel but to a team comprising nurses, occupational therapists, psychologists, psychiatrists, family doctors, a health services manager and director of mental health services, a clinical director, and a research and statistical officer. Added to this list, the social worker was consistently in communication with the VAC caseworker, who represented the agency's interests where Daniel was concerned. In these types of settings, it is not uncommon for social workers to be at odds with their colleagues. In terms of our responsibility to our clients, our professional values explicitly challenge inequality and domination, and prompt us to work toward social justice. However, in terms of our accountability to others within the organization, we are often positioned near the bottom of the professional hierarchy—a reality that persists despite the near identical clinical tasks assigned to both social workers and psychologists.

In Daniel's case, accessing culturally and socially relevant occupational therapy required the critical clinical social worker to rationalize the referral to an interdisciplinary team charged with Daniel's care. To access occupational therapy for Daniel, the social worker was not only required to provide a rationale for this additional service, but also a rationale for why they would be deviating from the original treatment protocol (which does not involve using an occupational therapist to assist with in vivo exposures). To effectively present a case to the team, with the aim of having client needs met, it is imperative that the critical clinical social worker be prepared to discuss all aspects of the client's care that are of interest to the various disciplines represented on the team (psychology, psychiatry, nursing, general medicine, occupational therapy, management, and research), and that they do so in a manner that is comprehensible to those team members. Given professional hierarchies and the manifold tasks and responsibilities broadly assigned to the role of social worker, we are in a unique position to be particularly adaptive and perhaps even cunning in our dealings with agencies. Learning the disciplinary language of the other professional groups with which we work, determining their objectives, and establishing alliances with those who share our values or are sympathetic to them are necessary and effective means of striking a balance between fair, socially just treatment for our clients and the mandates of government agencies. When such an approach fails, the social worker must be prepared to advocate for treatment that is responsive not to the needs of the agency, but to the social, emotional, and economic needs of the client. As critical clinical social workers we also need to assert our knowledge and training and resist the subordination of our professional approach to working with people. In the case of Daniel, the therapist reviewed with the team the aspects of the case that made the standard approach a challenge and argued that he was at risk of not actually benefitting from the treatment. Although the team members presented strong points to demonstrate that this modification to the treatment protocol would likely lengthen the course of treatment, they were eventually swayed by this reasoning.

Despite its proximity to government (or perhaps because of it), access to care for veterans avoids what Terris (1999) has labelled the neoliberal triad of anti-health reforms: government budget cutting, deregulation, and privatization. This, in large part, follows from the status afforded to veterans as veterans, and the unique relationship they have to the federal state, which is differently responsible for their care. Yet, even though they are entitled to care, and despite the fact that most veterans have health insurance and regular access to a medical doctor, veterans tend to have worse health, higher levels of (dis)ability, and higher rates of mental ill-health relative to the general Canadian population—conditions often attributed by veterans to their military service (Thompson et al., 2011). At the same time, many veterans experience that bureaucracy, otherwise intended to provide for them, as alienating and their engagements with the system as compounding their mental health challenges, rather than alleviating them. In part, this is an outcome of what many veterans experience as a counterintuitive process that is simultaneously circular and rigid. For Daniel, this process was, at once, familiar (in light of his 25-year service) but foreign. Like many, he avoided seeking out mental health services. Moreover, like many, he was aware of the ways in which his progress—as defined by his clinical team—might influence his ability to access benefits if he was deemed able to return to work. Such was the broad objective of Daniel's scheduled reassessment: to determine if he was well enough to be employed. The job of the critical clinician is to recognize this tension, and to act in the best interest of the client—not the state, and not the precarious labour markets it bolsters through workfare-style welfare programs.

CONCLUSION

The process and prospect of working with trauma-related issues, as has been illustrated in Daniel's case, is fraught for those who, on the one hand, wish to minimize their symptoms and be well, and on the other, are truly (by virtue of age, experience, and trauma) unable to return to regular employment. Exacerbating this concern for Daniel was the nature of the employment he would be returning to and his experiences of the sector, and more precisely, his encounters with racism. The clinician in this context, leading up to reassessment, is called upon to redress "problematic" symptoms in the service of the reintegration of an otherwise "unproductive" subject. Once well (or well enough), this newly activated worker enters into a labour market that is, itself, traumatizing: low-waged, insecure, and stratified in ways that reflect and reproduce profound inequality. These realities and what they represent to veterans, and more precisely veterans of colour, are significant. Read through the lens of denied or reduced benefits, the intervention itself appears punitive. Even a positive outcome (remedy or reduction of symptoms) brings with it negative consequence. Moreover, where the system is experienced as circular and the process convoluted, the effectiveness of the clinician may be called into question. Here, the therapeutic alliance is potentially undermined by the intent assigned to the clinician by the veteran. Who, phrased differently, is the client? The veteran or the system? And what is the objective of the intervention if its outcome determines access to monetary resources? To communicate their centrality and to undermine client mistrust, the critical social worker must effectively work within and against this system. This means developing effective strategies that recognize the social, economic, and cultural context from which marginalization emerges, and the manifold ways in which our clients can be informed by and excluded from that context. In the case of Daniel, the clinical social worker was largely constrained; her capacity to be innovative, creative, and critical in her approach was dramatically undercut by the institutional framework that dictated treatment. And yet, mindful of the operations of capital in the context of her client's life as an African Nova Scotian man, she—albeit at times subtly—operationalized the tenets of critical political economy as a means of reorienting that framework in the service of Daniel. In so doing, she made room for his anger and frustration, to acknowledge the realities and outcomes of white supremacy, while providing Daniel with the necessary supports to improve the quality of his life (an outcome that he could exercise in tandem with his care for his community), while not undermining his ability to access his benefits.

REFERENCES

Archibald, B. P. (1989). Sentencing and visible minorities: Equality and affirmative action in the criminal justice system. *Dalhousie Law Journal, 12,* 377.

Beagan, B. L., Etowa, J., & Bernard, W. T. (2012). "With God in our lives he gives us the strength to carry on": African Nova Scotian women, spirituality, and racism-related stress. *Mental Health, Religion and Culture, 15*(2), 103–120.

Brown, L. S., & Ballou, M. (Eds.). (1992). *Personality and psychopathology: Feminist reappraisals.* New York: Guilford Press.

Corrigan, P., & Leonard, P. (1978). *Social work practice under capitalism: A Marxist approach.* London: Palgrave Macmillan.

DiAngelo, R. (2011). White fragility. *International Journal of Critical Pedagogy, 3*(3), 54–70.

Egdell, V., & McQuaid, R. (2016). Supporting disadvantaged young people into work: Insights from the capability approach. *Social Policy and Administration, 50*(1), 1–18.

Este, D., & Bernard, W. T. (2006). Spirituality among African Nova Scotians: A key to survival in Canadian society. *Critical Social Work, 7*(1), 1–22.

Ferguson, I., & Lavalette, M. (2006). Globalization and global justice: Towards a social work of resistance. *International social work, 49*(3), 309–318.

Ferguson, I., & Lavalette, M. (2013). Crisis, austerity and the future(s) of social work in the UK. *Critical and Radical Social Work, 1*(1), 95–110.

Foa, E. B., & Kozak, M. J. (1985). Treatment of anxiety disorders: Implications for psychopathology. In A. H. Tuma & J. D. Maser (Eds.), *Anxiety and the anxiety disorders* (pp. 421–452). New York: Lawrence Erlbaum Associates.

Fook, J., & Gardner, F. (Eds.). (2012). *Critical reflection in context: Applications in health and social care*. New York: Routledge.

Fudge, J. (2005). After industrial citizenship: Market citizenship or citizenship at work? *Relations Industrielles/Industrial Relations, 60*(4), 631–656.

Garrett, P. M. (2009). Marx and "modernization": Reading capital as social critique and inspiration for social work resistance to neoliberalization. *Journal of Social Work, 9*(2), 199–221.

Gazso, A. (2012). Moral codes of mothering and the introduction of welfare-to-work in Ontario. *Canadian Review of Sociology/Revue canadienne de sociologie, 49*(1), 26–49.

Gazso, A., & McDaniel, S. A. (2010). The risks of being a lone mother on income support in Canada and the USA. *International Journal of Sociology and Social Policy, 30*(7/8), 368–386.

Harvey, D. (2005). *The new imperialism*. Oxford: Oxford University Press.

Heron, B. (2005). Self-reflection in critical social work practice: Subjectivity and the possibilities of resistance. *Reflective practice, 6*(3), 341–351.

Herring, C. (2019). Between street and shelter: Seclusion, exclusion, and the neutralization of poverty. In J. Flint & R. Powell (Eds.), *Class, ethnicity and state in the polarized metropolis: Putting Wacquant to work* (pp. 281–305). Cham, Switzerland: Palgrave Macmillan.

Hyslop, I. (2012). Social work as a practice of freedom. *Journal of Social Work, 12*(4), 404–422.

Jones, C. (1983). *State social work and the working class*. London: Macmillan International Higher Education.

Khenti, A. (2014). The Canadian war on drugs: Structural violence and unequal treatment of Black Canadians. *International Journal of Drug Policy, 25*(2), 190–195.

Knott, C., & Scragg, T. (Eds.). (2016). *Reflective practice in social work*. London: Sage; Learning Matters.

Kondrat, M. E. (1999). Who is the "self" in self-aware: Professional self-awareness from a critical theory perspective. *Social Service Review, 73*(4), 451–477.

Mandell, D. (2008). Power, care and vulnerability: Considering use of self in child welfare work. *Journal of Social Work Practice, 22*(2), 235–248.

Mattsson, T. (2014). Intersectionality as a useful tool: Anti-oppressive social work and critical reflection. *Affilia, 29*(1), 8–17.

Maynard, R. (2017). *Policing Black lives: State violence in Canada from slavery to the present*. Black Point, NS: Fernwood.

McCurdy, H. (1995). Africville: Environmental racism. In L. Westra & B. E. Lawson (Eds.), *Faces of environmental racism: Confronting issues of global justice* (pp. 95–112). Lanham, MD: Rowman and Littlefield.

Melamed, J. (2015). Racial capitalism. *Critical Ethnic Studies, 1*(1), 76–85.

Mirrlees, T. (2018). The alt-right's discourse on "cultural Marxism": A political instrument of intersectional hate. *Atlantis: Critical Studies in Gender, Culture and Social Justice, 39*(1), 49–69.

Nelson, J. (2000). The space of Africville: Creating, regulating and remembering the urban "slum." *Canadian Journal of Law and Society/La Revue Canadienne Droit et Société, 15*(2), 163–185.

Newman, J. (2007). The "double dynamics" of activation: Institutions, citizens and the remaking of welfare governance. *International Journal of Sociology and Social Policy, 27*(9/10), 364–375.

Palacios, L. (2016). Challenging convictions: Indigenous and Black race-radical feminists theorizing the carceral state and abolitionist praxis in the United States and Canada. *Meridians, 15*(1), 137–165.

Peck, J. (2001). *Workfare states.* New York: Guilford.

Peck, J. (2002). Political economies of scale: Fast policy, interscalar relations, and neoliberal workfare. *Economic Geography, 78*(3), 331–360.

Perry, B., & Scrivens, R. (2016). Uneasy alliances: A look at the right-wing extremist movement in Canada. *Studies in Conflict and Terrorism, 39*(9), 819–841.

Pollack, S., & Rossiter, A. (2010). Neoliberalism and the entrepreneurial subject: Implications for feminism and social work. *Canadian Social Work Review/Revue canadienne de service social, 27*(2), 155–169.

Powell, F. W. (2001). *The politics of social work.* London: Sage.

Raeymaeckers, P., & Dierckx, D. (2012). To work or not to work? The role of the organisational context for social workers' perceptions on activation. *British Journal of Social Work, 43*(6), 1170–1189.

Ramon, S. (2008). Neoliberalism and its implications for mental health in the UK. *International Journal of Law and Psychiatry, 31*(2), 116–125.

Robinson, C. J. (2000). *Black Marxism: The making of the Black radical tradition.* Chapel Hill: University of North Carolina Press. (Original work published 1983)

Rose, N. E. (1995). *Workfare or fair work: Women, welfare, and government work programs.* New Brunswick, NJ: Rutgers University Press.

Rossiter, A., & Heron, B. (2011). Neoliberalism, competencies, and the devaluing of social work practice. *Canadian Social Work Review/Revue canadienne de service social, 28*(2), 305–309.

Sassen, S. (1996). *Losing control? Sovereignty in the age of globalization.* New York: Columbia University Press.

Scrivens, R., & Perry, B. (2017). Resisting the right: Countering right-wing extremism in Canada. *Canadian Journal of Criminology and Criminal Justice, 59*(4), 534–558.

Shamir, R. (2008). The age of responsibilization: On market-embedded morality. *Economy and Society*, *37*(1), 1–19.

Teghtsoonian, K. (2009). Depression and mental health in neoliberal times: A critical analysis of policy and discourse. *Social Science and Medicine*, *69*(1), 28–35.

Terris, M. (1999). The neoliberal triad of anti-health reforms: Government budget cutting, deregulation, and privatization. *Journal of Public Health Policy*, *20*(2), 149–167.

Thompson, J. M., MacLean, M. B., Van Til, L., Sudom, K., Sweet, J., Poirier, A., & Pedlar, D. (2011). Survey on transition to civilian life: Report on regular force veterans. Ottawa: Research Directorate, Veterans Affairs Canada, and Director General Military Personnel Research and Analysis, Department of National Defence.

van Berkel, R., Caswell, D., Kupka, P., & Larsen, F. (Eds.). (2017). *Frontline delivery of welfare-to-work policies in Europe: Activating the unemployed*. New York: Routledge.

Wacquant, L. (2010). Crafting the neoliberal state: workfare, prison fare, and social insecurity. *Sociological Forum*, *25*(2), 197–220.

Wacquant, L. (2017). The punitive regulation of poverty in the neoliberal age. In V. Dashvantha, K. Venkateswara, & K. R. Krishna (Eds.), *Insights on global challenges and opportunities for the century ahead* (pp. 85–88). Andhra Pradesh, India: BS Publications.

Weinberg, M. (2016). *Paradoxes in social work practice: Mitigating ethical trespass*. New York: Routledge.

CHAPTER 7

Safety, Belonging, and Voice: Critical Clinical Practice with Girls and Women Struggling with Substance Use

Nancy Ross and Jean Morrison

INTRODUCTION

In this chapter, we will describe the most meaningful perspectives that we have learned from working with girls and women to reduce the harm of alcohol and drugs to live full and meaningful lives with dignity. Drawing on the feminist literature, we are aware that substance use is often adaptive and a form of coping while often causing women problems. Among girls and women, the links between substance use and sexual victimization are staggering and profound (Ross, Morrison, Cukier, & Smith, 2015). We will assert that it is essential to use an intersectional and critical feminist lens to inform a trauma responsive paradigm when working with girls and women who are challenged by substance use problems. We also have found the dislocation theory of substance use problems helpful in recognizing structural and cultural interlocking forms of oppression that impact the development of substance use problems. Many girls and women who are susceptible to substance use problems experience a general feeling of inadequacy and a sense of disconnection (Ross et al., 2015). Alongside feminist approaches to substance use problems among women, dislocation theory centres the importance of relationships and meaningful connections and engagement in community life, while fully recognizing the social and political context.

As you read this chapter, ask yourself the following questions:

1. In what ways does the neoliberal conceptualization of what it means to be a successful individual discount the challenges girls and women experiencing substance use problems may face?

2. Why is the experience of safety, belonging, and having a voice central to healing from adverse childhood experience, trauma, and substance use problems?

3. What does an intersectional feminist lens reveal about the unique experiences of girls and women who are struggling with substance use problems?

4. How might a critical clinical approach incorporate biomedical advances in neuroscience in practices that empower girls and women, and what are the dangers of the dominant neoliberal focus on biomedicine?

The metaphors of "safety," "belonging," and "voice" have been a central aspect of feminist approaches to working with women and reflect the most important elements in our work with women and girls impacted by substance use problems. We suggest that these metaphors signify aspects of trauma-informed critical clinical practice and processes of healing from oppression, trauma, and substance use problems that have been refined by feminist approaches to working with women over the past 30 years (Covington, 2008; Herman, 1992; Kasl, 1992; Najavits, 2002; Schmidt, Poole, Greaves, & Hemsing, 2018). Feminist theory helps clarify the unique and frequently traumatic pathways girls and women traverse to substance use problems and their distinctly gendered and embodied experiences. It rejects postfeminist arguments that depoliticize and de-gender girls' and women's experiences to posit that a feminist lens is no longer required by recognizing historical, embodied, and daily experiences of sexism (Ahmed, 2015). Throughout this chapter, we critique neoliberalism and postfeminist theories that suggest agency is exercised by making informed and healthy individual choices to promote a gendered and politicized analysis of social contexts (Gill, 2008; O'Neill, 2015).

Safety, the first metaphor, implies not only finding a way to secure physical safety, but also embodies the search to feel at home in the world, to feel acceptance such that it is possible to trust oneself and others in one's identified family and community (Najavits, 2002). Such efforts embody critical perspectives by helping girls and women recognize the ways in which the world can be hostile, unjust, and unsafe, while clinical practices can help them improve their safety physically, emotionally, culturally, and in relationship with others. The emergence of scholarship regarding "cultural safety" implies the need for non-Indigenous practitioners to take responsibility for their own learning of Indigenous history and ways of Knowing, Being, and Doing that involves collaboration and consultation with community (Duthie, 2019). This places a responsibility on the critical clinical practitioner to learn to practice in ways that do not retraumatize Indigenous girls and women.

The second metaphor is a sense of belonging. It is equated with obtaining psychosocial integration. This is a step toward forming connection with oneself and others to claim a meaningful and full life as a component of healing from substance use problems (Alexander, 2008; Mate, 2008). The term *psychosocial integration* describes a process of people exhibiting "a renewed stake in conventional life and in their social relationships and a new identity to go with it" (Cloud & Granfield, 2004, p. 200). Ideally, this life would include connections with those who enhance the values of an individual that is unhampered by the dictates of substance use problems. Alexander (2008, p. 161) states that those who find belonging in the social, cultural, and personal dimensions of a non-addictive life are most likely to heal and recover from substance use problems.

NEOLIBERALISM

Neoliberalism, a political philosophy that favours free-market capitalism, has been influential in Canada since the 1980s. It results in policies that support the wealthy and deepens the marginalization of those citizens who are already disadvantaged.

Within neoliberal frameworks, the focus is on the individual to act responsibly, drink responsibly, make rational choices, and exercise self-discipline, rather than on the social context in which people live (Gillingham, 2006; Haydock, 2014; Liebenberg, Ungar, & Ikeda, 2013; Lupton, 2005; Scourfield & Welsh, 2002; Swadener, 2010). For example, the dominant culture of alcohol normalizes the consumption of alcohol by teens and adults, while neoliberalism interprets problems with alcohol as personal and individual failures that are deeply shameful. Girls and women who are challenged with substance use issues may become silenced by a sense of stigma and shame that is particularly gendered.

Voice, the third metaphor, signifies agency and transformation from passive "object" to be acted on, to one of appreciation for agency, influence, and resistance. As a metaphor, when a person no longer has a sense of voice, they can experience a loss of humanity; a falling out of touch with meaning and the disappearance of significance. Voicelessness creates the experience of being numb, without a capacity to feel, to touch, or to be in touch (Lederach & Lederach, 2010).

This chapter highlights the ways in which a critical clinical practitioner works with girls and women to help them restore a sense of "safety," "belonging," and "voice" in the healing process. This involves the integration of feminist critical perspectives to demonstrate how they can assist girls and women to author their identity, facilitating an understanding of social factors that influence their lives. We position this within a brief discussion of theories of substance use problems and highlight the merits of the dislocation theory of substance use problems in helping to create a contextualized narrative of substance use issues. Like feminist theory, this theory describes the ways in which cultural and structural factors can sway the lives of girls and women to create a vulnerability to substance use problems that, we argue, is exploited by alcohol and pharmaceutical corporations. We then discuss the influence of childhood adversity and trauma in girls' and women's lives. The lens of neuroscience often reflects the growing neoliberal emphasis of biomedicalism, which operates to obscure social and structural inequities (Morrow & Weisser, 2012). We argue that while the dominant neuroscience focus is individualistic and decontextualized, it can also be valuable to increase girls' and women's embodied self-awareness of the effects of trauma in a critical clinical approach, while also emphasizing the ways in which social inequity impacts their lives. We then return to the guiding metaphors of safety, belonging, and voice and discuss how our work as critical clinical social workers is informed by this paradigm. Throughout, we demonstrate how a women's group can play an essential role in the recognition of social and relational factors that can contribute to these processes.

The voices of women in a film, *Women of Substance*, are highlighted, with specific attention to the challenges women encountered in re-authoring their identity (Ross, 2012). The women, who were members of a women's recovery group in Nova Scotia, chose to participate in this film to exercise their agency and "voice" to reduce stigma and influence a societal shift in attitude toward women who experience substance use issues. For example, the film begins with a description of how unsafe it feels to be a woman with substance use issues:

> As a woman you don't want people to look at you like *that* ... you're a mom. You don't want to admit it. You don't want your kids to know, because you think they don't know, but they know. A woman has more shame and guilt. Shame of physical, sexual abuse. You don't have the resources. You know babysitters ... you've got the schools looking at you differently. You're supposed to be the role model more so than a man.

The speaker recognizes the importance of claiming her identity and using her "voice" in healing from this gendered stigma:

Everybody has a voice. Everyone has the ability to stand up and say, you know, I am a person. I am not that addiction. I am not the little girl that was hurt as a child or abused. You are more than that.

Another woman describes the importance of feeling safe:

When you feel safe enough to offer yourself to others in whatever capacity you feel you have ... you're a great typist, you're a painter, you're a great flower arranger, you make great pies, you make excellent soup ... whatever it is when you hear the call of something in the community and you decide that what you have to offer is worth offering, you do so much more than you think you are doing. By being honest with one's self and feeling things deeply you can't help but touch others.

It was the words of these women that encouraged us to embrace the metaphors of "safety," "belonging," and "voice" for our work in the following years. A critical clinical social work approach will be demonstrated in our case study of Sally (a pseudonym representing a composite of women impacted by substance use problems). This case allows us to illustrate the themes of safety, belonging and voice in a way that is similar to how they were raised by women in the film. Other themes raised included stigma, mothering, shame, guilt, sexual and physical childhood abuse, women's inability to process alcohol as efficiently as men, opioids and pain, experiences of youth, and the need for safety and to exercise one's voice, offering one's contribution to the community and helping others. This chapter will demonstrate through Sally the ways in which a critical clinical approach informed by intersectional feminist theory and the dislocation theory of substance use problems can be helpful in linking the "personal" with the "political" to inform a gendered response.

GIRLS' AND WOMEN'S SUBSTANCE USE PROBLEMS: THE DISLOCATION THEORY OF SUBSTANCE USE PROBLEMS

The prevalence rates of girls' and women's substance use problems have steadily increased within the past few decades (Lal, Deb, & Kedia, 2015; S. C. Wilsnack,

2012; R. W. Wilsnack, S. C. Wilsnack, Gmel, & Kantor, 2018). Alcohol is the substance most commonly used by girls and women. Underage girls are drinking at ratios equivalent to boys in many high-income countries (Poole & Greaves, 2007; Thomas, 2012). Prescription drug use by girls and women has been on the rise at an alarming rate for the past two decades (Hemsing, Greaves, Poole, & Schmidt, 2016; Peteet, Mosley, Miler-Roenigk, McCuistian, & Dixon, 2019). For example, in Canada the use of opioids continues to be slightly higher for females (13.9 percent) than males (12.1 percent), women are twice as likely to use prescription sedatives (14 percent compared to 7 percent for men), and prescription stimulant use is increasing among young women (Health Canada, 2017). One study found that women were 48 percent more likely than men to use any prescription drugs and also more likely to be prescribed opioids (Simoni-Wastila, 2000). In the United States, 4.6 million adult women had problem use of prescription drugs in 2013 (Peteet et al., 2019). The application of a feminist intersectional lens reveals that among women there are differences. For example, older women are more frequently prescribed sedatives, particularly Indigenous women (Currie, 2004).

Despite these prevalence rates within the problem substance use field, 90 percent of the gender-specific research has emerged only since 1990 (Brady, Back, & Greenfield, 2009). Prior to this period, most literature related to substance use problems was largely based on men's experiences and heavily influenced by Alcoholics Anonymous 12-step programs (Kasl, 1992).

SUBSTANCE USE PROBLEMS

The term *substance use problems* refers to "a state of a person as a whole" and is an overwhelming involvement with an activity or substance (including, but not limited to, alcohol and drugs) despite the harms it causes.

Charlotte Kasl (1992) was among the first writers to critique Alcoholics Anonymous as an insufficient approach to address the complexity of women's lives. She noted that 12-step programs begin by asking people to admit they are powerless to exercise control over their substance use problems (or addictive behaviour) and that this approach was often unhelpful for women who experienced multiple oppressions. She argued that women's social context and lived realities were not accounted for within 12-step programs. For example, women are disproportionately held responsible for multiple caregiving roles, including parenting (Poole & Greaves, 2012; Ross et al., 2015). Women experience greater levels of stigma for substance use problems. This is complicated by less access to the social determinants of health and the shorter time period, called the telescoping effect, of negative health impacts from substance use issues (Lal et al., 2015; Mancinelli, Vitali, & Ceccanti, 2009; Najavits, 2002).

The majority of women accessing substance use treatment programs have prior experiences of trauma that include childhood physical and sexual abuse (C. Brown, 2008; Covington, 2008; Najavits, 2002, 2004; Poole & Greaves, 2012). Women's experiences of substance use issues have been under-researched, including hidden and frequently related experiences of interpersonal violence (Najavits, 2002; World Health Organization, 2013). Status of Women Canada (2018) states that gender-based violence is a product of gender inequality rooted in patriarchal social structure. Gender-based violence intersects with and is intensified by other forms of systemic oppression, including colonialism, racism, ableism, heterosexism, transphobia, ageism, and poverty. Feminist theory has long asserted that experiences of interpersonal violence need to be politicized, thereby resisting tendencies to silence it (Stanley & Wise, 1993). The profound links between prior experiences of trauma and violence and women's subsequent substance use issues and mental health challenges have been witnessed in the direct (30 years combined) practice of the authors. This is also reported in research that has found women to be more likely to use substances after a traumatic experience (Collins Reed & Evans, 2009; Kendler et al., 2000).

Two prominent models of substance use problems that have been influential in shaping a narrow understanding of substance use problems are commonly referred to as the medical or disease model and the moral or skeptical model. A feminist approach to women's use of alcohol and other substances seeks to avoid these two approaches. The biomedical approach medicalizes and pathologizes women's struggles and efforts at coping without looking at the social context of their lives. The moral model view is also problematic, as it focuses on individual deficit reflected in poor choices (Alexander, 2008; Carter, Hall, & Capps, 2009; Heyman, 2009; Smith & Seymour, 2004). This position is not aligned with women-centred harm reduction approaches that work effectively with girls and women to reduce the harm they experience from substance use problems (Schmidt et al., 2018). Both of these dominant approaches to substance use problems are divested from a social analysis and aligned with the neoliberal emphasis on individual responsibility that can exacerbate the impact of stigma and criminalization of substance use for women. Therefore, treatment approaches are "grounded in neoliberal discourses of personhood and citizenship rooted in ideologies of efficiency, individualism, and self-responsibility" (Schlosser, 2018, p. 191).

Haydock (2014) underscores common features of a neoliberal approach. Neoliberalism emphasizes market rationality located in regulatory and state structures and in the mode of the ideal citizen. For those citizens who do not perform as ideal members of society, "this approach to government focuses on 'technologies of citizenship' to shape people's behaviour" (Haydock, 2014, p. 263). Here, Haydock references Michel Foucault (1988, p. 18) to explain that these technologies focus on the individual's responsibility to make rational choices and exercise self-discipline if provided with the appropriate information, rather than on the regulatory environment in which people act. Such understandings of substance use problems preclude a wider focus on the environment and lack an intersectional feminist lens that is essential to understanding the embodied and psychosocial stress women experience that is often rooted in trauma both in childhood and adulthood.

The medical model describes substance use problems as a psychiatric disorder or disease that requires treatment (Smith & Seymour, 2004; Mate, 2008; Carter et al., 2009). Popular acceptance of this model was boosted by Alcoholics Anonymous, which, in the introductory chapter of the *Big Book of Alcoholics Anonymous*, describes the disease of alcoholism as "an allergy of the body and a compulsion of the mind" (Smith & Seymour, 2004, p. 13). The main strength of the medical or disease model is a movement away from penalizing the individual and toward the provision of therapeutic and treatment programs. Most of the criticism of this model arises from a belief that substance use problems need to be understood more broadly as a societal, political, and economic problem. For example, feminists note that medicalized programs fail to appreciate the complexity of women's lives because they do not acknowledge that many women seeking treatment for substance use problems have suffered past trauma, are single parents, and have limited access to the social determinants of health (C. Brown, 2008; Kasl, 1992; Najavits, 2002).

DISEASE MODEL OF SUBSTANCE USE PROBLEMS

The disease model of substance use problems explains substance use problems as a chronic, primary disease. The focus is individual pathology and not the social context or lived experience of girls and women.

Consistent with a feminist approach, the dislocation theory of substance use problems differs from moral and medicalized explanations of substance use problems by focusing on social context. This theory describes "the loss of psychological, social and economic integration into family and culture [and] a sense of exclusion, isolation and powerlessness" (Mate, 2008, p. 261) as precursors to substance use problems. The first principle of this theory states, "psychosocial integration is an essential part of human well-being, and that dislocation—the sustained absence of psychosocial integration—is excruciatingly painful" (Alexander, 2008, p. 86). In advancing the dislocation theory of substance use problems, both Alexander (2008) and Mate (2008) suggest that increasing rates of substance use problems in Canada, and elsewhere, can be linked to a growing sense of alienation and disconnection that they claim is fuelled by globalization and free market economies. In his sustained critique of the neoliberal globalized agenda, Alexander (2008) describes the myriad ways in which individuals compete for employment and financial success, ways that often result in their separation from family, community, and culture. To curb growth in substance use problems, this theory points to structural and cultural change to promote psychosocial integration and a sense of belonging as the goal of human development, both personal and societal.

DISLOCATION THEORY OF SUBSTANCE USE PROBLEMS

The dislocation theory of substance use problems suggests that rates of substance use problems increase in social contexts dominated by colonialism, patriarchy, and capitalism, resulting in mass dislocation and alienation.

Psychosocial integration, a concept originating with the work of Erikson's (1968) theory of lifespan development and developed by feminist thinkers, speaks to identity formation and the importance of choice, agency, and opportunities to define one's life (Alexander, 2008; C. Brown, 2017; Syed & McLean, 2015). This concept can be linked to our description of the importance of voice, noted in the women's decision to participate in the film *Women of Substance*. Erikson's (1968) theory and narrative therapeutic approaches emphasize relational and societal processes in which other people are crucial in constructing personally coherent identity narratives (C. Brown, 2017). Although theories of substance use problems have historically focused on individual factors as described in the medical and moral models, research continues to show that social factors play an important role and are involved in every stage of the development of and "recovery" from a substance use problem (Alexander, 2008; Dingle, Cruwys, & Frings, 2015; Mate, 2008; Poole & Greaves, 2012). In so doing, this research moves beyond individual explanations for the origins of substance use problems to emphasize the role of relationships, communities, and influential social and cultural factors.

In the next sections of this chapter, we argue that establishing safety, a sense of belonging, and opportunities for voice are three pillars of a woman's substance use treatment paradigm and are best informed by a critical intersectional feminist lens and the dislocation theory of substance use problems.

GIRLS' AND WOMEN'S SUBSTANCE USE PROBLEMS: AN INTERSECTIONAL CRITICAL FEMINIST LENS

Increased consumption of alcohol and prescription drug use by girls and women has been influenced by successful marketing strategies used by the alcohol and pharmaceutical industries that are referred to as "Big Alcohol" and "Big Pharma" (Chan, 2013; Ross et al., 2015). Consumption of alcohol by underage girls matches or exceeds that by underage boys in Canada (Health Canada, 2018). Heavy drinking among all age groups was higher for males (65.1 percent) than females (52.2 percent) (Health Canada, 2017). Prescription drug use has been on the rise at an alarming rate for the past two decades (Hemsing et al. 2016; Peteet et al., 2019). Canadian women are more likely to abuse prescription medications than Canadian men (Health Canada, 2017). Despite a greater burden of substance use and "relapse," prior to Peteet and colleagues (2019) systematic review, no identified studies had methodically reviewed the literature exploring prescription drug use among adult women.

The addictive nature of benzodiazepines, also known as tranquilizers or sedatives, and their profound effects on the brain and body have been known for over 40 years, yet these drugs are among the most widely prescribed in Canada and the world today. The over-prescription of benzodiazepines to women in Canada was first identified as a critical health care issue in the 1970s and yet in 2000 there were more than 15.7 million prescriptions for benzodiazepines filled by Canadian retail pharmacies (Currie, 2004). In the research that exists, it is repeatedly demonstrated that women who have prior experiences of marginalization, dislocation, and trauma are more susceptible to substance use problems (Najavits, 2002; C. Brown, 2008; Covington, 2008;

Hemsing et al., 2016; Peteet et al., 2019). There are also important differences among women and further research incorporating an intersectional and gendered lens is required. Attention to race, gender, and other identity categories help us better acknowledge and understand these differences (Crenshaw, 1991). Trans women of colour are, for example, among the most targeted victims of violence in the LGBTQIA+ community (Cox, 2014). This vulnerability also influences a susceptibility to substance use problems (Perspectives in Public Health, 2015). Colonial oppression is also a factor in a vulnerability to substance use issues among Indigenous women. However, Poole and Dell (2005) caution against making assumptions, as these can serve as a barrier to health care among poor women and women of colour who are more frequently screened for substance use when accessing perinatal care than middle-class and Caucasian women.

Greenfield and Picard (2009, p. 290) write that the significant differences between men and women who are experiencing substance use problems include "risk factors, natural history, presenting problems, motivations for treatment and reasons for relapse." When compared to men, women are less likely to seek treatment and when they do it is more likely to be from a mental health practitioner (Greenfield & Picard, 2009). Girls and women are less likely to seek treatment for substance use because of the greater stigma they experience and the profound fear of losing custody of their children (Greenfield & Picard, 2009; Johnston, 2014). The impact of this stigma and fear is felt individually by the women and girls who neither seek treatment nor are adequately screened for substance use. The impact of stigma in society includes fewer allocated resources (Yang et al., 2017) meaning less research and policy initiatives. An intersectional feminist approach can help professionals who work alongside women who use substances to incorporate a women-centred and harm reduction lens to better respond to their needs. We argue that feminist theory (Ahmed, 2015; Crenshaw, 1991; Grosz, 1990; Stanley & Wise, 1993) is essential to critical practice with women in two ways. First, feminist theory assists girls and women to critique and challenge sexism existing in prevailing social, political, and theoretical relations. Second, feminist theory offers a way forward to create feminist alternatives. It can provide a sense of agency and voice.

For instance, feminist theory can help girls and women critique the ways in which they are targeted by Big Alcohol and Big Pharma. As an example, it is helpful to explore pediatrician Flegel's (2013) concern related to adolescent girls' consumption of alcohol. He suggests that adolescents need information about the intent of alcohol advertising:

> They need to be taught that the purpose of advertising is to create a demand where there is no need. When advertising reaches a vulnerable group, such as adolescent girls, they need to understand what it means to be duped by an adult influence that does not have their interest at heart. (p. 859)

His statements offer sharp critique of government approaches that fail to limit alcohol advertising and media that target youth. Feminist theory can assist girls to be armed against these industry tactics to discern when they are duped by adult and corporate influences.

Feminist theory helps girls and women recognize how neoliberalism and globalization can influence cultural values in film, social media, and advertising in ways that can undermine their sense of self-worth. Kilbourne's (2000) huge body of work critiques the way images of women are portrayed in advertising generally and alcohol and tobacco advertising specifically. Social work researcher Brené Brown's (2012) lecture "Listening to Shame" is featured on YouTube and has been viewed by more than seven million individuals.

Many of the women featured in *Women of Substance* had also written pieces for a column published in the *Lighthouse Log*, a newspaper (with a circulation of 60,000) in Bridgewater, Nova Scotia, between 2004 and 2012. Both the newspaper column and the film evolved from the weekly women's recovery group that met in Bridgewater between 2002 and 2012. During one group meeting, we discussed what could be a title for the newspaper column and chose *Coming Home: Stories of Women in Recovery*. This title reflected aims of both the column and the women's group. The goals were to reduce stigma and silence regarding women's substance use issues and to encourage women in the community to seek help if they felt it was needed. Approximately 20 articles were published, each of which reflected the voice of a woman telling her story about what steps she had taken to rewrite the narrative of her life in "coming home."

TRAUMA AND ADVERSE CHILDHOOD EXPERIENCES

Many girls and women who access treatment for mental health and substance use problems have experienced trauma and/or adverse childhood experiences. The Adverse Childhood Experiences Study, the world's largest longitudinal health study on this subject, began in 1995 as a joint initiative of Kaiser Permanente and the Centers for Disease Control and Prevention in the United States. It aimed to better understand the relationships between adverse childhood events and the development of health and social problems as adults. This study made connections between chronic stress caused by early adversity and the profound impact on the developing brains and bodies of children that resulted in later-life health issues (Felitti et al., 1998). In the initial study, over 17,000 health maintenance organization members from Southern California receiving physical exams completed confidential surveys regarding their childhood experiences and current health status and behaviours. The majority of these individuals were Caucasian, middle class, and university educated. The study looked at 10 categories of childhood adversity that included physical, sexual, and emotional abuse and physical and emotional neglect, and 5 measures of household dysfunction that included domestic violence, parental mental illness and/or substance use problems, an incarcerated relative, and separation/divorce. The Adverse Childhood Experiences Study had two striking findings. First, adverse childhood experiences were incredibly common—67 percent (two out of three) of the study participants had at least one adverse childhood experience and 13 percent (one out of eight people) had four or more adverse childhood experiences. Second, there was a dose-response relationship between adverse childhood experiences and numerous health problems. This means that the more adverse childhood experiences a child has, the higher the risk of developing chronic illnesses such as heart disease, obesity, chronic obstructive pulmonary disease (COPD), depression, and cancer (Felitti et al., 1998). Today, a significant body of evidence continues to demonstrate a powerful dose-response relationship between adverse childhood experience scores and a wide array of significant health and social problems in adulthood (Anda et al., 2006; Douglas et al., 2010; Dube et al., 2003; Edwards et al., 2001; Felitti et al., 1998; Logan-Greene, Green, Nurius, & Longhi, 2014; McDonald, Kingston, Bayrampour, & Tough, 2015). Women have been found to have experienced higher rates of childhood sexual abuse in many of the adverse childhood studies and these experiences were found to increase the probability of having experienced other adverse childhood experiences (Baglivio et al., 2014; Banyard, Williams, & Siegel, 2001; Cavanaugh, Petras, & Martins, 2015). Accurate rates of childhood sexual abuse are unavailable. The studies that have been completed suggest that although both girls and boys experience childhood sexual abuse, the rate is thought to be three to five times higher for girls (Finklehor, Statluck, Turner, & Hamby, 2013; Harrison, Fulkerson & Beebe, 1997). The association of childhood sexual abuse with later substance use problems appears to be greater for women than men (Widom, Marmorstein, & White, 2006).

Girls' and women's experiences of trauma and adverse childhood experiences are often hidden and internalized as individualized experiences that are alienating and shameful. However, adverse childhood experiences research tells a collective story that signals the need for community healing, thereby helping girls and women recognize they are not alone. Feminist theory can be influential in "clinical" approaches that are responsive to individual needs, while also highlighting the importance of advocating for social justice. In this way, the personal becomes the political. There is now considerable evidence that effective treatment approaches can help offset negative health and social consequences of adverse childhood experiences and that this framework can influence policy and legislation in efforts to reduce adverse childhood experiences (Korotana, Dobson, Pusch, & Josephson, 2016; Larkin, Felitti, & Anda, 2014). Childhood experiences of abuse and trauma often result in not feeling safe, relational injury and disconnection, and a struggle to voice the pain of these experiences (Herman, 1992, 2015). These early experiences of trauma are often dealt with in adulthood through the use of substances in order to numb the pain (C. Brown & Stewart, 2008). Through discussing Sally's experience, I will highlight the metaphors of safety, belonging, and voice.

Sally

Sally, age 38, is a white, working-class woman living in a small rural community. She has limited education and is seasonally employed. She has struggled with an alcohol problem since she was 13. Her substance use increased as she got older to include problems of opiates and benzodiazepines. She has been in both individual and group treatment at a women's substance use problems centre. She is divorced and a single parent to one child, age 11. She has described feeling powerless and a deep sense of shame regarding her substance use problems, which have resulted in some involvement with the police. Sally experienced emotional, physical, and sexual abuse during her childhood, as well as subsequent abuse in her marriage by her former partner who also struggled with substance use problems. Sally reports feeling like she is a bad mother and expresses a deep sense of isolation, insecurity, and loneliness. She believes that her child's teachers also think she is inadequate as a parent and that they do not feel the same way about the father of her child, who has limited involvement with their lives.

She has struggled with precarious employment, poverty, and feelings of anxiety and depression for as long as she can remember.

Clinical critical social work practice, with its unique focus on the individual within their social context, blends clinical approaches with a critical perspective that perceives how unjust social contexts marginalize individuals and advocates for social justice. Feminist theory can help girls and women recognize the ways in which trauma and adverse childhood experiences are both personal and political. This means it can validate girls' and women's experiences and provide guideposts to help them define a narrative in their life that makes sense of their past while pointing to steps they can take as individuals to heal. For example, Sally thought there was something personal about her that resulted in her experiences of abuse, and this thinking had contributed to internalizing a deep sense of loss and shame regarding the abuse she had experienced. When she began to realize that she was not alone in these experiences and that the abuse she had suffered was perpetrated by a man influenced by patriarchal values who had also experienced childhood trauma, she perceived her experiences of childhood abuse differently. Her feelings of shame lessened as she began to engage in a process of counterviewing her past. Catrina Brown (2017) describes this process as a way to view stories differently by unpacking what has been assumed as truth, critiquing dominant social discourse to facilitate counterstories that emphasize agency and self-compassion. A feminist clinical critical social work approach to Sally's experiences of adversity in childhood assisted her to externalize what was perceived as an intractable part of individual experience. She chose to exercise her agency to influence social change by taking this step to reduce stigma and increase recognition in her community of factors that contribute to substance use problems for women. Taking this step within her community can be described as politicizing what had been experienced as personal.

SALLY: SAFETY, BELONGING, AND VOICE

Table 7.1 demonstrates how centring the metaphors of safety, belonging, and voice within an intersectional and critical feminist lens is helpful to guide our work with Sally. Within a critical clinical framework, Sally's experiences are understood as influenced by community and societal influences.

While prioritizing safety for individuals who have experienced prior violence may appear self-evident, Najavits (2002) and Lederach and Lederach (2010) describe steps to feel safe as moving beyond assurances of physical security to include a search to find a way to feel at home in the world. This includes

TABLE 7.1: SALLY: SAFETY, BELONGING, AND VOICE

	SELF	COMMUNITY	SOCIAL
Safety	Are you physically safe from harm? Do you have a safe place to live? Do you have access to resources? Do you have someone to look after you if needed? Have you learned skills that help you feel safer? Do you have knowledge and skills to cope with possible physiological responses (flight, fight, or freeze) when you remember a traumatic event?	Do you have supportive people/services in your life to help you cope with your feelings of anxiety and depression? Do you feel that those around you can be trusted? Do you have places within your community where you feel safe, valued, and respected?	While recognizing factors that can contribute to social injustice do you experience cultural safety? Are you in a place where the societal and cultural values that influence your life are consistent with your own values?
Belonging	Do you feel connected to others? Do you have a friend? Do you like yourself? Can you share your experiences with others?	Are there groups of people or community organizations that foster a sense of connection to others? Do you receive and reciprocate good invitations?	Do you have cultural and/or spiritual practices that are important to you that are shared with others with whom you are connected?
Voice	Do you have a sense of agency? Can you observe and describe yourself and your situation?	Do you have groups or community organizations that will help you meet your goals? Are there safe places to meet where you can share your experiences?	Do you have opportunities to use your influence to have a voice in society to advocate for social justice in matters that are important to you? Do you know how to effectively use your influence?

Sally learning to trust herself and others. As a metaphor, safety is described as a container (Lederach & Lederach, 2010).

A sense of belonging is the antidote to disconnection, dislocation, and trauma. Sally found herself feeling connected to others as she shared her story in the group. In making the decision to participate in the film, Sally is exercising a sense of agency and voice, fuelled by a belief that sharing her story will make a difference.

SAFETY, BELONGING, AND VOICE: FOCUSING ON BOTH THE INDIVIDUAL AND SOCIAL CONTEXT

Research on adverse childhood experiences has been instrumental in helping individuals understand the ways in which the developing brain and nervous system respond to childhood adversity and trauma. Cognitive processing takes place in the neocortex. It includes functions of analyzing, strategizing, reasoning, making meaning of situations, and human language (Ogden & Fisher, 2014). When we describe in words our ideas and experiences, we use the neocortex. In other words, this is a place of "voice." When situations are outside our window of tolerance for stress, it is challenging to access cognitive functioning.

To be at our best we need to stay within our window of tolerance for stress so that we can function optimally in all three levels of information processing: sensorimotor, emotional, and cognitive. When we are playful, creative, and confident there is a coordination of brain functions (van der Kolk, 2014). Considering the prevalence of stress and trauma in the lives of women who use substances, it is not surprising that attending to the need to create a place where women can experience safety and belonging and then be given the opportunity to find and use their distinctive voice is so effective in clinical work. Understanding the brain is helpful to working with people with past traumatic experiences. For example, it helps us realize the need for safety when a woman is triggered into feeling like a traumatic event may be happening in the moment despite all evidence to the contrary.

CONCLUSION

When women decide to seek help for and safety from substance use problems, they risk more stigma than men, including receiving the label "bad mother." In some cases, women risk having their children removed from their care.

In seeking to diminish the stigma barrier for women in their community, the "women of substance" spoke of their experiences with alcohol and drugs first in the local newspaper and later on film so that other local women would know that they were not alone. By filming their reflections in *Women of Substance*, they hoped to make it easier for other women to seek services for substance use problems. This was the collective effort of women from various backgrounds working together to make their communities safer for all. It was a bold, compassionate action that promoted a healthier alternative than hiding and continuing substance use problems.

In Nova Scotia, Women's Services positions were developed in 2002 by the Nova Scotia Health Authorities to address the specific gendered needs of women and girls and redress the tendency to provide generalist services that often neglected to focus on those specific needs. As is often the case, the grassroots work has not yet resulted in policy changes that will protect women and girls in local communities from developing substance use problems.

So often we consider therapy an experience in which the therapist evokes change within the client. Less often do we acknowledge that this is a two-way street. The words of the women of substance have had a lasting resonance in our work. In a few brief words, the women of substance charted a road map of recovery. It was after the film was complete that the authors of this chapter encountered the metaphor of safety, belonging, and voice and realized that it had been the road map described in the film, group work, and many therapeutic conversations.

In this chapter, we have described how the concepts of safety, belonging, and voice fit with the dislocation theory of substance use problems, an intersectional critical feminist lens, and the research on adverse childhood experiences and trauma. As we return to the paradigm of safety, belonging, and voice to complete this chapter, we are reminded of the words of T. S. Eliot (1959, p. 49): "We shall not cease from exploration, and the end of all our exploring will be to arrive where we started and know the place for the first time."

REFERENCES

Ahmed, S. (2015). Introduction: Sexism—A problem with a name. *New Formations: A Journal of Culture/Theory/Politics, 86*(1), 5–13.

Alexander, B. (2008). *The globalisation of addiction: A study in poverty of the spirit.* New York: Oxford University Press.

Anda, R. F., Felitti, V. J., Bremner, J. D., Walker, J. D., Whitfield, C., Perry, B. D., ... Giles, W. H. (2006). The enduring effects of abuse and related adverse experiences in childhood: A convergence of evidence from neurobiology and epidemiology. *European Archives of Psychiatry and Clinical Neuroscience, 256*(3), 174–186.

Baglivio, M., Epps, N., Swartz, K., Sayedul Huq, M., Sheer, A., & Hardt, N. S. (2014). The prevalence of adverse childhood experiences (ACE) in the lives of juvenile offenders. *Journal of Juvenile Justice, 3*, 1–23.

Banyard, V. L., Williams, L. M., & Siegel J. A. (2001). The long-term mental health consequences of child sexual abuse: An exploratory study of the impact of multiple traumas in a sample of women. *Journal of Traumatic Stress, 14*(4), 697–715.

Brady, K., Back, S., & Greenfield, S. (2009). *Women and addiction: A comprehensive handbook.* New York: Guilford Press.

Brown, B. (2012). *Listening to shame* [Film]. TED Talks. Retrieved from https://www.ted.com/talks/brene_brown_listening_to_shame/transcript?language=en

Brown, C. (2008). It's not cut and dry: Women's experiences of alcohol use, depression, anxiety and trauma. Halifax: Dalhousie University.

Brown, C. (2017). Creating counterstories: Critical clinical practice and feminist narrative therapy. In D. Baines (Ed.), *Doing anti-oppressive practice: Building transformative, politicized social work* (3rd ed., pp. 212–232). Halifax: Fernwood.

Brown, C. G., & Stewart, S. H. (2008). Exploring perceptions of alcohol use as self-medication for depression among women receiving community-based treatment for alcohol problems. *Journal of Prevention and Intervention in the Community, 35*(2), 33–47.

Carter, A., Hall, W., & Capps, B. (2009). What is addiction? In EMCDDA Monographs. *Addiction neurobiology: Ethical and social implications* (pp. 21–28). Luxembourg: Office for Official Publications of the European Communities.

Cavanaugh, C. E., Petras, H., & Martins, S. S. (2015). Gender-specific profiles of adverse childhood experiences, past year mental and substance use disorders, and their associations among a national sample of adults in the United States. *Social Psychiatry and Psychiatric Epidemiology, 50*(8), 1257–1266.

Chan, M. (2013). WHO Director-General addresses health promotion conference. Opening address at the 8th Global Conference on Health Promotion, Helsinki, Finland.

Cloud, W., & Granfield, R. (2004). Life course perspective on existing addiction problems: The relevance of recovery capital in treatment. In P. Rosenqvist, J. Blomqvist, A. Koski-Jannes, & L. Ojesjo (Eds.), *Addiction and life course* (pp. 185–202). Helsinki, Finland: Nordic Council for Alcohol and Drug Research.

Collins Reed, S., & Evans, S. M. (2009). Research design and methodology in studies of women and addiction. In K. T. Brady, S. E. Back, & S. F. Greenfield (Eds.), *Women and addiction* (pp. 14–31). New York: Guilford Press.

Covington, S. (2008). Women and addiction: A trauma-informed approach. *Journal of Psychoactive Drugs*, SARC Supplement 5, 377–385.

Cox, L. (2014). Laverne Cox on bullying and being a trans woman of color [Video file]. *Afropunk*. Retrieved from https://afropunk.com/2014/01/laverne-cox-on-bullying-and-being-a-trans-woman-of-color/

Crenshaw, K. (1991). Mapping the margins: Intersectionality, identity politics, and violence against women of color. *Stanford Law Review*, *43*(6), 1241–1299.

Currie, J. (2004). Manufacturing addiction. *Canadian Women's Health Network*, 6/7(4/1), 16–19.

Dingle, G., Cruwys, T., & Frings, D. (2015). Social identities as pathways into and out of addiction. *Frontiers in Psychology*, *6*(1795), 1–12.

Douglas, K. R., Chan, G., Gelernter, J., Arias, A. J., Anton, R. F., Weiss, R. D., ... Kranzler, H. R. (2010). Adverse childhood events as risk factors for substance dependence: Partial mediation by mood and anxiety disorders. *Addictive Behaviors*, *35*(1), 7–13.

Dube, S. R., Felitti, V. J., Dong, M., Chapman, D. P., Giles, W. H., & Anda, R. F. (2003). Childhood abuse, neglect, and household dysfunction and the risk of illicit drug use: The adverse childhood experiences study. *Pediatrics*, *111*(3), 564–572.

Duthie, D. (2019). Embedding Indigenous knowledges and cultural safety in social work curricula. *Australian Social Work*, *72*(1), 113–116.

Edwards, V. J., Anda, R. F., Nordenberg, D. F., Felitti, V. J., Williamson, D. F., & Wright, J. A. (2001). Bias assessment for child abuse survey: Factors affecting probability of response to a survey about childhood abuse. *Child Abuse and Neglect*, *25*(2), 307–312.

Eliot, T. S., (1959). Little gidding. In *Four quartets*. London: Faber and Faber.

Erikson, E. (1968). *Identity: Youth and crisis*. New York: Norton.

Felitti, V. J., Anda, R. F., Nordenberg, D., Williamson, D. F., Spitz, A. M., Edwards, V., ... Marks, J. S. (1998). Relationship of childhood abuse and household dysfunction to many of the leading causes of death in adults: The Adverse Childhood Experiences (ACE) Study. *American Journal of Preventive Medicine*, *14*(4), 245–258.

Finklehor, D., Statluck, A., Turner, H., & Hamby, S. (2013). The lifetime prevalence of childhood sexual abuse and sexual assault assessed in late adolescence. *Journal of Adolescent Health*, *55*(3), 329–333.

Flegel, K. (2013). Big Alcohol catches up with adolescent girls: Editorial. *Canadian Medical Association Journal*, *185*(10), 859.

Foucault, M. (1988). The ethic of care for the self as a practice of freedom. In J. W. Brenauer & D. M. Rasmussen (Eds.), *The final Foucault* (pp. 1–20). Cambridge, MA: MIT Press.

Gill, R. (2008). Culture and subjectivity in neoliberal and postfeminist times. *Subjectivity*, *25*, 432–445.

Gillingham, P. (2006). Risk assessment in child protection: Problem rather than solution? *Australian Social Work*, *59*(1), 86–98.

Greenfield, S., & Picard, S. (2009). Gender-specific treatment for women with substance use disorders. In K. T. Brady, S. E. Back, & S. F. Greenfield (Eds.), *Women and addiction* (pp. 289–306). New York: Guilford Press.

Grosz, E. (1990). Contemporary theories of power and subjectivity. In S. Gunew (Ed.), *Feminist knowledge: Critique and construct* (pp. 59–121). London: Routledge.

Harrison, P. A., Fulkerson, J. A., & Beebe, T. J. (1997). Multiple substance use among adolescent physical and sexual abuse victims. *Child Abuse and Neglect*, *21*, 529–539.

Haydock, W. (2014). The rise and fall of the "nudge" of minimum unit pricing: The continuity of neoliberalism in alcohol policy in England. *Critical Social Policy*, *34*(2), 260–269.

Health Canada. (2017). *Canadian Tobacco, Alcohol and Drugs Survey: Summary of results for 2016*. Ottawa: Government of Canada.

Health Canada. (2018). *Canadian Student Tobacco, Alcohol and Drug Survey*. Ottawa: Government of Canada.

Hemsing, N., Greaves, L., Poole, N., & Schmidt, R. (2016). Misuse of prescription opioid medication among women: A scoping review. *Pain Research and Management: The Journal of the Canadian Pain Society*, Article ID 1754195.

Herman, J. L. (1992). *Trauma and recovery* (1st ed.). New York: Basic Books.

Herman, J. L. (2015). *Trauma and recovery: The aftermath of violence—from domestic abuse to political terror* (2nd ed.). New York: Basic Books.

Heyman, G. M. (2009). *Addiction: A disorder of choice*. Cambridge, MA: Harvard University Press.

Johnston, A. (2014). *Drink: The intimate relationship between women and alcohol*. New York: Harper Wave.

Kasl, C. (1992). *Many roads, one journey: Moving beyond the 12 steps*. New York: Harper Perennial.

Kendler, K. S., Bulik, C. M., Silberg, J., Hettema, J. M., Myers, J., & Prescott, C. A. (2000). Childhood sexual abuse and adult psychiatric and substance use disorders in women: An epidemiological and cotwin control analysis. *Archives of General Psychiatry*, *57*, 953–959.

Kilbourne, J. (2000). *Can't buy my love: How advertising changes the way we think and feel*. New York: Simon and Schuster.

Korotana, L., Dobson, K., Pusch, D., & Josephson, T. (2016). A review of primary care interventions to improve health outcomes in adult survivors of adverse childhood experiences. *Clinical Psychology Review*, *46*, 59–90.

Lal, R., Deb, K. S., & Kedia, S. (2015). Substance use in women: Current status and future directions. *Indian Journal of Psychiatry*, *57*(Suppl 2), S275–285.

Larkin, H., Felitti, V. J., & Anda, R. F. (2014). Social work and adverse childhood experiences research: Implications for practice and health policy. *Social Work in Public Health*, *29*(1/2), 1–16.

Lederach, J. P., & Lederach, A. J. (2010). *When blood and bones cry out: Journeys through the sound scape of healing and reconciliation*. New York: Oxford University Press.

Liebenberg, L., Ungar, M., & Ikeda, J. (2013). Neoliberalism and responsibilisation in the discourse of social service workers. *British Journal of Social Work*, *45*(3), 1006–1021.

Logan-Greene, P., Green, S., Nurius, P. S., & Longhi, D. (2014). Distinct contributions of adverse childhood experiences and resilience resources: A cohort analysis of adult physical and mental health. *Social Work in Health Care*, *53*(8), 776–797.

Lupton, D. (2005). Lay discourses and beliefs related to food risks: An Australian perspective. *Sociology of Health and Illness*, *27*(4), 448–467.

Mancinelli, R., Vitali, M., & Ceccanti, M. (2009). Women, alcohol and the environment: An update and perspectives in neuroscience. *Functional Neurology*, *24*(2), 77–81.

Mate, G. (2008) *In the realm of hungry ghosts: Close encounters with addiction*. Toronto: Alfred A. Knopf.

McDonald, S., Kingston, D., Bayrampour, H., & Tough, S. (2015). Adverse childhood experiences in Alberta, Canada: A population-based study. *Medical Research Archives*, *3*(3), 1–18.

Morrow, M., & Weisser, J. (2012). Towards a social justice framework of mental health recovery. *Studies in Social Justice*, *6*(1), 27–43.

Najavits, L. (2002). *A woman's addictions workbook*. Oakland, CA: New Harbinger Publications.

Najavits, L. (2004). Assessment of trauma, PTSD and substance use disorder: A practical guide. In J. Wilson & T. Keane (Eds.), *Assessment of psychological trauma and PTSD* (pp. 466–491). New York: Guilford Press.

Ogden, P., & Fisher, J. (2014). *Sensorimotor psychotherapy: Interventions for trauma and attachment*. New York: Norton.

O'Neill, R. (2015). Whither critical masculinity studies? Notes on inclusive masculinity theory, postfeminism and sexual politics. *Men and Masculinities*, *18*(1), 100–120.

Perspectives in Public Health. (2015). The health of 25 million transgender people worldwide is reliant on transgender rights. *Perspectives in Public Health*, *136*(5), 258.

Peteet, B., Mosley, C., Miller-Roenigk, B., McCuistian, C., & Dixon, S. (2019). Transnational trends in prescription drug problems among women: A systematic review. *International Journal of Drug Policy*, *63*, 56–73.

Poole, N., & Dell, C. (2005). *Girls, women and substance use.* Ottawa: Canadian Centre on Substance Abuse and BC Centre of Excellence for Women's Health.

Poole, N., & Greaves, L. (2007). Introduction. In N. Poole & L. Greaves (Eds.), *Highs and lows: Canadian perspectives on women and substance use* (pp. xix–xxv). Toronto: Centre for Addiction and Mental Health.

Poole, N., & Greaves, L. (2012). *Becoming trauma informed.* Toronto: Centre for Addiction and Mental Health.

Ross, N. (Producer). (2012). *Women of substance* [Film]. Retrieved from https://www.facebook.com/WomenofSubstanceNovaScotia/videos/644519342271322/ [link no longer available]

Ross, N., Morrison, J., Cukier, S., & Smith, T. (2015). Consuming carcinogens: Women and alcohol. In D. Scott (Ed.), *Our chemical selves: Gender, toxics, and environmental health* (pp. 188–230). Vancouver: University of British Columbia Press.

Schlosser, A. (2018). "They medicated me out": Social flesh and embodied citizenship in addiction treatment. *Contemporary Drug Problems, 45*(3), 188–207.

Schmidt, R., Poole, N., Greaves, L., & Hemsing, N. (2018). *New terrain: Tools to integrate trauma and gender informed responses into substance use practice and policy.* Vancouver: BC Centre of Excellence for Women's Health.

Scourfield, J., & Welsh, I. (2002). *New times or same old story? Risk, reflexivity and social control in child protection.* Working Paper Series, Paper no. 23. Cardiff, UK: Cardiff University School of Social Sciences.

Simoni-Wastila, L. (2000). The use of abusable prescription drugs: The role of gender. *Journal of Women's Health and Gender-Based Medicine, 9*(3), 289–297.

Smith, D., & Seymour, R. (2004). The nature of addiction. In R. Coombs (Ed.), *Handbook of addictive disorders: A practical guide to diagnosis and treatment* (pp. 3–30). New Jersey: Wiley and Sons.

Stanley, L., & Wise, S. (1993). *Breaking out again: Feminist ontology and epistemology.* London: Routledge.

Status of Women Canada. (2018). *Breaking the silence: Final report of the engagement process for the federal strategy to address gender-based violence.* Retrieved from https://www.swc-cfc.gc.ca/violence/strategy-strategie/breaking-briser-en.html

Swadener, B. B. (2010). "At risk" or "at promise"? From deficit constructions of the "other childhood" to possibilities for authentic alliances with children and families. *International Critical Childhood Policy Studies, 3*(1), 7–29.

Syed, M., & McLean, K. (2015). Understanding identity integration: Theoretical, methodological, and applied issues. *Journal of Adolescence, 47,* 109–118.

Thomas, G. (2012). *Levels and patterns of alcohol use in Canada.* Alcohol Price Policy Series, Report 1. Ottawa: Canadian Centre on Substance Abuse.

van der Kolk, B. (2014). *The body keeps the score: Brain, mind, and body in the healing of trauma*. New York: Penguin.

Widom, C. S., Marmorstein, N. R., & White, H. R. (2006). Childhood victimization and illicit drug use in middle adulthood. *Psychology of Addictive Behaviour, 20*, 394–403.

Wilsnack, R. W., Wilsnack, S. C., Gmel, G., & Kantor, L. W. (2018). Gender differences in binge drinking. *Alcohol research: Current Reviews, 39*(1), 57–76.

Wilsnack, S. C. (2012). The GENACIS project: A review of findings and some implications for global needs in women-focused substance abuse prevention and intervention. *Substance Abuse and Rehabilitation, 3*(Suppl 1), 5–15.

World Health Organization. (2013). *Global and regional estimates of violence against women: Prevalence and health effects of intimate partner violence and non-partner sexual violence*. London School of Hygiene and Tropical Medicine, South African Medical Research Council.

Yang, L., Wong, L. Y., Grivel, M. M., & Hasin, D. S. (2017). Stigma and substance use disorders: An international phenomenon. *Current Opinion in Psychiatry, 5*, 378–388.

Zlotnick, C., Lawental, M., & Pud, D. (2017). Double whammy: Adverse childhood events and pain reflect symptomology and quality of life in women in substance abuse treatment. *Social Work in Health Care, 56*(3), 189–201.

CHAPTER 8

Animal-Informed Social Work: A More-Than-Critical Practice

Cassandra Hanrahan and Darlene Chalmers

> If we are intertwined with the rest of the natural world in a process of becoming, then politics cannot end at the boundary of the human species, but the rest of the natural world must also be an active part of the polis. Furthermore, as planetary creatures, with planetary connections and planetary problems (such as climate change), politics cannot end at the boundary of specific locations or nations but must connect through planetary flows. In order to think about the planetary polis, we must also begin to think about new stories. (Bauman, 2018, p. 386)

INTRODUCTION

Animal-informed social work[1] is an approach that enables more effective and comprehensive pedagogies and practice because, at its core, it "understands humans as part of the rest of the planet" (Bauman, 2018, p. 386). Social work can no longer ignore non-human animals and the diverse environments we co-inhabit. It must reconceptualize its social justice mission to include the more-than-human world that shapes our living, not as a special interest add-on, but as inhabitants and habitats, animated by radical relationality and affirmative politics and ethics (Braidotti, 2018; Goodley, Lawthom, & Runswick Cole, 2014), of a porous and pluralistic planetary polis, the primary aspiration of which "is that it attends to diversity and remains open to not-yet-imagined possibilities for planetary becoming" (Bauman, 2018, p. 387).

To this end, the first part of this chapter discusses how human-animal interaction, as embodied and embedded relationships and dynamics, is intrinsic to humanity and, as such, to the myriad contexts wherein social work is practised. We believe "the welfare of nonhuman animals and the health of the natural environment are inextricably connected to the well-being of humans" (Faver, 2009, p. 374). Appreciation of this basic premise is fundamental to social work's relevance and efficacy in a world of entangled and intensifying global pressures and local tensions characterized by complex socio-political-economic issues including increased conflict and poverty, mass migration, war, food insecurity and toxicity, climate change and other environmental degradation, species extinction, increased numbers of more-than-human families and hybrid relationships, an expanding awareness of violence including animal cruelty and animal "processing" as food, and an increased emergence of zoonoses (diseases transmissible between people and other species).

The larger ethical dimensions that shape these issues and the salience of human-animal interaction to cultures, politics, societies, identities, and ways of life are richly explored across the humanities and social sciences. Today, an expanding body of scholarship is "rethink[ing] the prominence of the 'human' in our accounts of the world by exploring the category less as an individualised essence and more as a temporal process of becoming … [in which] being human is a process of becoming 'with,' operating through interactions with others, including non-human others" (Kirk, Pemberton, & Quick, 2019, p. 75). While some trans-disciplinary, trans-methodological conversations are easier than others, a primary interest in "being well" is shared between the medical or health humanities and animal studies, for instance. Within the latter, a prominent theme is peaceful cohabitation, "to understand how to live with other species so that all prosper within a mutually beneficial, although not necessarily equal, collective (often expressed through the language of 'flourishing')" (p. 75). Similarly, both critical disability studies and a feminist ethics of care literature shift understandings of the unitary subject and even critical concepts on "being" toward an ethics and ontology of *becoming*, bringing to life "an enlarged sense of inter-connection between self and others by removing the obstacle of self-centered individualism" (Braidotti, 2013, p. 49). Elsewhere, authors of the Truth and Reconciliation Commission of Canada (2015) contend:

> Reconciliation requires talking, but our conversations must be broader than Canada's conventional approaches. Reconciliation between Aboriginal and non-Aboriginal Canadians, from an Aboriginal perspective, also requires reconciliation with the natural world. If human beings resolve problems between themselves but continue to destroy the natural world, then reconciliation remains incomplete.… Reconciliation will never occur unless we are also reconciled with the earth. (p. 13)

Reconciliation with the earth and all its inhabitants was raised by Wolf (2000) in social work two decades ago in an article boldly called "Social Work and Speciesism" that highlighted the conspicuous absence of speciesism in social work theory and practice. Understood as an ideology that upholds and validates a particular social order and economic system (Nibert, 2002, 2013; Sorenson, 2014), and as a form of discrimination based on species membership, Wolf argued because attention to marginalized groups is a "defining feature of the social work profession, we must consider what groups we are not serving" (p. 88). In an unprecedented move, Wolf further argued that because appreciation and respect for the inherent dignity of all persons is a core social work value (of, for example, the National Association of Social Workers and Canadian Association of Social Workers), "it is worth deliberating over whether our treatment of other species … is associated with our own sense of dignity and self-respect" (p. 88). Building on the case of why animals matter to social work and what they and our interactions with them, including those that are violent, reveal about us, Risley-Curtiss (2010) argued 10 years later:

> Given the ever-growing body of evidence supporting the importance of human–other animal relationships in early identification of potential problems and regarding the potential for companion animals to help individuals and families build resiliency, it is incumbent on the social work profession to join other professions and disciplines in efforts to delve into and build on this bond. If social work practice is to be truly anti-oppressive and ecologically grounded (which requires one to see humans in the context of their environments and as constantly in reciprocal interaction with significant others), then the inclusion of the [human–companion animal bond] is essential. (p. 44)

The second part of the chapter presents animal-informed social work, a therapeutic approach that when conducted in a mutually beneficial way contributes to the health and well-being of individuals and their surrounding communities—across species—and ultimately to a "better and more inter-subjective way of relating" (Chagani, 2014, p. 432). Through a case example we highlight the unique critical clinical skills of animal-informed social work, which includes the burgeoning field of animal-assisted interventions. We also position animal-informed social work as a beginning framework for expanding the scope and depth of social work such that companion animals are "integrated into social work research, education, and practice because of their interconnectedness with humans" (Risley-Curtiss, 2010, p. 39). Because interconnectedness and intersectionality are core concepts of critical social work, animal-informed practice is methodologically aligned. The challenge arises in confrontation of the *species barrier*, characterized by a closed ontological position based on "the singular and bounded model of the human subject" (Chagani, 2014, p. 425) within social work. Our goal is to invite a new and creative approach to social work that extends the critical theory of intersectionality toward species-inclusiveness, recognizing human oppression of other animals is intensely intertwined with the oppression of other humans. It is an approach that broadens the circle of compassion and, at the same time, "assists us in the process of learning to think differently about ourselves" (Braidotti, 2018, p. 4), acknowledging that "social life is always lived in more-than-human contexts" (Irvine & Cilia, 2016, p. 8). Our aim is to provide an understanding of a basic level of preparedness for becoming an animal-informed social worker, premised on the notion that human and non-human health are inseparable.[2] We also assert "a need [for] an ethics of the Anthropocene" (Jamieson, 2017, p. 16) or "Ecocene" (Ulmer, 2017, p. 844). In so doing, we hope to contribute to the many post-humanist perspectives that "represent contemporary efforts to reconceptualize the human condition" (Rose & Walton, 2018, p. 92), such that social work becomes a sustainable practice in a sustainable world, redressing its historic complicity in violent divisive practices and become truly holistic in its commitment to justice and to cause no harm.

As you read this chapter, ask yourself the following questions:

1. Why is it important for critical clinical social workers to develop a critique of humanism, with its fixation on the *human* as the measure of all things, and of the ways human privilege is imbricated in and informs multiple and intersecting forms of oppression?
2. How might a client benefit from receiving assistance from an animal-informed social worker with appreciation of the more-than-human world?
3. What skills are needed for animal-informed social workers to work with and support a client's bond with their companion animal?

THE ANIMAL AS THERAPEUTIC AND THEORETIC IN SOCIAL WORK

Non-human animals occupy a curious place in social work. On the one hand, there is a long-standing interest in animals as therapeutic adjuncts, with a history older than the social work profession itself. In a historical overview of animal-assisted interventions, Serpell (2010, p. 27) argues that "relations with animals played such a prominent role in human evolution that they have now become integral to our psychological well-being." A growing body of research from the health sciences supports a range of benefits of mutually positive human–companion animal interactions or human-animal bonds on human health across all dimensions, including physical, psychological, social, and emotional, and with a range of populations across the life course. "Positive physiological measures, such as lower blood pressure and cholesterol levels," in addition to increased immune systems responses, are significant. Remarkably, "the presence of a pet was found to be more effective than that of a spouse or friend in ameliorating the cardiovascular effects of stress" (Walsh, 2009a, p. 466). Not surprisingly, animal-assisted interventions comprise a growing field.

THE HUMAN-ANIMAL BOND

The human-animal bond is "a mutually beneficial and dynamic relationship between people and [other] animals that is influenced by behaviors considered essential to the health and well-being of both. The bond includes, but is not limited to, emotional, psychological, and physical interactions of people, animals, and the environment" (American Veterinary Medical Association, n.d.).

The first documented case of animal-assisted interventions dates back to 1792 and the York Retreat, an 18th-century asylum in England run by the Society of Friends. Founder William Tuke incorporated farm animals into treatments for patients with mental illness in the belief that their inclusion could "enhance the humanity of the emotionally ill" (Beck & Katcher, 1996, p. 132). As a method of organizing and engaging patients, Tuke understood that the presence of animals reduced the use of medicines and restraints (Urichuk & Anderson, 2003). The introduction of animals into institutional care facilities became widespread during the 19th century (Fine, 2015; Lee, 1984), until a subsequent displacement of early and preliminary uses of animal-assisted therapy "due to the discovery of psychotropic medications" (Urichuk & Anderson, 2003, section 1.2) during the early part of the 20th century. Notably, contemporary studies have found heart attack victims with companion animals experienced prolonged life (Friedmann & Thomas, 1995), and patients with chronic stroke and aphasia improved their language abilities with animal-assisted therapy while baselines remained the same with conventional speech therapy (Macauley, 2006). While the American

Veterinary Medical Association officially recognizes that the human-animal bond has existed for thousands of years and is important to clients (person and other animal) and community health, professional ethics and standards for human health and social service providers do not recognize the vital significance of this relationship to practice.

ANIMAL-ASSISTED INTERVENTIONS

Animal-assisted interventions are goal-oriented and structured interventions that intentionally incorporate non-human animals in health, education, and human services for the purpose of therapeutic gains and improved health and wellness. Well-designed animal-assisted interventions are of mutual benefit to all animals engaged, with provisions and safeguards for their health and well-being. Animal-assisted therapies, education, and activities are all forms of animal-assisted interventions, in which the animal may be part of a volunteer therapy-animal team working under the direction of a professional or an animal that belongs to the professional.

Western clinical perspectives on the therapeutic presence of companion animals, and other positive social and health effects from interactions with them, were reintroduced later in the 20th century by renowned child psychologist Boris Levinson (1961, 1965, 1969), the first well-known practitioner, who, in the early 1960s, inadvertently "pioneered the use of pets in therapy, [having] observed that a pet could be a lifeline for those who were especially vulnerable" (Walsh, 2009a, p. 469). Today, this research draws on several health disciplines, including medicine and nursing (Friedmann, Son, & Saleem, 2015; Friedmann & Thomas, 1995), clinical psychology (Walsh, 2009a, 2009b), gerontology (Barak, Savorai, Mavashev, & Beni, 2001; Gee, Mueller, & Curl, 2017), public health (Beck & Meyers, 1996; Rock, 2013, 2017), counselling (Chandler, 2017), and social work (Hoy-Gerlach & Wehman, 2017; Risley-Curtiss, 2010; Sable, 1995). In exploring the relational significance of companion animals in her therapeutic work with families, Walsh (2009a, 2009b) discusses the ways the unique interactions between people and companion animals contribute to good health across the life cycle. This includes psychological well-being, recovery from serious illness, and success in psychological and physiological therapeutic interventions aimed at prevention, as well as rehabilitation and education, all of which are now well documented.

The unremitting growth of interest in the clinical applications and practice of animal-assisted interventions is evidenced by an ever-expanding body of academic/clinical literature. The topics range from the various goals and strategies of interventions and the therapeutic roles non-human animals have in assisted and informed approaches (Arkow, 2004; Tedeschi, Fitchett, & Molidor, 2005), to more recent developments regarding competencies, standards, and ethics of practice (Fine, 2015; Iannuzzi & Rowan, 1991; Stewart, Chang, Parker, & Grubbs, 2016; A. Taylor, 2003; N. Taylor, Fraser, Signal, & Prentice, 2016). Correspondingly, animal-assisted interventions today are also prominently supported by an ever-growing number of training, education, and research programs around the world dedicated to supporting and deepening our understanding of human-animal interaction.[3]

In contrast to the historically seated appeal and expanding knowledge of the therapeutic benefits of all animals, there remains a significant ignorance in social work of the non-human animal as a theoretical construct that mediates our material and imagined realities. The mental health field is likewise characterized by a disconnect in which human-animal interaction is absent from health education curricula, clinical training, and research programs "despite the abundant evidence of their importance over the millennia, their centrality in contemporary lives, their therapeutic value in health and mental health research, and their deep meaning for human companions over the life course" (Walsh, 2009a, p. 476). This absence of the non-human animal as a theoretic and ubiquitous relational being is astonishing when one considers all the ways in which they are embodied in people's lives and societies within the Anthropocene from food to symbol to family members, the more-than-human environments that shape the geographies and spaces in-between that we all inhabit, and the ways companion animals in particular figure in the lives of so many—within client populations and among practitioners alike.

Hanrahan (2011, p. 283) has argued the following:

[Just as] "civilizing missions produce the 'Other' in need of help, thereby sustaining the identity of the helper as good, innocent, and helpful," (Rossiter, 2001, p. 2)[,] ... challenging speciesism and the anthropocentrism of social work is a de-civilizing undertaking, one that calls attention to our very culpability as a species in instigating and participating in the oppressive politics of "othering." By bringing into focus the connections between speciesism, interpersonal violence and animal abuse, slavery, and misogyny, research in the field of human-animal interactions and relationships has fundamental implications for critical AOP [anti-oppressive] social work.

Indeed, as Weil (2010), who traced the significance of the animal turn in critical theory, argued, "if animal studies have come of age, it is perhaps because nonhuman animals have become a limit case for theories of difference, otherness, and power" (p. 3). These authors similarly argue that social work—including critical anti-oppressive scholars and practitioners—can no longer ignore the theoretical and ethical dimensions of human privilege, anthropocentrism, and speciesism.

> Like trauma studies, animal studies thus stretch to the limit questions of language, of epistemology, and of ethics that have been raised in various ways by women's studies or postcolonial studies: how to understand and give voice to others or to experiences that seem impervious to our means of understanding; how to attend to difference without appropriating or distorting it; how to hear and acknowledge what it may not be possible to say. (Weil, 2010, p. 4)

SPECIESISM

The term *speciesism* was coined by British clinical psychologist and animal rights activist Richard D. Ryder in *Speciesism* (1970).[4] Ryder was an original member of the Oxford Group, now the prestigious Oxford Centre for Animal Ethics, which was concerned with the emerging concept of animal rights within a frame of relational ethics. For views on speciesism and anthropocentrism in non-Western cultures, see Noske (2008) and Serpell (1996); in social work, see Ryan (2011).

Speciesism brings into relief the converse power dynamic of human privilege, or "human exceptionalism" (Haraway, 2008)—a notion that "humanity alone is not [part of] a spatial and temporal web of interspecies dependencies" (p. 11). The spectre of speciesism in social work that was first raised 20 years ago by David Wolf (2000) in *Social Work and Speciesism* belongs to a growing critique of liberal humanism that invisibilizes human privilege and the anthropocentrism that posit the human being, but not all people, as measure of all things. Earlier feminist research on the intersecting oppressions of speciesism, racism, and sexism include Marjorie Spiegel's book *The Dreaded Comparison: Human and Animal Slavery* (1988/1997) and Carol Adams's book, *The Sexual Politics of Meat* (1990). A more recent example is Bénédicte Boisseron's book, *Afro-Dog: Blackness and the Animal Question*

(2018), which examines how the relations of power that inform dynamics and experiences of racialization and animalization provide insights into interlinked forms of oppression, more so than trivializing Black pain. Recent writings examining concurrence between Indigenous worldviews and critical animal studies include two chapters from *Critical Animal Studies: Towards Trans-Species Social Justice* (Matsuoka & Sorenson, 2018): Margaret Robinson's "The Roots of My Indigenous Veganism" and Ruth Koleszar-Green and Atsuko Matsuoka's "Indigenous Worldviews and Critical Animal Studies: Decolonization and Revealing Truncated Narratives of Dominance."

ANTHROPOCENTRISM

Anthropocentrism "puts the observer, and the group he/she belongs to, in a superior position in relation to the group observed" (Martinelli, 2008, p. 80), into a binary opposition that produces a dualistic (as opposed to a pluralistic) interpretation of reality, based on static or fixed criteria of difference.

While the rational case for animals has historically been absent from social work and generally understated within academia, today the *question of the animal* (Wolfe, 2003) is at the centre of two burgeoning transdisciplinary fields known as animal studies and critical post-humanism that "challenge the politics of knowledge and the ways knowledge discipline and shape different bodies differently" (Bauman, 2018, p. 386). Individual and institutional resistance in social work to this scholarship is perplexing given the profession's history of eclecticism, commitment to intersectional analysis, and mission to respond to diversity. Moreover, given the incursions being made elsewhere by these bold and progressive fields, social work's general silence contradicts its avowed commitment to context and environment. To explain this phenomena, Hanrahan (2011, p. 278) describes

anthropocentrism as the central organizing principle of western social work ... [which] limits the profession's value framework, as well as the long-term sustainability of mainstream, even critical anti-oppressive theoretical practice approaches because it informs and supports a point of view that prioritizes and exalts humans over other animals, nature, and the planet.

This particular arrangement is what Martinelli (2008, p. 80) calls binary anthropocentrism, described as

> the fact of being a different entity from the object observed (human, rather than another animal), which produces a dualistic (as opposed to a pluralistic) interpretation of reality, based on criteria of difference … and/or a strongly hierarchical identity, which puts the observer, and the group he/she belongs to, in a superior position in relation to the group observed.

Thus, while leveraging the human-animal bond to improve human health and well-being contributes to a corollary improvement in quality of life for individual animals and increases the public profile of companion animals within society, the too common explicit and implicit construction of non-human animals in animal-assisted interventions as "tools," albeit within a welfarist framework of humane treatment, ultimately limits latent potential of animal-assisted interventions (Glenk, 2017). For example, Harm (2005, p. 1) proposed "it may be beneficial to incorporate the presence of companion animals in ecological assessments and consider those relationships as potential resources." Well intentioned as it is, this particular approach is too often tempered by the humanist conceptualization of human-animal relationships as resources. It follows that despite the increased attention to issues of animal welfare in the designs and operation of interventions, the moral status of non-human animals and corresponding protections are "under considered" (N. Taylor et al., 2016, p. 142). Correspondingly, we suggest the moral status of persons is overstated.

We argue that non-human animals in animal-assisted interventions must be seen as *relational agents* whose emotional and physical labour are central to the therapeutic relationship.[5] Rather than as a "unique human quality or force, which acts upon the world," we extend an understanding of agency as "an action that is shared with the world" (Rose & Walton, 2018, p. 96). In other words, the notion of "agency is not seen as an *attribute* of human beings or of caregivers and care receivers, as in for example their autonomy, but rather agency is exercised through affecting and being affected by others, meaning that it is an *enactment* between humans (and also between humans and nonhumans, or more-than-humans)" (Lenz Taguchi, 2010, as cited in Hugman & Carter, 2016, p. 82). From this posthumanist lens, we proffer a focus on affirmative political and ethical action. Like Faver (2009, p. 374), we contend that "in order to fulfill our professional obligation to promote the welfare of society as well as individuals [human and non-human], social workers must attend to humans' relationships [among other interactions] with non-human animals and the environment"

HUMAN-ANIMAL INTERACTIONS IN SOCIAL WORK: WHY THEY MATTER

Animal-assisted interventions comprise only one domain within the field of human-animal interaction in relation to individual and public health and social services. Other areas of interest highlight not only the partial and contingent nature of species interactions within shared ecosystems, but also the connected larger ontological, epistemic, and spiritual concerns intrinsic to human social customs, beliefs, activities, and meaning. This section will review these areas of interest, drawing attention to their relevance to social work and as such to the astonishing lack of consideration within the profession. The following section will introduce a clinical case example, highlighting unique dynamics of animal-informed social work.

Other foci in the field of human-animal studies with implications for both micro (individual/personal) and macro (material/structural/discursive) practice include the link between animal cruelty and other forms of human violence (Arkow, 2003, 2013; Ascione, 2008); animal (mal)treatment in industrial food production; bereavement and disenfranchised grief regarding the loss of animal companions (Strand et al., 2012); the feminist care tradition and animal ethics (Adams & Donovan, 2007; Besthorn, 2002; Faver & Strand, 2003; Glasser, 2011); ecological injustice such as climate change, environmental racism, and food (in)security; compassionate conservation (Bekoff, 2013); posthuman disability studies (Goodley et al., 2014; Kirk, Pemberton, & Quick, 2019); trans-species justice (Matsuoka & Sorenson, 2014); animals and the law (Francione, 2000; Sankoff, Black, & Sykes, 2015); zoonoses (Akhtar, 2013); and the politics and ethics of species (Corbey & Lanjouw, 2013; Coulter, 2015; Donaldson & Kimlicka, 2011; Ryan, 2011). Like renowned ethologist Mark Bekoff (2007), who declared it is simply bad biology to deny the existence of animals' emotions (pp. xvii–xviii), this chapter argues that social work remains prejudicial and inadequate in its exclusive view of the human that simultaneously homogenizes and "others" people.

Despite the growing ubiquity of non-human animals in family systems and in relationships as significant others with humans, and in research knowledge on human-animal bonds, other interactions, and human health, there remain significant gaps in the literature and in educational curricula on how the health professions, including social work, respond to real-world issues. While the links between violence to humans and violence to other animals are documented, such connections have yet to translate into systemic education, practice, and policy. Despite the prolific research correlating interpersonal violence and family breakdown with child and adult animal cruelty (Flynn, 2000; Long, Long, & Kulkarni, 2007), there is no service coordination between child welfare and animal protection agencies, and only one empirical study to date investigating cross-sector training and reporting (Zilney & Zilney, 2005). This disconnect ignores how violence to animals is a known indicator of other forms of human violence, often concurrent with domestic violence (N. Taylor & Fraser, 2019).

The anthropocentrism of social work and its dominant perspectives, including the conventional person-in-environment (PIE) and the "progressive" structural and critical anti-oppressive (AOP) approaches, limits an inclusive approach to violence. Anthropocentrism further limits the scope of social work's current value base, code of ethics, theoretical frameworks, and standards that directly inform education and practice (Hanrahan, 2011; Ryan, 2011). Fundamentally, to ignore animal oppression and cruelty is to ignore human violence. As such, we support the inclusion of animal protection in public health and social policies (Akhtar, 2013).

Regarding homelessness and housing security, core social work issues, services for the homeless with companion animals are few. While a small number of studies highlight the unique circumstances surrounding homelessness and companion animals (Labrecque & Walsh, 2011; Lem, Coe, Haley, Stone, & O'Grady, 2016), there is not enough information on how shelters for the homeless, transition housing, and other services can more holistically respond to clients and their companion animals. With the exception of Lem and colleagues (2016), few studies explore this issue in Canada or from the perspectives of youth and/or women living in shelters. Despite the research that has identified that "homeless individuals' attachments to their animals are stronger compared with the general population" (Labrecque & Walsh, 2011, p. 83), there remains a pervasive gap between homelessness research, policy, and service delivery regarding meeting the needs of potential shelter guests involved in human-animal attachment-based relationships. Another area characterized by a dearth in companion-species services is animal hoarding, which, according to the Hoarding of Animals Research Consortium (2010), is about "satisfying a human need," and associated with other forms of violence, such as elder abuse, child abuse, and self-neglect. Surprisingly, social workers as front-line mental health workers, who are in a position to witness animal hoarding first-hand, are not educated on this complex psychosocial phenomenon and are rarely involved in such cases. This, despite the reality that "social work folklore is replete with stories of animal neglect and/or abuse." As noted by Ryan (2011, pp. 3–4), "it is often implicit in much casework experience, but infrequently made explicit."

The following section provides a brief introduction to animal-assisted interventions, making explicit the animal question in social work by recognizing that "being well" is a process of "becoming with." We present a short micro-level case study illustrating how "families are, and always have been, constituted as 'more-than-human,'" rather than as preconstituted entities (Irvine & Cilia, 2016, p. 8). We provide practical strategies that, upon integration, can shift practice to becoming animal-informed. At minimum, these strategies are considered necessary aspects of critical clinical practice.

ANIMAL-INFORMED SOCIAL WORK PRACTICE

The influence of the human-animal bond on the psychosocial and physiological benefits of interaction with companion animals has been proposed to occur through activation of the oxytocin system (Beetz, Unvas-Möberg, Julius, & Kotrschal, 2012; Miller et al., 2009). Friendly interactions with a dog can activate hormonal changes in humans by eliciting a decrease in the stress hormone cortisol and an increase in oxytocin, the hormone that makes us feel happy (Odendall & Meintjes, 2003). Studies also demonstrate that human-animal bonds can positively impact changes to physical health (Matchock, 2015; Wells, 2009), such as lowered heart rate and decreased blood pressure through stroking an animal (Shiloh, Sorek, & Terkel, 2003) and an association between human-animal companionship and cardiovascular disease treatment and prevention (Friedmann et al., 2015). Human-animal companionship can contribute to psychological benefits derived from a multitude of social benefits for children and adults that can include, for example, an increase in social capital (Arkow, 2013; Wood et al., 2015). Acknowledging the existence of human-animal bonds and understanding their impacts on human health is also imperative for appreciating how and why animal-assisted interventions "work" (Barker, Rogers, Turner, Karpf, & Suthers-Mccabe, 2003; Fine & Beck, 2015).

Animal-assisted intervention is an umbrella term that captures an array of approaches specifically defined as "any intervention that intentionally includes or incorporates animals as part of a therapeutic or ameliorative process or milieu" (Kruger & Serpell, 2006, p. 25). Approaches are various and offered across numerous populations with a variety of species, although dogs, and to a lesser degree horses, are most commonly involved. Animal-assisted interventions inform literacy and reading programs for children (Fung, 2016), prison animal programs (Dell, Chalmers, Stobbe, Rohr, & Husband, 2019), university student wellness initiatives (Dell et al., 2015), equine programs with veterans (Duncan, Critchley, & Marland, 2014), visitation programs for seniors and others in care facilities, and youth in treatment for substance abuse (Adams et al., 2015). With the proliferation of animal-assisted interventions over the decades, definitions for therapeutic approaches involving animals have also evolved. Currently this is problematic as there is a lack of clarity within the field, which has implications for professionalization, standards of practice, and safety, particularly when an approach is implemented that may not be well understood (Fine, Tedeschi, & Elvove, 2015).

Aside from formalized and increasingly recognized approaches, the integration of animal-assisted interventions as a critical and integral component of social work practice is virtually non-existent. The inclusion of animals in practice is not readily taught in social work curricula. We recognize that the availability of social workers who are credentialed in animal-assisted interventions as therapeutic specialists, or who work alongside handler/animal teams with training in this area, may be limited.[6] Additionally, not all practitioners will have an interest in animal-assisted interventions per se, nor in animals for that matter, and not all clients, depending on the type of relationship they have with their companion animals, will necessarily perceive them as playing an important role in their day-to-day lives. However, it is important to include animals in practice; undoubtedly for those clients where animals are central or are a barrier to their well-being (Hodgson & Darling, 2011; Hoy-Gerlach & Wehman, 2017; MacNamara & Moga, 2014), and simply in general terms, because as living beings, they act and are acted upon within a multiplicity of contexts, be they social, cultural, spiritual, or economic.

Drawing on the work of MacNamara and Moga (2014) and Moga (2019) we propose that animal-assisted interventions can be an integral component of critical social work by shifting the focus from "animal-assisted" to "animal-informed" practice (Moga, 2019, p. 261). Our perspective is that such a shift represents the integration of both a theoretical lens and practice approach. In practice, a key difference is the involvement of the clients' own animals as adjuncts in interventions, which may enhance consistency, accessibility, and purposeful engagement for the client in the therapeutic process and outcome (MacNamara & Moga, 2014). We also incorporate *zooeyia*[7] as part of our proposed animal-informed practice framework. Zooeyia is the philosophical construct of the human-animal bond with an evidence base that demonstrates the benefits of relationships with companion animals in four key health promotion areas. They include animals as: builders of social capital, agents of harm reduction, motivators for health behaviour change, and active participants in treatment plans (Hodgson et al., 2015, p. 527). Thus, animal-informed social work practice recognizes human-animal bonds and the myriad ways they facilitate the exploration of client and community challenges and the identification of strengths, and support change.

The Case

Bill, a 63-year-old cisgender, white male who has been single his entire life, lives with Rosie, his 5-year-old miniature schnauzer, and does not have children. He has a cognitive disability due to a head injury when he was a child. Bill has lived on the upper floor of a rental unit in a small urban community for 30 years. He had worked for decades at the same business but retired two years ago, as working with the customers became increasingly stressful. Bill has a limited income through disability supports. His elderly parents were a primary support, but both had passed in the previous five years. His sibling and two acquaintances check in occasionally, but he prefers to be alone. He recently saw a doctor due to lethargy he believed was connected to the flu. He did not share with the physician that he was having mobility issues, especially using the short flight of stairs in his apartment building. The doctor referred Bill to your community-based agency for counselling support as he believed Bill was experiencing depression.

As Bill's clinical social worker, where would you start? We provide initial insights into this case and then pose questions for thinking through next steps. To begin, building rapport and establishing a therapeutic alliance is fundamental to the client–social worker relationship, the change process, and therapeutic outcomes. Bill indicated during the referral that he lives with his companion dog, Rosie. The process of developing a relationship with Bill can include the "pet query" developed by Hodgson and colleagues (2015). This question simply asks: "Are there companion animals in the home?" and, if yes, "Who cares for them?" This can open a non-threatening conversation about the client's home life that is holistic, client-centred, and animal-informed (p. 531). Asking this question readily positions the social work practitioner as valuing an important relationship in the client's life, which can enhance the therapeutic alliance. It can also give insight into where Rosie fits into Bill's immediate environment and larger system, how her presence may affect his day-to-day functioning, and how she may be influential in any future intervention process (Hoy-Gerlach & Wehman, 2017; MacNamara & Moga, 2014).

Upon further assessment, it is learned that Bill will require more routine care than initially indicated. His mobility issues and the use of stairs are also making it dangerous for him to get out with Rosie. His daily walks with her are important for their physical activity and being around other people (Toohey, McCormack, Doyle-Baker, Adams, & Rock, 2013). It is learned that Rosie is an important facilitator in addressing Bill's loneliness (Stanley, Conwell, Bowen, & Van Orden, 2013). However, Bill expresses insight that he may have to move due to a need for additional personal support, but also his concern that he will lose Rosie (Johnson & Bibbo, 2015). While many settings importantly encourage visiting animals, such as in animal-assisted activities, fewer permit residents to live with their companion animal. Animal-informed social work requires knowledge of policies governing animals residing in assisted-living settings, particularly those for older adults (Morley & Fook, 2005). Critical clinical practice also includes challenging oppressive or systemic barriers and advocating on behalf of a client's best interests. To assist Bill in remaining at home if feasible and maintaining his valued relationship with Rosie, an animal-informed social worker will also want to speak with Bill's support network, and community groups like ElderDog Canada about supporting Bill by providing dog care assistance in order for him to stay with his canine companion at home. We suggest educating a client's support network about the benefits of the human-animal bond. Knowledge of organizations like ElderDog, for example, whose mission is to honour and preserve the human-animal bond through programs that include help for seniors with daily dog care activities, foster care and adoption of older dogs, and long-term care planning for companion dogs, is an important component of an animal-informed social worker's toolkit.

What other sources of information will you need to practice using an animal-informed social work framework? How can your knowledge of the human-animal bond and Bill's relationship with Rosie be a motivator for Bill's behaviour change? How can Rosie be incorporated as an active part of Bill's intervention plan? Given Bill's relationship with Rosie, are there opportunities for building his social capital?

As an animal-informed social worker, it is important to know the following additional information to be able to address a range of client issues. Building relationships with veterinarians can be an important resource around the health of a client's animal and the well-being of the relationship for both. Given Bill's limited income, identifying veterinarians that provide sliding scale or pro bono care is essential for individuals and families who may not be able to access this care for their companion animals, nor their own health care. Clinics like Community Veterinary Outreach (n.d.) offer "human health services and health education alongside preventative veterinary care" for marginalized or at-risk populations, drawing on the human-animal bond to increase health access for humans and animals. Such a clinic might be an important resource in your community. If one does not exist, an animal-informed practitioner can advocate for the development of a community veterinary outreach to better the health of people and animals.

Bill also indicates that he has been unable on occasion to purchase enough food to feed Rosie and himself. Knowledge of food banks in the community, and those that carry pet food is important. This can be discovered by contacting local food banks to check on their availability of pet food. Pet food–specific food banks are an emerging trend that can prevent pets from being relinquished to animal shelters when a person is experiencing financial stress or poverty. Knowledge about no-kill animal shelters may provide additional relief to clients in situations where they may need to surrender their companion animals. Knowing they will not be euthanized but cared for in the shelter until adopted may possibly facilitate the difficult decision and limit potential concern. Additional stressors for individuals and their companion animals are environments that place both at risk due to intimate partner violence. An animal-informed social worker will be aware of the way perpetrators of violence have been known to exercise control and power over human family members by leveraging threats and/or enacting harm on the family's companion animal. They will also be aware of local community shelters and transitional homes that accommodate both people and their animal companions. In addition, a key animal-informed advocacy role to increase understanding of the human-animal bond at the community level could include presenting at a food bank or a shelter to highlight the multitude of roles that animals may play in clients' lives.

In the case example we presented, Bill lives with a companion animal. However, not all older adults are able to keep an animal for a multitude of health-related reasons (Gee et al., 2017). In fact, many adults, children, and youth may not have access to the therapeutic benefit of animals generally and a companion animal may not be an option. Seeking out volunteer opportunities for clients at humane societies, wildlife rehabilitation organizations, and animal sanctuaries will augment your list of resources. Other options exist that do not require access to formalized programs but can support clients in connecting with animals and nature, such as therapeutic walks outdoors, local parks with benches in safe sunny and shaded areas, or meeting in settings with other life forms such as plants or aquariums (Besthorn, Wulff, & St. George, 2010).

Creating awareness of social workers and other professionals who have training in human-animal bonds in your community can be a valuable asset. An animal-informed social worker should have knowledge of clinicians who are trained in animal-assisted interventions to be able to make appropriate referrals on behalf of clients. A beginning knowledge of the human-animal bond, its role in animal-assisted interventions, and the breadth of animal-assisted intervention approaches is necessary to ensure that your referrals will meet the client's needs. Asking questions of the practitioner to determine their knowledge on integrating an animal through a visiting or structured treatment program will be important in ensuring that safety is a priority for the animals and humans involved.

It is important to note that there are differences in the requirements of handler/dog teams when engaged in the practice options outlined within animal-assisted interventions, specifically assisted activities and therapies. These differences mainly relate to the purpose and intention of the intervention and, importantly, the knowledge and understanding of the practitioner or handler as it relates to the animal-assisted intervention, the human(s) and animals involved, the role and purpose of the animal in the intervention, and the relevant competencies and standards. The key differences between an animal-assisted activity and therapy is that the former is typically a planned, informal visiting program that is social in nature and not guided by structured therapeutic goals, but is therapeutic given the shared connection that a client and therapy animal may experience. Animal-assisted therapy is a structured, goal-oriented process on behalf of the client that is facilitated by a licensed practitioner working within the scope of their professional practice. Animal-assisted therapy can be considered an adjunct to counselling and therapy, and a practice approach that can be integrated into various theoretical counselling frameworks and techniques (O'Callaghan & Chandler, 2011).

Regardless of the animal-assisted intervention approach used, attention to animal welfare is critical (Glenk, 2017). Animal well-being in the context of animal-assisted interventions refers to the handler having knowledge of the animal and ensuring the mental and physical needs of the animal are being met, regardless of the species. Animals should be healthy prior to inclusion in animal-assisted intervention programs, which includes receiving regular veterinary care. They should also be monitored during intervention sessions to ensure their safety and comfort (Iannuzzi & Rowan, 1991). Shani (2017) states that therapists and/or handlers hold the responsibility to ensure that the animal's physical and mental needs are being met during their involvement in animal-assisted intervention work. Doing this, then, requires a personal knowledge of the animal, which allows for a deeper understanding of their behaviour and needs and thus, their welfare (Hart, 2000).

Finally, a critical component of animal-informed social work is the recognition of the importance of the human-animal bond and health and well-being for people *and* other animals. From a one-health perspective, it has been proposed that health for humans and companion-animals may share parallel social determinants that affect the well-being of both (Card, Epp, & Lem, 2018). Furthermore, regardless of the inclusion of a handler/dog team through a formalized animal-assisted intervention program or integration of the client's own animal as a resource in therapeutic practice, "ethically justifiable [animal-assisted interventions] should generate an added value in health and wellbeing for humans as well as animals and avoid any suffering in both" (Hediger, Meisser, & Zinsstag, 2019, p. 2).

CONCLUSION

Animal-informed social work is vitally hopeful of new world possibilities. Social work is well positioned to incorporate animal-informed theory and practice because of its orientation toward intersectionality and justice, and because several theoretical models used in social work, such as strengths perspective, ecosystems theory, and family systems theory, further support the inclusion of human-animal interactions in practice (Hoy-Gerlach & Wehman, 2017, p. 7). In reality, however, only a small number of social workers in Canada consider animals or integrate animal-assisted interventions in practice. This is in part because schools of social work in Canada do not provide curriculum on human-animal bonds and other interaction, animal-assisted interventions, or speciesism as a form of human oppression of non-human animals that informs and intersects with the oppression of other humans, and consequently there are few organized practicum placements for students, and little to no awareness among employers within social work settings of the intersections of human-animal interaction with social work issues.

While needs assessments regarding human–companion animal interaction in social work have identified interests among practitioners but major gaps in education and training (Chalmers, 2019; Hanrahan, 2013; Risley-Curtiss, 2010), and the call by Zilney and Zilney (2005) for cross-training and cross-reporting among front-line child welfare and mental health workers and animal welfare workers, highlighted violence to animals as concomitant with other forms of violence such as child abuse, human-animal interactions and interventions in social work continue to be generally regarded as representing special interest topics, if regarded at all. It is, however, not a matter of whether one is interested in animal-informed practice or not, or whether one likes or dislikes, fears or embraces, animals. That is beside the point. It is a question of ethical behaviour: "it is up to us whether to willfully intensify the human domination of the [more-than-human world], accept it, or try to reduce it" (Jamieson, 2017, p. 16). Seen perhaps to be on the wrong side within "binary anthropocentrism," advocates of species-inclusive intersectionality and trans-species justice in social work, including these authors, are "participating in the search for more livable 'other worlds' (autres-mondialisations) inside earthly complexity" (Haraway, 2008, p. 41). Animal-informed social work is an effort to align the profession within the current historical moment—to generate greater relevancy —in a world where "how we live, eat, drink, breathe, commute, hear, see, smell, touch, sense, and experience life are inextricable from our local ecologies" (Ulmer, 2017, p. 833). In an evolving world, we can no longer accept that "knowledge frameworks that privilege the human at the expense of the more-than human" (p. 833), including anthropocentric critical practice and transformative theories, are enough to move people toward sustainable progressive action. In a world still deeply divided along multiple spaces, geographies, and bodies, specific politicized standpoints are required, but "put simply, more-than-critical methodologies are needed for a more-than-human world" (p. 843).

NOTES

1. The distinction between humans and animals is a false dichotomy. Humans are mammals. The human/animal binary informs many worldviews, including the Enlightenment and its attendant philosophy of humanism. It trades on the same power dynamics as other predominant binaries, such as man/woman, White/Black, heterosexual/gay, and society/nature that continue to shape the civilizing mission of modernity. The historical system of classification that "naturalized" human privilege and assigned superiority in relation to the more-than-human world is the same one that privileges and thus renders man, whiteness, heteronormativity, and affluence among other markers as characteristics of the "normative" human. The term *non-human animal* came into use to underscore the reality that humans *are* animals and the dividing lines separating us from nature are

about power rather than essential properties. For some, *non-human animal* reifies the privileged category of human and as such they continue to use the term *animal* to refer to non-human animals while recognizing the biases inherent in this language choice. The choice here to use the terminology of "animal-informed social work" is intentional, aimed at redefining the social in social work as inclusive and relational rather than exclusive and atomistic. Both *non-human animal* and *animal* are used throughout to refer to species other than human and are determined by context and intent.

2.   See Hoy-Gerlach and Wehman (2017) for a recent comprehensive social work guide to human-animal interventions, and Ryan (2011) for a discussion of the moral imperative in social work to include non-human animals in the profession's code of ethics and an example of a revised trans-species code.

3.   Pet Partners (n.d.), a non-profit organization that promotes mutually beneficial relationships between companion animals and people in order to help people improve their health, independence, and quality of life, is considered to be the leading North American organization in animal-assisted interventions. The International Association of Human-Animal Interaction Organizations (n.d.) also promotes the unique role animals play in human well-being and quality of life through research and education about human-animal interaction. The longest-standing organization is the Latham Foundation, established in 1918 to promote respect for all life through education. Education programs include the Institute for Human-Animal Connection and the Veterinarian Social Work Program at the Graduate Schools of Social Work, University of Denver and University of Tennessee, respectively. Other centres supporting scientific research are the leading Animals and Society Institute and the Human-Animal Bond Research Initiative Foundation. The latter funds and shares scientific research about the positive health impacts of animals on people in mental health, post-traumatic stress and trauma, cancer, cardiovascular health, child health and development, autism spectrum disorder, healthy aging, Alzheimer's disease and dementia, workplace health, and allergies and immunity. The Kerulos Center for Nonviolence is organized around a broader mission to inspire radical change to align humanity with nature through research, education, and sanctuary so that animals may live in dignity and peace.

4.   This is a privately printed leaflet, which was distributed at the University of Oxford in 1970 in protest against animal experimentation.

5.   For an innovative discussion on nonhuman animal labour, see Coulter (2015).

6.   We recognize the term *handler* as problematic in that it perpetuates a view of animals as inanimate objects or non-agentic beings, but because it is a technical term unique to a subspecialty, and because we have not yet developed an alternative, we have chosen to use it here with this caveat.

7.   This term was coined by Hodgson and Darling (2011).

REFERENCES

Adams, C. (1990). *The sexual politics of meat: A feminist vegetarian critical theory.* New York: Continuum.

Adams, C., Arratoon, C., Boucher, J., Cartier, G., Chalmers, D., Dell, C., … Wuttunee, M. (2015). The helping horse: How equine assisted learning contributes to the wellbeing of First Nations youth in treatment for volatile substance misuse. *Human-Animal Interaction Bulletin, 1*(1), 52–75.

Adams, C., & Donovan, J. (Eds.). (2007). *The feminist care tradition in animal ethics: A reader.* New York: Columbia University Press.

Akhtar, A. (2013). The need to include animal protection in public health policies. *Journal of Public Health Policy, 34*(4), 549–559.

American Veterinary Medical Association (n.d.). The human-animal interaction and human-animal bond. Retrieved from https://www.avma.org/KB/Policies/Pages/The-Human-Animal-Bond.aspx

Arkow, P. (2003). *Breaking the cycles of violence: A guide to multi-disciplinary interventions; A handbook for child protection, domestic violence and animal protection agencies.* Alameda, CA: Latham Foundation.

Arkow, P. (2004). *Animal-assisted therapy and activities: A study resource guide and bibliography for the use of companion animals in selected therapies.* Stratford, NJ: Self-published.

Arkow, P. (2013). The impact of companion animals on social capital and community violence: Setting research, policy and program agendas. *Journal of Sociology and Social Welfare, 40*(4), 33–56.

Ascione, F. R. (2008). *The international handbook of animal abuse and cruelty: Theory, research, and application.* West Lafayette, IN: Purdue University Press.

Barak, Y., Savorai, O., Mavashev, S., & Beni, A. (2001). Animal-assisted therapy for elderly schizophrenic patients: A one-year controlled trial. *American Journal of Geriatric Psychiatry, 9*(4), 439–442.

Barker, S. B., Rogers, C. S., Turner, J. W., Karpf, A. S., & Suthers-Mccabe, H. M. (2003). Benefits of interacting with companion animals: A bibliography of articles published in refereed journals during the past five years. *American Behavioral Scientist, 47*(1), 94–97.

Bauman, W. A. (2018). Religion, science, and nature: Doing without human exceptionalism. *Religious Studies Review, 44*(4), 383–388.

Beck, A. M., & Katcher, A. H. (1996). *Between pets and people: The importance of animal companionship.* West Lafayette, IN: Purdue University.

Beck, A. M., & Meyers, N. M. (1996). Health enhancement and companion animal ownership. *Annual Review of Public Health, 17*, 247–257.

Beetz, A., Unvas-Möberg, K., Julius, H., & Kotrschal, K. (2012). Psychosocial and psychophysiological effects of human-animal interactions: The possible role of oxytocin. *Frontiers in Psychology*. Retrieved from https://www.frontiersin.org/articles/10.3389/fpsyg.2012.00234/full

Bekoff, M. (2007). *The emotional lives of animals*. Novato, CA: New World Library.

Bekoff, M. (Ed.). (2013). *Ignoring nature no more: The case for compassionate conservation*. Chicago & London: University of Chicago Press.

Besthorn, F. (2002). The oppression of women and nature: Ecofeminism as a framework for an expanded ecological social work. *Families in Society: The Journal of Contemporary Human Services, 83*(3), 221–232.

Besthorn, F., Wulff, D., & St. George, S. (2010). Eco-spiritual helping and postmodern therapy: A deeper ecological framework. *Ecopsychology, 2*(1), 23–32.

Boisseron, B. (2018). *Afro-dog: Blackness and the animal question*. New York: Columbia University Press.

Braidotti, R. (2013). *The posthuman*. London: Polity.

Braidotti, R. (2018). A theoretical framework for the critical posthumanities. *Theory, Culture, and Society* [online], 1–31.

Card, C., Epp, T., & Lem, M. (2018). Exploring the social determinants of animal health. *Journal of Veterinary Medical Education, 45*(4), 437–447.

Chagani, F. (2014). Critical political ecology and the seductions of posthumanism. *Journal of Political Ecology, 21*, 424–436.

Chalmers, D. (2019). The importance of including animals in social work practice. *Saskatchewan Social Worker, 30*(1), 13.

Chandler, C. (2017). *Animal-assisted therapy in counseling* (3rd ed.). New York: Routledge.

Community Veterinary Outreach. (n.d.). Our mission. Retrieved from https://vetoutreach.org/about-us/

Corbey, R., & Lanjouw, A. (Eds.). (2013). *Politics of species: Reshaping our relationships with other animals*. Cambridge, UK: Cambridge University Press.

Coulter, K. (2015). *Animals, work, and the promise of interspecies solidarity*. Basingstoke, UK: Palgrave Macmillan.

Dell, C., Chalmers, D., Gillett, J., Rohr, B., Nickel, C., Campbell, L., … Brydges, M. (2015). PAWSing student stress: A pilot study of the St. John Ambulance Therapy Dog program on three Canadian campuses. *Canadian Journal of Counselling and Psychotherapy, 49*(4), 332–359.

Dell, C., Chalmers, D., Stobbe, M., Rohr, B., & Husband, A. (2019). Animal-assisted therapy in a Canadian psychiatric prison. *International Journal of Prisoner Health, 5*(13), 209–231.

Donaldson, S., & Kimlicka, W. (2011). *Zoopolis: A political theory of animal rights*. Oxford & New York: Oxford University Press.

Duncan, C., Critchley, S., & Marland, J. (2014). CAN PRAXIS: A model of equine assisted learning (EAL) for PTSD. *Canadian Military Journal, 14*(2), 64–69.

Faver, C. (2009). Seeking our place in the web of life: Animals and human spirituality. *Journal of Religion and Spirituality in Social Work: Social Thought, 28*, 362–378.

Faver, C. A., & Strand, E. B. (2003). Domestic violence and animal cruelty: Untangling the web of abuse. *Journal of Social Work Education, 39*, 237–253.

Fine, A. (2015). Handbook on animal-assisted therapy: Foundations and guidelines for animal-assisted interventions (4th ed.). London: Elsevier.

Fine, A., & Beck A. (2015). Understanding our kinship with animals: Input for health care professionals interested in the human-animal bond. In A. Fine (Ed.), *Handbook on animal-assisted therapy: Theoretical foundations and guidelines for practice* (4th ed., pp. 3–10). San Diego: Elsevier.

Fine, A., Tedeschi, P., & Elvove, E. (2015). Forward thinking: The evolving field of human-animal interactions. In A. Fine (Ed.), *Handbook on animal-assisted therapy: Theoretical foundations and guidelines for practice* (4th ed., pp. 21–35). San Diego, CA: Elsevier.

Flynn, C. P. (2000). Why family professionals can no longer ignore violence toward animals. *Family Relations, 49*, 87–95.

Francione, G. (2000). *Introduction to animal rights: Your child or the dog?* Philadelphia: Temple University Press.

Friedmann, E., Son, H., & Saleem, M. (2015). The human-animal bond: Health and wellness. In A. Fine (Ed.), *Handbook on animal-assisted therapy: Theoretical foundations and guidelines for practice* (4th ed., pp. 73–88). San Diego: Elsevier.

Friedmann, E., & Thomas, S. A. (1995). Pet ownership, social support, and one-year survival after acute myocardial infarction in the cardiac arrhythmia suppression trial (CAST). *American Journal of Cardiology, 76*, 1213–1217.

Fung, S. (2016). Canine assisted reading programs for children with special educational needs: Rationale and recommendations for the use of dogs in assisting learning. *Educational Review, 69*(4), 435–450.

Gee, N., Mueller, M., & Curl, A. (2017). Human-animal interaction and older adults: An overview. *Frontiers in Psychology, 8*, 1–7.

Glasser, C. L. (2011). Rational emotions: Animal rights theory, feminist critiques and activist insight. In C. Blazina, G. Boyra, & D. Shen-Miller (Eds.), *The psychology of the human–animal bond: A resource for clinicians and researchers* (pp. 307–319). New York: Springer.

Glenk, L. (2017). Current perspectives on therapy dog welfare in animal-assisted interventions. *Animals, 7*(2), 7.

Goodley, D., Lawthom, R., & Runswick Cole, K. (2014). Posthuman disability studies. *Subjectivity, 7*(4), 342–361.

Hanrahan, C. (2011). Challenging anthropocentricism in social work through ethics and spirituality: Lessons from studies in human-animal bonds. *Journal of Religion and Spirituality in Social Work: Social Thought, 30*(Special edition), 272–293.

Hanrahan, C. (2013). Social work and human animal bonds and benefits in health research: A provincial study. *Critical Social Work, 14*, 63–79.

Haraway, D. (2008). *When species meet*. Minneapolis: University of Minnesota Press.

Harm, N. (2005). Guest editorial. *Journal of Family Social Work, 9*(4), 1–10.

Hart, L. A. (2000). Understanding animal behavior, species, and temperament as applied to interactions with specific populations. In A. Fine (Ed.), *Handbook on animal-assisted therapy: Theoretical foundations of and guidelines for practice* (pp. 81–97). New York: Academic Press.

Hediger, K., Meisser, A., & Zinsstag, J. (2019). A One Health framework for animal-assisted interventions. *International Journal of Environmental Research and Public Health, 16*(4), 1–6.

Hoarding of Animals Research Consortium. (2010). Home page. Retrieved from http://vet.tufts.edu/hoarding/

Hodgson, K., Barton, L., Darling, M., Antao, V., Kim, F. A., & Monavvari, A. (2015). Pets' impact on your patients' health: Leveraging benefits and mitigating risk. *Journal of the American Board of Family Medicine, 28*, 526–534.

Hodgson, K., & Darling, M. (2011). Zooeyia: An essential component of "One Health." *The Canadian Veterinary Journal, 52*(2), 189–191.

Hoy-Gerlach, J., & Wehman, S. (2017). *Human-animal interactions: A social work guide*. Washington, DC: NASW Press.

Hugman, R., & Carter, J. (2016). Rethinking values and ethics in social work. London: Palgrave Macmillan Education.

Iannuzzi, D., & Rowan, A. (1991). Ethical issues in animal-assisted therapy programs. *Anthrozoös, 4*(3), 154–163.

International Association of Human-Animal Interaction Organizations. (n.d.). Meet our members. Retrieved on from http://iahaio.org/aaizoo-the-netherlands/

Irvine, L., & Cilia, L. (2016). More-than-human families: Pets, people, and practices in multispecies households. *Sociology Compass, 11*(2), e12455.

Jamieson, D. (2017). The Anthropocene: Love it or leave it. In U. K. Heise, J. Christensen, & M. Niemann (Eds.), *The Routledge Companion to the Environmental Humanities* (pp. 13–20). London & New York: Routledge.

Johnson, R., & Bibbo, J. (2015). Human-animal interaction in the aging boom. In A. Fine (Ed.), *Handbook on animal-assisted therapy: Theoretical foundations and guidelines for practice* (4th ed., pp. 249–260). San Diego: Elsevier.

Kirk, R. G. W., Pemberton, N., & Quick, T. (2019). Being well together? Promoting health and well-being through more than human collaboration and companionship. *Medical Humanities, 45*, 75–81.

Kruger, K., & Serpell, J. (2006). Animal-assisted interventions in mental health: Definitions and theoretical foundations. In A. Fine (Ed.), *Handbook on animal-assisted therapy: Theoretical foundations and guidelines for practice* (2nd ed., pp. 21–38). San Diego: Elsevier.

Labrecque, J., & Walsh, C. A, (2011). Homeless women's voices on incorporating companion animals into shelter services. *Anthrozoös, 24*(1), pp. 79–95.

Lee, D. (1984). Companion animals in institutions. In P. Arkow (Ed.), *Dynamic relationships in practice: Animals in the helping professions* (pp. 229–236). Alameda, CA: Latham Foundation.

Lem, M., Coe, J. B., Haley, D. B., Stone, E., & O'Grady, W. (2016). The protective association of pet ownership and depression among street-involved youth: A cross-sectional study. *Anthrozoös, 29*(1), 123–136.

Lenz Taguchi, H. (2010). *Going beyond the theory/practice divide in early childhood education: Introducing an intra-active pedagogy.* Abingdon, UK: Routledge.

Levinson, B. (1961). The dog as "co-therapist." Annual Meeting of the American Psychological Association, New York City.

Levinson, B. (1965). Pet psychotherapy: Use of household pets in the treatment of behavior disorder in childhood. *Psychological Reports, 17*, 695–698.

Levinson, B. (1969). *Pet-oriented child psychotherapy.* Springfield, IL: Charles C. Thomas.

Long, D., Long, J., & Kulkarni, S. (2007). Interpersonal violence and animals: Mandated cross-sector reporting. *Journal of Sociology and Social Welfare, 34*(3), 147–163.

Macauley, B. (2006). Animal-assisted therapy for persons with aphasia: A pilot study. *Journal of Rehabilitation Research and Development, 43*, 357–366.

MacNamara, M., & Moga, J. (2014). The place and consequence of animals in contemporary social work practice. In T. Ryan (Ed.), *Animals in social work: Why and how they matter* (pp. 151–166). Basingstoke, UK: Palgrave Macmillan.

Martinelli, D. (2008). Anthropocentrism as a social phenomenon: Semiotic and ethical implications. *Social Semiotics, 18*(1), 79–99.

Matchock, R. L. (2015). Pet ownership and physical health. *Current Opinion in Psychiatry, 28*, 386–392.

Matsuoka, A., & Sorenson, J. (2014). Social justice beyond human beings: Trans-species social justice. In T. Ryan (Ed.), *Animals in social work: Why and how they matter* (pp. 64–79). Basingstoke, UK: Palgrave Macmillan.

Matsuoka, A., & Sorenson, J. (Eds.). (2018). Critical animal-studies: Towards trans-species social justice. London & New York: Rowman and Littlefield.

Miller, S. C., Kennedy, C. C., DeVoe, D. C., Hickey, M., Nelson, T., & Kogan, L. (2009). An examination of changes in oxytocin levels in men and women before and after interaction with a bonded dog. *Anthrozoös, 22*, 31–42.

Moga, J. (2019). Integrating clients' animals in clinical practice: Insights from an animal-informed therapist. In L. Kogan & C. Blazina (Eds.), *Clinician's guide to treating companion animal issues: Addressing human-animal interaction* (pp. 253–266). San Diego: Academic Press.

Morley, C., & Fook, J. (2005). The importance of pet loss and some implications for services. *Mortality, 10*(2), 127–143.

Nibert, D. (2002). *Animal rights, human rights: Entanglements of oppression and liberation.* New York: Rowman and Littlefield.

Nibert, D. (2013). *Animal oppression and human violence.* New York: Columbia University Press.

Noske, B. (2008). Speciesism, anthropocentrism, and non-Western cultures. In C. Flynn (Ed.), *Social creatures: A human and animal studies reader* (pp. 77–87). New York: Lantern Books.

O'Callaghan, D., & Chandler, C. (2011). An exploratory study of animal-assisted interventions utilized by mental health professionals. *Journal of Creativity in Mental Health, 6,* 90–104.

Odendall, J., & Meintjes, R. (2003). Neurophysiological correlates of affiliative behavior between humans and dogs. *Veterinary Journal, 165*(3), 296–301.

Pet Partners. (n.d.). Who we are. Retrieved from https://petpartners.org/about-us/who-we-are/

Risley-Curtiss, C. (2010). Social work practitioners and the human-companion animal bond: A national study. *Social Work, 55*(1), 38–46.

Rock, M. (2013). Pet bylaws and posthumanist health promotion: A case study of urban policy. *Critical Public Health, 23*(2), 201–212.

Rock, M. J. (2017). Who or what is "the public" in critical public health? Reflections on posthumanism and anthropological engagements with One Health. *Critical Public Health, 27*(3), 314–324.

Rose, E. J., & Walton, R. (2018). Factors to actors: Implications of posthumanism for social justice work. In K. R. Moore & D. P. Richards (Eds.), *Posthuman praxis in technical communication* (pp. 91–118). New York & Abingdon, UK: Routledge.

Rossiter, A. (2001). Innocence lost and suspicion found: Do we educate for or against social work? *Critical Social Work, 2*(1). Retrieved from https://ojs.uwindsor.ca/index.php/csw/article/view/5628/4598

Ryan, T. (2011). *Animals and social work: A moral introduction.* Basingstoke, UK: Palgrave Macmillan.

Sable, P. (1995). Pets, attachment, and well-being across the life cycle. *Social Work, 40*(3), 334–341.

Sankoff, P., Black, V., & Sykes, K. (2015). *Canadian perspectives on animals and the law.* Toronto: Irwin Law.

Serpell, J. (1996). *In the company of animals: A study of animal-human relationships* (2nd ed.). New York: Cambridge University Press.

Serpell, J. (2010). Animal-assisted interventions in historical perspective. In A. Fine (Ed.), *Handbook on animal-assisted therapy: Theoretical foundations and guidelines for practice* (3rd ed., pp. 17–32). San Diego: Elsevier.

Shani, L. (2017). Animal-assisted dyadic therapy: A therapy model promoting development of the reflective function in the parent-child bond. *Clinical Child Psychology and Psychiatry, 22*(1), 46–58.

Shiloh, S., Sorek, G., & Terkel, J. (2003). Reduction of state-anxiety by petting animals in a controlled laboratory. *Anxiety, Stress and Coping, 16*(4), 387–395.

Sorenson, J. (2014). *Critical animal studies: Thinking the unthinkable.* Toronto: Canadian Scholars' Press.

Spiegel, M. (1997). *The dreaded comparison: Human and animal slavery* (2nd ed.). Philadelphia: New Society Publishers. (Original work published 1988)

Stanley, I., Conwell, Y., Bowen, C., & Van Orden, K. (2013). Pet ownership may attenuate loneliness among older adult primary care patients who live alone. *Aging in Mental Health, 18*(3), 394–399.

Strand, E., Poe, B., Lyall, S., Yorke, J., Nimer, J., Allen, E., & Nolen-Pratt, T. (2012). Veterinary social work practice. In C. Dulmus (Ed.), *Social work fields of practice: Historical trends, professional issues and future opportunities* (pp. 245–272). Hoboken, NJ: Wiley.

Stewart, L. A., Chang, C. Y., Parker, L. K., & Grubbs, N. (2016). *Animal-assisted therapy in counseling competencies.* Alexandria, VA: American Counseling Association, Animal-Assisted Therapy in Mental Health Interest Network.

Taylor, A. (2003). *Animals and ethics: An overview of the philosophical debate.* Peterborough, ON: Broadview Press.

Taylor, N., & Fraser, H. (2019). *Companion animals and domestic violence: Rescuing me, rescuing you.* London: Palgrave Macmillan.

Taylor, N., Fraser, H., Signal, T., & Prentice, K. (2016). Social work, animal-assisted therapies and ethical considerations: A programme example from central Queensland, Australia. *British Journal of Social Work, 46*, 135–152.

Tedeschi, P., Fitchett, J., & Molidor, C. E. (2005). The incorporation of animal-assisted interventions in social work education. *Journal of Family Social Work, 9*(4), 59–77.

Toohey, A. M., McCormack, G. R., Doyle-Baker, P. K., Adams, C. L., & Rock, M. J. (2013). Dog-walking and sense of community in neighborhoods: Implications for promoting regular physical activity in adults 50 years and older. *Health Place, 22*, 75–81.

Truth and Reconciliation Commission of Canada. (2015). *Canada's residential schools: Vol. 6. Reconciliation*. Montreal & Kingston: McGill-Queen's University Press. Retrieved from http://nctr.ca/assets/reports/Final%20Reports/Volume_6_Reconciliation_English_Web.pdf

Ulmer, J. B. (2017). Posthumanism as research methodology: Inquiry in the Anthropocene. *International Journal of Qualitative Studies in Education, 30*(9), 832–848.

Urichuk, L. J., & Anderson, D. (2003). *Improving mental health through animal-assisted therapy*. Edmonton, AB: Chimo Project.

Walsh, F. (2009a). Human-animal bonds I: The relational significance of companion animals. *Family Process, 48*(4), 462–480.

Walsh, F. (2009b). Human-animal bonds II: The role of pets in family systems and family therapy. *Family Process, 48*(4), 481–499.

Weil, K. (2010). A report on the animal turn. *Differences: A Journal of Feminist Cultural Studies, 21*(2), 1–23.

Wells, D. L. (2009). The effects of animals on human health and well-being. *Journal of Social Issues, 65*, 523–543.

Wolf, D. (2000). Social work and speciesism. *Social Work, 45*(1), 88–93.

Wolfe, C. (Ed.). (2003). *Zootologies: The question of the animal*. Minneapolis: University of Minnesota Press.

Wood, L., Martin, K., Christian, H., Nathan, A., Lauritsen, C., Houghton, S., … McCune, S. (2015). The pet factor: Companion animals as a conduit for getting to know people, friendship formation and social support. *PLOS ONE, 10*, 1–17.

Zilney, L. A., & Zilney, M. (2005). Reunification of child and animal welfare agencies: Cross-reporting of abuse in Wellington County, Ontario. *Child Welfare, 84*, 47–66.

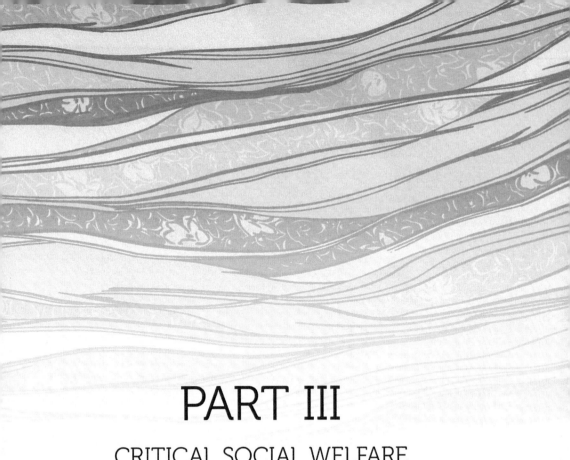

PART III

CRITICAL SOCIAL WELFARE
AND INSTITUTIONAL PRACTICES

CHAPTER 9

The Whole or Part? Postcolonial Theory versus Clinical Approaches to Marginalized Groups' Quest for Social Services

Ifeyinwa Mbakogu

INTRODUCTION

Recent social work literature focuses on decolonizing approaches for addressing mental health as a process that is aimed at inclusion of several currently underserved populations. This chapter explores a broader frame of reference to question if social work can engage in these decolonizing discussions without acknowledging its foundation of power and knowledge, which is not situated within ethnically diverse clients and professionals, who are confined to approaches that are rooted in Western ways of knowing in the postcolonial. This lack of acknowledgement of foundations of power and knowledge accentuates concerns of inequitable mental health service delivery, lack of culturally suitable services (Etowa, 2016), and lack of diversity training for health service providers to respond to the needs and help-seeking behaviours of ethnically diverse service users (Codjoe, 2001; Cooper, 2016; Etowa, 2016). This chapter explores how mental "illness" and treatment and the clients or objects of interventions are perceived and understood. I situate this chapter within a postcolonial analysis, while weaving in a case study, practice notes, and interventions with an actual client as a frame to interrogate the relevance and application of critical clinical social work. The discussions within this chapter address three key areas: (1) "power" and the nature and extent of social services, (2) service users' perceptions of the nature and manner of care provided and received, and (3) postcolonial theorizing and the voices and experiential knowledge of clients. I conclude by advocating for balance within the client-worker relationship.

As you read this chapter, ask yourself the following questions:

1. What informs and shapes how I view the ethnically diverse client in my clinical engagements?
2. What approach is sought by the client and what approach is favoured, provided, or made accessible to the client?
3. How do I make decisions about resources that are needed by the client?
4. Do the processes for arriving at this decision reinforce the client's knowledge and allow mutual learning and transformation?

POWER AND THE NATURE AND EXTENT OF SOCIAL SERVICES

What are the epistemological questions behind the dominant understandings of mental health problems and ways to work with people experiencing them? This chapter explores a case from the author's field placement that is relevant for students engaging in international social work and could serve as a reference point for interactions with other clients. The chapter and the case scenario do not make generalizations about situations affecting clients of African Descent and strategies for working with these clients. Indeed, every problem affecting a particular client should be treated and recognized on its own merits, rather than fitting all clients with "similar" attributes into the same box. The case study, and the discussions and interventions that are explored, provide a basis for social work students to interrogate their engagement with diverse clients and the contexts that inform the services that clients receive, while also questioning if clinical practice can reinforce social justice yet satisfy the health needs of clients. The case study of Mr. T, a young man diagnosed as schizophrenic, begins as follows:

A referral letter for an unkempt young man wandering within the premises of a university hospital was received by the social worker at the psychiatric unit. A member of the catering staff, Mrs. X, who had offered the man daily meals, clothing, and money, brought him to the psychiatric unit, where he was immediately admitted on humanitarian grounds. The young man, Mr. T, said that he was 28 years old and had attended a prominent academy for his elementary and high school education. He mentioned that he had enrolled in a social science program after graduating high school, but dropped out in his second year due to ill health. Mr. T maintained that he had always been healthy before attending university, but he was admitted to hospital twice before his second semester exams. Mr. T said that when he collapsed while sitting for an exam, his cousin, a student at the same university, carried him to the health centre. From there he was referred to two neuro-psychiatric hospitals. Mr. T added that he became an outpatient and occasionally collected drugs from the hospital. He said that five years later, he enrolled for evening classes at a different university to earn his degree.

Several notions shape this chapter; these include building the knowledge and assumptions that shape service providers' understanding of how help and care should be provided for the mentally ill client of African Descent; understanding if mental health problems should be seen to stand alone, apart from the individual within their holistic, individualistic, or collective interpretation of self and healing; and how power takes shape or form to be interpreted as either power that benefits the client or power over the client.

I will provide a simple description of mental "illness" before delving into the assumed help-seeking behaviour of clients of African Descent. According to the Canadian Mental Health Association (2019), mental "illness" is "a collection of disorders such as … bipolar disorder, depression, and anxiety. The symptoms can range from loss of motivation and energy, changed sleep patterns, extreme mood swings, disturbances in thought … or overwhelming obsessions or fears … often leading to social isolation." African clients often consult traditional healers to deal with mental health problems because of the perceived interaction of mental health problems with the supernatural, magic, and religious and/or spiritual beliefs. These beliefs guide clients' interpretations of the cause of their mental health problems, identified symptoms, and the treatment directions they will explore. These perceptions of the help-seeking pattern of African clients are informed by the media and literature (Benning, 2015; Corrigan, 2004) and erode the state of mental health in Africa in the postcolonial. They also undermine the state of clinical practice and the needs of clients that differ from the norm—that is, those who do not attribute mental health problems to primitive associations with misfortune, bewitchment, and sorcery (Burns, Jhazbhay, & Emsley, 2011; Cooper, 2016). Moreover, considering individual differences among clients, it is flawed to assume that irrespective of their social status, gender, religion, and educational background, clients of African Descent will share similar beliefs and help-seeking behaviours (Cooper, 2016). Since critical clinical practice is motivated by social justice and the attempt to understand why certain oppressive practices persist to enable social workers to design flexible and inclusive treatment approaches that are centred on the client, one may wonder how it is operationalized with ethnically diverse clients. Building within a limited frame for understanding the client, the interaction with Mr. T reinforces the critical clinical practice resolve to prioritize client's stories, histories, contexts, and approach to their mental health problems.

Mr. T said that his father is a 63-year-old owner of a thriving farm, while his mother is 50 years old and undergoing evangelical training. Mr. T mentioned that his parents are separated and that his father has remarried. Mr. T said that he is the second son in a family of three boys and one girl.

The problem that trailed the client, Mr. T, is not peculiar to this case. Those engaged in clinical practice are quick to be directional about what the client needs without giving attention to the "missing pieces" that inhibit the client's ability to be themselves away from the problem. We cannot aspire to critical clinical practice when power is exerted in directing clients toward long- and short-term goals that should be theirs to design, manage, and commit to for their own emancipation. Social action should originate from the client, be directed by the client using their own words and action plans for engaging with the worker. The client is the expert on their problem and course of action, while the worker is the learner.

Mr. T talked a lot about his family; however, he mentioned that he has lost touch with his parents but would like to return home. When asked, Mr. T said that everyone was kind to him in the psychiatric unit but could not understand what his problem was. Putting the client's interests and his right to self-determination first requires that the client articulate the path to self-care on their own. Mr. T articulated his main desire as returning home to his family; to achieve this required more meetings with me to understand the nature of his mental health problem. As a social worker who is invested in client advocacy, I articulated to my supervisor, Mr. F, the need to build the client's strength to allow him to stand on his own and, with that, consent was provided to work more closely with Mr. T.

The resolution was to "work with the client" to trace his relatives and gain insight into his mental health problem. Negative perceptions of clients, their way of life, knowledge, and care inhibit treatment and approaches to their problems. This is compounded in terrains where interventions are structured toward educating clients to understand causes, symptoms, and treatment of mental health within "more refined Western approaches." It is evident from this case that the client did not understand the nature of his mental health problem. Moreover, the majority of clients may be exploring other culturally appropriate resources, such as spiritual connections with family, friends, and neighbours to deal with health outcomes (Codjoe, 2001; Etowa, 2016; Mattis & Jagers, 2001). From conversations with Mr. T, it was discerned that family, and the strength it represents, provides huge support for healing.

WESTERN SUPREMACY

Western supremacy refers to Western approaches that pathologize non-Western traditions and fail to support client comfort or alignment with the diagnosis, care, or trust of professionals and interventions they provide. An evidence of Western supremacy is the use of the *Diagnostic and Statistical Manual of Mental Disorders* (DSM) as the standard for understanding mental health problems for people living in countries and encountering socio-economic circumstances that may differ from those informing the manual (Akomolafe, 2012).

Every approach has its appeal marked by its impact on client health. The manner in which the *Diagnostic and Statistical Manual of Mental Disorders* (DSM) is used and applied presents structural basis for clinical exclusion. One wonders whether there should be a single foundation for clinical knowledge and, building from this, knowledge sharing and understanding of patient care. Knowledge production that serves to help the clinical client of African Descent find a new lease on life should be structurally competent by recognizing policies, agency practices, and rules that marginalize the minority client within practices that are accepted and projected by the majority. Not much progress is made when care is provided using clinical language that excludes, confines, or forces certain clients to fit, thus creating power imbalances on a path that should lead to client wellness and empowerment.

PERCEPTION OF CARE FROM THE SERVICE USER'S PERSPECTIVE

Saraceno and colleagues (2007) engaged with international mental health professionals in selected low- and middle-income countries to ascertain the barriers for improving mental health services. Their findings indicate that respondents felt that advocacy for mental health is ineffective because of the invisibility of patients and their family members; large psychiatric institutions that isolate patients from family members who are their prime sources of care; and scarcity of mental health services. The findings encouraged training in the use of formal (trained professionals) and informal community mental health services that build from participatory action methods (Saraceno et al., 2007), while reinforcing the impact of social factors on client's mental health and well-being.

How do we incorporate social support–directed advocacy in our clinical engagement? It involves seeking those missing pieces that are ignored in hasty decisions made for the client by working hand-in-hand with the client to seek strategies that advance their well-being. With meetings that built on trust and mutual respect, Mr. T provided some missing information, including the following:

- *the address and telephone number of his family house*
- *the telephone number of the closest facility, patronized by his father and through which his father could be contacted*
- *the address of his father's farm*
- *his mother's maiden name*
- *his church pastor's name and residential address*

I began by checking the consistency of the addresses and telephone numbers provided. This was achieved by pretending daily that I had lost the addresses and telephone numbers. Each time, Mr. T quietly provided new and similar addresses. I followed up with some of these leads: some were dead ends, while others provided new insight for contacting Mr. T's relatives.

After discussing Mr. T's case with Mr. F and obtaining his consent, I began the visits that would likely reunite the family, but this process would have been impossible without validating the client's stories and giving him strength by checking in with him and receiving confirmation and direction before any action was taken.

I arrived at the farm and it was everything Mr. T had described. I met Mr. T's stepmother, Mrs. K, who told me that Mr. T had disappeared from home, causing his father unnecessary upset. I asked why Mr. K never came to visit his son in the hospital, since the owner of the facility patronized by her husband confirmed that Mr. T had telephoned relaying that information. Mrs. K replied that the message was never relayed to them; the last they heard of Mr. T was when her husband's friend in City J said Mr. T was a resident with his family. Mrs. K provided a chronicle of the psychiatric hospitals, churches, and specialists that Mr. K had consulted to find solutions to his son's problem. She said Mr. K was contemplating barring Mr. T from the farm. I cautioned against this move, which could aggravate Mr. T's problems.

Apart from their mental health diagnosis, the client who is institutionalized must deal with physical symptoms of avoidance, rejection, and even violence that are associated with their mental health problems (Wright, Gronfein, & Owens, 2000). These physical symptoms affect how they function emotionally and socially. Most times we deal with the internal symptoms of the problem but fail to attend to the stigma of diagnosis of mental "illness" especially with clients from racially diverse communities. Stigma can refer to things that set one apart from others (Bryne, 2000), with negative connotations that impact the affected person's social relations, interactions with others, societal adjustment, and well-being. Some clients conceal their mental health problem or treatment (Botha, Koen, & Niehaus, 2006), which means that they are inclined to poorer outcomes because their social networks (social, cultural and economic resources) are reduced due to secrecy and seclusion due to stigma.

STEREOTYPES

Stereotypes—"the belief that all members of a group are the same" (Bishop, 2002, p. 52)—are often judgmental and oppressive, and breed prejudice. Stereotypes of mentally ill patients originate from our environments, family, and media representations that shape our beliefs and values. With these stereotypes come the associated attributes—such as believing that all schizophrenic patients are violent, mad, unreasonable, or in need of sympathy. The stigma ascribed to one person, in a collective culture especially, is shared by all—immediate or extended family and the community.

Mrs. K complained that Mr. T was lazy, because he was not interested in working on the farm. Mr. T said he was more interested in completing his university education. In addition, while Mrs. K maintained that Mr. T was using drugs while in university, Mr. T denied using drugs, instead attributing his malady to a form of mental juju sent by some envious friends. Mrs. K provided contact details of Mr. T's close relatives and explained that Mr. T's mother does not own an automobile company as Mr. T claimed. Mrs. K maintained that Mr. T's passion for cars spurred such fantasies.

Understanding stigma and its associated markers is important for determining interventions for care management for clients. Stigmatization of the mentally ill is part of both Western and traditional cultures. To curtail stigma and ease client adjustment and reintegration, professionals advocate diversifying care within communities, or what Wright and colleagues (2000) refer to as "community mental health treatment," which reduces the effects of stigma resulting from a client's encounter with large state mental treatment hospitals. In addition, clinical services should deviate from the reinforcement of discrimination and stigma through asking questions that build on rigid foundations of the origin of mental health problems as either biological or psychological (Eisenberg, 1995), while eliminating other structural triggers in society (Corrigan, 2004). Diagnosis of mental "illness" presents a variety of consequences in some racially diverse communities that affect client, family, and community wellness. These include:

- contending with the cultural connotations of what a diagnosis of mental "illness" means;
- contending with the underlying beliefs around the status, associations, and treatment of people perceived as "mentally ill"; and
- Contending with the discrimination and marginalization faced by those considered "mentally ill."

The critical clinical perspective reinforces both questioning and moving beyond diagnosis to look at implications of the client's problem (especially in contexts where associations with "mental illness" are fraught with deficits rather than strengths) and accommodating both less pathologizing and more culturally sensitive and inclusive interventions that invite rather than discourage ethnically diverse clients to access mental health services.

Mr. T's younger brother, Mr. Y, said he was only 19 months at the time of his parent's separation. Besides, owing to several accusations, his father was reluctant to take him to meet his mother. Mr. Y said he is unable to assist with locating his mother. Nevertheless, Mr. Y suggested that his paternal uncle, Mr. U, could elucidate on the genesis of Mr. T's problem and plead with his father to pay Mr. T's hospital bills. Mr. Y accompanied me to Mr. U's office, but Mr. U was away on business.

Ideally, social work students are expected to move beyond the comfortable and safe to experience the uncomfortable (Boler & Zembylas, 2003) that is beyond their cultural and emotional boundaries. However, social work educators tend to eliminate conflict-provoking readings and topics in their classrooms in the hope of maintaining a comforting, stress-free environment that does not exist in real life. How do we prepare students for a beginning discussion of the uncomfortable issues that constitute the lives of their clients if we keep some voices and situations away from our classrooms? Situating this discussion within social justice is to engage in transforming the client to understand the nature of their problem and be an advocate for both self and others with similar problems. It is anticipated that professionals extend their role by motivating rather than asking, demanding, or directing clients to build social networks of friends and others that are often silenced by the secrecy and discrimination constituting service delivery that destabilize clients' self-esteem and well-being. It is important to understand the experiences of families with mental health problems and the services they are able to access and receive, particularly regarding the conflict between Western and traditional services.

Mr. U mentioned the numerous hospitals and spiritual homes visited by his brother, Mr. K, in search of solutions to Mr. T's problem. He regretted that his brother, though touched by our concern, was uninterested in visiting his son at the hospital or offsetting his hospital bills. When asked if Mr. T's mother could be encouraged to take responsibility for her son, Mr. U explained that she had remarried, had several children, and was finding it difficult to make ends meet. Mr. U said that Mr. T was a promising and loving young man. In fact, he was the closest to his father (among his siblings), constantly travelling to be with him on the farm. After his acceptance to university, he was always seen with a gang in the city. It was only after several hospital admissions that Mr. K confessed that to prevent his son (then a first-year student) from visiting home frequently, he had given him a large sum of money to keep in his bank account. Apparently, the young man associated with the wrong friends and began a habit of drug use. Mr. U said he would pressure Mr. K. to visit his son in hospital and give him another chance at treatment.

Critical clinical practice requires that our clients are recognized as people meriting understanding, attention, and occasionally, alternative patterns of care. Ensink and Robertson (1999) looked at the experiences of South African psychiatric patients and their family members. They reported that out of about 62 African patients included in their study, the majority (61 percent) had consulted Indigenous healers within 12 months of the study. Different help providers could be consulted—diviners or healers (herbalist or faith healers). Of the 42 patients that used Indigenous names to describe their ailment, a large number received a combination of Western and Indigenous services. Other clients' problems were a blend of psychosocial, religious, and Indigenous factors commonly associated with failure to engage in a ritual or affiliation with evil spirits or spells. Others who did not consult Indigenous services felt they were not needed or that they conflicted with their religious/Christian beliefs. Some who received psychiatric services considered them insufficient, as they were not provided with a name for their ailment—and even when diagnoses were provided, they revolved around "acute psychosis, organic syndromes, parasuicide or mood disorder" (Ensink & Robertson, 1999, p. 34). The clients complained that without a name for their ailment, they would be unable to seek further help or services elsewhere.

While it is crucial to understand how some clients of African Descent could interpret their mental health problems and who they are likely to consult for care and support, it is also important to know how practitioners explain clients' problems to them, and how clients describe themselves and their problems to others based on that client-worker interaction. Such feedback amplifies our understanding of the reach and benefit of different types of counselling encounters, especially with clients advocating for family-focused approaches to counselling (Ensink & Robertson, 1999). These can be integrated into mental health counselling plans for ethnically diverse groups, considering also that a large percentage of clients felt that their unemployment status and reliance on overstretched caretakers contributed to their mental health problems (Ensink & Robertson, 1999).

POSTCOLONIAL THEORIZING AND THE VOICES AND EXPERIENTIAL KNOWLEDGE OF CLIENTS

IDENTITIES

Recognition of the power of client identities is crucial to social work, as they determine the way individuals seeking social services are seen and problematized, and how discourses and ideologies take shape and the images we assign to those fitting within them. Essentially, when we focus on identities, we draw links to language, culture, and structural associations that determine who is "othered" and excluded, and who is "superior" and included.

In the field of mental health, little attention is given to how colonial legacies endure to influence how clients are categorized and provided with services, and who is excluded or included in the mapping of services (Joseph, 2015). The lack of attention to the history of mental health and its impact on clients further contributes to the silencing of mental health clients. For instance, *mad* is a term that has been used through history to denote those perceived as different or abnormal, as evidenced by their thoughts and behaviours (Porter, 1987). Mad is also a way of documenting the experiences and treatment of people fitting within this category. Foucault (1965) outlines developments across history that led to the construction of mad persons as people warranting confinement and seclusion because of the threat they pose to the socio-economic development of other "more rational" members of the society. In other words, it benefits society to keep them hidden away. Their difference justifies the violence meted out to them. This could also be society's way of keeping the mentally ill and their family members safe from the stigma associated with their diagnosis. Clinical practice is implicated by not promoting broader culturally sensitive models. The individual is usually set apart and blamed for their identified deficits, because psychiatry is not interested in changing society, but in changing the individual to fit into society.

Five months later, I received a message from the consultant handling Mr. T's case that my previous field supervisor, Mr. F, needed my assistance in locating Mr. T's father. Apparently, Mr. T had presented a cheque running into millions of naira with the forged signature of the university's president. He was arrested and handed over to the police. During interrogation, Mr. T claimed to be a medical student at the university's hospital. Upon ascertaining at the hospital that he was a patient in the psychiatric unit, the police officers handed him over to the medical social worker for immediate admission.

The restricted analysis of social problems and interventions reinforces the relevance of postcolonial theory. As Abrahamsen (2003, p. 190) argues, "the recognition of the relationship between power, discourse and political institutions and practices have cast new light on colonial and postcolonial experiences, that provide for more comprehensive understanding of how past and present relations of inequality are constructed and maintained." In discussions of postcolonial theory, a lot is mentioned about the "other," which Said (1978) describes as the Western way of maintaining some form of authority that is achieved by presenting an image of the person or society that is different from what they are or the way they would like to be portrayed. In other words, knowledge and power dwell with the Occident and are wielded in a way that reinforces Western authority. What then is African social work following interaction with Western colonization and professionalism? It appears that the interaction with Western social work stripped Africa of much of its traditional practices of care. Western social work demanded new form and shape that eroded the protective "collective" while centring on the individualistic. The interaction between the African and Western provided structures that were more organized, with personnel recruited and paid to coordinate care previously provided freely by families and communities, but the price was forfeiting the collective, communal, affective nature of that which existed previously. Through critical reflection, social workers are able to interrogate self, their values, and beliefs in relation to others.

During my chat with Mr. T, I found that his health had deteriorated. Mr. T was adamant that Mr. K was no longer his father but a guardian, whereas the Ooni of Ife, Bill Cosby, and Bill Clinton were his natural fathers. Mr. T said that only his mother could resolve the controversy over his biological father. Mr. T also accused several doctors with new cars, his consultant included, of looting his showroom. Mr. F had arranged for an ambulance to take him and Mr. T to the farm. But Mr. T had disappeared. Since Mr. F did not know the location of the farm, I had to accompany him.

To increase mental health care seeking, care patterns and attitudes of ethnic minority groups need to be accommodated. This requires understanding how the problem is recognized, care initiated, and treatment followed up (Corrigan, 2004) with interaction with those that impact the client's well-being. Further, we relate this to Africentricity that enjoins social workers to integrate approaches to healing that build from rich, collective, spiritual, holistic approaches that are embedded into familiar cultural interactions for the client, their family, and community because they enhance mutual learning and transformation (Bernard & Marsman, 2010; Schiele, 1997).

Mr. K adopted a hostile stance. He said he had spent a fortune on Mr. T and would provide receipts from places visited as evidence. He emphasized that he was unprepared to waste more money on a lazy, ambitionless young man who preferred aimless wandering to productive living. We explained to Mr. K. that the recent forgery case involving his son was a clear indication that Mr. T needed immediate help and that, since his arrest, the social welfare department had spent a lot of money on him and was ill equipped to pay more. But Mr. K. was emphatic that stealing was alien to his lineage and that thieves are burnt alive. Mr. K. apologized for his unfriendliness and promised to collect his son from the hospital the next day.

Several situations and circumstances jump out from the case study that could be simply words on paper, but have meaning for understanding the histories of structural stigma or trauma for both client and family. What does the client's mental health mean to the family? What does the arrest and accusation of forgery or stealing mean within their cultural interpretation? The family's interpretation is crucial to the therapeutic process and client health. Practice interactions should accommodate the cultural practices and beliefs that clients bring into the client-worker relationship. Following from the case study, students on international social work placements could have a different outlook on social issues affecting their clients. When working with clients from non-Western cultures, practitioners must be free of assumptions that build on Western models of practice that are adopted to interpret and confront problems facing their clients. Practitioners should recognize cultural imperialism (Gray & Fook, 2004), dominant pathologizing discourse, and inappropriate cultural interventions, and avoid professional imperialism when dealing with the mental health problems of clients, especially as there is no universal approach to these problems.

UNVEILING AND VIEWING THE CLINICAL SUBJECT

Critical social work perspectives stress attention to institutions, social structures, policies, practices, and processes (Mullaly & West, 2017) because social workers cannot aspire to find solutions to clients' problems without recognizing the context within which the client and their problems are located. Social workers must consider the following: What impedes or promotes positive outcomes, what was the nature of previous interventions, what should be the new focus, who should be included or excluded in engaging with the client? There should be shifts in social work practice with diverse clients to reflect how clients (not social workers) define their problems, how their problems are discussed in client-worker encounters, and how treatment is moderated.

Within the realm of clinical practice in postcolonial Africa, it is essential to ascertain the client's needs and the extent of their voice and contribution to interventions within the confusing narratives of the client as "expert." Is the client really the expert? The client is the expert when their voice is heard and their expressed needs used to direct resources that are shaped to provide the services they need and use, rather than those workers assume they need but were unable to express effectively (Swartz, 2005). The nature of our critical reflection assists in knowing if we consciously or unconsciously silence the client before the client-social worker encounter begins:

- How do you see your client?
- Who is the client?
- Who is the professional?

These are questions that the professional often ignores or feels they have attended to prior to, within, and after the encounter. Is it more important to close the file and move on or to invest in understanding the client and their histories, which inform care that allows the client to function on their own? The client's life may be a sequence of stories rooted in psychotic innuendoes of institutional treatment of clients and their situations without attention to the client's experiences of their mental health problems. The case study appears similar to several situations that may afflict institutional clients across social, economic, gender, and racial divides, because the client appeared to have limited voice in the nature of treatment received. Can Mr. T speak? Are we able to hear when Mr. T speaks? Or do we only hear what we think Mr. T should be saying that serves our own immediate or long-term treatment interests that align with our understanding of his mental health problem? How often do we speak for our clients, rather than allow them to speak for themselves? The reach of the worker's voice advances the power they command and the power of structures (services, resources, and policies) they represent. Our perception of our clients is evident in the way we write our case histories and the way we allow the voice of the client to filter through these records. Often, our notes project our own voices and perceptions of the client—we let our biases, opinions, and directions for the client walk into that initial insight. Our clinical practice encourages this process by allowing workers to hear only what they are trained to hear (Swartz, 2005). In most cases, this is the power to move clients from one point of despair to the next point of hope as only social workers appear able to do. That is not empowerment but a new form of dependency.

When clients command an audience, it is seen as oppositional and destabilizing of power, which again questions the role of the critical clinical framework. This framework advocates that social workers disrupt prior power imbalances that promote equitable service delivery rather than previous structures in which clients from ethnically diverse groups are perceived as unreal or as something to be interrogated and shaped in ways that produce people that can better function in society. In essence, the critical clinical framework within postcolonial theorizing should be an attempt to listen to those voices rendered silent because the realm of discourse is dominated by the elite, with inhibited access to those considered subordinate, inferior, or ordinary (Said, 1978; Spivak, 1988) by their positionality in society, and their mental health struggles.

VOICE

If we want the client to speak, then there should be an attempt to understand the client's "language." We cannot expect the clinical subject to speak about their experiences using the colonizer's language or the colonizer's understanding of their problems, symptoms, and diagnosis.

Language is essential in interpreting the settlement and adjustment of clients before, within, and after the clinical interaction. Clients of African Descent are not expected to function when their histories (especially approach to care) are rewritten to fit with the colonizer's views of self and path to health. If the clinical subject should be allowed to speak and direct interventions in ways that are transformative, then encounters should:

- be respectful;
- create room to hear, accommodate, and validate clients' experiences;
- be questioning of self and others;
- be flexible—allowing for adjustment and evaluations of relationships after each encounter;
- be open to education—since the client is the expert, the worker should be open to learn; and
- move beyond colonizer theories to those that promote the functioning of the culturally diverse client.

Our clients speak but we do not listen. When we imagine what our clients say or should be saying, we ultimately engage in inappropriate interventions.

Mr. K was at the psychiatric unit with a pile of receipts he claimed was Mr. T's only inheritance from him. He expressed a readiness to pick up his son, but Mr. T had absconded on notification of his father's arrival. Mr. F was unable to convince Mr. K to keep his son in the hospital for about a month and sought the assistance of Mr. T's consultant. The consultant explained that since the patient had been off medication for several months, he needed close monitoring and judicious treatment for at least one month. Mr. K reluctantly consented to his son's one-month hospital admission. Mr. T appeared to say goodbye after he was told that he would not be travelling to the farm with his father.

Clinicians also have the training to listen for information that satisfies and fits the mould—for example, separation anxiety and childhood trauma—while exploring different approaches to obtain information. Some approaches could be client centred. Allowing the client to share their stories as they come to them unfiltered, uninterrupted, and without inhibitions, while the professional provides direction, in a non-judgmental manner without room for otherness in politicized relationships (Swartz, 2005).

On a visit to the hospital during a major strike, it was gladdening that though some patients had been discharged, Mr. T was present and responding to therapy. His only complaints were boredom and an insatiable appetite, known side effects of his current medication.

Practitioners account for other lives and experiences that deviate from their own. It remains that those experiencing the problems should be allowed to present them. The client speaks, but their words could be erased from clinical records when they do not align with clinical training—subalterns speak to each other, and their experiences and encounters count within those spaces.

Advocating a Balance within the Client–Social Worker Relationship

Social work students sometimes engage in what are considered "heroic" statements of the reach of their role as potential social workers (Marston & McDonald, 2012); these often begin with how they found themselves in social work. Some claim that "they were those who always helped others." This claim gets somehow reinforced within educational programs where their interpretation of client wellness or adjustment is framed around achieving client "empowerment" within their perceived intervention. It is questionable if social work clients have achieved empowerment when there is a lingering sense of dependency on the worker. How then do we deconstruct social work to reimage these traditions to ensure that client's transformation is both contextual and transformative irrespective of the worker's lens (clinical, community, policy)? This thought is reinforced by Viruru (2005, p. 9) who maintains that postcolonial theory is not entirely concerned with exploring how previous colonial territories have fared after colonization; it also strives to adopt "an activist position, seeking social transformation" (p. 9). It requires an extension of the cultural competency lens to recognize that, depending on the client's problem, there should be a blend of structural competency with the individualistic nature of Eurocentric approaches—individual, organizational, policy, societal:

- Social workers should "truly" act in the interest of the client. Client's agency should be an inclusive part of the process, with their strengths identified and social workers vested in acting in their best interest.
- Social workers should address structures that impede progress in achieving clients' short- and long-term goals.
- To improve clients' standards of living, social workers must recognize the social, political and economic factors impeding on these and the role of social workers in ameliorating or compounding situations.
- Social workers must rejuvenate their role as policy-makers—currently a forgotten, ignored, or downgraded practice function.

CONCLUSION

Social work practice that operates within the clinical critical lens projects a respectful engagement with the client to unmask the voiced and unvoiced within a judicious and holistic approach that includes, rather than excludes, and respects, rather than undermines, the client and their family network. Since it is projected that mental health should be considered a public health priority, this implies that clinical care should include community training, understanding, and respect of the basic rights of clients (Saraceno et al., 2007). Advocacy should include research into strategies for improving mental health services in ways that are clear, informative, and focused.

REFERENCES

Abrahamsen, R. (2003). African studies and the postcolonial challenge. *African Affairs*, *102*(407), 189–210.

Akomolafe, A. (2012). Decolonizing the notion of mental illness and healing in Nigeria, West Africa. *Critical Psychology in Changing World*, 726–740.

Benning, T. (2005). Western psychiatry and traditional healing: Postcolonial perspectives. *International Journal of Psychosocial Rehabilitation*, *19*(2), 3–11.

Bernard, W., & Marsman, V. (2010). The Association of Black Social Workers (ABSW): A model of empowerment approach. In S. F. Hick, H. I. Peters, T. Corner, & T. London (Eds.), *Structural social work in action* (pp. 191–208). Toronto: Canadian Scholars' Press.

Bishop, A. (2002). *Becoming an ally: Breaking the cycle of oppression in people* (2nd ed.). Halifax: Fernwood.

Boler, M., & Zembylas, M. (2003). Discomforting truths: The emotional terrain of understanding difference. In P. Trifonas (Ed.), *Pedagogies of difference: Rethinking education for social justice* (pp. 115–138). New York: Routledge.

Botha, U. A., Koen, L., & Niehaus, D. J. (2006). Perceptions of a South African schizophrenia population with regards to community attitudes towards their illness. *Social Psychiatry and Psychiatric Epidemiology, 41*(8), 619–623.

Burns, J. K., Jhazbhay, K., & Emsley, R. A. (2011). Causal attributions, pathway to care and clinical features of first-episode psychosis: A South African perspective. *International Journal of Social Psychiatry, 57*(5), 538–545.

Byrne, P. (2000). Stigma of mental illness and ways of diminishing it. *Advances in Psychiatric Treatment, 6*(1), 65–72.

Canadian Mental Health Association: Toronto. (2019). Understanding mental illness. Retrieved from https://toronto.cmha.ca/understanding-mental-illness/

Codjoe, H. M. (2001). Fighting a "public enemy" of Black academic achievement: The persistence of racism and the schooling experiences of Black students in Canada. *Race Ethnicity and Education, 4*(4), 343–375.

Cooper, S. (2016). Research on help-seeking for mental illness in Africa: Dominant approaches and possible alternatives. *Transcultural Psychiatry, 53*(6), 696–718.

Corrigan, P. (2004). How stigma interferes with mental health care. *American Psychologist, 59*(7), 614.

Eisenberg, L. (1995). The social construction of the human brain. *American Journal of Psychiatry, 152*(11), 1563–1575.

Ensink, K., & Robertson, B. (1999). Patient and family experiences of psychiatric services and African Indigenous healers. *Transcultural Psychiatry, 36*(1), 23–43.

Etowa, J. (2016). Diversity, racism and eurocentric-normative practice in healthcare. *International Journal of Health Sciences and Research, 6*(1), 278–289.

Foucault, M. (1965). *Madness and civilization: A history of insanity in the age of reason.* New York: Pantheon Books.

Gray, M., & Fook, J. (2004). The quest for a universal social work: Some issues and implications. *Social Work Education, 23*(5), 625–644.

Joseph, A. (2015). The necessity of an attention to Eurocentrism and colonial technologies: An addition to critical mental health literature. *Disability and Society, 30*(7), 1021–1041.

Marston, G., & McDonald, C. (2012). Getting beyond "heroic agency" in conceptualising social workers as policy actors in the twenty-first century. *British Journal of Social Work, 42*(6), 1022–1038.

Mattis, J. S., & Jagers, R. J. (2001). A relational framework for the study of religiosity and spirituality in the lives of African Americans. *Journal of Community Psychology, 29*(5), 519–539.

Mullaly, R., & West, J. (2017). *Challenging oppression and confronting privilege: A critical approach to anti-oppressive and anti-privilege theory and practice.* New York: Oxford University Press.

Porter, R. (1987). A social history of madness: Stories of the insane. London: Weidenfeld and Nicolson.

Said, E. (1978). *Orientalism.* New York: Penguin.

Saraceno, B., van Ommeren, M., Batniji, R., Cohen, A., Gureje, O., Mahoney, J., … Underhill, C. (2007). Barriers to improvement of mental health services in low-income and middle-income countries. *The Lancet, 370*(9593), 1164–1174.

Schiele, J. H. (1997). The contour and meaning of Afrocentric social work. *Journal of Black Studies, 27*(6), 800–819.

Spivak, G. (1988). Can the subaltern speak? In C. Nelson & L. Grossberg (Eds.), *Marxism and the interpretation of culture* (pp. 271–313). Urbana: University of Illinois Press.

Swartz, S. (2005). Can the clinical subject speak? Some thoughts on subaltern psychology. *Theory and Psychology, 15*(4), 505–525.

Viruru, R. (2005). The impact of postcolonial theory on early childhood education. *Journal of Education, 35*, 7–29.

Wright, E., Gronfein, W., & Owens, T. (2000). Deinstitutionalization, social rejection, and the self-esteem of former mental patients. *Journal of Health and Social Behavior, 41*(1), 68–90.

CHAPTER 10

Critical Intercultural Communication and Practice: Applying Knowledge and Skills to Prevent Entry or Re-Entry of Children and Youth into State Care

Sara Torres, Monique Nutter, Donna-Mae Ford, Yvonne Chiu,
and Kathi Campbell

INTRODUCTION

In the highly contested field of child intervention, immigrant and refugee populations along with Indigenous Nations are calling on the child welfare system to enter into collaboration and negotiation to address their historical overrepresentation in child welfare settings and children and youth in care (Blackstock, 2010; Choate & Lindstrom, 2018; Este & Sao, 2018). Racism and systemic discrimination, poverty, and lack of intercultural understanding have been shown to be factors in this overrepresentation (Trocmé, Knoke, & Blackstock, 2004). Research indicates that children of African descent are at least five times as likely to become youth in care as other children. They exit foster care most frequently through adoption or "aging out" of the system, while white children exit most frequently through reunification with families (Ontario Association of Children's Aid Societies, 2015).

Many immigrant and refugee families experience high levels of stress and vulnerability, often resulting from pre-migration factors and post-migration conditions. Exposure to war, poverty, differing child-rearing practices, cultural distance from service providers, and challenges in navigating new social and cultural contexts potentially heighten the risk of child welfare involvement (Campbell, Nutter, Chiu, & Torres, 2018; LeBrun et al., 2016).

In this chapter, we discuss the collaboration and negotiation between cultural brokers and child welfare workers in supporting Mira and family's encounter with the child welfare system in Edmonton, Alberta. We discuss the multiple factors affecting the case: Mira's family cultural background, their pre- and post-migration history, the child welfare worker's knowledge of migration context, and the impact of social determinants of health. We provide a detailed description, and theoretical explanation, of how cultural brokers use critical clinical practice to negotiate between immigrant and refugee families and child welfare workers, and the openness of child welfare workers to participating in the process of preventing the entry or re-entry of children into provincial care. We illustrate, through Mira's experiences, the need to shift from a style of caring for children as vulnerable, isolated individuals (the forensic approach) toward a model of care that recognizes that families live in a web of relationships that have a fundamental impact on their well-being (the family and community–based approach).

As you read this chapter, ask yourself the following questions:

1. What is the children's services assessor doing to make the collaboration successful?
2. What is the cultural broker doing to make the collaboration successful?
3. What is the family doing to make the collaboration successful?
4. What are the individual, community, and systemic barriers and supports to social inclusion?

A CHALLENGING MIGRATION AND SOCIETAL CONTEXT

Currently in Alberta, 18 percent of individuals are foreign-born and 20 percent of Edmontonians are foreign-born. Statistics Canada projects that by 2036, one in two Albertans will either be immigrants or children of immigrants (Statistics Canada, 2016). As cities become more diverse, this creates intersections of culture, language, religion, gender, and racialization that expose rifts in understanding and perspectives (Schalge & Rudolph, 2007). In the context of addressing family violence, for example, the following factors have been identified as contributing to this "perspective gap": cultural distance from the dominant culture; cultural norms and expectations; geographic and social isolation; length of residency in the host country; loss of socio-economic status; loss of culture, family structures, and community leaders; power imbalances between partners and children; stress associated with migration; post-migration strain and stigma; strict or changing gender roles; traditional patriarchal beliefs; unresolved pre-migration trauma; victim/survivor immigration status; and intra- and external discrimination and racism (Maiter & Stalker, 2011; Yohani, 2013). Unfortunately, there is no data collected on the immigration status or ethnocultural background of victims of domestic violence by police or courts in Alberta.

FEAR OF REPORTING

Many immigrant and refugee women have unique risk factors related to their immigration status and policy that might deter them from reporting spousal violence. For example, women who are sponsored by a spouse/partner to come to Canada may face threats of having their sponsorship revoked if they do not "behave." This power over the woman is often used by abusive spouses to make the women stay in relationships, with women not knowing their rights (Canadian Council for Refugees, 2018). In actuality, if a sponsored spouse or partner is experiencing abuse or neglect by the sponsor or their family, they do not have to remain in that abusive situation (Government of Canada, 2017).

A CHALLENGING AND UNRESPONSIVE CHILD WELFARE CONTEXT

Research indicates that the fundamental shortcoming in child protection is "system misdesign" (Melton, 2009). The child welfare system came into being in the United States with a seminal publication on "battered child syndrome" in the 1960s, when the term *child abuse* also came into being. In Canada, the first child protection act was passed in Ontario in the 1890s; mandatory reporting came to Alberta in 1966 (Tonmyr, Mathews, Shields, Hovdestad, & Afifi, 2018). The hallmark of this system is mandatory reporting and investigation of cases of child maltreatment—in essence, case-finding. According to Melton (2009), a case-finding focus results in a system that is designed to answer the question "What happened?" not "What can we do to help?" Research indicates that it has become far easier to pick up the telephone to report one's neighbour for child abuse than it is for that neighbour to pick up the telephone and trigger help before the abuse happens. Vast resources are spent on law enforcement–style investigations by child protection workers. This is referred to as a "forensic approach" (Lonne, Parton, Thomson, & Harries, 2009).

While there is a place for a forensic approach, the vast majority of cases require supports to address social and economic problems (MacLaurin et al., 2013), cultural understanding of non-Eurocentric child-rearing practices (Choate & Lindstrom, 2018), and collaboration between the child welfare system and other community actors (Este & Sao, 2018). In the case of Indigenous children, a Eurocentric approach to child protection has been identified as a reason for overrepresentation in the system (Trocmé, Knoke, & Blackstock, 2004). For example, a report by the Black Community Action Network of Peel (2015) in Ontario identified eight key risk or causal factors that contribute to racial disproportionalities in child welfare: anti-black racism, racialized poverty, immigration stress, biased decision-making, agency-system factors, placement dynamics, policy impacts, and lack of culturally relevant services.

A Call for a Focus on Family Well-Being

Lonne and colleagues' (2009) seminal work, *Reforming Child Protection*, proposes a shift away from a forensic approach toward an approach centring on family well-being. The authors highlight the importance of working on the strengths and supports that families require for the well-being of their children and youth. This involves assessing the needs, strengths, and hopes of family members, including access to the social determinants of health. It also means focusing on prevention and addressing root causes and embedding programs within neighbourhoods and communities. Lonne and colleagues also foster a relationship-based practice and encourage partnerships with children and parents. This enhances family well-being and mitigating adverse circumstances, which are fundamental for the support of children (Choate & Lindstrom, 2018).

Alberta's Child Welfare System: The Beginning of a Change Process

In recent years, the child intervention system in Alberta has implemented some promising innovations, including the Child Intervention Practice Framework (CIPF). The CIPF came about through listening to front-line staff about new, innovative, and best practices in serving at-risk children, youth, and families (Government of Alberta, 2016). It provides guidance for the day-to-day decisions of front-line workers, ensuring that family strengths are recognized and all children and youth are respected, valued, and supported (Government of Alberta, 2016). The CIPF fosters critical practice by embedding "a family centered and strengths-based practice early into the assessment process through slowing down and critically thinking through decisions, involving parents as active partners and engaging extended family and natural supports early in the process of safety planning for children and youth" (ALIGN Association of Community Services, 2018, p. 1).

The framework acknowledges that Indigenous Peoples have always had their own ways of ensuring that vulnerable community members, including children, are safe, protected, and nurtured. The recognition of the Indigenous experience is crucial, given the fact that approximately 70 percent of children in care in Alberta come from Indigenous families (Government of Alberta, 2016). It reinforces collaboration between Children's Services in regions across the province and Delegated First Nations Agencies, starting at the assessment phase and continuing throughout the life of the file. Given the increasing number of immigrants and refugees coming to Alberta, and the complexity of issues lived by families, including family violence, collaboration with immigrant and refugee families involved with child welfare authorities calls for nuanced understanding of the relationship between child welfare workers and families within Alberta's legislative framework (Government of Alberta, 2016).

A COMMUNITY-DRIVEN CRITICAL CLINICAL PRACTICE

The Multicultural Health Brokers Co-op (MCHB) is the organization that recruits and trains cultural/liaison brokers. The MCHB is 20 years old and offers more than 10 programs to support families on multiple issues linked to the social determinants of health. Currently, there are 102 cultural/liaison brokers supporting more than 10,000 immigrant refugees in Edmonton. On average, 15,704 new immigrants settled in Edmonton annually between 2011 and 2016 (Statistics Canada, 2017).

Cultural brokers are often natural leaders from the same background of the communities with whom they work (Torres, 2013; Torres, Spitzer, Labonté, Amaratunga, & Andrew, 2013). Cultural brokering, a mid-range theory that comes from nursing and anthropology, is inherently intercultural. "Cultural brokering is the act of bridging, linking, or mediating between groups or persons" (Jezewski, 1995, p. 20) to reduce conflict or to produce change.

WHO IS A CULTURAL BROKER?

Cultural brokers share evolving knowledge and skills through fostering and facilitating critical intercultural communication with Children's Services workers and immigrant and refugee families in Canada. This critical intercultural negotiation and development of intercultural competence influence cultural brokers' and child welfare workers' ability to work from each other's strengths to prevent the entry or re-entry of children and youth into provincial care. Cultural brokers support Children's Services workers and immigrant and refugee families to stay connected even through conflict. They catalyze change at family, community, and system levels.

In 2003, via the doctoral studies of one of its members, and using a grounded theory approach, MCHB created its own multicultural health brokering theory to guide the organization's work (Ortiz, 2003). From its origins, MCHB's practice has been centred on developing equal and non-hierarchical relationships with families. In this relationship, it is assumed that the family (client) and worker (cultural broker) have knowledge, skills, and expertise that are valuable to achieving successful outcomes (MCHB, 2004). From the outset, cultural brokers seek to share control in the working relationship as a means of achieving "social justice, equity, and democracy" (MCHB, 2004, p. 16).

Interculturalism

Interculturalism informs cultural brokers' practice because it is a concept that encompasses macrosocial and microsocial policies and social relations (Bouchard, 2015). The macrosocial level embodies a concept or a general philosophy of ethnocultural relationships, expressed "in orientations, policies, and programs for which the government and major institutions of a society or nation are responsible" (Bouchard, 2015, p. 31). At this level, interculturalism encompasses social inequalities that immigrants and refugees experience in Canada owing to power differentials, discrimination, and racism (Bouchard, 2015). From a macrosocial perspective, the Government of Alberta CIPF (2016) exemplifies an approach that fosters interculturalism.

At a microsocial level, interculturalism informs cultural brokers' practice because they focus on "establishing ways of living with ethnocultural diversity in the daily functioning of public and private institutions (education, health, business, and the like) and in community life in general" (Bouchard, 2015, p. 31). From a microsocial perspective, cultural brokers foster the negotiation of ethnocultural differences and collaboration between immigrant and refugee families and child welfare workers.

The Third Space

Cultural brokers' theory-informed practice defines them as agents of change who intentionally place themselves in the "third space" or "middle space," a space that acknowledges and attempts to balance power to enable authentic conversation to stay connected even through conflict (Fishbane, 2001; Michie, 2014). Cultural brokers are sought for their unique location—that is, being "in the middle"/ negotiating between formal (authoritative) knowledge of child welfare systems and informal (experiential) knowledge of immigrant and refugee communities (MCHB, 2008c; Torres, 2013).

A Culturally Appropriate Collaborative Family-Intervention Model

This innovative collaborative model has been co-created over the past 16 years by the MCHB and Edmonton and Area Children's Services. The model places cultural/liaison brokers side by side in collaborative relationships with Children's Services, collaborative service delivery organizations, and families (Nutter, Chiu, & Ford, 2017). Cultural brokers are constantly negotiating with Children's Services workers, and many times feel they have to defend some immigrant or refugee communities' cultural practices and protocols (Torres, 2013). Children's Services workers (assessors) also identify regularly to managers their lack of knowledge on how to work with culturally diverse families and ask for support to help improve their practice (Campbell, 2017, personal communication).

The collaborative model comprises (1) the co-location (co-assignment) of cultural/liaison brokers in Children's Services Neighbourhood Centres across Edmonton with high numbers of immigrant and refugee families; (2) a joint casework protocol outlining clearly the responsibilities of all actors involved in the process, including families; (3) cross-staff training and support between MCHB brokers and Children's Services workers; and (4) referrals between agencies involved in the collaborative model (North East Neighbourhood Centre et al., 2016). Through a contractual relationship, Children's Services provides funding for a team of cultural/liaison brokers to be located on site at their offices to pursue intercultural practices, and for a portion of the holistic family support provided by a diverse group of brokers to prevent child intervention (Torres, Labonté, Spitzer, Andrew, & Amaratunga, 2014).

Children's Services finances the brokers' pre-intervention work with families. The MCHB supports families in the short and long term through project funding and is constantly looking for additional support to sustain its long-term involvement with families, which seeks to prevent their entry or re-entry into provincial care.

APPLYING KNOWLEDGE AND CRITICAL CLINICAL SKILLS TO SUPPORT MIRA AND HER FAMILY

The Report

One morning, Mira, a woman from South Asia, runs to a local temple with her two young children, seeking safety from a violent husband. After supporting Mira to make a report to the police, temple leaders engage an older couple who happened to be praying at the temple, and they agree to take Mira into their home. As there are children involved, the police report to Children's Services. The file is assigned as a one-day response to Megan, a child protection assessor. Megan invites Prita, the cultural broker co-located in the Children's Services office, to come along.

The Response

By recognizing that there may be cultural distance, linguistic barriers, and power and privilege differentials, and the cultural broker's complementary knowledge and skills, Megan is engaging in critical clinical practice and demonstrating cultural humility. An intercultural approach to family violence requires a negotiation that honours cultural perspectives of those most affected (interculturalism). The cultural broker supports the explicit articulation of these perspectives. At the same time, the Children's Services assessor articulates and upholds the standards set out in law (Government of Alberta, 2019). This requires reciprocity and mutual accommodation and being mindful of relations of power.

ENABLING PRACTICE STRATEGIES

Alberta's *Practice Strategies for Lifelong Connections* enables critical clinical practice. This document explicitly calls on workers to acknowledge the power that derives from their position, and the privilege that results from such things as ethnicity, gender, social class, language, and educational achievement. It also includes the clear statement that "relationship is the single most important factor in the capacity for healing and resilience" (Government of Alberta, 2018, p. 4).

The First Step: Securing Engagement

Before going out, Prita stresses to Megan the importance of calling the family that is hosting Mira and her children to prepare them for the impending visit. Choosing to share power and modify standard practice to respect cultural protocols and allow the broker to bridge cultural distance and power differentials, Megan agrees. Prita calls the couple (Sana and Amir), thanks them, and explains to them, in their first language, that the Children's Services team will be coming to their house. The couple is worried: "Will the police come too?" "Will we be in trouble because we have 'informal' renters living downstairs?" "Will our own grandchildren be safe?" Prita allays their fears, an important step in engaging and developing Mira's support system.

When the team arrives, Mira is in the bedroom crying and clinging to her young children (who are five years and two months old). She doesn't want to talk to anyone from Children's Services because she is so afraid of her children being apprehended. Repeatedly, Mira asks Prita, "Are you being honest with me?" Prita emphasizes that Mira can trust her and that she will be beside her through the process. Prita approaches Mira gently, talking with her in her first language. She explains the role of Children's Services in Canada and her role as a broker, reassuring Mira that the intention is not to take her children away. She explains that it is better for Mira to work co-operatively with Children's Services, and that they will work with her to make sure her children stay safe.

Social bonds between the broker, family, and host family allow trusting relationships that are important for effective practice to form quickly. This trust begins to bridge the relationship between Mira and Megan, and link this cultural, linguistic, and racialized minority family to equitable service provision. Explaining the role of Children's Services in the family's first language and allowing Mira and the host family to express themselves in their first language, while simultaneously providing cultural guidance to both sides, balances power and supports fuller agency on the part of the family. When Mira eventually comes out to meet Megan, she has become calm, but is still distrustful, answering only yes or no to questions. Normally the team would collect more information about Mira and the family she is staying with at this stage, but because trust is still so tenuous and Prita knows it will feel invasive, she suggests to Megan that they leave it until later. Megan, recognizing the hard work toward trust, agrees. Prita is consciously working to create the "third space"—a space in which one is able to have both clarity about one's own needs and desires, and a readiness for the relational ... a willingness to be moved by the other, to see and be seen, to stay connected even through conflict, to hear the other's narrative even while articulating one's own, and to negotiate differences without resorting to "power over" tactics. Readiness for the relational also entails relational accountability to the other, and an openness to being affected by the other's response. (Fishbane, 2001, p. 276)

The assessor is allowing herself to be affected by Mira's response. Megan says "no" to power over, by "slowing down" and modifying her approach. This allows Mira the space to come into relationship.

THREE TYPES OF SOCIAL CAPITAL

1. *Social bonds*: connections within groups—family, like-ethnic community, refugee community organizations.
2. *Social bridges*: connections between groups—friendliness of neighbours, shared activities, sports, worship, community groups.
3. *Social links*: connections between individuals and structures of the state—ensuring levels of access to government services in line with other residents (Ager & Strang, 2008).

The Assessment: Highlighting Relevant Cultural and Contextual Factors for Signs of Safety

Over the next week, Prita visits Mira daily, hearing her story and identifying factors related to immigration and culture that are of particular relevance to a comprehensive mapping. Prita understands the social marginalization experienced by immigrant and refugee families. Holistic assessment includes things beyond the mandate of Children's Services, and good assessment with migrant, immigrant, and refugee families must account for multiple layers, including pre-migration history, immigration pathway and status, and socio-economic, cultural community, and family context, as well as individual factors. The cultural broker provides complementary assessment-gathering information that addresses the whole family situation including the social determinants of health. This level of responsiveness to the whole person in their whole situation empowers the person to trust, open up, and be vulnerable after many traumatic and adverse experiences. Reflecting back, Mira states, "The thing I liked was that with [Prita] if I called her, she would respond right away—a response right away! And with my culture she was understanding my situation and not judging. She was like a big sister to me, who I trusted right away."

Enabling Framework
Alberta's Child Intervention Practice Framework (CIPF) articulates principles that enable critical clinical practice:

- Indigenous experience: Indigenous peoples have always had their own ways of ensuring that vulnerable members, including children, are safe, protected and nurtured. We honour this by recognizing their expertise in matters concerning their children, youth and families. [This method of approaching culturally distinct ways can easily be related to cultural minority families.]
- Preserve family: Children and youth should be safe, healthy and live with their families therefore we focus on ... building on the capacity of extended family and communities to support children, youth and families.
- Strengths-based: Our approach is reflective, culturally responsive and strengths-based.... We recognize and support the right and responsibility of parents to share in the decision-making process for them and their children.
- Connection: Children and youth are supported to maintain relationships that are important to them, be connected to their own culture, [and] practice their religious or spiritual beliefs.
- Collaboration: We are child-focused and family-centered. We collaborate with families, community agencies, and other stakeholders in building positive, respectful partnerships across integrated multidisciplinary teams and providing individualized, flexible and timely services to support these efforts.
- Continuous improvement: Our casework is transparent, and we share information appropriately.... We support innovative practice, evaluate our performance and strive for continuous improvement. (Government of Alberta, 2019)

Pre-Migration History
Because Mira's family was poor and her mother died when she was young, she entered her marriage with few assets and only a modest dowry. Because of her

relatively low status, she was ill treated by her in-laws in her home country, and, over the course of her marriage, there has been intermittent physical abuse. The couple has a third child, a girl now 10 years old, who was born in their country and is living with Mira's in-laws there. When Mira threatens to report her husband or leave, he threatens harm to their daughter. He has already left her off their application for permanent residence. Prita is able to understand where Mira is coming from and why she might not have reported the violence to the police earlier. Brokers understand the terrain of the home country as well as the landscape of cultural understandings in Canada, so can bridge the cultural distance between the family and the home country context and Children's Services workers with their expectations and standards.

Immigration Pathway and Status

Mira and her husband came from South Asia, via Europe, about six months ago on temporary work permits. Their employer has been unable to renew these. Prita knows this means the family has fallen into "non-status" with no health care, no Canada child benefit, no employment insurance, an inability to secure formal work, and an intense fear of being deported. She also knows, on the basis of her intimate knowledge of the culture and rural life in the country of origin, that should Mira return, her life and that of her daughter would be in danger. When Prita shares this information with Megan, she arranges emergency funding while Prita works with community members to help Mira find employment. Brokers have a nuanced understanding of the structural factors, such as immigration policies and statuses, that impact the situation and are able to share this with Children's Services workers. Thus, brokers are able to articulate the asymmetries of power between the dominant culture and marginalized populations. Despite her marginalized status, it is recognized that Mira has strengths (in line with the CIPF). She is frightened to work as she risks deportation, but is also not eligible for income support because she has no immigration status. Rather than leaving her in this Catch-22 (dilemma), Megan, Prita, and Mira work together to address the social determinants of health, sharing risks, resources, and rewards, a hallmark of authentic collaboration. Together, they accomplish things none could do on their own. This expectation of reciprocity, mutual sharing of gifts and assets, aligns with interculturalism.

Present Context of Family Challenges

Loss of status, unemployment issues, and social isolation seem to have contributed to Mira's husband's growing addiction issues (using both alcohol and cocaine). Any pre-existing family stability has been undermined and episodes of family violence have become more frequent and severe. Prita explains to Mira, in an accessible way, Canada's laws about family violence. At the same time, Prita recognizes and accepts that the temple leaders, in line with their values, feel it important to bring the couple together to attempt mediation. These attempts eventually pave the way for the temple leaders to support the couple to stay separated. Prita bridges cultural distance and helps Mira understand her rights in the new context. This balances power in gender relations and empowers Mira to have more agency in deciding how to move forward in the midst of community pressure and her husband's threats if she does not return to him. This bridging and balancing begins to mitigate some of the intersectional factors leading to Mira's extremely marginalized position.

Parenting Strengths
Having spent many hours with Mira and the children, Prita is able to report that she is consistently gentle, tender, and attentive to her children's needs. She has also reached the point of a firm commitment to remain separate from her husband for the sake of the children, despite his ongoing threats. Prita validates to the Children's Services assessor Mira's parenting skills, and the fact that Mira is learning about the law in Canada, how to get an emergency protection order (EPO), and the appropriate use of police and community. Brokers are able to identify strengths so crucial to Children's Services assessors' ability to implement CIPF. Mira is empowered to take an active role in providing and increasing safety for her children and herself. Prita is linking social capital with Mira to be able to benefit from formal systems.

Supportive Network through Ethnic Community
Although Mira has been very isolated, there is a great potential for the development of a network of support through the South Asian community, especially those members of her own ethnic community who live in the neighbourhood near the temple. That she has already reached out to them shows her trust. Prita also fosters the involvement of Mira within her own community. Social bonds (Staeheli, 2003) are an important element to build intrafamilial wellness, a key foundation for social inclusion. Social bonds provide a milieu in which to build competence and confidence to bridge with other communities (Enns, Kirova, & Connolly, 2013).

Addressing "Wonderings" of the Children's Services Team
Prita and Megan have worked together before and have a strong working relationship. Thus, Megan feels free to bring her "wonderings" to Prita: "How could this Mom [Mira] really not have known about 911?" "Why didn't she just call 911,

rather than running to the temple in the middle of winter?" Prita explains that Mira does not understand English, has not been in Canada very long, and that she has been very socially isolated, even within her own community. About family violence in South Asia she shares: "We don't call the police—it's the family or community [who we turn to]. And since [Mira] had no family here, she ran to the community [temple]." A broker is a cultural guide not only for families to understand the Canadian context, but also for workers to understand the multifold layers of the family's context. Megan also worries about the meaning of Mira's reserve and wonders if she could be concealing relevant family information. Prita explains that it's her distrust of Children's Services, fueled by stories circulating in the community, that leaves her guarded, and that a failure to open up does not necessarily imply she has anything to hide. In fact, in Mira's own view, she was being very open, "I felt like I could tell them anything because [Prita] was there. She [Prita] said, 'Yes … you go ahead and tell them your story.'" Together, Megan's questions and Prita's explanations allow Children's Services to understand Mira's perspectives; this curiosity and openness is a hallmark of cultural humility, and balances power rather than simply interpreting Mira's story through the dominant Western cultural lens. Another issue arose with Mira feeding her baby, Taj, porridge, even though he is only two months old. Culturally bridging, Prita talks about traditional feeding practices and how, especially in a time of crisis, Mira will want to nurture her children in culturally familiar ways. Megan and Prita agree that while a conversation about feeding practices is important, it is not the priority at this time. Prita points out the strengths of Mira's devotion to her children. Megan recognizes these strengths, shares power by engaging in intercultural negotiation to prioritize issues, and modifies standard practice.

Seamless Cultural Connections for Cultural Continuity and a Network of Sustainable Support

Because Mira initially feels scared and alone, she relies heavily on Prita to help her know who she can trust. Prita reflects, "It was like I was the middle person—to validate that this person [from the community] was okay—'you don't have to worry, you can trust them.'" Prita supports connection with community for housing and child care, and the temple for spiritual support and couples' mediation. Prita also connects with the school, which agrees to allow her older son, Abri, to remain enrolled even though he has no status. Community members brought culturally familiar food in times of stress. A community landlord provided transportation for Abri to and from school. A lawyer from the South Asian community supported her in completing immigration applications. Community members provided her with jobs and child care. Prita reflects,

> In every crisis, we found someone who helped deal with the crisis ... the temple, the community members, the hotel—yes [you could say] they took advantage, but at least they gave her a job.... The husband would follow her everywhere and harass her employers, threatening that he would tell on them. But then she would get work somewhere else in the community—everybody helped ... [At one stage] she worked seven days a week, 12 hours per day. The kids were raised by community members. She would leave when the kids were sleeping and come back when they were sleeping. But the community looked after them.

Edmonton's Domestic Abuse High Risk Team (DAHRT) social worker and police officer supported with safety planning, and, in light of the relentless threats from Mira's husband, with criminal charges, no contact orders, and eventual deportation of Mira's husband.

Prita's intimate working knowledge of South Asian communities in Edmonton allow her to act as a connector, so that she could help Mira develop a support network. Making and sustaining cultural and community connections was a key feature of this case throughout the child protection assessment phase (which lasted about two months) and later when the file was closed and handed back to MCHB. Prita worked with Mira on an ongoing basis for more than two years, developing and strengthening social bonds. Prita's ability to form supportive connections is enhanced by shared culture and being a well-respected and trusted member of the South Asian community. Prita also takes a critical approach to social links and builds equitable access by advocating with the school to ignore policies that would deny extremely vulnerable, marginalized children access to education. She further enables connection with the DAHRT team by providing linguistic and cultural interpretation, without which Mira could not benefit from the service. With this sustainable foundation for healing in place, Mira's own strength and resilience, her faith, cultural capital, aspiration for a better life, and commitment to the well-being of her children contribute immensely by enabling respectful acceptance of needed support from the people and institutions that stepped forward to offer it. Mira also works hard to provide for her children and follows through on every aspect of the plans she develops in collaboration with the broker, Children's Services worker, DAHRT team, and community members.

Consistent, Reliable Emotional Support Rooted in Shared Culture

Mira explained that Prita's accessibility and reliability helped to sustain her mental health in the many times of crisis: "Without her, I would have lost it!" Prita's sisterly attentiveness and cultural understanding allowed Mira a safe, non-judgmental space in which to release her fears and worries, regain perspective, and ultimately, follow through with the plans for safety. Prita likewise emphasized that the pace of change in Mira's life was rapid and very taxing: "She would have had a mental breakdown if not for a consistent presence in her life." The model of cultural brokering is rooted in holistic family support, which attends to physical, emotional, social, cultural, and spiritual support of the family. The shared culture and social bonds between broker and client allow Mira to articulate her hopes for herself and her children, to be understood, and to build ever greater agency in her own life.

Steps toward Social Inclusion: From Extreme Marginalization to Empowered Sense of Belonging

Mira now has a work permit, with an application for permanent residence pending. She has also applied to sponsor her daughter so that she can join her in Canada. Her husband has been deported, and Mira, Abri, and Taj are safe from immediate violence and harassment. Mira has a secure nine-to-five job and a driver's licence—she is able to provide for the basic needs of her children and to be at home with them in the evenings and on weekends. Mira's children have remained at home and within their cultural community through times of instability. At no point have they been separated from their culture, language, or religion. Mira feels safe, demonstrates good parenting skills, and appropriately reaches out for Prita and others in her community for support at critical life junctures. Abri has been able to remain at the same school throughout family upheaval. Taj is cared for by a community member while Mira works and will soon be in daycare. This family was only involved with Children's Services under assessment for two months and has had no subsequent involvement despite being in such a tenuous and vulnerable situation.

The collaboration between Children's Services and MCHB gives marginalized families a chance to connect with someone who will actively work toward their social inclusion. When contact was first made with Mira, her husband, and her children, they were experiencing social exclusion, which is marked by barriers to access, such as literacy and numeracy skills; availability of time;

scarcity of resources (such as affordable housing); proximity, remoteness, and the availability of transportation; financial considerations; health, wellness, and disability; social support; and stigma and discrimination (Westfall, 2011). Sadly, Mira's husband faced the ultimate in social exclusion: deportation. While cultural brokers normally work with the whole family, including both parents and all children, due to his active addictions and threats of violence, there were safety issues in connecting Mira's husband with a broker who is embedded in the community and could become a target of violence. Further, insufficient funding means there are not enough brokers to serve all the families encountering child protection who could benefit. However, exacerbating Mira's husband's social exclusion are also a lack of culturally safe/culturally relevant addiction treatment programs, a lack of services for men perpetrating domestic violence, and an even greater dearth of culturally relevant services for cultural minority men. While the temple leaders made attempts to counsel Mira's husband and mediate, they did not have the specialized skills to support him to address his addictions and abusive behaviours, and they could see nowhere to connect him for help. In contrast, while Mira still faces barriers of language and literacy, scarcity of financial resources, and stigma and discrimination, she has made progress toward social inclusion.

> A social inclusion framework focuses attention on the differential life experiences of all citizens within a community and in so doing, highlights the need to remove barriers to equal participation, free from discrimination. A socially inclusive society is thus one that develops the talents and capacities of all members, promotes inclusive participation in all walks of life, actively combats individual and systemic discrimination, and provides valued recognition to groups such as ethno-racial communities. (Scott, 2009, p. 29)

This case example really demonstrates the need to appreciate the cultural capital present in cultural minority communities, specifically in terms of their strong community relations, commitment to collective well-being, and spiritual support.

Social inclusion is also fundamentally about access and participation. In Mira's case, community members provided housing at reduced cost, as well as food, transportation, emotional support, protection, spiritual guidance and mediation, informal work opportunities—all of this was provided in the context of ongoing threats and pressure from Mira's husband. Without the holistic support the community was able to provide, Mira would not have had the foundation supporting her to achieve the greater access to nutritious food, suitable housing, essential material goods, and medical care (Westfall, 2011). Mira's experience of social inclusion also improved in terms of participatory activities such as formal employment, and her children's entitlements to education. However, she is still far from accessing other participatory activities including continuing education (e.g., English language learning), arts and cultural activities, sports and recreation, elections, consultations, and decision-making (Westfall, 2011).

Furthermore, the classroom her children enter may implicitly exclude them by not reflecting or appreciating their culture, which could contribute to alienating them from their home culture and possibly their mother in their desire to "fit in." Mira's work, although formal, is still at a minimum-wage level. While Mira and her family have come a long way, demonstrated many strengths and resilience, and established a sense of belonging within their own cultural minority community, which adds to their resilience and provides a foundation to bridge beyond, their journey to true social inclusion is still long and their path sure to be set with hurdles, systemic barriers, and structural violence.

CONCLUSION: A STARTING POINT FOR FURTHER WORK

In this chapter, we illustrated cultural brokers' and Children's Services workers' critical clinical practice in working with Mira and her family. By working with and through Mira's encounter with the child welfare system, we illustrated how cultural brokers use cultural humility, social bonds, signs of safety, cultural brokering, the third space, and interculturalism to negotiate between immigrant and refugee families and child welfare workers. Cultural brokers' critical clinical practice aligns with the call to move from a forensic approach toward a model focused on collaboration with communities and families (Este & Sao, 2018). Cultural brokers' practice resonates with the growing imperative in child welfare to embrace a critical analysis that acknowledges the multiple layers creating social, political, and economic marginalization. Their practice empowers women and mobilizes families and communities to address protective factors, enhancing their health and well-being. The collaborative model and the support by Alberta's CIPF, with its focus on family preservation, strengths, connection, and collaboration, are key in fostering healthy and strong relationships between communities and the child welfare system. The collaborative model holds a great deal of promise for actually bringing to life the principle of Indigenous experience and the related concept of multicultural experience. This model could be used to inform social work practice by developing culturally appropriate academic curricula and complementary culturally appropriate community training materials dealing with child welfare and marginalized populations. Other elements of such an approach would entail integrating culturally appropriate graduate and undergraduate student practicum supervision and privileging community engagement and intercultural social work practice.

REFERENCES

Ager, A., & Strang, A. (2008). Understanding integration: A conceptual framework. *Journal of Refugee Studies, 21*(2), 166–191.

ALIGN Association of Community Services. (2018). Practice strategies for lifelong connections. Retrieved from https://alignab.ca/caregiver-network-resources/ alberta-ps4llc-caregiver-information-package-2018/

Black Community Action Network of Peel. (2015). *Pathways and prevention of African Canadian disproportionalities and disparities in the child welfare system: A position paper.* Brampton, ON: Author. Retrieved from http://www.bcanpeel.com/wp-content/ uploads/2014/03/BCAN-Position-Paper_2015-12-08.pdf

Blackstock, C. (2010). The Canadian Human Rights Tribunal on First Nations child welfare: Why if Canada wins, equality and justice lose. *Children and Youth Services Review, 33*(2011), 187–194.

Bouchard, G. (2015). *Interculturalism: A view from Quebec.* Toronto: University of Toronto Press.

Campbell, K., Nutter, M., Chiu, Y., & Torres, S. (2018, October). *Child welfare involvement with immigrant and refugee populations collaborative service delivery with ministry and non-profit organizations.* Paper presented at the Future of Child Welfare in Canada: National Child Welfare Conference, Calgary.

Canadian Council for Refugees. (2018). Violence against newcomer women. Retrieved from https://ccrweb.ca/en/violence-against-women

Choate, P. W., & Lindstrom, G. (2018). Inappropriate application of parenting capacity assessment in the child protection system. In Dorothy Badry, H. M. Montgomery, D. Kikulwe, M. Bennet, & D. Fuchs (Eds.), *Imaging child welfare in the spirit of reconciliation: Voices from the Prairies* (pp. 94–115). Regina, SK: University of Regina Press.

Enns, R., Kirova, A., & Connolly, D. (2013). Examining bonding and bridging activities in the context of a common spaces approach to integration. *Canadian Ethnic Studies, 45*(3), 39–63.

Este, D., & Sao, C. (2018). A strained relationship: Southern Sudanese communities and child welfare systems in two urban centres in western Canada. In D. Badry, H. M. Montgomery, D. Kikulwe, M. Bennet, & D. Fuchs (Eds.), *Imaging child welfare in the spirit of reconciliation: Voices from the Prairies*. Regina, SK: University of Regina Press.

Fishbane, M. D. (2001). Relational narratives of the self. *Family Process, 40*(3), 273–291.

Government of Alberta. (2016). Introduction to signs of safety. Calgary: Author.

Government of Alberta. (2018). Practice strategies for lifelong connections. Edmonton: Author. Retrieved from https://alignab.ca/wp-content/uploads/2018/11/Practice-strategies-for-lifelong-connections-full-booklet.pdf

Government of Alberta. (2019). Child intervention practice framework. Retrieved from https://www.alberta.ca/child-intervention-practice-framework.aspx

Government of Canada. (2017). Notice: Government of Canada eliminates conditional permanent residence. Retrieved from https://www.canada.ca/en/immigration-refugees-citizenship/news/notices/elminating-conditional-pr.html

Jezewski, M. A. (1995). Evolution of a grounded theory. *Advances in Nursing Science, 17*(3), 14–30.

LeBrun, A., Hassan, G., Boivin, M., Fraser, S.-L., Dufour, S., & Lavergne, C. (2016). Review of child maltreatment in immigrant and refugee families. *Canadian Journal of Public Health, 106*(2), eS45–eS56.

Lonne, B., Parton, N., Thomson, J., & Harries, M. (2009). *Reforming child protection.* New York: Routledge.

MacLaurin, B., Trocmé, N., Fallon, B., Sinha, V., Feehan, R., Enns, R., … Budgell, D. (2013). *The Alberta incidence study of reported child abuse and neglect (AIS-2008): Major findings*. Calgary: University of Calgary. Retrieved from http://cwrp.ca/provincial-studies/alberta-incidence-study

Maiter, S., & Stalker, C. (2011). South Asian immigrants' experience of child protection services: Are we recognizing strengths and resilience? *Child and Family Social Work, 16*(2), 138–148.

Melton, G. (2009). Community program successful in preventing child abuse: Marks child abuse prevention month; Five questions for Gary Melton. Retrieved from https://www.apa.org/news/press/releases/2009/04/melton.aspx

Michie, M. (2014). *Working cross-culturally: Identity learning, border crossing and culture brokering.* Rotterdam, Netherlands: Sense Publishers.

Multicultural Health Brokers Co-op. (2004). *Draft competency framework for the multicultural health brokering practice.* Edmonton: Author.

Multicultural Health Brokers Co-op. (2008). *Enhancing community capacity to engage and involve immigrant and refugee families: A model for inclusive collaboration.* Unpublished project report.

North East Neighbourhood Centre, Edmonton Region Child and Family Services, Multicultural Health Brokers, Ubuntu Children and Families, & Delivery, C. S. (2016). *Joint casework protocol: Overview*. Edmonton: Multicultural Health Brokers Co-op.

Nutter, M., Chiu, Y., & Ford, D. M. (2017). *Multicultural Health Brokers Co-operative (MCHB): Submission to Child Intervention Panel*. Edmonton: Multicultural Health Brokers Co-op.

Ontario Association of Children's Aid Societies. (2015). *Race matters in the child welfare system*. Retrieved from http://www.oacas.org/wp-content/uploads/2015/09/Race-Matters-African-Canadians-Project-August-2015.pdf

Ortiz, L. M. (2003). *Multicultural health brokering: Bridging cultures to achieve equity of access to health*. Unpublished doctoral dissertation, University of Alberta, Edmonton.

Schalge, S. L., & Rudolph, C. E. (2007). Race as cultural construction, race as social reality, mothering for contradictions and ambiguities. *Journal of the Association for Research on Mothering, 9*(2), 9–19.

Scott, K. (2009). *Community vitality: A report of the Canadian Index of Wellbeing*. Canadian Ottawa: Council on Social Development.

Staeheli, L. A. (2003). Women and the work of community. *Environment and Planning, 35*, 815–831.

Statistics Canada. (2016). *Immigration and ethnocultural diversity in Canada: Census program*. Statistics Canada Catalogue no. 99-010-X2011001. Retrieved from https://www12.statcan.gc.ca/nhs-enm/2011/as-sa/99-010-x/99-010-x2011001-eng.cfm

Statistics Canada. (2017). Table 1: Geographic distribution of immigrants and recent immigrants and their proportion within the population of census metropolitan areas, Canada, 2016. *The Daily*. Retrieved from https://www150.statcan.gc.ca/n1/daily-quotidien/171025/t001b-eng.htm

Tonmyr, L., Mathews, B., Shields, M. E., Hovdestad, W. E., & Afifi, T. O. (2018). Does mandatory reporting legislation increase contact with child protection? A legal doctrinal review and an analytical examination. *BMC Public Health, 18*(1021). doi:10.1186/s12889-018-5864-0.

Torres, S. (2013). *Uncovering the role of community health worker/lay health worker programs in addressing health equity for immigrant and refugee women in Canada: An instrumental and embedded qualitative case study*. Doctoral thesis, University of Ottawa.

Torres, S., Labonté, R., Spitzer, D. L., Andrew, C., & Amaratunga, C. (2014). Improving health equity: The promising role of community health workers in Canada. *Healthcare Policy, 10*(1), 71–83.

Torres, S., Spitzer, D. L., Labonté, R., Amaratunga, C., & Andrew, C. (2013). Community health workers in Canada: Innovative approaches to health promotion outreach and community development among immigrant and refugee populations. *Journal of Ambulatory Care Management, 36*(4), 305–318.

Trocmé, N., Knoke, D., & Blackstock, C. (2004). Pathways to the overrepresentation of Aboriginal children in Canada's child welfare system. *Social Service Review, 78*(4), 577–600.

Westfall, R. (2011). *Dimensions of social inclusion and exclusion in Yukon, 2010.* Whitehorse, YT: Department of Health and Social Services, Bureau of Statistics.

Yohani, S. (2013). Educational cultural brokers and the school adaptation of refugee children and families: Challenges and opportunities. *International Migration and Integration, 14*, 61–79.

CHAPTER 11

Epistemic (In)Justice in Child Welfare Risk Assessment

Marjorie Johnstone

INTRODUCTION

In 2008, Family Youth and Child Services of Muskoka (Ontario, Canada) removed Tammy Whiteman's two daughters from her home. This was done on the grounds that they had serious concerns about the safety and well-being of the children due to the mental health and child-rearing ability of their sole parent, Tammy. Hair-strand drug testing performed by Motherisk hair lab in Toronto's SickKids Lab, had produced results indicating that Tammy was using large amounts of alcohol. Her protestations that this was incorrect went unheard and she was told she was in denial and must attend counselling. Several years later, after continuing tests "proved" that she was still using alcohol in excess, and as her children continued to reside in foster care placements, she and her lawyer set up a house arrest monitor with technology that could measure alcohol use and after 90 days she had the drug hair-strand test completed again. This resulted in another finding of heavy alcohol use. When the lawyer challenged this test result (with the powerful counter-evidence from an alternative monitoring technology that showed she had consumed no alcohol during the 90-day period), it was then discovered that the test was actually measuring the alcohol content in her hairspray. Tammy said, "I was shocked. I cried for the first couple seconds and then thought, 'Why am I crying?' This is a good thing, this is actually proving to people that I wasn't wrong, that I wasn't incorrect and … and I wasn't lying." (In this declaration Tammy clearly articulates the injury and the pain caused by being disbelieved and not listened to.) This type of test was being used by child welfare agencies in child protection cases in five provinces in Canada. It was regarded as scientific evidence of substance abuse and was a pivotal factor in numerous child removal decisions (Mayor, 2017).

Critical philosopher Miranda Fricker (2007) contributes some useful concepts for considering power, inequity, and injustice in human interactions. She postulates that "epistemic injustice" is a fundamental wrong done to someone specifically in their capacity as a knower/subject of knowledge. Adams, Dominelli, and Payne (2009) suggest that critical social work practice involves upholding the view of vulnerable people who are often unheard and then considering more than one approach to a person's problem. They stress the importance of reflecting critically "on different perspectives and options before deciding on 'best practice'" (p. 3). A critical clinical approach to social work practice guards against essentialism, subjectivism, and the reification of dominant discourses by using therapeutic approaches that focus on respecting the uniqueness of individual lives and the constraints of dominant social ideas and structural inequities (C. Brown, 2017; Mullaly, 2010). I suggest that we can mobilize Fricker's concepts as a way to critically reconsider the child protection assessment process and explore how we can enrich and enhance our practice by incorporating the clinical implications of Fricker's work into our practice. By honouring human dignity and worth while we work collaboratively with vulnerable families, we can be guided by the principles of epistemic justice, and work toward achieving a more successful balance between identifying risk and protecting family integrity.

EPISTEMIC INJUSTICE

Epistemic injustice accompanies oppression. It has different forms, but they all involve a fundamental wrong done to someone in their capacity as a knower. It could involve unequal access to knowledge practices, damaged credibility in testimonial interactions (i.e., not being believed because you are assumed to be an unreliable informant—because you are, for example, a convicted criminal or have been diagnosed with a mental illness), or hermeneutic marginalization (i.e., not being understood as there is no previous conceptualization of your experience). Fricker (2007) says that when epistemic injustice occurs there is a double injury—the subject is not only degraded as a knower, but the person is also degraded as a human being. Thus, openness to differences— both your own differences as well as the differences of others—is key to being epistemically responsible (Fricker, 2007; Medina, 2013).

I began with a case example that I will discuss throughout the chapter. I then briefly explore current practices in child welfare risk assessment, before describing the work of Miranda Fricker on epistemic justice. For the remainder of the chapter, I discuss in detail how the principles of epistemic justice can be applied to our child welfare clinical practice to ensure that all voices of the family are heard and that we provide a just and equitable service that supports families and children.

As you read this chapter, ask yourself the following questions:

1. How do child protection service workers commonly complete their assessments? How do they make decisions?
2. What are the primary responsibilities of child protection workers?
3. Are there other ways we can do this work that might mitigate the kind of injury that Tammy Whiteman and her family have suffered?
4. How can we ensure that the voices of families, including children, are incorporated into the child protection assessment process?
5. How do we use a critical clinical approach to social work practice by including the principles of epistemic justice into the process?

LOCATING CANADIAN APPROACHES TO CHILD WELFARE RISK ASSESSMENT

Approaches to child welfare assessment are influenced by competing epistemological positions. Science, scientific method, and knowledge generated through science are central to modernity. The belief is that good science reveals the laws of nature, and the findings of science (knowledge resulting from a rigorous application of scientific methods) represent objective reality and truth. A critical postmodern approach questions this idea that reality is fixed, stable, unchanging, and therefore predictable, universal, and inevitable. Postmodernists posit that things are always changing, and there are multiple realities, multiple stories, and multiple ways of seeing the world. This competing epistemological position suggests that what we know is constructed by us, and this fundamental epistemological difference changes the way we think practice should be done.

An example of practice that grows out of a positivist (modern) epistemology and scientific method is evidence-based practice. This is practice that is based on research and empirical evidence, where current best evidence is built into practice decision-making (Gibbs, 2003). In the 1980s in the field of child welfare, this resulted in the development of risk assessment measures that are empirically based predictors of events or dysfunction and were designed to make the decision-making process in child protection cases "scientific," standardized, and efficient (Leshied, Chiodo, Whitehead, & Marshall, 2003). In the 1990s, risk assessments were widely used to try to increase the match between the intervention and the individual's need, but the results were not encouraging. As a result, scholarship on risk assessment shifted from the risk prediction tool to considering the decision-making ecology that surrounds the use of the assessment tool. Current child welfare evidence-based scholarship has begun using an ecological framework that examines case factors, organizational factors, external factors, and decision-making factors. There is a recognition that risk assessment as a singular focus does not engage the broader objectives of child protection (such as the well-being of the child and permanence in their lives) and may even serve to increase out-of-home placements, as when risk is identified, the organization itself is "at risk" if it fails to act (Shlonsky & Mildon, 2017).

ECOLOGICAL FRAMEWORK

An ecological framework combines general systems theory with an ecological viewpoint that is centred on the environment. This approach argues that connections between the person and the environment are complex and non-linear. The goal of this approach is to promote adaptation between the person and their environment, and to recognize that this is complex and multi-faceted. Application of this theory has not been developed through empirical research, and a focus on function and exchange can leave out questions of structural justice and power imbalance. For example, family systems approaches were critiqued by feminists because they relied on the exploitation of women's labour, but this injustice was not recognized within the systems analysis, which only acknowledged the role of women's labour (Healy, 2014).

In a critique of the risk assessment approach to child protection, critical social work scholars Swift and Callahan (2009) observe that the professional literature often presents risk as a very real thing that can be observed, measured, identified, and managed. They express concern that this reification of risk can result in child protection workers viewing identified risk as something static, fixed, and "real" that must then be "fixed," rather than viewing a reported family configuration as an identified point in time that can be changed to lower or manage risk. They express concern that clients labelled as "at risk" can then internalize their risk status as fixed and their identity as risky. In addition, this assessment label remains on file, so even if the circumstances in the subject's life change dramatically, this rating will not change. For a family/child that has once been assessed as "at risk," this itself becomes a risk factor if further assessment is completed. It appears that this is what happened in the Tammy Whiteman case, where the results of a "scientific" test overrode all other assessment tools—the Whiteman family was judged to be "at risk" and the children were removed, and further review of the case continued to be based on the Motherisk lab tests.

The media is a seminal actor in child welfare procedures. When workers are vilified by the media, public confidence deteriorates, and this in turn further increases the strain on child protection workers. Child deaths are the subject of widespread media coverage and mobilize strong public opinions, and child death review recommendations influence policy and legislation. Peter Choate, an assistant professor of social work at Mount Royal University, has an extensive history of assessment practice in child welfare and has appeared as an expert witness in child protection matters in provincial courts in Calgary, Red Deer, and Edmonton over 150 times. Choate (2016) conducted a review of 91 child protection reports and used grounded theory methods to identify themes within them. He noted that the reports did not dig into the data to identify systemic factors that might be associated with these tragedies. He described blame-focused or deficit-focused inquiries, which identified the child protection worker as at fault. He noted that the reports failed to consider the toll that this difficult and complex work has on workers and to document structural factors such as high caseloads, high turnover, challenging caseloads, and inadequate supervision. The practice outcomes of these deficit-focused enquiries include workers leaving this area of practice and increases in the number of children placed in care, as workers act in the direction of caution. Choate also identified some practice errors that appeared repeatedly in the inquiry reports: poor co-operation and communication between systems serving children; weak assessments in which the credibility of data is unquestioned and there is an absence of child perspective; and a repeated identification of inadequate child protection services for Indigenous children.

The tasks confronting child protection workers are complex and challenging and place them in forensic and authority-based roles. At times the work is investigative and involves policing parents, removing children from their homes, and working against the wishes of the parents. However, after years of child protection work experience, Dumbrill (2011) points out that most investigations are less dramatic and that the primary work is engaging families in a process of protective change. He outlines an anti-oppressive approach to child protection work that is relationship based, emphasizing the central importance of working on building an alliance and common ground between the worker and the family and approaching each case as unique and individual. In using this approach, Dumbrill avoids essentializing the problem and works collaboratively with the family toward building a safe and improved parenting configuration.

A THEORETICAL FRAMEWORK: EPISTEMIC JUSTICE

Critical philosopher Miranda Fricker (2007) pursues the idea that there is a distinctly epistemic form of injustice. By this term she does not mean the unfair distribution of epistemic goods such as information or access to education; rather she is referring to a wrong done to another in their capacity as a knower. She has developed a conceptual framework of two main types of epistemic injustice—*testimonial injustice* when prejudice prevents a hearer from believing or listening attentively to what is being said (e.g., a known drug addict claims sobriety), and *hermeneutic injustice* where there is a gap in collective interpretive resources so that someone is denied the opportunity to make sense of their social experience (e.g., someone suffering from post-traumatic stress disorder before the syndrome has been identified). In the Tammy Whiteman case, testimonial injustice is clearly at play. Tammy was known to the child protection workers to have a history of substance misuse and, furthermore, a "scientific" test seemed to support this, so it appears she was not listened to attentively. She was known to have used drugs in the past, so her "identity" reduced her credibility. Testimonial injustice often occurs because of this kind of prejudice in interpersonal interactions.

Each of these forms of epistemic injustice has ethical implications and is related to social power. It is often social marginalization that results in being at an epistemic disadvantage; Fricker points out that in the Anglo-American tradition, it is feminist epistemology that has highlighted this point very effectively. Fricker (2007, p. 9) defines social power as "a capacity we have as social agents to influence how things go in the social world." A subset of this is *identity power*—this is the power that derives from a shared imagined conception of a social identity and it can be exercised passively or actively. For example, if you are a child protection worker, then your passive presence in a family home might be sufficient to silence conversation and if you comment on what might be considered a good parenting practice, this observation will have greater power in the interaction than if a neighbour made the same comment. Identity power usually operates in conjunction with other forms of social power such as class, gender, race, ability, and age. This then creates *identity prejudice*, which is the social identity that follows a subject through different dimensions of social activity—economic, educational, professional, sexual, legal, political, religious, and so on. While this can be both positive and negative, "the central case of testimonial injustice is ... a credibility deficit owing to identity prejudice in the hearer—so the central case of testimonial injustice is *identity-prejudicial credibility deficit*" (Fricker, 2007, p. 28; italics in original). What this means is that if you have a social identity that is negatively valanced (e.g., drug addict, criminal, bad parent, welfare client, sex worker, racialized person, woman), then your testimony may have decreased social power (credibility). We know that Tammy Whiteman was judged by the identity prejudice of "addict," and it is likely that some other accompanying social identities, such as bad parent, welfare client, single mother, were also present during her interactions with child protection services.

Fricker elaborates on the harm done when this testimonial injustice occurs both in a one-to-one context and as a structural phenomenon. She identifies rationality as the core function that lends humanity its distinctive value, and so she comments that "no wonder that the powerful will be sure to undermine the powerless in just that capacity, for it provides a direct route to undermine them in their very humanity" (2007, p. 44). Thus, when epistemic injustice occurs there is a double injury—the subject is not only degraded as a knower, but the person is also degraded as a human being. If this attack on intellectual confidence is sustained over time as in the case of structural identity-prejudice, where a prejudice is pervasive throughout an institution (e.g., racism in the police/correctional or education system or sexism in public attitudes toward sex workers), then the credibility deficit can have long-lasting effects and "genuinely inhibit the development essential aspect of a person's identity" (Fricker, 2007, p. 54). This sustained personal injury is powerfully described by Lynda Thomas (2015) in her account of growing up as a Black child in Halifax, surrounded by white people. She describes ongoing experiences of racism and exclusion, particularly in the school system in the 1960s and yet, despite this, she highly valued education. As a mature student in the 1980s she attended Dalhousie University to complete a social work degree. At the time, Lynda was the only Black student in the classroom and on an ongoing basis she experienced professors assuming that she wouldn't understand and paradoxically expecting her to be an authority on Black issues and to speak on behalf of the Black community. She describes her experience during a field placement: "I felt my faculty field advisor talked to me in a way that was very disrespectful. I found that she didn't value my experience, didn't even respect that I had the ability to lay out my own learning objectives" (2015, p. 128). This is a good example of structural identity-prejudice: Lynda was assumed to not have any worthy knowledge of her own or to have the competence to manage her own learning. Iris Marion Young (1992, p. 58) describes this form of oppression as "the disadvantage and injustice some people suffer not because a tyrannical power intends to keep them down, but because of the everyday practices of a well-intentioned liberal society." Fricker (2007, p. 54) also notes that "somebody subject to this sort of injustice may not have the sort of community in which to find resources for resistance, since the formation of such a community is itself a social achievement and not a social given."

HERMENEUTICS

Hermeneutics means a theory of interpretation. This is a conceptual way of trying to make sense of the world. It is the study of experience—we reflect, we try to make sense of what happened, and we develop a language to describe it. Until this has been achieved, there is what Fricker calls a "hermeneutic gap." This means that there is no epistemology developed to explain something and there is no special vocabulary to describe the concepts. Fricker gives the example of sexual harassment. Until this was identified by feminists in the 1970s, it did not exist epistemically. This does not mean it did not happen—women were experiencing harassment and the discomfort and sense of violation that accompanies it, but they could not name what was happening. On a structural level, there were no laws, policies, or rules to protect women from this form of victimization because the concept had not been named. This is a hermeneutic gap and it is a significant form of epistemic injustice (Fricker, 2007).

In the case of hermeneutic injustice, social power impacts collective social understandings. A good example of this is the history of women. Prior to the women's movement, much of women's experience was collectively unknown and it was through speak-outs and consciousness-raising that this began to change. In her memoir of the women's liberation movement, Susan Brownmiller (1990, p. 149) documents the following:

In my group people started talking about postpartum depression. In that one forty-five minute period I realized that what I had been blaming myself for, and what my husband had blamed me for, wasn't my personal deficiency. It was a combination of physiological things and a real societal thing, isolation. That realization was one of those moments that makes you a feminist forever.

As can be seen from this short piece, the collective hermeneutic gap regarding postpartum depression meant that no one understood this particular syndrome—there was a gap in collective hermeneutic resources—so when symptoms emerged the woman was blamed for the occurrence. But the collective understanding of the shared phenomenon provided a hermeneutic breakthrough and Brownmiller was able to understand her own experience and the social experience of which it was a part. Hermeneutic injustice is "having some significant area of one's social experience obscured from collective understanding owing to hermeneutic marginalization" (Fricker, 2007, p. 158).

For a person who is victim to hermeneutic injustice, there will be dissonance between the mainstream understanding of their experience and their own sense of experience and this in turn challenges their faith in their ability to make sense of the world. Fricker (2007) suggests that this hermeneutic injustice can be so significant that it damages the development of self. To counter this, Fricker (2007, p. 169) suggests that we must listen very carefully and have a "reflexive awareness on the part of the hearer, for a speaker whose communicative efforts are hampered by hermeneutical injustice may seem to be making no sense at all to the hearer." Fricker suggests that we should reserve judgment, keep an open mind as to credibility, and perhaps seek corroborating evidence to counter uncertainty.

In the case of Tammy Whiteman, she found support for her position from her lawyer, and notably not from child protection services. After her children were removed, she experienced hermeneutic injustice, as child protection services bases its service provision around the location of the child; once her children were removed, Tammy was alone and forced to try to make sense of what was happening without any support or the opportunity for epistemic justice (i.e., to have her testimony listened to respectfully).

Child protection services workers informed Tammy that she was in denial and that she should attend counselling. Once Tammy and her lawyer had proved that the Motherisk tests were wrong, retired Court of Appeal justice Susan Lang investigated the lab's procedures and her findings confirmed that the tests were unreliable. Lang expressed amazement that in the 15 years that these tests were used to substantiate child removal, no one in child protection services ever challenged the test results, even when numerous desperate parents were certain the results were dead wrong. This is a telling observation and reflects that the child protection practice was rooted in a belief that the workers were the experts and were always right and demonstrates that they did not regard client testimony as credible or even worth investigating. Fred and Julie, a Halifax couple who had their son removed as a result of Motherisk tests, reported shock and dismay when they were told the results of the investigation into the tests. Of their child protection worker, they said, "He talked in riddles kind of. Nobody understood the science he was speaking, so he sounded like he knew what he was talking about." A Superior Court judge found the worker credible, reliable, and knowledgeable, and Fred and Julie lost not only custody of their son, but also access to him. Later, when the unreliability of the tests was announced, Fred and Julie applied for the return of their son, but the boy's adoption had already been finalized. If child protection workers had been conducting assessments with a goal of epistemic justice and respect for the knowledges of the people they were working with, I believe that the investigation into the Motherisk tests would have begun decades earlier, as child protection workers would have been repeatedly confronted with assessment evidence that was in contradiction to client testimony.

APPLYING PRINCIPLES OF EPISTEMIC JUSTICE TO CHILD WELFARE ASSESSMENT

Active and Empathetic Listening

Psychotherapy scholars concur regarding the fundamental importance of empathetically listening to a client's story (Berzoff, Flanagan, & Herz, 2016; Norcross, 2011), which not only builds the therapeutic alliance, but also enables the communication of respect and the establishment of trust. For the assessment process this is crucially important, as the focus of the interaction is the future of the child and the family. It is widely agreed that engagement with the family is of critical importance to achieving a collaborative working relationship and establishing a level of trust and respect (Dumbrill, 2011; Fargion, 2014). Participation is achieved through openness, warmth, and empathy toward the situation of the family. Listening, summarizing, and paraphrasing are key skills in this process. However, effective empathetic listening also requires that the understanding that is being reached is conveyed back to the client(s). In a study of parents in the child protection system, Smithson and Gibson (2017) interviewed parents and heard that they felt prejudged and that the social worker did not take the time to find out about their situation (a good description of testimonial injustice). Furthermore, these parents spoke about the lack of compassion or empathy or even awareness of the emotional strain of the child protection process as a whole on them and their children (perhaps an example of hermeneutic injustice as this parental/family experience of participating in the child protection process is underexplored and underreported). Parents reported feeling minimized and silenced as they felt they could offer no challenge for fear of the possible consequences for their family (examples of the enormous power imbalance in the child protection system). One family described being given a copy of the assessment report at the beginning of a meeting and being asked to read it, but they were so nervous they could not comprehend it, and thus left the meeting feeling inadequate and defeated as they had not been able to engage in the discussion about their family's future. Parents described being cut off when speaking, belittled, and dehumanized. Forrester, Westlake, and Glyn (2012) described how child protection workers often used a confrontational and authority-based communication style with parents as they attempted to balance being empathetic with what they feared might be colluding with behaviours that were unsafe for children. Parents reported that an unfairly negative impression of them was contained in the assessment and then all plans were based on this.

A critical clinical approach in social work acknowledges openly power differentials and includes discussion of legal and procedural requirements, while at the same time communicating an awareness of social inequalities, and most importantly, being available, accessible, and non-judgmental (H. Brown, 2009). Conveying respect by addressing the client as a good informant and communicating respect for the client's knowledge and experience establishes a communication groundwork that is rooted in epistemic justice (Fricker, 2007). Conveying understanding requires that the social worker use summarizing and paraphrasing to repeat back to the client what they understand and then being open to feedback on that. It is much more complicated than making unqualified statements such as "I understand" or "I get it," as this claim to understanding provides no evidence that true understanding is present. Communicating respect for client knowledge and experience does not mean that you must agree with them or that you must praise them when you do not think their behaviour is praiseworthy. What it does mean is listening carefully to their account of a situation or another family member and asking clarifying and probing questions to ensure you understand what happened. These kinds of questions communicate your wish to understand and to be clear about the client's experience.

In child protection work, families are often in conflict and there are mis-understandings and hurt feelings, and sometimes a particular family member will have become the focus of blame and anger. Michael White (2006) sug-gests using externalizing conversations to begin a conversation in which the effects of the problem the family is experiencing can be discussed and mapped. Externalizing conversations are a way to ensure that the focus of the conversa-tion is the problem and not the person. White provides an example of this in a single-mother family with a seven-year-old boy who has become school-phobic and has persistent insomnia. Michael meets with both the boy, Richard, and his mother, Jane, and begins by inviting Richard to introduce him to these fears. When Richard is lost for words, he gives him art materials and suggests that he draw his fears, and then begins the interview:

> M: No-one who had fears like this running around in their lives would be able to get any sleep at all.
> R: Well, I hardly get any sleep myself!
> M: Well, is that fair?
> R: What?
> M: Do you think that it is fair that these fears take your sleep away?
> R: No, it's not fair. It's really not fair.
> M: Are the neighbour's getting any sleep with these fears on the loose at night?
> R: Uh.
> M: Are the neighbours …
> R: What do you think Mum?
> J: Maybe you could ask them? (White, 2006, pp. 3–4)

By externalizing the fears, the conversation became a collaborative one between the child, parent, and social worker to work together on how to address the problem. The ensuing conversation with Richard generated ways he could take action against the fears that were interfering in his life. White and Morgan (2006) provide a detailed explanation and description of narrative therapy with children and their families in their book. This is a therapeutic approach that dovetails very well with the principles of epistemic justice.

Missing Voices: The Voice of the Child and Working with the Entire Family

The United Nations Convention on the Rights of the Child (UNCRC) was ratified in Canada in 1991. Enshrined in this convention are four principles:

(1) the right to the best interests of the child, (2) the right to nondiscrimination, (3) the child's right to life, survival, and development, and (4) the child's right to be heard. Bernstein (2016) makes some recommendations on ways we could all work to enhance the rights of children. He recommends that we modernize child welfare language to reduce stigma. Specifically, he addresses language such as "apprehension," "custody," "adoption probation," "runaway," and "society and crown wardship," and notes that this language conjures up penal and mental health institutionalization and serves to promote discrimination. The right to be heard is Article 12 of the UNCRC, and a Child's Rights Impact Assessment (CRIA) has been developed by the UNCRC that can be used by agencies and individuals to access specific issues (e.g., health supports, age-appropriate access to justice). Bernstein suggests that we need to bring child welfare out from the shadows and in from the margins by which he means that we should be more transparent about child welfare issues and challenges. Risk assessments in child protection cases are usually completed by a social worker and often exclude the voice of the child, who is the one designated as at risk.

The Tammy Whiteman case suggests that the children were not involved in the assessment process. If they had been interviewed, they would have provided corroborating evidence that their mother was not using alcohol in the household and I predict they would also have provided a lot of information on Tammy's parenting strengths. Given that she never stopped fighting to get her children back, Tammy demonstrates a high level of investment in her family and love for her daughters. She eventually got her two daughters back, but she reported that they were not the same. Her daughter Krista said she was moved nine times after she was taken from her mother and when she first returned to her mother's care, she refused to leave the house for two months for fear that she would be "removed" again.

White (2006) identifies many of the normative and developmental ideas about children that are deeply entrenched in Western thinking as responsible for the frequent exclusion of children from the proceedings. For example, there is the idea that nurturing, caretaking, and supervising are exclusively adult roles, so pathologizing language such as "parentified child" or "this child is being robbed of their childhood" or "arrested development" is often applied to children who are viewed as being forced into adult roles and therefore as needing protection. In order to further protect children from this "harm," they are excluded from these painful adult conversations. White reports that in his experience children are resilient and are well able to articulate in a family conference what effects the abusive or neglectful behaviours have had on them and what they would like to see changed. Using principles of epistemic justice, it is imperative to listen very carefully to a child's account and to honour their experience and knowledge.

Domains of Resistance

In 2008, Forrester, McCambridge, Waissbein, and Rollnick conducted a study on the responses of child protection workers to cases involving alcohol abuse. They discovered a pervasive use of confrontational challenges and an authority-based conversational style, where imposing the agency agenda was at the forefront and issues raised by parents were ignored or minimized. Empathy was almost absent from the interactions and clients were reported to be resistant, unengaged, in denial, and in some cases, threatening. These findings are consistent with the picture evoked in the Tammy Whiteman story. It appears no one listened to Tammy, and her denial that she was abusing alcohol was immediately pathologized and recorded as further evidence of her need for counselling.

Parental resistance is considered to be a challenging feature of child and family social work. A breakdown of reasons parents might be resistant includes social context, social power, child protection context, shame, stigma, and the skill level of the social worker. A critical clinical approach alerts us to the dangers of subjectivism, where we assume that individuals have a fixed identity, are untouched by social forces, and have little or no ability to change (C. Brown, 2017). In his anti-oppressive approach to child protection casework, Dumbrill (2011, p. 61) places weight on all of these factors and speaks of "the gentle art of merging perspectives," where he describes working with parents' stories and agency mandates. An epistemically just approach to child protection services requires that the first task is to listen to the testimony of the client family, including all the members, as the starting point. Dumbrill (2011) emphasizes the importance of including issues such as unemployment, poor housing, lack of daycare, poverty, and isolation as part of that initial assessment plan, with thought being given to how to respond to these issues. In her article "Reconciliation Means Not Saying Sorry Twice: Lessons from Child Welfare in Canada," Cindy Blackstock (2008) notes that risk assessments do not account for risks that are located outside a family unit (factors such as poverty, unemployment, inadequate housing, poor community resources, and so on). This results in the child welfare system making individual families accountable for structural risk factors that they have little ability to influence by themselves. It is at a later point in the child protection assessment process that the mandate of the agency can be introduced into the conversation and can then become a topic of discussion in light of what is known about the family's perception and the social context of the difficulties.

Social Context

Populations that are involved with the child welfare system are some of our most vulnerable, most marginalized, and most affected by the neoliberal climate of individualizing, cutbacks, precarious employment, and the retrenchment of the welfare state. Swift and Callahan (2009, p. 210) say we are "identifying the less fortunate and more vulnerable people among us as 'risky' individuals and legitimizing various forms of 'education' and control in our treatment of them." As social workers, we are required to implement child welfare legislation, which asks that we "balance society's wish to protect children from abuse while maintaining the family as the bastion of liberty" (Regehr & Kanani, 2006, p. 48). These competing demands mean that social workers have the difficult task of completing assessments that identify the risk/safety of a child and decide on what would be in the best interests of the child. At the same time that social workers have been enlisted to identify and manage difficult populations, they have also themselves come under public surveillance and control (Dustin, 2016; Swift & Callahan, 2009).

Child Protection Context

Currently there is an overrepresentation of racialized children in care. Indigenous, Black, and immigrant children are apprehended and placed in out-of-home locations in disproportionate numbers (Kikulwe, 2016). This is, in part, a reflection of the social context of most child protection cases as identified in this chapter. In a study of child protection work with Black families and immigrant families, Kikulwe (2016) identified that families were often involved in the child welfare system because of their use of physical punishment. Kikulwe surmised that this could be because of the impact of slavery, as slave masters used physical punishment to control and manage their slaves. In discussing absentee fathers, he noted that during slavery the husband did not belong to the family and could be sold elsewhere. This meant that mothers and their children were left alone as a family unit, albeit an unstable arrangement as children could also be sold. A parallel was noted in the current surveillance of single Black mothers, who are now accused of poor parenting and are at risk of having their children removed from them. Kikulwe (2016) noted that for these immigrant families, social support networks are absent, when they often come from a tradition of extended kin relationships, and in their settlement process in Canada, children often act as language and cultural interpreters, often assuming "adult-like" family roles.

In working with immigrant families, it was noted that child protection workers are tasked with teaching these families about "parenting in Canada"

and "Canadian parenting law." Racialized child protection workers were challenged by the overrepresentation of racialized children in care, "a problem that
they felt should receive public attention" (Kikulwe, 2016, p. 202), and they actively used their role as gatekeepers to try to slow down the admission of children into care. A reported problem is that it is not uncommon for immigrant
children to threaten their parents with child welfare authorities. Child protection social workers described role modelling for newcomer parents and teaching
them about Canadian racialized stereotypes (e.g., incompetent parents, drug users, violent mothers and fathers) and then encouraging them to use "Canadian"
disciplinary techniques in order to avoid this stereotyping.

Skill Level of the Social Worker

Dumbrill (2011) describes a scenario where an Indigenous father retrieved his
adolescent daughter from a bar by dragging her out, physically leaving bruises on
her arms. This resulted in assault charges being laid. In a follow-up encounter,
Dumbrill enquired as to how things were. The father responded that he ignores his daughter now as he is too afraid to do anything and be charged again.
Clearly there is a big problem here and a great deal of family conference work
needs to be done to reach agreed-upon ways of keeping the daughter safe and
honouring parenting practices for the father.

In her discussion of cross-cultural competence in social work, Ruth Dean
(2001) suggested that we cannot become competent at something that is continually changing and proposes a model based on acceptance of one's lack of
competence: "I would propose that it is not so much knowledge but rather understanding that is basic to successful clinical work" (p. 628). Dean proposes
that we adopt a position of "not knowing" and explore the contexts and histories
surrounding the experience of our clients. She suggests that our "knowing" must
always be tentative and must incorporate a reflexive awareness of our own cultural and theoretical assumptions. This does not mean that we abandon responsibility for our own positioning and for our critical awareness of the content we
are listening to. Feminist philosopher Donna Haraway (1988) calls this "partial
knowing," where there is a recognition that both the client and the social worker
bring knowledge to the conversation. Similarly, in her examination of cultural
safety and child welfare systems, Eveline Milliken (2012) critiques the social
work practice model of cultural competence, which focuses on the practitioner's
consciousness and skill set rather than on the "definitions, priorities, perceptions, and responses to the client" (p. 101). She emphasizes that there needs to

be a shift from examining our own practice to listening to the other. In other words, Milliken, like Dean, is proposing that we aspire to epistemic justice and that we honour the vulnerable persons we work with by inviting their experience and knowledge into the conversation.

Milliken observes that the model of cultural competence places social work practitioners outside a relationship with the client and gives them the social power to decide and control what is appropriate for the client. She suggests that it is imperative that vulnerable persons in the social work encounter need to be able to define for themselves what safety looks like. She warns that "the marginalized often cannot articulate what is missing, and given their vulnerability, even if they could, would they? The outsider-other, who already is feeling powerless, marginalized, and voiceless, frequently can respond only by sitting in silence" (p. 105). In her identification of the challenge for the marginalized to articulate what is missing, Milliken is accurately describing what Fricker calls hermeneutic injustice. Fricker (2007) advises that when we are in the presence of a hermeneutic gap (when the client is attempting to put words to an experience where there is little or no common understanding to draw on), it is doubly important to attend closely, to assist the client to describe and explain the experience, and to listen respectfully (i.e., to treat the client as a good informant).

In the case of Tammy Whiteman, we have only a media-generated account of the "flawed Motherisk hair test" and so we do not know the details of the entire child protection process that resulted in her children being placed in foster homes. However, we are presented with the information that it was her lawyer who came up with a creative way to check the hair-test results. This demonstrates that it was the lawyer who treated Tammy as a good informant and was willing to consider other ways of investigating her protestations that she was not using alcohol. In the media account, we are told that the child protection practitioners interpreted her testimony as denial and instructed her to attend counselling and rehabilitation programs. This is an example of what Fricker calls *identity-prejudicial credibility deficit*, where Tammy's previous history and social status, in combination with the results of a "scientific" test, were the foundation for the decision-making process and the recommendations. By practising the principles of epistemic justice, the lawyer was able to discover that the scientific Motherisk hair test was flawed. (By 2015, 35,000 hair tests had been completed across Canada, and this finding meant that hundreds of child protection cases had to be reviewed.)

IDENTITY-PREJUDICIAL CREDIBILITY DEFICIT

Fricker (2007) describes identity-prejudicial credibility deficit as the social situation where a person has been given an identity that is accompanied by a lowered credibility or believability status. For example, if someone is labelled as a criminal, in the justice system the evidence provided by someone who is a "known criminal" will have very low credibility in contrast to a police officer, who will have high credibility. These unequal epistemic statuses are then very significant factors in the weighing of evidence. Similarly, persons diagnosed with a mental illness experience a significant credibility deficit and must navigate the world with this ongoing epistemic disadvantage.

The Tammy Whiteman story is not only a story of how a particular scientific test was flawed, it is also a story of how, when social workers become dependent on such tests and sources of information and do not practice according to social justice principles (including epistemic justice for our clients, deep and thoughtful listening, and respect for clients' experience and testimony), we are not upholding the commitments of our profession to promote social justice.

CONCLUSION

While child protection work is important, challenging, and complex it also has the potential to be rewarding and progressive and to make a significant contribution to family and community well-being. Currently, a risk assessment model where the focus is on caution and a safety model that places weight on standardized signs of risk and child removal are widely used. A critical clinical approach to child protection work is informed by an understanding that uncertainty and complexity are part of the territory and that while working within mandated constraints is challenging, trying to limit the process to standardized signs, indicators, and responses invites abuse of power and injustice. I have argued that we need to enrich and supplement our approach to this work with a relation-based assessment foundation that is grounded in the principles of epistemic justice and honours the lived experience of families, including the children who are the focus of these inquiries and yet are often not even consulted. I suggest that we must build on existing strengths and coping strategies within families and within communities to increase parental confidence and strength, and that this approach should be foundational with risk assessment as an additional tool rather than a fundamental practice.

REFERENCES

Adams, R., Dominelli, L., & Payne, M. (Eds). (2009). *Critical practice in social work* (2nd ed.). New York: Palgrave.

Bernstein, M. (2016). Honoring the twenty-fifth anniversary of the United Nations Convention on the Rights of the Child: Transforming child welfare in Canada into a stronger rights-based system. In M. Montgomery, D. Badry, D. Fuchs, & D. Kikulwe (Eds.), *Transforming child welfare: Interdisciplinary practices, field education, and research* (pp. 3–27). Regina, SK: University of Regina Press.

Berzoff, J., Flanagan, L. M., & Herz, P. (2016). *Inside out and outside in: Psychodynamic clinical theory and psychopathology in contemporary multicultural contexts* (4th ed.). New York: Jason Aronson.

Blackstock, C. (2008). Reconciliation means not saying sorry twice: Lessons from child welfare in Canada. In Aboriginal Healing Foundation, *From truth to reconciliation: Transforming the legacy of residential schools* (pp. 163–179). Ottawa: Dollco Printing.

Brown, C. (2017). Creating counter-stories: Critical clinical practice and feminist narrative therapy. In D. Baines (Ed.), *Doing anti-oppressive practice: Social justice social work* (pp. 212–232). Halifax: Fernwood.

Brown, H. (2009). Safeguarding adults. In R. Adams, L. Dominelli, & M. Payne (Eds.), *Critical practice in social work* (2nd ed., pp. 303–311). New York: Palgrave.

Brownmiller, S. (1990). *In our time: Memoir of a revolution*. New York: Dial Press.

Choate, P. (2016). Child protection inquiries: What are they teaching us? A Canadian perspective. In M. Montgomery, D. Badry, D. Fuchs, & D. Kikulwe (Eds.), *Transforming child welfare: Interdisciplinary practices, field education, and research* (pp. 61–87). Regina, SK: University of Regina Press.

Dean, R. (2001). The myth of cross-cultural competence. *Families in Society, 82*(6), 623–630.

Dumbrill, G. (2011). Doing anti-oppressive child protection casework. In D. Baines (Ed.), *Doing anti-oppressive practice: Social justice social work* (2nd ed., pp. 51–63). Halifax: Fernwood.

Dustin, D. (2016). *The McDonaldization of social work*. New York: Routledge.

Fargion, S. (2014). Synergies and tensions in child protection and parent support: Policy lines and practitioners cultures. *Child and Family Services Social Work, 19*(1), 24–33.

Forrester, D., McCambridge, J., Waissbein, C., & Rollnick, S. (2008). How do child and family social workers talk to parents about child welfare concerns? *Child Abuse Review, 17*(1), 23–35.

Forrester, D., Westlake, D., & Glyn, G. (2012). Parental resistance and social worker skills: Towards a theory of motivational social work. *Child and Family Social Work, 17*(2), 118–129.

Fricker, M. (2007). *Epistemic injustice: Power and the ethics of knowing*. Oxford: Oxford University Press.

Gibbs, L. (2003). *Evidence-based practice for the helping professions: A practical guide with integrated multimedia*. Pacific Grove, CA: Thomson Brooks Cole.

Haraway, D. (1988). Situated knowledges: The science question in feminism and the privilege of partial perspective. *Feminist Studies, 14*(3), 575–599.

Healy, K. (2014). *Social work theories in context* (2nd ed.). London: Palgrave Macmillan.

Kikulwe, D. (2016). Boundaries and identities: Racialized child welfare workers' perspectives of their histories and perspectives when working with diverse families. In M. Montgomery, D. Badry, D. Fuchs, & D. Kikulwe (Eds.), *Transforming child welfare: Interdisciplinary practices, field education, and research* (pp. 187–211). Regina, SK: University of Regina Press.

Leshied, A., Chiodo, P., Whitehead, D., & Marshall, L. (2003). The empirical basis of risk assessment in child welfare: The accuracy of risk assessment and clinical judgement. *Child Welfare, 82*(5), 527–540.

Mayor, L. (2017, October 19). "It's a tragedy": How the flawed Motherisk hair test helped fracture families across Canada. *CBC News*. Retrieved from https://www.cbc.ca/news/canada/motherisk-hair-testing-families-1.4360577

Medina, J. (2013). *The epistemology of resistance. Gender and racial oppressions, epistemic injustice, and resistant imaginations*. New York: Oxford University Press.

Milliken, E. (2012). Cultural safety and child welfare systems. In D. Fuchs, S. McKay, & I. Brown (Eds.), *Awakening the spirit: Moving forward in child welfare* (pp. 93–117). Regina, SK: CPRC Press.

Mullaly, R. (2010). *Challenging oppression and confronting privilege* (2nd ed.). New York: Oxford University Press.

Norcross, J. C. (2011). *Psychotherapy relationships that work* (2nd ed.). New York: Oxford University Press.

Regehr, C., & Kanani, K. (2006). *Essential law for social work practice in Canada*. Don Mills, ON: Oxford University Press.

Shlonsky, A., & Mildon, R. (2017). Assessment and decision-making to improve outcomes in child protection. In M. Connolly & N. Parton (Eds.), *Beyond the risk paradigm in child protection*. London: Palgrave.

Smithson, R., & Gibson, M. (2017). Less than human: A qualitative study into the experience of parents involved in the child protection system. *Child and Family Social Work, 22*, 565–574.

Swift. K., & Callahan, M. (2009). *At risk: Social justice in child welfare and other human services*. Toronto: University of Toronto Press.

Thomas, L. (2015). Partnering for connectedness in the community. In W. R. Bernard (Ed.), *Still fighting for change* (pp. 123–133). Lawrencetown, NS: Pottersfield Press.

White, M. (2006) Narrative practice with families with children: Externalizing conversations revisited. In M. White & A. Morgan (Eds.), *Narrative therapy with children and their families* (pp. 1–57). Adelaide, Australia: Dulwich Centre Publications.

White, M., & Morgan, A. (2006). *Narrative therapy with children and their families.* Adelaide, Australia: Dulwich Centre Publications.

Young, I. M. (1992). *Justice and the politics of difference.* Princeton, NJ: Princeton University Press.

CHAPTER 12

AIDS Quarantine Revisited in British Columbia's Treatment as Prevention: Possibilities for Critical Clinical Social Work in the Era of HIV Criminalization[1]

Eli Manning and MT O'Shaughnessy

INTRODUCTION

On September 3, 1998, the Supreme Court of Canada ruled on the *R. v. Cuerrier* case, Canada's precedent-setting case of HIV non-disclosure criminalization. Based in British Columbia, the *Cuerrier* case established that people living with HIV/AIDS (PWAs) are criminally liable if they do not disclose their HIV status to their sexual partners before "engaging with them in activities that pose a 'significant risk of serious bodily harm' (i.e. HIV transmission)" (Mykhalovskiy, 2011, p. 669). In practice, this meant that PWAs didn't need to disclose their HIV status to their sexual partners *if* they used a condom. However, in October 2012, the Supreme Court of Canada issued another ruling, revising the *Cuerrier* ruling, which intensified life for PWAs. This ruling meant that if PWAs did not want to disclose their status to their sexual partners, they needed to not only use a condom, but also have a low viral load to avoid criminal prosecution. Current substantial advocacy efforts, in the courts and with the attorney general, are challenging the 2012 Supreme Court ruling, so it is not the final word on disclosure. Yet before either of these rulings, PWAs were subject only to public health measures that ranged from voluntary to coercive, including voluntary counselling, cease and desist orders, and isolation. Critiques of both the 1998 and 2012 Supreme Court rulings are well established and convincingly argue against criminalization, opting for public health interventions (Cameron, 2009; Canadian HIV/AIDS Legal Network, 2012; Gagnon, 2012; Kotiswaran, 2014; McClelland, 2013; Mykhalovskiy, 2011, 2014; Mykhalovskiy & Betteridge, 2012; Mykhalovskiy, Betteridge, & McLay, 2010; Wilson, 2013). To be clear, we are not arguing for criminalization; rather, we will demonstrate some of the problems with coercive public health measures. Our analysis will show the challenges of using public health interventions like British Columbia's Public Health Act.

PEOPLE LIVING WITH HIV/AIDS (PWAs)

We use PWA intentionally in this chapter rather than persons living with HIV (PLWH) for political reasons. MT fought for the identity of PWA, to be recognized as a person living with HIV/AIDS as a political entity. PWAs also self-identified as PWAs in the Denver Principles, which was the first self-proclaimed manifesto by and for people living with HIV/AIDS.

Today's criminalization of PWAs for HIV non-disclosure may evoke urban legends of AIDS quarantine. However, in British Columbia the connection between today's criminalization and yesteryear's quarantine is not an analogy, but a reality. While British Columbia may have a unique history directly linked to AIDS quarantine, we argue that this context bears significant similarity to other Canadian provinces, which have similar public health legislation. In this chapter, we map provincial public health legislation and regulations enacted during the first decade of the epidemic that allowed for quarantining PWAs through to the present-day Public Health Act and its regulations, as well as discuss the present-day implications for PWAs under HIV criminalization. We discuss the history of British Columbia's Public Health Act as a site of policy change with real-life implications for people living with HIV and critical clinical implications for the social workers who work with them. We detail how policy change impacts PWAs and how critical clinical social workers can intervene. We begin by briefly describing the differences between these various forms of containment, followed by the 1987 scare for enacting AIDS quarantine in British Columbia. Next, we dissect the Public Health Act and examine how the AIDS quarantine bill was renewed in the 2009 legislation. You will see that we have analyzed these policies, but also included historical AIDS activists, and civil rights defenders' responses as well as MT's first-person responses to these policies. We do this because part of critical clinical social work practice for Eli is centring people's lived experiences. MT's experiences give a sharp reality check to how policy impacts PWAs, which is essential for critical clinical social workers to understand. Detailing a clinical encounter from the perspective of a person living with HIV, we examine critical clinical social work practice that includes lived experience and critical policy analysis. Policies are never neutral, and it is our job to not only see how they impact the people we serve, but also critique and change them.

As you read this chapter, ask yourself the following questions:

1. How does policy guide, limit, and/or expand my critical clinical social work practice?
2. How do social workers respond to ethical dilemmas imposed by policy changes?
3. How can critical policy analysis, first-person histories, and their contemporary experiences inform and shape our critical clinical practice?
4. How do we work with the people we support when policy changes work against them?

American legal scholar Lawrence Gostin (2004, pp. 179–184) eloquently distinguishes between the various types of containment to clarify who is targeted in civil/public health and criminal confinement. With regards to public health forms of confinement, Gostin describes the differences between quarantine and isolation: the former applies to those who have been exposed to the communicable disease, while the latter applies to those who know infected people. Both forms of civil containment seek to prevent disease transmission. Gostin goes on to specify that there are two notable forms of isolation: status-based isolation, which is associated with one's HIV status, and behaviour-based isolation, which is related to PWAs engaging in dangerous behaviour (p. 183). Criminal containment, or imprisonment, is the result of a criminal conviction and sentence. In theory, the purpose of imprisonment is to prevent harm to others and to punish those that have caused harm. Therefore, it is vital to understand how using criminal procedures, prosecutions, and sentences in public health shifts the focus from disease prevention to punishment.

Gostin (2004, p. 185) details three distinguishing factors related to civil and criminal applications used to confine people: clarity, objectivity, and safeguards. He argues that public health often mobilizes broad categories such as "dangerous," or as we will show, "health hazard," whereas "criminal law must specify the behaviour prohibited" (p. 185). With regard to the objective of the indicted person, civil confinement can be based on future predictions of behaviour whereas criminal prosecution must be based on acts that have already occurred. In terms of safeguards, criminal convictions must be proven beyond a reasonable doubt whereas civil interventions just need to provide a convincing argument and evidence. Another safeguard that the criminal process offers that public health interventions may not is that the former has clear guidelines for the duration of the sentence whereas the latter may not (Gostin, 2004).

TIMELINE OF HIV-RELATED HEALTH LEGISLATION IN BRITISH COLUMBIA

July 7, 1987: First reading of Bill 34, Health Statutes Amendment Act, presented by Honourable Mr. Dueck on behalf of the lieutenant-governor (British Columbia Legislative Assembly, 1987a)

November 24, 1987: Second reading of Bill 34 (British Columbia Legislative Assembly, 1987b)

November 25, 1987: Committee stage of Bill 34 (British Columbia Legislative Assembly, 1987c)

December 3, 1987: Third reading of Bill 34 (British Columbia Legislative Assembly, 1987d)

December 17, 1987: Royal assent of Bill 34, changing the Health Act (Legislative Assembly of the Province of British Columbia, 1987)

May 29, 2008: Royal assent of new Public Health Act (Legislative Assembly of the Province of British Columbia, 2009)

March 31, 2009: Repeal of Health Act

THE 1987 AIDS QUARANTINE BILL: HEALTH STATUTES AMENDMENTS ACT, BILL 34

The Health Statutes Amendment Act, also known as Bill 34, was ascended into law on December 17, 1987, effectively changing the Health Act in British Columbia (Legislative Assembly of the Province of British Columbia, 1987). While this bill did not specify quarantining PWAs or those potentially exposed to the virus that causes AIDS, it was proposed at the height of the AIDS scare. For the purposes of this discussion, we focus on particular Bill 34 propositions that prompted civil rights concerns, primarily from AIDS activists (Coalition for Responsible Health Legislation, 1987a, 1987b, 1987c; Smith & Hughes, 1987a,

1987b). Specifically, we discuss two problematic proposed amendments to the Health Act that effectively introduced vague terminology subject to political interpretation and extended the powers of medical health officers.

While quarantine and isolation were already in health legislation in British Columbia, it was the combination of timing, politics, and implications that raised concern for AIDS activists and human rights defenders. As we show, the changes to the Health Act proposed in Bill 34 not only impacted quarantine and isolation, but also expanded governmental power and limited the privacy of PWAs.

Introducing the Vague Terminology of Health Hazards

AIDS activists raised concerns about adding a new, vague term, "health hazard," which was defined in the Health Statutes Amendment Act as

> a condition or thing that does or is likely to (a) endanger the public health, or (b) prevent or hinder the prevention or suppression of disease and includes a prescribed condition or thing or a prescribed condition or thing that fails to meet a prescribed standard. (Legislative Assembly of the Province of British Columbia, 1987)

Related to the "health hazard" definition, the Vancouver Gay and Lesbian Community Centre (VGLCC) and the ad hoc Coalition for Responsible Health Legislation (CRHL) also objected to the variable definition left in the hands of selected members of the government of the day (CRHL, 1987a, 1987b, 1987c). Specifically, the VGLCC and the CRHL argued that this "sweeping legislation ... leaves the definition of words ... up to a small group of politicians who may respond to the paranoia and hysteria of an ill-informed public" (Smith & Hughes, 1987a, 1987b). Condemning the broadness proposed in the bill, they further stated, "past experience in this country and this province does not leave us with any sense of security. One only has to reflect upon the treatment of Canadians of Japanese ancestry during the Second World War" (Smith & Hughes, 1987a, 1987b). In the end, this section of Bill 34 ascended to law unchanged.

Extending the Powers of Medical Health Officers

Bill 34's initial proposal of enhancing the role of medical health officers was what led to the scare of British Columbia enacting legislation that enabled AIDS quarantine. Its initial wording charged medical health officers with the power to isolate or quarantine any person with a "reportable communicable disease" (as then defined by Cabinet) who "is likely to expose others to the disease or the agent" (Smith & Hughes, 1987a, 1987b). In short, this allowed medical health officers to impose testing, treatment, and/or confinement of any person with HIV/AIDS. Boldly, the VGLCC and the CRHL stated that this amendment was "clearly designed for people testing positive for antibodies to the AIDS virus. There is no other explanation" (Smith & Hughes, 1987a, p. 4). The British Columbia Civil Liberties Association (BCCLA) echoed concerns that this bill targeted PWAs, but suggested a particular amendment to the proposed legislation: "If the legislation is designed to deal with those who are willfully or carelessly spreading AIDS (or any other communicable disease) it should say so" (BCCLA, 1987a). Following this suggestion, the legislation passed with the BCCLA's amendment and added an additional clause: "the person is likely to, willfully, carelessly or because of mental incompetence" (Legislative Assembly of the Province of British Columbia, 1987). With the enactment of the Health Statutes Amendments Act, the worst-case scenario, outright quarantine of PWAs, did not manifest; however, its implications for PWAs, as well as public health, still significantly impact public health policy in British Columbia today. In this section, we centred the historical objections of AIDS activists and civil rights defenders to the AIDS quarantine bill.

PUBLIC HEALTH ACT

In the following section, we examine the current public health legislation that replaced the Health Statutes Amendment Act and the Health Act. Along with our critique, MT's first-person experiences of living with HIV offer insight into AIDSphobia in the present-day public health policy.

In 2009, the Public Health Act replaced the Health Act in British Columbia. In 2008, the Public Health Act repealed all sections outlined in Bill 34 except for the section on Research Information, which remained relatively unchanged except for minor changes such as updating the name of the British Columbia Cancer Agency. To be clear, the sections empowering the lieutenant-governor in council to define public health terms and outlining the powers of the minister of health, lieutenant-governor in council, provincial health officer, and medical health officers were deleted from the Health Act (Legislative Assembly of the Province of British Columbia, 2009). Yet, they were not erased from legislation. Instead, they were modified in the new Public Health Act. In this section, we outline the legislative transition from the Health Act to the Public Health Act, noting how the Health Statutes Amendment Act was carried through to present-day public health legislation. We will examine several specific sections of the Public Health Act that legislate sections comparable to those that AIDS activists contested in Bill 34.

Definitions and Authority

The term *health hazard* came into BC public health legislation with the Health Statutes Amendment Act passed in 1987 and was carried through in the Public Health Act of 2009; this is one way the AIDS quarantine bill carries through to present-day public health legislation. The definition of health hazard in the Public Health Act has shifted slightly to include the idea of likelihood, such as "a condition, a thing or an activity that endangers, or *is likely to* endanger, public health" (Legislative Assembly of the Province of British Columbia, 2009; emphasis added). Adding likelihood to the definition of health hazard, while it may seem insignificant, opens up the possibility of more expansive applications. There is no specification as to how broadly this could be applied; for example, the legislation does not require medical testing or assessment to determine the likelihood of infection or exposure.

Similarly, *health hazard* gets attached to numerous sections of the Public Health Act, effectively broadening the reason for intervention to now include anyone who has "likely been exposed" to an infectious agent or hazardous material. In addition new terms were added including *infected person*, which describes a person who "(a) is or is likely infected with, or has been or has likely been exposed to, a prescribed infectious agent, or (b) is or is likely contaminated with, or has been or has likely been exposed to, a prescribed hazardous agent" (Legislative Assembly of the Province of British Columbia, 2009). These broad definitions effectively enact a wider scope for the application of public health legislation than even originally proposed in Bill 34; broad application was a central feature of AIDS activists' contestations of Bill 34, but the new Public Health Act met with no recorded objections in 2009.

The Public Health Act also defines the terms *health impediment, infectious agent,* and *preventative measures*, offering broad-based definitions of these. For example, preventative measures are actions "(a) preventing illness, (b) promoting health, (c) preventing transmission of an infectious agent, or (d) preventing contamination by a hazardous agent" (Legislative Assembly of the Province of British Columbia, 2009). Further preventative measures include "being treated or vaccinated" or "taking preventive medication" (Legislative Assembly of the Province of British Columbia, 2009). Under Section 27 of the Public Health Act, the medical health officer is charged with the power to "issue an order ... only if the medical health officer reasonably" believes that a person is infected, and an order is "necessary to protect public health." So, if the medical health officer believes a person meets the criteria, the medical health officer can then, "order a person to do *anything* that the medical health officer reasonably believes is necessary" (Legislative Assembly of the Province of British Columbia, 2009; emphasis added).

In sum, if the medical health officer believes a person is infected, they can order that person to do "anything" to prevent transmission. What this legislation has potentially set into motion is the possibility of legally mandating HIV treatment for prevention. There are no limits, such as time frame, considerations, or circumstances, set out in the Public Health Act to curb the possibility of mandatory HIV treatment. While the possibility of forced treatment may seem extreme or unlikely, given the trend in treatment as prevention (TasP) to use more coercive measures, we raise concerns about the possibility of mandatory treatment for the purposes of enacting and enforcing TasP.

A FIRST-HAND ACCOUNT OF THE IMPACT OF THE PUBLIC HEALTH ACT ON PWAs

When I came out, the process of letting people know I was gay struck me as odd. It was accepted that at some point to be "authentic," among other reasons, you had to let people know. I feel as conflicted now about disclosure of my HIV status as I did about "needing" to have a very public conversation about what essentially felt like a revelation of who I slept with. Who, exactly, is served and who is impacted by this process?

In both cases, I feel that it is a process that *other* people expect from me for purposes that have nothing to do with my well-being. I have to deal with casual, offhanded discrimination in situations of telling people my HIV status, for instance. Usually it is centred on some vague sense of what "could" happen. Often people believe either an act I might engage in (touching, handshake, etc.) or simply something about *having* HIV is a threat to them in some way no one has ever been able to articulate to me. It has led to the odd realization that my existence is linked to the concept of contagion. Inevitably in conversations it is disheartening to realize there is a level of suspected intent by simply having HIV. My status is, in other words, a moral evaluation of my personality and intentions, not my health.

When placed in the context of Canadian law and the prevailing attitude about so-called best practices in medicine, there is a dangerous nebulousness to "potential health hazard" as a foundation for policy. While often people tell me about whether or not this has been or will be utilized, I have actually lived through a period of history and personal experience that has taught me that, at some point, this open doorway will be walked through. And, shockingly, unlike the rest of our legal precedents, there is a lack of clarity as to what constitutes a hazard, let alone who judges that and on what criteria. All of which allows an almost countless number of situations in which we are confronting personal freedoms and human rights issues with no guidance or oversight beyond what we know at this moment about a disease. And that does not even begin to cover that we have failed to discuss autonomy of the individual as more than a disease status.

I often think of the early days of HIV/AIDS, when everyone was doing everything they could to try to get people to survive. In those days, the consensus was that we provide people with a drug or process that *seemed* to work. If we assume that our current approaches will not need to be altered in the future, we ignore the evolution of our understanding of this disease, pre-emptively closing the door on considering what may actually work.

Containment and Forced Treatment

To understand who can order a person to comply with the Public Health Act, it is important to understand the authority of the various positions charged with this power. The definition of a health officer is expanded in the Public Health Act to include not only a provincial health officer, who "is the senior public health official for British Columbia" (S.64), but also a medical health officer, who is a physician with a specialization in community health or someone recommended by the provincial health officer (S.71), and an environmental health officer (S.77). The Public Health Act deals with when orders can be made and allows the "medical health officer to issue an order under this Division only if the medical health officer reasonably believes that a person is an infected person" and "the order is necessary to protect public health." Yet this language erases the specificity that the BCCLA suggested in the amendment of the Health Act. The BCCLA requested that the language be amended to those who are "willfully or carelessly spreading AIDS (or any other communicable disease)," and the legislation passed with the BCCLA's amendment and an additional clause, "or because of mental incompetence" (BCCLA, 1987b). But in the new Public

Health Act, that specific wording is completely absent, reverting back to the excessive broad language originally proposed in Bill 34.

The new legislation makes no mention of "willfully or carelessly" or "mental incompetence." The judgment of the health officer is the measure used to enact a public health order. Given the Vancouver Coastal medical health officer's enthusiasm for TasP (described later in the chapter), and the reiteration of the threat that those unaware of their HIV status and those not on HIV treatment pose to public health, it is not unreasonable to think that she may use her powers to enact orders against non-adherent PWAs.

Section 32 governs what a health officer may order a person to do to comply with the public health order. Section 42 declares that a "person named or described in an order made under this Part must comply with the order" (Legislative Assembly of the Province of British Columbia, 2009; emphasis added). Division 6 deals with order enforcement and outlines procedures of how a health officer may seek a warrant, "without notice to any person," to "enter and search a place" (S.47) and an injunction from a judge of the Supreme Court, "without notice to any person," "restraining a person from contravening, or requiring a person to comply" with the act. Section 49 outlines the general procedures for enforcing an order, which may include the "apprehension of the person and transportation of the person to a place" (S.4), as well as

> detention of the person, including setting the location of detention, the terms of detention and expiry of the order, and order the person to submit to an examination, preventive measures, or any other thing necessary to ensure that the person will not be a danger to public health. (Legislative Assembly of the Province of British Columbia, 2009)

Understandably, the legislation emphasizes public health; however, what measures are put in place to protect individuals? What recourse do PWAs have to protect their individual rights, including their right to refuse treatment?

A PWA's REALITIES OF TREATMENT TO PROTECT THE PUBLIC VERSUS FOR THEIR OWN HEALTH BENEFIT

Again, I am often reassured by people who say, "but that would never happen." When I describe my personal experiences, I am always met with a conversation about my perception of the situation. About a year ago, I was part of the program here in British Columbia that "allowed" people who had stable viral loads and CD4 counts for at least six months to call an automated phone line to renew their antiretroviral medications. The rules are simple—every 90 days you get a blood test and call in for a refill. Anything indicating that medications either are no longer being taken or they aren't working, like upward spikes of viral loads or sudden lowering of CD4 counts, results in a request for a consultation with either a primary care provider or a pharmacist to assess what's going on. Otherwise, you go and grab your medications.

> ## VIRAL LOAD
>
> Viral load measures how much the HIV virus has replicated in your blood; it is a key measurement that is now associated with how infectious PWAs are. The lower the viral load, the less likely they could transmit the virus. CD4 counts measure how active one's immune system is; this measurement is key to the health of PWAs. Antiretrovirals (or ARV medication) are the complex treatment regimen PWAs can take to reduce the negative impacts of the virus on their health and bodies.

In this case, I was one day late.

What followed was a conversation with a pharmacist informing me that if I "failed" even so much as one more time (this was my first with this program), I would be removed from the program because they did not have time to do follow-up calls for everyone. And because of their largess, which I was assured no one else would grant me, I would have my medications available that day.

After 20 minutes of slowly coming to a boil in a conversation where I was told calmly and clearly that I was creating a problem for being even one dosage off, and that my "privilege" of not needing to see a pharmacist would be revoked if I continued like this, I simply handed the medications back. I have had HIV since 2004 and have been stable and had virtually unchanged numbers for the last decade. Apparently, that was not enough. Nor was it seen as unusual for me, a patient, to be threatened if I did not meet an exact standard—contradicted by several studies showing a single dose missed in a 90-day period is not treatment failure. And argument or even disagreement, depending on semantics, on my part was seen as hostility or could lead to a charge under the current Public Health Act.

One of the aspects of getting my medications every three months—despite clinical guidelines indicating that it could actually be done every six months—is supplication. It has never failed to feel like I am seeking approval from pharmacists to continue to receive my medications. What is worse is the realization that the situation does nothing to accommodate a patient having an issue with the personality or presentation of the pharmacist. Most pharmacists are backed by a series of policies that allow them all the authority in a situation, which, to be honest, is about the medications that stop me from dying.

As a white male, admittedly gay, with a job and a stable housing situation, I am the least likely to cross the line by necessity. But when the system at its *best* treats patients as hostile by default, what then of people with more complicated lives and restrictions? Having to constantly deal with this attitude means that for me, at the most basic level, the authority given to health care professionals to determine the so-called "best interests" for patients or community can be frightening. Add in legislation that specifically broadens their capacity to dictate my actions regardless of my choices? I am convinced it has an almost inevitable potential for disaster.

Use of Peace Officers

Section 90 of the Public Health Act authorizes the use of a peace officer for

> the purposes of taking an action authorized under this or any other enactment, including, without limitation, either of the following purposes: (a) making or enforcing an order or carrying out an inspection; (b) assisting a person to comply with an order of the health officer. (Legislative Assembly of the Province of British Columbia, 2009)

To be clear, a peace officer is "a mayor, sheriff and sheriff's officer"; "a warden, correctional officer, and any other officer or permanent employee of a penitentiary, prison, correctional centre or youth custody centre"; or "a police officer, police constable, constable or other person employed for the preservation and maintenance of the public peace" as defined in the province's Interpretation Act. Let us be explicitly clear, under no circumstances were peace officers authorized under the Health Act or the Communicable Diseases Regulations to enforce public health orders. This enactment of peace officers to enforce public health orders begins to blur the lines between the goals of public health and the goals of the criminal justice system. While the enforcement of public health orders are not criminal charges, using the police to protect public health certainly reinforces the perception of force and punishment should one not comply with medical orders.

A PWA's Response to Police in Public Health

I think what concerns me most is the unquestioned aspect of some of the decisions we as Canadians are making these days, specifically that we are developing and implementing responses to an issue of health through criminal and civil legislation without ever discussing the ramifications of that, or even what thinking led us to this point. In the middle of this we are thinking of expanding the powers of police departments and officers to enforce those laws as if they constitute care. How is an officer of the law, exactly, trained to provide health care? And why are we framing interactions with people who have HIV/AIDS as needing law enforcement *because* of their HIV status?

As a member of one of the many minorities that exist within Canada—specifically as a gay man—I am more than aware of the lack of discussion over developing laws to regulate behaviour and now, more than ever, to respond to a disease often conflated with behaviour.

Again, I am not only brought back to the concerns around the ill-defined nature of half of these laws and their consequences, but the apathy toward the very real underpinning of all of these perspectives that is adversarial. Laws to protect an undefined "us" against an ever-widening "them." The focus is kept squarely on what I could or might be able to do to … who? The assumption is not only paternalistic in that I might not be "able" to make decisions without oversight, but also in that my inherent decision-making process is subject to the best interests of others.

When empowering police officers to land squarely in the middle of this already complicated discussion, as if it is a done deal with clear lines, which it in no way has, elicits an immediate uprising of concern. What would it be like for people in far more vulnerable situations than me? Even for myself, the idea that the police would be given authority over any part of health care seems counterintuitive on the face of it. Any offer to explain it as "just trying to help" seems disingenuous at best and threatening at worst.

PUBLIC HEALTH ACT REFLECTIONS

Over the last 30 years, public health law and regulations have undergone significant changes in British Columbia. The concerns of AIDS and civil rights activists of the late 1980s should still resonate in relation to today's legislation. And, as MT aptly points out, there are numerous current concerns, but one in particular:

Ultimately, my deepest concern as a PWA is that a series of powers and authorities have been granted and none of them have been truly tested, challenged, or defined. I conclude that relying on a vague point of reference of "what is best" without ever truly forging a clear definition *may not* actively be dangerous to my health and rights as a human being. Yet, the *potential* harm of relying on the moral and ethical compasses of other people to always, *always* match my interests is not only foolish in the absence of a framework to compare terms, it is negligent to all of our rights as individuals. It assumes that providers I interact with will uniformly reach the exact same conclusions. Each and every time.

While the blatant quarantine of PWAs was avoided in Bill 34, what still exists is strengthened today by broad-based definitions that can be enacted across a wide range of situations. "Health hazards" have a central role in broadening the reasons for public health interventions. Health hazards have replaced the language proposed by the BCCLA of "willfully and carelessly" spreading disease. Intent is not considered in the Public Health Act. The discretion and "reasonable belief" of health officers allows for significant latitude in enacting orders. Under the Public Health Act, the medical health officer may order a person to undergo testing, examination, or preventative treatment. If an individual fails to abide by the order of the medical health officer, the officer may escalate their intervention using more forceful techniques, including seeking detainment and the services of peace officers. Granted that the health officer needs support from the courts to enforce more extreme measures of public health orders, health officers are not obligated to notify the person against whom they seek the warrant or injunction, leaving challenges to the order to occur after the enforcement. Use of police to enforce orders blends the goals of public health with law enforcement, which reinforces the criminalization of PWAs. We are not arguing for or against one particular intervention over another, be it civil or criminal. Rather, we are pointing out the legislative leeway in British Columbia to enact particularly coercive measures in the name of public health, the seemingly more humane approach than HIV criminalization. Given the persuasiveness of the British Columbia Centre for Excellence in HIV/AIDS (BCCfE) to have the province endorse and promote TasP as *the* provincial HIV prevention initiative, it is not unreasonable to be concerned about how our present-day public health legislation and regulations may be enacted for those non-adherent patients. As it stands, public health legislation would not require any significant changes in order to enact mandatory treatment, so long as a medical health officer "reasonably believes" that public health is at risk.

IMPLICATIONS FOR CRITICAL CLINICAL SOCIAL WORK PRACTICE

Although the connection between legislation, policy, and critical clinical practice may seem thin, we are adamant that critical clinical social workers must be well versed in the legislation of the jurisdictions in which they practice and particularly in how these policies impact the people we serve. This attention to legislation is of the utmost importance, especially in this era of HIV criminalization and in places where public health measures can be severe. This is also intensified where AIDS service organizations and clinical settings are shy to engage with PWAs about the implications of criminal law for their lives. Using the example of a man who was charged under the Public Health Act in August 2018, we outline four specific focuses for critical clinical social work practice with PWAs and offer critical clinical interventions for this case study.

In August 2018, the Vancouver medical health officer, Dr. Reka Gustafson, charged an HIV-positive man, let's call him Joe, under the Public Health Act for not complying with treatment. Media reports state that the man failed "to collect medication and fail[ed] to attend clinic appointments" (Proctor, 2018). Because his viral load had reached a certain level, which made him potentially infectious, he was supposed to attend daily medical appointments. In a CBC article, Gustafson is quoted as saying, "the person would be required by the courts to take whatever prevention measures would be needed to reduce the probability of transmission" (Proctor, 2018). We think this actual case example speaks directly to our public health policy concerns and MT's experiences with BC health care providers.

First, we must not sever discussions of public health from care for individual PWAs. We do not see a dichotomy between public health and personal care, but rather an integrated and contextual discussion to address all needs, holding the PWA's health as priority. We suggest that critical clinical social workers consistently work with PWAs to understand and uphold *their* priorities. While care can be complex and involve multiple pressures, like maintaining organizational goals and meeting reporting measures, critical clinical social workers must prioritize the needs of PWAs. Remember that PWAs have to live with the care decisions and the consequences of the care priorities. As a critical clinical social worker working with Joe, this would mean prioritizing his health care needs and critically examining the concept of public health risk. How could you advocate with/for him and reframe his actions so that public health officials would not consider him a risk to public health? If he was non-adherent to his medication, what arguments can you make to assert his treatment rights, including his right to refuse treatment?

As HIV is a reportable disease nationally, our second point is related to public health legislation and people's right to confidentiality and to know how their information and tissues (in this case, blood) are used. We see this tension between public health reporting and PWAs' right to confidentiality as an ethical dilemma. Given our previous point, we come down on the side of PWAs. However, critical clinical social workers will need to wrestle with their own ethics in these practice situations. At the very least, we advocate for critical clinical social workers to understand where people's information and tissues go and are stored, and how they are used. We encourage practitioners to share this information with PWAs and discuss the possible implications of engaging with health care services, so PWAs can make informed decisions about their care and life. In the case of British Columbia, PWAs are given little to no information about where and how their information and tissues are used and stored, or who can access them. We believe this is unethical, regardless of the fact that the present-day public health legislation enacts this practice. Given this, PWAs' choices might not be your own. The clinical priority to share information between agencies could be a source of anxiety for PWAs. Maintaining adherence may have broader contextual implications for the client than you understand. In short, when offering options, understand that simply because the patient chooses an option that is not in line with policy does not constitute a failure or misguided choice.

In Joe's case, we hypothesize that the threat to public safety that he supposedly posed because of his non-adherence to treatment was not the only reason he was charged under the Public Health Act. Understanding the multitude of systemic reasons why adherence in British Columbia is important is essential to unpacking why he may have been charged. One example connects to MT's experience of the punishment of being denied access to treatment because he was one day late with his medication refill. The BCCfE uses medication refills as their marker for adherence, which also becomes their scientific basis for making particular claims about the utility of TasP. A critical clinical social worker would understand that markers of adherence are not solely for the patient's benefit, but also represent institutional interests that can complete or compromise patient autonomy.

Third, we also advocate for critical clinical social workers to collectively push back regarding the lack of confidentiality in public health legislation, particularly in cases where people's specific consent to research has been legislatively revoked. We reiterate that the care of PWAs should be our first priority, not research that may or may not directly benefit them. As a critical clinical social worker, how can you prioritize Joe's confidentiality despite the lack of it as a result of the public health charges? Based on discussions with Joe, what concerns of confidentiality has he raised and what protection might you offer him? For example, if he is concerned about his name being released to the media, does he want you to intervene with journalists? What arguments could you make to protect his privacy?

Lastly, as a direct care provider, we emphasize again that your clients' care is your priority, not research, not how their health impacts others, not the general public. We are not saying that you should completely disregard these other priorities, but instead place them in a constellation with rather than opposition to the patient's priorities. We encourage critical clinical social workers to centre their practice on how patients define what is best for them and how we can best support them. Given that the Public Health Act removes the right to notice, how might a critical clinical social worker advocate for Joe's right to representation during the process of the public health injunction? How can you as a critical clinical social worker advocate for transparency and clarity in the process? How might legal representation or advocacy from other institutions like the BCCLA be in Joe's best interest and prioritize his care, autonomy, and informed consent?

CONCLUSION

In this chapter, we engaged with critical historical policy analysis to understand how the AIDS quarantine bill still impacts current BC public health legislation. Based on historical AIDS activists' and human rights defenders' objections, we can see how they are still applicable in today's context. MT's lived experience also highlights how individual concerns persist despite the lack of overt response to the Public Health Act changes in 2009. By understanding the policy implications and the lived experiences of those who are targets of public health policy, as critical clinical social workers we are better positioned to respond both individually and systemically to PWAs' rights to care, autonomy, and informed consent.

NOTE

1. Part of this chapter comes from Eli's dissertation (Manning, 2016), but it has been expanded on and developed further through our (Eli and MT's) ongoing conversations about quarantine, AIDS activism, and clinical care in British Columbia.

REFERENCES

British Columbia Civil Liberties Association. (1987a). *Bill 34 and AIDS: A Fresh Approach*. Vancouver: Author.

British Columbia Civil Liberties Association. (1987b, April 11). Health Bill 34: AIDS quarantine legislation. Retrieved from https://bccla.org/our_work/ health-bill-34-aids-quarantine-legislation/

British Columbia Legislative Assembly. (1987a). *Official report of the debates of the Legislative Assembly* (34th Parliament, p. 2236). 1st Reading. Victoria: Queen's Press.

British Columbia Legislative Assembly. (1987b). *Official report of the debates of the Legislative Assembly* (34th Parliament, pp. 2634–2652). 2nd Reading. Victoria: Queen's Press.

British Columbia Legislative Assembly. (1987c). *Official report of the debates of the Legislative Assembly* (34th Parliament, pp. 2667–2678). Committee Reading. Victoria: Queen's Press.

British Columbia Legislative Assembly. (1987d). *Official report of the debates of the Legislative Assembly* (34th Parliament, p. 2793). 3rd Reading. Victoria: Queen's Press.

Cameron, E. (2009). Criminalization of HIV transmission: Poor public health policy. *HIV/AIDS Policy and Law Review, 14*(2), 63–75.

Canadian HIV/AIDS Legal Network. (2012). *HIV non-disclosure and the criminal law: An analysis of two recent decisions of the Supreme Court of Canada*. Toronto: Author.

Coalition for Responsible Health Legislation. (1987a). *Bill 34: The Health Statutes Amendments Act*. Vancouver: Author.

Coalition for Responsible Health Legislation. (1987b, November 16). No AIDS Quarantine, Says Coalition. Vancouver: Author.

Coalition for Responsible Health Legislation. (1987c). *Position paper for effective action on AIDS*. Vancouver: Author.

Gagnon, M. (2012). Toward a critical response to HIV criminalization: Remarks on advocacy and social justice. *Journal of the Association of Nurses in AIDS Care, 23*(1), 11–15.

Gostin, L. O. (2004). *The AIDS pandemic*. Chapel Hill: University of North Carolina Press.

Health Act, RSBC 1996, c. 179. Retrieved from http://bclaws.ca/Recon/document/ID/ freeside/00_96179_01

Interpretation Act, RSBC 1996, c. 238. Retrieved from http://www.bclaws.ca/civix/ document/id/complete/statreg/96238_01

Kotiswaran, P. (2014). Beyond the allures of criminalization: Rethinking the regulation of sex work in India. *Criminology and Criminal Justice, 14*(5), 565–579.

Legislative Assembly of the Province of British Columbia. Health Statutes Amendment Act (1987), 36.

Legislative Assembly of the Province of British Columbia. Public Health Act (2009). Retrieved from http://www.bclaws.ca/civix/document/id/complete/statreg/08028_01

Manning, E. (2016). *The Treatment as Prevention® empire: HIV treatment adherence as the new war on AIDS*. Doctoral dissertation, Department of Gender, Sexuality, and Women's Studies, Simon Fraser University, Vancouver, BC. Retrieved from https://theses.lib.sfu.ca/thesis/etd9867

McClelland, A. (2013). Research at the medico-legal borderland: Perspectives on HIV and criminal law. *Somatosphere*, 1–9. Retrieved from http://somatosphere.net/2013/10/research-at-the-medico-legal-borderland.html

Mykhalovskiy, E. (2011). The problem of "significant risk": Exploring the public health impact of criminalizing HIV non-disclosure. *Social Science and Medicine*, *73*(5), 668–675.

Mykhalovskiy, E. (2014). The public health implications of HIV criminalization: Past, current, and future research directions. *Critical Public Health*, *25*(4), 373–385.

Mykhalovskiy, E., & Betteridge, G. (2012). Who? What? Where? When? And with what consequences? An analysis of criminal cases of HIV non-disclosure in Canada. *Canadian Journal of Law and Society*, *27*(1), 31–53.

Mykhalovskiy, E., Betteridge, G., & McLay, D. (2010). *HIV non-disclosure and the criminal law: Establishing policy options for Ontario.*

Proctor, J. (2018, August 24). Vancouver man charged with ignoring medical health officer's orders for HIV treatment. *CBC News*. Retrieved from https://www.cbc.ca/news/canada/british-columbia/hiv-medical-public-health-risk-1.4795491

Smith & Hughes. (1987a). *Brief on the Health Statutes Amendment Act (Bill 34)*. Vancouver: Coalition for Responsible Health Legislation.

Smith & Hughes. (1987b). *Excerpts from brief on the Health Statutes Amendments Act (Bill 34) (Final)*. Vancouver: Vancouver Gay and Lesbian Community Centre.

Wilson, C. (2013). The impact of the criminalization of HIV non-disclosure on the health and human rights of "Black" communities. *Health Tomorrow*, *1*, 109–143.

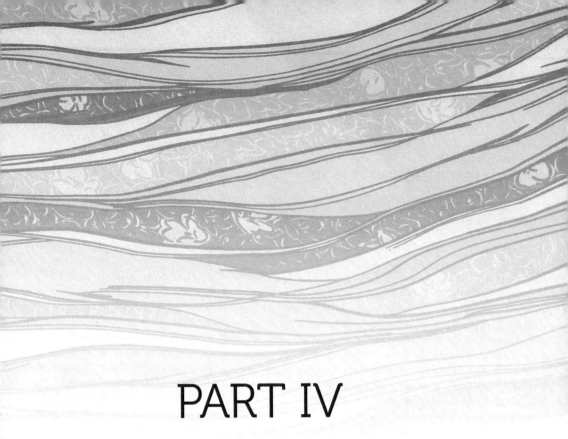

PART IV

WORKING IN THE CONTEXT
OF MARGINALIZATION, OPPRESSION,
AND DIVERSITY

CHAPTER 13

Spirituality as a Resource for Well-Being in African Canadian Communities

Wanda Thomas Bernard, Josephine Etowa, and Barbara Clow

INTRODUCTION

It has been well documented that most African Nova Scotian women are not using the health care services available to them through the publicly funded health care system (Beagan, Etowa, & Bernard, 2012; Bernard, 2005; Etowa, Wiens, Bernard, & Clow, 2007; James et al., 2010). For example, while Black people make up the largest proportion of the visible minority population in Nova Scotia and constitute 4 percent of its population overall, health practitioners report that few, if any, of those seeking their services are African Nova Scotian women. Their limited use of available services may be explained in part by the lack of cultural responsiveness of the services compounded by the physical distance from and geographic location of services, especially for those living in rural areas.

The Nova Scotia Department of Health's *Cultural Competence Guidelines* (Government of Nova Scotia, 2005) were established to advance and support cultural competency in primary health care. Nationally, there has been a push from non-governmental organizations to move to the second stage of medicare, where the emphasis is on inequities in health, accessibility, patient centredness, and population health. In spite of such initiatives, we see little change in the type of health services being provided or how services are delivered in rural Nova Scotia, particularly in reference to African Nova Scotian women.

The On the Margins research project brought together qualitative and quantitative research indicating the need to further investigate the content and context of rural African Nova Scotian women's health and well-being.[1] As Enang (2002) found in her literature review, data and analysis pertaining to African Nova Scotian women's health were limited, and there was even less research on women in rural communities. Research undertaken in the United States provides insight into the experiences of African American women, but these findings do not necessarily pertain to the Canadian context. Meanwhile, extant Canadian studies indicate that the provision of culturally competent services continues to create barriers to care. Transportation and the availability of health care services are also big challenges in rural Nova Scotia. If affordable transportation is available, Black women in rural Nova Scotia are much more likely to seek services outside their own communities (Enang, 2002). Further, Black women, in general, tend not to utilize services except in a time of crisis or emergency, in part because they find that the health, education, and justice systems are often hostile, or at best uncomfortable, due to racism (Enang, 2002). Thus, Black, rural Nova Scotian women experience the compounded effects of many intersecting challenges: poor health, low self-esteem, limited levels of education, isolation of rural communities, racism, and discrimination due to gender and culture (Enang, 2002).

Significant work needs to be done to involve Black Nova Scotian women in their health care communities. Broad-scope health services must become accessible, culturally competent, and culturally safe in terms of effectively addressing the needs of rural African Nova Scotian women. The overall findings of the On the Margins study broaden the focus of research attention concerning rural women of African descent and their awareness of and access to health care in their communities. In this chapter, we look at one element of the On the Margins study: how rural African Nova Scotian women articulate the links between their health and spirituality. The chapter begins with some background information, followed by a brief discussion of the research methodology and our findings. It concludes with a discussion of implications for critical clinical practices in health care policy and practice.

As you read this chapter, ask yourself the following questions:

1. How might the ways in which African Canadian women define health impact the critical clinical perspectives that I might consider in practice?
2. What is the role of spirituality in African Canadian communities and how might this influence their experiences with health care services?
3. How can health and social service providers integrate spirituality into critical clinical practices with African Canadian women?

BACKGROUND

Although people of African descent have lived in Nova Scotia for centuries, and African Nova Scotians comprise one of the largest visible minority groups in both Nova Scotia and Canada, Black Nova Scotians remain socially, economically, and politically disadvantaged. Many are unemployed or underemployed and live in poverty; most have limited access to appropriate social, economic, and health services; and all are underrepresented in health care delivery, in health research, and in the design and implementation of health policy (Este & Bernard, 2006; McGibbon & Etowa, 2009). Like their urban counterparts, African Nova Scotians living in rural and remote regions encounter serious cultural barriers to appropriate health care, but in contrast to urban Black people, their situation is compounded by geographic isolation (Etowa, Bernard, Clow, & Wiens, 2012). Kisely, Terashima, and Langille (2008) used administrative data spanning the period from 1996 to 2005 to investigate three health conditions—circulatory disease, diabetes mellitus, and psychiatric disorders—in a predominantly African Nova Scotian community. This study compared the health experience of these African Nova Scotians with the White population in similar communities in the province. Their study revealed that the incidence rates for all three conditions in the African Nova Scotian community were 13 to 43 percent higher than for Nova Scotia as a whole, and the incidence rates were also higher than for the comparison communities (Kisely et al., 2008).

Even when African Nova Scotians in rural and remote communities have the financial and social resources to gain access to health services, they may not find culturally responsive providers, programs, or facilities within a reasonable distance (Etowa, Bernard, Clow, & Adongo, 2017). This mesh of corrosive conditions has a predictable impact on the health of rural African Canadians. Evidence from other regions of Canada suggests that Black people are disproportionately affected by many serious illnesses, including diabetes mellitus, cardiovascular and cerebrovascular diseases, cancers, HIV/AIDS, lupus, and sarcoidosis (Husbands et al., 2013; Remis, Swantee, & Liu, 2012). Mortality among Black infants is also more than double that of Caucasian infants (Office of Minority Health, 2019). Despite this increased burden of illness, African Canadians are less likely than White Canadians to seek and receive health services in a timely manner (Etowa, Beagan, Bernard, & Eghan, 2017). For example, some studies have shown that African Nova Scotians are more likely to access health care services for conditions such as renal disease at the end stage of the illness than at earlier, often more treatable, stages (Bernard, Maddalena, Smith, & Njiwaji, 2014; Maddalena et al., 2010).

Although still in its infancy, there is a growing body of research and literature regarding spirituality in social work and in health care (Bowen-Reid & Smalls, 2004; Canda, 2008; Johnson, Elbert-Avila, & Tulsky, 2005), particularly in African American communities (Este & Bernard, 2006). Recognizing that more research into spirituality in health care needs to be conducted, Johnson and colleagues (2005, p. 718) suggest:

> Future research should focus on the use and development of reliable and valid measures exploring the association between spirituality, culture, and ethical decision making; the inclusion of national samples of subjects of diverse ages, ethnicities, and illnesses; and the relative influence of spirituality and other factors.

Two key themes emerge in the literature on religion, spirituality, and health: first, spirituality differs from religion and second, spirituality is used as a resource for health in African American and African Canadian communities. These themes are explored in depth in the following sections.

Spirituality Differs from Religion

The differences between spirituality and religion are well documented. Spirituality is defined as a connectedness with a sense of a higher being or power that governs one's existence by serving as a source of meaning and purpose through which people interpret their lives and experiences (Bowen-Reid & Smalls, 2004; Canda, 2008; Este & Bernard, 2006; Johnson et al., 2005). This definition remains consistent in both African Canadian and African American studies. Johnson and colleagues' (2005) study of African Canadian people facing illness and death revealed that spirituality was significant to those journeys. Este and Bernard (2006) also cited the work of Wheeler, Ampadu, and Wangari (2002, p. 77), suggesting, "spirituality is deeply embedded in the healthy lifespan development of people of Africa and the African Diaspora." In a later work, Bernard (2009) defined spirituality as the essence of our being, the innate, invisible, and sustaining force in one's life, which is separate from but not necessarily unrelated to one's participation in organized religion.

In contrast, religion is often understood as a formal involvement and commitment that is organized within a particular institutional structure, such as churches and mosques (Bowen-Reid & Smalls, 2004; Canda, 2008; Este & Bernard, 2006; Johnson et al., 2005). For many Canadians of African descent, involvement in organized religion has been significant to their survival in this country (Pachai, 1990; Pachai, 1997; Saunders, 1994; Winks, 1997). For African Nova Scotians in particular, the significance of the Baptist Church and the African United Baptist Association (AUBA) has been identified as central to their resilience and survival (Este & Bernard, 2003; Walker & Thorvaldson, 1979). In fact, the AUBA website (2015) states:

> The AUBA has a long and distinguished history in serving the Black Community throughout Nova Scotia. The AUBA has played an important part in nurturing the spirit for many Black Nova Scotians. This organization is far more than a religious organization—it has served as a centre for education opportunities, a trailblazer for social change and remains a strong voice for hundreds of black families throughout Nova Scotia.

While the current and historical significance of organized religion, especially the AUBA, is clear, differences between religion and spirituality must be further explored by researchers and health care providers. It is essential that health care providers understand that, for some clients, spirituality may be different from religion.

Spirituality Is an Important Resource for Health in African American and Canadian Communities

A second theme that emerges in the literature is the concept of spirituality as a resource for health in African American and Canadian communities. For example, in a study by Bowen-Reid and Smalls (2004), African American participants with high spirituality and religious salience scores reported better health-promoting behaviours compared to participants with moderate-to-low spirituality scores. The study also revealed that respondents with higher spirituality scores and lower levels of stress tended to report better nutrition, spiritual growth, interpersonal skills, and overall health-promoting behaviours. Similarly, the 40 studies reviewed by Johnson and colleagues (2005) highlight that spiritual beliefs and practices are particularly salient for African Americans, especially regarding their spirituality as guidance for overcoming an illness or coping with end-of-life treatments. The researchers extracted four themes that support the notion of spirituality as a resource for health: (1) the importance of spiritual beliefs and practices in coping with illness, (2) the power of spiritual beliefs and practices to promote healing, (3) the belief that God is ultimately responsible for physical and mental health, and (4) the belief that the physician is God's "instrument" to promote healing (p. 713). These findings indicate that people of African descent use spirituality as a resource for health.

These themes are reiterated in the Canadian literature. For example, Maddalena and colleagues (2013) noted that spirituality is a significant factor in the experiences of both the caregiver and the person receiving care when dealing with cancer. Similarly, Bernard and colleagues (2014) asserted that at the end of life, those who have a solid spiritual base seem to face death with a more positive attitude and the dying process is less stressful than for those who lack this spiritual base. Furthermore, they noted that those who are both spiritually anchored and involved with organized religion have more support from their faith communities during this final stage of life than those who are not. Beagan and colleagues (2012) also found that spirituality and religion helped African Nova Scotian women cope not only with illness, but also with difficult life transitions and everyday stress, including the stress of racism. Este and Bernard (2006) and Bernard and colleagues (2014) highlighted the significance of culturally appropriate spirituality in the lives of African Canadians. All of these studies support the notion that spirituality is a resource for health promotion and for coping with health issues, including palliative care and death (Este & Bernard, 2006; Maddalena et al., 2013).

Similar themes arise in literature concerned with other Africans in the Diaspora (Banerjee & Pyles, 2004; Giger, Appel, Davidhizar, & David, 2008; Holt, Schulz et al., 2011; Holt, Wang et al., 2011). The evidence highlights the significant role of spirituality and/or religion in the lives of African people, especially when they are dealing with illness and health concerns.

It is evident from the literature that spirituality is an important resource for health. Furthermore, from an Africentric social work theoretical perspective, spirituality is a key principal to use in practice (Bernard et al., 2014; Este & Bernard, 2006; Schiele, 1996). However, for African Canadians living in rural communities, holistic health care and critical clinical practice is woefully absent (Etowa, Wiens et al., 2007; Etowa, Bernard et al., 2017). This chapter is based on findings from a study that investigated the health status of and health care delivery for African Canadian women living in rural and remote regions of Nova Scotia, specifically the towns and villages along the south and west shores of the province from Liverpool through Yarmouth to Annapolis Royal. Through an innovative program of research conducted over three years, the On the Margins project resulted in a rich combination of quantitative and qualitative data and community action.

The principles of Africentricity and participatory action research guided the process of this mixed method research comprising both quantitative and qualitative traditions. Researchers of African descent were meaningfully engaged through the design, implementation, and knowledge translation phases of the project (Asuquo & Etowa, 2016; Etowa, Bernard, Clow, & Oyinsan, 2007). In phase one of the study, three African Nova Scotian community facilitators who worked on the project as research assistants conducted community consultations to inform the questions and methods. In phase two, the facilitators completed 270 in-depth, individual interviews with African Nova Scotian women living in the southwest region of Nova Scotia. Of these, 237 were deemed analyzable and transcribed. The research team, including the community facilitators, conducted the analysis of this rich body of data. Following the analysis of the interview data, the community facilitators held four focus groups to further explore issues around the major themes that had emerged from the data.

Thematic analysis guided the interpretation of the data from the interviews and focus groups. ATLAS.ti computer software facilitated the management of the large amounts of qualitative data. SPSS and Excel were used for the quantitative data mining and to generate descriptive statistics.

SPIRITUALITY

The theme of spirituality emerged in the data in different ways. First, several participants included spirituality in their definitions of health and emphasized the importance of believing in a higher power. Second, many women identified spirituality as a strategy for managing their health. Finally, for some women, prayer was identified as a specific manifestation of spirituality. Each of these themes is discussed below, using excerpts from the women's narratives to elaborate and highlight main points.

SPIRITUALITY

Spirituality, or higher power, is a strategy for managing health, including individual and collective prayer.

Spiritual Health as an Integral Component of Health Definitions

Spiritual health was important to the women in the study, as was access to church as a space for nurturing their spirituality. In discussing their health concerns, some women recognized a need for and the importance of having a church within the community. Others suggested that not only was the presence or absence of a church important, but that a *culturally specific* church and/or church leader was very significant for health. One woman spoke about the need for a Black minister, saying, "It would be nice … if we could get our own minister.… We usually always get a good minister." Lack of access to a place to share spirituality due to churches moving outside the Black community also presented a health concern for many women in the study and their families. Another woman shared:

> You know when it's not, when it's not a Black church you can't go and be yourself, you can go into a white church and you can fellowship. But you can't sit down and tell them your deepest darkest secrets and concerns … they are not going to understand.… You don't feel like you can let your guard down. You feel like you have to put on your … best behaviour and put on a front. And that, I think that contributes to bad health.… If you can't be yourself what is that doing to your health if you gotta be somebody else all the time?

Not only was access to culturally specific places of worship identified as important for spiritual health, but the lack of such spaces was associated with adverse effects on spiritual health. This finding is supported by the published literature. James and colleagues (2010) stressed that one of the impacts of racism on the lives of African Canadians is damage to their spiritual health. Similarly, Este and Bernard (2006) and Bernard and colleagues (2014) stress the importance of culturally specific spiritual practices to the health of African Canadians.

Spirituality as a Strategy for Managing Health

The narratives of the women in this study revealed multiple strategies that Black women use to manage their health concerns and conditions despite the obstacles they must overcome and challenges they face as they interact with the health system. Spirituality was identified as one of those coping strategies. As discussed in the literature review, spirituality is a fundamental component of Black women's experiences (Etowa, Bernard et al., 2017). Black women turn to a spiritual being for guidance, healing, and support. Women in this study likewise talked about the importance of spirituality and prayer.

For some, spirituality was used as a strategy for dealing with grief, providing a sense of hope in very challenging circumstances. For many of the women, the greatest help was having both a positive attitude and a spiritual base. Other participants stressed how important faith was in their lives and expressed that their spiritual beliefs helped them to cope with unbearable stress and medical issues. For example, one person said:

> Through my faith and trust and belief in the ____ [name for God].... That's how I was healed. In his words I learned that he gave us a book just like the one [when] we buy a computer, or whatever we get a book to show how it operates. We all come with a book, and that's the Bible. And in there is things telling us what we have to do, and I believe with my faith I believe in what it says ____ [quoting the Bible verse] by Christ's stripes I was healed.... And I will hold that until the day that I die. Until I take my last breath, I feel so much better now ... and the doctor told me that I would be in a wheelchair. I am sitting here and you see me walking.

Another woman shared, "When I walk away from church, I take hope with me. I bring hope. And I find ... it is my strength, it is." For this woman and others like her, spirituality and religious practices help to foster hope in the face of difficult and challenging situations.

Similarly, a sense of critical hope (James et al., 2010) helps many women who survive against the odds to continue to believe that their needs will be met. Critical hope involves an understanding of the forces that produce injustice, an ability to imagine what the world might look like without these forces, and a commitment to engage in a process of transformative systemic change (James et al., 2010). James and colleagues (2010, p. 28) state that "hope has the power to restore, regenerate and heal." Moreover, they state that "a sense of hope, rooted in an understanding of the history of Black People, continues to sustain those who are Black and offers a buffer against the wounds and pain of racism" (p. 28).

According to participants, spirituality also fosters a positive outlook on life and a good attitude, which helps them cope with everyday stressors in life. For example, some women in the study noted that a strong spiritual background helped them feel thankful and appreciative for all that they have, even if their situations are not viewed as optimal by others. One person shared:

> You know I got so much to thank and praise to God for.... My mother died at 68. My oldest sister died at 69. And here we are up in our seventies

and eighties. You see how blessed we are? It must be somebody up there giving us strength ... to be living this long and they wasn't able to. We are really blessed is right, and that is what you have to thank and praise the Lord for. That is so nice.

Prayer for Healing and Coping

A consistent theme amongst participants was the link between spirituality, prayer, and healing. As noted in the review of the literature, spirituality is abstract and people live out or put into action their spirituality in myriad ways. Bernard and colleagues (2014) highlighted the different ways that spirituality is expressed by those at the end of life, including music, individual prayer, meditation, and collective prayer. In this study, many participants identified individual and collective prayer as strategies to practice their spirituality and help to manage their health. Many of the narratives make distinctions between different types of prayers and the purpose of prayer, such as prayer for support or prayer of thanksgiving; however, the overarching theme was prayer for healing and help with coping.

One participant described the importance of prayer in her quest for the healing of loved ones and respite for herself. It is important to note that participants focused on prayer for healing for others as well as themselves. As one woman shared:

> There's times I'm telling you, sweet, that I walk the floor, I pray if I'm walking, if I go outdoors I'm walking, especially when he was sick, I'd go outdoors, I'd walk the floor, I'd pray going to bed, pray myself to sleep, get up in the morning and say thank you, Jesus, I'm alive. Oh I'm telling ya.... And I put my faith where it should be and I get a lot better, I really do.

Two specific points regarding prayer that emerged from the data are the power of collective prayer and the capacity of prayer to relieve stress and help manage mental health. These are discussed in detail in the following sections.

Collective Prayer

Some women in the study talked about the healing effects brought about by collective prayer. For some, this entailed "prayer circles" or the "laying on of hands" organized by members of their church community. Several women talked about how supportive they found prayers from other church members to be. One woman, when speaking about the church as a space for collective prayer and support, added, "The church also had its own way ... of being that neutral ... ground ... where people ... can let go a little bit you know."

Several women reported having witnessed answers to collective prayers, and how significant the collective prayers were for individuals' healing. However, many of the women shared that prayer was most helpful as a stress-reliever.

Prayer as a Stress-Reliever and as a Coping Mechanism for Mental Health Issues

Similar to findings from other studies, many of the women in this study shared that they live with everyday stress triggered by a number of sources and they use prayer as a way to help them cope. For example, one woman said:

> If I'm feeling down, I pray, I pray, I pray and I pray. You've got to pray.... Strength comes from in here [pointing at her heart]. In here, it's not in your arms.... I don't care if it's your son, your husband, who it is in the family, something goes wrong, who do they run to, they run right to mom. And you might not even be around and know what they're talking about, but they all come to you anyway. You are the centre of the family.... You are the centre, and sometimes that's an awful load to hold up but as I said praying.... I'm telling you, I, I have learned that there is a greater force than I ... or any man on earth. I have learned that. And sometimes it takes a lot.... And I have now learned, there is somebody stronger than me and mightier than me. Pray to him and I'm telling you things have lightened up, these are things like I can run into something like, like it's almost like a brick wall and you think, oh my God, how am I going to get over this? Just give a little prayer.... He, he hears ya.

A number of women in the study said that prayer helps them to cope with larger mental health issues such as depression. One woman had a number of health conditions in the past couple of years, including surgery to remove a cancerous tumour in her stomach and surgery to remove her gall bladder. While she said that she did not feel as well as before these operations, she found that she was able to cope through prayer. Another woman who injured her arm in the past and had not been able to work for several years related how prayer helped her deal with the depression that accompanied her physical health problems and subsequent disability:

Well, some days I get a little down but then I say to myself, I thank the Lord that I could have broke my neck when I fell. Like I mean I could have been in a wheelchair for life. So I thank the Lord. I look at it like I do have my health in that sense, and I am able to move around and go out and about. But … some days I get a little depressed. But then again I say to the Lord, well, you done it for a reason…. I'll sit for a while and then I'll say to myself the Lord has been good to me so far and he'll see me through. So I just leave it in his hands.

One woman who experienced severe depression that led to a nervous break-down and psychotic episodes had the following to say about her road to recovery:

I always deal with depression on a daily basis and some days are worse than others. It is just something I learned to live with. Something I've learned to deal with. I am a very spiritual person like I am not really faithful of God right now, but you know I pray … and you know that helps me a lot…. A lot of people don't realize when they are having a nervous breakdown … it takes so many steps to get to that point. One thing I will say about it, it made me a better person. I don't know I'm just stronger. I … got closer to God.

In dealing with her husband's illness, one of the participants said that she valued prayer and, even more than that, the "inner strength that always comes out," stating that she prayed and "I never ever thought I could do it. But I did it. And I prayed and I done it and I, and I, got it done."

Clearly, for these women participants, spiritual health is as important to maintain as physical and mental health. Their action-based spirituality, as mani-fested in prayer, is a solid resource for managing overall health and well-being, whether they are dealing with a critical health issue or everyday stress. Similarly, Este and Bernard (2006) noted that Black women found strength and comfort through daily prayer.

Spirituality has been identified as a coping mechanism and a resource for managing health. Critical clinical social workers could look to Africentric the-ory in considering the role of spirituality in addressing health issues with people of African descent. Principles of Africentricity include the interconnection of all things, the spiritual nature of human beings, the importance of collective iden-tity, and the recognition of affective dimensions (James et al., 2010). Africentric theory is not yet a mainstream theoretical framework. It has been built from the margins. Although grounded in African American/African Canadian experiences, its principles are transferable to other groups. A key principle is centring the client/consumer in the experience. Africentrism is built on three central beliefs: (1) human identity is a collective identity and context is central to this identity, (2) spirituality is as important as material aspects of life, and (3) affective knowledge is valid and essential in understanding the lived experiences of all people (Schiele, 1996). Central to this chapter is the significance of spirituality, which has also been stressed by other scholars, such as Beagan and colleagues (2012), Bernard and colleagues (2014), and Este and Bernard (2006). Africentric theory is an example of best practices in social work, which include validating lived experiences, focusing on strengths of the individual, and designing community and collective solutions to issues. Walton and Shepard Payne (2016, p. 650) suggest that social workers "receive training regarding cultural nuances [and] identify culturally relevant protective factors [such as] social support and spirituality." The authors also note that "only through tapping into the experiential world of individuals … can social work practitioners come to truly understand" (p. 651).

This builds on the work of Davis, Williams, and Akinyela (2010), James and colleagues (2010), and Este and Bernard (2003), who stress the importance of culturally specific programming. Davis and colleagues (2010, p. 338) also highlight the inherent risks of "social work researchers complicating social problems and biasing solutions if they do not follow culturally relevant principles and approaches." They affirm, "the insider/outsider dilemma must be taken seriously if we are to move beyond superficial connections of race, class, and gender … and respect for the history, culture, and knowledge of African-descendant people," (pp. 342–343). Africentric social work practice also builds critical consciousness and critical hope through practices that are grounded in community values, ethics, and commitment to social justice, which are all key tenets of Africentrism (James et al., 2010; Warner, 2006). Africentric principles valuing lived experiences and taking them seriously as a form of knowledge (James et al., 2010, p. 23) are significant in this work. We concur with Bernard and Smith (2018) that understanding community is central to the Africentric perspective and to the creation of meaningful real solutions to real problems. Furthermore, as Bernard and Smith (2018) assert, a holistic approach through Africentric practice helps to heal the harm done through the alienation of culturally irrelevant policy and practice.

We assert that we can and should lead the charge that to use Africentric theory in critical clinical practice is to "study the world and its people, concepts, and history from an African worldview" (Asante, 1991, p. 171) or "to place Africans and the interest of Africa at the center of our approach to problem solving" (Asante, 1987, p. 17, cited in James et al., 2010, p. 23). Considering the results of this study, one could explore the use of spirituality as a resource for health when working with African Canadians.

CRITICAL CLINICAL CASE

The case of Jennifer Jones is one that was eventually taken to the Nova Scotia Human Rights Tribunal. It involved discrimination based on sex and race, where the complainant was a Black and Métis woman who experienced unwanted sexual advances and reprisal from her employer. Jennifer testified that her stress level had been rising throughout the two years prior to her filing the complaint, and stated that she was really stressed out. Symptoms of her stress included crying at home, snapping at her husband and children, and frequently skipping meals and beginning to avoid food. As a result, she began losing hours at work, because she skipped days and couldn't get up to go to work. Despite the toll the job was taking on her, she did not quit as she needed the income. She was having stomach pains, vomiting, and thought she had an ulcer. She was also experiencing depression, found it difficult to focus, and just wanted to give up on life. When Jennifer filed her human rights complaint, her caseworker strongly suggested that she see a medical doctor to examine her physical symptoms of stress and also that she see a social worker to address the depression.

Jennifer sought counselling at the local mental health clinic and also visited her family doctor. Her doctor immediately put her off work on stress leave so that she could focus on restoring her health. At the mental health clinic, she saw a social worker who used an Africentric critical clinical perspective to first understand her experiences, and then to help her navigate her journey to wellness while her human rights complaint was being investigated.

The social worker was able to investigate the complex issues in this case from an Africentric perspective, considering the underlying historical context and the intersectionality of race, class, gender, and colonialism and the implications these held for Jennifer. The worker also explored Jennifer's strengths and the coping mechanisms that she had used in the past to manage stress and challenges in her life.

Jennifer identified spirituality as a major source of strength, but noted that she had even stopped going to church because of the stress, depression, and discomfort she felt due to the sexual and racial harassment she endured at her workplace. Through her work with the social worker, Jennifer was able to restore her sense of critical hope and her spirituality. She started reaching out to her support systems and managed to find strength and comfort in her faith.

The Africentric critical clinical approach used in this case helped Jennifer to more effectively manage the stress of a two-year investigation of her complaint, which was resolved in her favour.

CRITICAL CLINICAL PRACTICES

Based on the findings of the On the Margins study and other literature, we advance to the following critical clinical practice strategies:

1. An Africentric critical clinical approach to health and wellness issues faced by African Nova Scotian women must be multi-faceted, including social, community, employment, and religious services, as well as health services.
2. Training to address culturally safe practices, including spirituality, as well as specific issues affecting Africans in the Diaspora, should be integrated into programs of study for health care practitioners using critical clinical practice.
3. Existing policy must be put into action. The Nova Scotia Department of Health's *Cultural Competence Guidelines* recommend that health care service providers work collaboratively to provide more effective program planning and service delivery in health care for African Canadians and other marginalized populations. Such initiatives must be implemented at the local level so that local health authorities can ensure more culturally safe practices are in place. In addition, the guidelines should pay more explicit attention to spirituality in relation to critical clinical health care services for African Canadians.

Spirituality was identified as a fundamental component of the Black women's lived experience. A major finding in this study was the inclusion of spirituality in the women's definitions of health and the significance they placed on believing in a higher power. The strong association between spiritual care and well-being was made especially clear when the women identified limited access to culturally specific spiritual leaders and churches in their communities as a health concern. The women's narratives, related through qualitative interviews, revealed that many turn to a spiritual being for guidance, healing, and support. Participants referred to the concepts of spirituality and prayer. The women's descriptions highlighted that spirituality can be considered a lifestyle or attitude. They saw prayer as an action that is an outcome of a spiritual attitude. For some, spirituality was a strategy for dealing with their grief, while for others it was a way of coping with everyday stress, including the stress of racism. Given these findings about the significance of spirituality for Black women, we suggest that it has potential as an important resource for critical clinical practice with people of African descent.

CONCLUSION

Spirituality and organized religion have been central to the lives of African Nova Scotians from the days of slavery and their arrival in Nova Scotia to present times (Este & Bernard, 2006). One could argue that given contemporary issues affecting African Nova Scotians, including systemic and institutionalized racism, spirituality and organized religion are more crucial to their continued survival and success than ever before. Spirituality should be included as a significant component of critical clinical practice, to be used as a vital resource for health care practice in African Canadian communities. Participants in the On the Margins study affirmed the need for a strong spiritual base to help them deal with critical life and health care issues. The importance of spirituality for health promotion and for healing and coping was clearly articulated in the women's narratives. Furthermore, the women showed that their spirituality and faith created a safe space for hope, comfort, and overall well-being in the face of uncertainty and challenges in multiple contexts. This includes the everyday stress of racism, which has been described as surviving "a thousand little cuts" (Hunn, Harley, Elliott, & Canfield, 2015).

Themes that emerged from the data illustrate the importance of spirituality as a sustaining life force for African Nova Scotian women in rural communities, or a "peace that surpasses understanding" (Beagan et al., 2012; Bernard et al., 2014; Este & Bernard, 2006; Maddalena et al., 2013).

Understanding the role of spirituality in the lives of African communities can be used as an effective tool when working with clients from the African

Diaspora, as illustrated in the case example. To work competently and efficiently with the African Nova Scotian community, health care service providers need to incorporate the spirituality that is embedded within this culture. Unfortunately, despite its importance for many African Nova Scotian women, spirituality has not been seriously considered a policy issue in health care. Este and Bernard (2006) assert that spirituality serves as a survival mechanism, source of strength, coping strategy, buffer against the everyday violence and trauma of racism, and tool of resistance for African Nova Scotians. They call on practitioners to explore the use of spirituality in both assessment and interventions when working with African Nova Scotian individuals and families. The findings in this study are aligned with these ideas. Critical clinical assessment processes could explore the meaning of spirituality, the role of spirituality, or the absence of spirituality, which could help to guide culturally safe intervention strategies.

NOTE

1. For further information on the study's findings, see Etowa, Wiens, Bernard, and Clow, 2007; Etowa, Bernard, Clow, and Oyinsan, 2007; Etowa, Bernard, Clow, and Wiens, 2012.

REFERENCES

African United Baptist Association. (2015). Home page. Retrieved from http://www.auba. ca/html/history.html

Asante, M. (1991). The Afrocentric idea in education. *Journal of Negro Education*, *60*(2), 170– 180.

Asuquo, E., & Etowa, J. (2016). Participatory action research (PAR): A strategy to achieve transformational change in nursing research and policy development in low and middle income countries (LMICs). *International Journal of Health, Wellness, and Society*, *6*(1), 11–21.

Banerjee, M. M., & Pyles, L. (2004). Spirituality: A source of resilience for African American women in the era of welfare reform. *Journal of Ethnic and Cultural Diversity in Social Work*, *13*(2), 45–70.

Beagan, B. L., Etowa, J., & Bernard, W. T. (2012). "With God in our lives he gives us the strength to carry on": African Nova Scotian women, spirituality and racism-related stress. *Mental Health, Religion and Culture*, *15*(2), 103–120.

Bernard, W. T. (2005). Black women's health in Nova Scotia: As viewed through a single case study. In S. Harding (Ed.), *First Nations women/Black women/women of colour and health* (pp. 47–70). Calgary: University of Calgary Press.

Bernard, W. T. (2009). Black men in the Diaspora: Resilient and surviving but still catching hell. In G. G. James, R. Ramsay, & G. Drover (Eds.), *International social work* (pp. 81–102). Toronto: Thompson Educational Publishing.

Bernard, W. T., Maddalena, V., Smith, D., & Njiwaji, M. (2014). The role of spirituality at end of life in Nova Scotia's Black community. *Journal of Religion and Spirituality in Social Work: Social Thought, 33*(3/4), 353–376.

Bernard, W. T., & Smith, H. (2018). Injustice, justice, and Africentric practice in Canada. *Canadian Social Work Review, 35*(1), 147–157.

Bowen-Reid, T. L., & Smalls, C. (2004). Stress, spirituality and health promoting behaviours among African American college students. *Western Journal of Black Studies, 28*, 283–291.

Canda, E. R. (2008). Spiritual connection is social work: Boundary violations and transcendence. *Journal of Religion and Spirituality in Social Work: Social Thought, 27*, 25–40.

Davis, S. K., Williams, A. D., & Akinyela, M. M. (2010). An Afrocentric approach to building cultural relevance in social work research. *Journal of Black Studies, 41*(2), 338–350.

Enang, J. E. (2002). Black women's health: Health research relevant to Black Nova Scotians. In C. Amaratunga (Ed.), *Race, ethnicity, and women's health* (pp. 43–82). Halifax: Atlantic Centre of Excellence for Women's Health.

Este, D., & Bernard, W. T. (2003). Social work practice with African Canadians: An examination of the African-Nova Scotian Community. In J. R. Graham & A. Al-Krenawi (Eds.), *Multicultural social work practice* (pp. 306–337). Oxford: Oxford University Press.

Este, D., & Bernard, W. T. (2006). Spirituality among African Nova Scotians: A key to survival in Canadian society. *Critical Social Work, 7*, 1–22.

Etowa, J., Beagan, B., Bernard, W., & Eghan, F. (2017) "You feel you have to be made of steel": The strong Black woman, health and wellbeing in Nova Scotia. *Health Care for Women International, 38*(4), 379–393.

Etowa, J., Bernard, W., Clow, B., & Adongo, L. (2017). On the margins: Racism and its impact on the health of African Canadian women in rural and remote communities. In T. LaVeist (Ed.), *Legacy of the crossing: Life, death and triumph among descendants of the world's greatest forced migration* (pp. 165–182). New York: Diasporic Africa Press.

Etowa, J., Bernard, W. T., Clow, B., & Oyinsan, B. (2007). Participatory action research (PAR): Improving Black women's health in rural and remote communities. *International Journal of Transcultural Nursing, 18*, 349–359.

Etowa, J., Bernard, W. T., Clow, B., & Wiens, J. (2012). Defining health: Perspectives of African Canadian women living in remote and rural Nova Scotia communities. In B. Liepert & B. Leach (Eds.), *Rural women's health in Canada* (pp. 287–303). Toronto: University of Toronto Press.

Etowa, J., Wiens, J., Bernard, W. T., & Clow, B. (2007). Determinants of Black women's health in rural and remote communities. *Canadian Journal of Nursing Research, 39*(3), 56–76.

Giger, J. N., Appel, S. J., Davidhizar, R., & David, C. (2008). Church and spirituality in the lives of the African American communities. *Journal of Transcultural Nursing, 19*(4), 375–383.

Government of Nova Scotia, Department of Health. (2005). *Cultural competence guidelines for the delivery of primary health care in Nova Scotia*. Retrieved from http://healthteamnovascotia.ca/cultural_competence/CulturalCompetenceGuidelines_SumSum08.pdf [link no longer available]

Holt, C. L., Schulz, E., Caplan, L., Blake, V., Southward, V. L., & Buckner, A. V. (2011). Assessing the role of spirituality in coping among African Americans diagnosed with cancer. *Journal of Religion and Health, 51*(2), 507–521.

Holt, C. L., Wang, M. Q., Caplan, L., Schulz, E., Blake, V., & Southward, V. L. (2011). Role of religious involvement and spirituality in functioning among African Americans with cancer: Testing a mediational model. *Journal of Behavioural Medicine, 34*(6), 437–448.

Hunn, V., Harley, D., Elliott, W., & Canfield, J. (2015). Microaggression and the mitigation of psychological harm: Four social workers' exposition for care of clients, students, and faculty who suffer "a thousand little cuts." *Journal of Pan African Studies, 7*(9), 41–54.

Husbands, W., Oakes, W., Ongoiba, F., Pierre-Pierre, V., Soje, P., McGee, F., & Mbulaheni, T. (2013). *Talking Black: Understanding the HIV-related needs, challenges and priorities of heterosexual African, Caribbean and Black men in Ontario, Canada*. Toronto: APAA and ACT.

James, C., Este, D., Bernard, W. T., Benjamin, A., Lloyd, B., & Turner, T. (2010). *Race and well-being: The lives, hopes, and activism of African Canadians*. Black Point, NS: Fernwood.

Johnson, K. S., Elbert-Avila, K. I., & Tulsky, J. A. (2005). Ethnogeriatrics and special populations: The influence of spiritual beliefs and practices on the treatment preferences of African Americans: A review of the literature. *Journal of the American Geriatrics Society, 53*, 711–719.

Kisely, S., Terashima, M., & Langille, D. (2008). A population-based analysis of the health experience of African Nova Scotians. *Canadian Medical Association Journal, 179*(7), 653–658.

Maddalena, V., Bernard, W. T., Etowa, J. B., Davis-Murdoch, S., Smith, D., & Marsh-Jarvis, P. (2010). Cancer care experiences and the use of complementary and alternative medicine at end of life in Nova Scotia's Black communities. *Journal of Transcultural Nursing, 21*(2), 114–122.

Maddalena, V., Bernard, W. T., Etowa, J. B., Davis-Murdoch, S., Smith, D., & Marsh-Jarvis, P. (2013). Assessing the knowledge of African Canadians regarding options available for palliative and end of life care using participatory research. *Journal of Transcultural Nursing, 24*(2), 144–152.

McGibbon, E. A., & Etowa, J. B. (2009*). Anti-racist health care practice.* Toronto: Canadian Scholars' Press.

Office of Minority Health. (2019). *Infant mortality and African Americans.* US Department of Health and Human Services. Retrieved from https://minorityhealth.hhs.gov/omh/browse.aspx?lvl=4&lvlid=23

Pachai, B. (1990). *Beneath the clouds of the promised land: The survival of Nova Scotia's Blacks: Vol. 2. 1800–1989.* Halifax: Black Educators Association.

Pachai, B. (1997). *People of the Maritimes: Blacks.* Halifax: Nimbus Publishing.

Remis, R., Swantee, C., & Liu, J. (2012). *Report on HIV/AIDS in Ontario 2009.* Toronto: Ontario HIV Epidemiologic Monitoring Unit.

Saunders, C. (1994). *Share and care: The story of the Nova Scotia Home for Coloured Children.* Halifax: Nimbus Publishing.

Schiele, J. (1996). Afrocentricity: An emerging paradigm in social work practice. *Social Work, 41*(3), 284–294.

Walker, J. W. St. G., & Thorvaldson, P. (1979). *Identity: The Black experience in Canada.* Toronto: Ontario Educational Communications Authority.

Walton, Q. L., & Shepard Payne, J. (2016). Missing the mark: Cultural expressions of depressive symptoms among African-American women and men. *Social Work in Mental Health, 14*(6), 637–657.

Warner, R. (2006). *Theoretical framework for the racism, violence and health project: A working paper.* Retrieved from http://rvh. socialwork.dal.ca/resources.html

Wheeler, E. A., Ampadu, L. M., & Wangari, E. (2002). Lifespan development revisited: African-centered spirituality throughout the life cycle. *Journal of Adult Development, 9*(1), 71–78.

Winks, R. (1997). *The Blacks in Canada: A history* (2nd ed.). Montreal & Kingston: McGill-Queen's University Press.

CHAPTER 14

(De)Colonizing Indigenous Social Work Praxis within the Borderlands

Gail Baikie

We have ... this big flat landscape that you can walk in summertime. They are very wet and they can also be quite dangerous sometimes. When you walk it looks like a place where you can put your foot, but if you put it there then you go through and you get stuck, and it's very hard to get the foot back up again, and can even be dangerous because in some places you can even go through and drown in this mud ... because it's wet and you have to know where to walk.... This is a kind of metaphor [for Indigenous social work praxis] that I've been using. Sometimes you are working there and you think you can do one thing and you put your feet there and then you go through past your knee and you are just on one foot and you have to work a lot to just get this foot back up, continue, but sometimes you know you see one place and you go there and it's risky, but it's the right place, and you can actually walk further on.... You have to know the landscape, you have to know exactly where to put your feet, which places, because all of them can look like this is very good, you can walk there but then you can't. (Judy, Indigenous social worker and research participant)

INTRODUCTION

Indigenous social worker interactions within the borderlands in between Indigenous and Euro-Western worlds and worldviews are (de)colonizing. Indigenous social workers use both their Indigenous knowledge and their knowledge of mainstream perspectives, systems, and institutions to strategically navigate practice situations. However, mainstream practice contexts are dominated by Euro-Western structures and ideas. Often the Indigenous ways of knowing, being, and doing are disregarded by non-Indigenous professionals and organizations. Euro-Western knowledge and skills can also infiltrate the minds and practices of Indigenous so-cial workers given that they are also socialized into the profession and the broader Canadian society. This is problematic if the Euro-Western perspective uncritically and unintentionally operates as the default standpoint for social work practices with Indigenous Peoples and communities.

I conducted a research project that demonstrated that the interactions of Indigenous social workers in everyday practice sites in which Indigenous and Euro-Western practices and perspectives intersect can either challenge or reify colonizing systems and ideologies, and can potentially do both. The research showed that Indigenous social workers naturally critically reflect to mindfully interrupt and disrupt colonizing and therefore oppressive influences on their praxis. In this chapter, I illuminate and demonstrate this phenomenon through the use of practice scenarios from my research. The quote to begin the chapter came from Judy, a participant in the study. It eloquently serves as a metaphor for the challenges faced by Indigenous social workers as they practice within the borderlands. It symbolizes the tenuous and risky nature of their praxis as they have to be careful and vigilant given that the application of Indigeneity is inherently risky to the Indigenous social worker and to Indigenous Peoples and knowledges more generally.

Consistent with Indigenous protocol, I first position myself as an Indigenous person, social worker, and scholar. I then theorize (de)colonizing praxis. I in-troduce my research, which investigated Indigenous social worker praxis from their borderland practice contexts. I emphasize decolonizing critical reflection, a method I developed and used for acquiring decolonized data. Finally, I profile results from my research that are relevant to critical clinical practice in the bor-derlands and discuss the implications for critical clinical practice.

As you read this chapter, ask yourself the following questions:

1. If you are an Indigenous social worker, do the borderland experiences of the Indigenous social workers' practice scenarios resonate with your own? How? How do you bring Indigenous ways of being, knowing, and doing into your borderland practices? How are these ways of knowing and practising responded to by non-Indigenous people and systems?

2. If you are a non-Indigenous social worker, have you ever found yourself in the borderlands in between worldviews? What did you think, feel, or do? What do you know from that experience? If you've never had that

experience, why might that be? How might you recognize if and when you are in the borderlands and how might you best respond to this realization?

3. How might your everyday interactions be (de)colonizing? In other words, how might your everyday interactions either reinforce or dismantle colonizing practices, systems, and institutions, or potentially do both?

4. How might the decolonizing critical reflection method help you examine your practice events for dominant Euro-Western influences on your praxis (thinking and action) and recognize the influence of Indigenous values, beliefs, and practices?

WHO AM I AND HOW DO I KNOW?

From an Indigenous perspective, the only way to know is from one's own experience. In addition, Indigenous Peoples traditionally existed in relation to all things, including land, animals, and other humans. Therefore, I position myself as an Indigenous person, social worker, and scholar, in order to respect my own way of knowing and to acknowledge the knowledge that I receive.

I identify as Inuk-settler, given that I am of both Inuit and European heritage. Pauktuutit (2006), the national Inuit women's organization in Canada, explains that "the term 'Inuit' means 'the people' in Inuktitut, the Inuit language…. 'Inuk' is the singular form of Inuit…. The term 'Eskimo' is no longer in common use and is considered offensive by some Inuit" (p. 2).

The meaning of the term *settler* is controversial. It has been argued that a settler is anyone who is non-Indigenous and has taken up residency on what was once Indigenous land. Settlers also benefit from the fact that Indigenous Peoples are deprived of their collective rights to land and resources (Snelgrove, Dhamoon, & Corntassel, 2014).

Indigenous people are traditionally connected to land. My territorial affiliation is in Labrador, historically with Nunatsiavut, a self-governing territory on the northern coast of Labrador. My Inuk grandfather was born there; however, being nomadic, he also travelled inland and eventually settled in North West River, a town that was established as a Hudson's Bay Company trading post in the 1700s. My grandfather had a trapline along the Churchill River. During his era, there were no opportunities for wage labour. This began to change with the Second World War, when the military became interested in the North for its geographic strategic significance.

Subsequently, the North also became the target for natural resource exploration and exploitation. As a result, while my father learned the ways of my grandfather and spent his life as a subsistence hunter and fisherman, he also became an electrician, thereby joining the first generation of wage labourers in the region. My mother, of British descent, came from the city of St. John's, Newfoundland, to teach in North West River.

I grew up in North West River and learned many of the traditional ways of the Indigenous people, spending much of my time on the land with my father, mother, and siblings. I was the second social worker from my territory to earn a BSW and the first to earn an MSW. I spent my earlier career working in the mental health and addictions field, often travelling for work in small airplanes to the small, isolated Indigenous communities in Labrador. I later moved to Nova Scotia but continued to work in policy and programming with respect to the health and well-being of Indigenous communities in the Atlantic region prior to entering academia in 2002, where I continue to focus on issues of relevance to Indigenous social work education, research, and practice.

BORDERLAND

Gloria Anzaldua (1999) explains that borders are "physically present wherever two or more cultures edge each other, where people of different races occupy the same territory" (in preface [n.p.]). She clarifies that

> borders are set up to define the places that are safe and unsafe, to distinguish us from them. A border is a dividing line, a narrow strip along a steep edge. A borderland [in contrast to a border] is a vague and undetermined place created by the emotional residue of an unnatural boundary. It is in a constant state of transition. (p. 25)

As a result of both my personal and professional experiences, I came to understand that I am positioned in the borderlands in between two worlds, a more traditional Indigenous context that I grew up within and a very Euro-Western context that I intersect with in my education and work life. However, despite many years of immersion into Euro-Western society, my early Indigenous socialization means I am still very much rooted in my Indigeneity, meaning that I have not assimilated, at least not fully, into Euro-Western society. I have come to recognize that other Indigenous social workers are similarly positioned within their personal and work lives. Often Indigenous people have to avail themselves of Euro-Western social services provided by practitioners trained in Euro-Western practices. Even most Indigenous-developed and -run services have to adhere to Euro-Western legislation, regulations, and standards of practice. At the very least, Indigenous services, such as an Indigenous child welfare agency, will undoubtedly have to interface with numerous non-Indigenous organizations and service providers.

The borderlands are a phenomenon of colonization, created by the invasion by European nations of what is now known as North America. These lands were already occupied by Indigenous Peoples who lived in intricate societies that included political and socio-economic systems. Colonization not only entailed the domination of Indigenous lands and resources, but also of their systems, institutions, spirituality, and perspectives. In some cases, the colonizer's explicit agenda was to exterminate, and in others to at least assimilate Indigenous Peoples into mainstream Euro-Western society. In Canada, a primary tool for assimilation was the residential school system. It is my contention that professional education, such as in social work, is also implicated in structural colonialism.

While colonization is associated with political and economic devastation of Indigenous communities and individual and collective trauma, Indigenous Peoples have resisted annihilation. There has been a resurgence of Indigenous cultures, along with the assertion of an Indigenous right to self-determination. This is the process of decolonization. Decolonization is about "the repatriation of Indigenous land and life" (Tuck & Yang, 2012, p. 1) and "is a process of centering the concerns and worldviews of the colonized Other so that they understand themselves through their own assumptions and perspectives" (Chilisa, 2012, p. 13). However, despite the reclamation of identity and autonomy, Indigenous Peoples have no choice but to navigate the interface of two worlds and worldviews. Yet social work education and practice has not fully acknowledged and recognized the borderland reality in which Indigenous social workers must practice and Indigenous Peoples must live. As a result, neither Indigenous nor non-Indigenous social workers are formally prepared to recognize this reality or to act in morally responsive, culturally safe, and anti-oppressive ways.

WORLDVIEW

A worldview is an ethnophilosophy consisting of sets of values, beliefs, and primary assumptions about the world and the nature of humans in relation to and within the world. These give rise to secondary assumptions that are the basis for institutionalized knowledge and practices (Jackson, 2008). The notion of worldview can be applied at the level of an individual, group, or society. Obviously, within a broader worldview there are multiple worldviews, but there is a more dominant perspective within a particular society. Furthermore, while there are multiple Indigenous worldviews, there tend to be common and consistent features among them.

THEORIZING (DE)COLONIZING PRAXIS

I used Giddens's (1986) structuration theory to theorize (de)colonizing praxis. Colonization/decolonization is conceptualized as an interactional-relational verb that occurs along a continuum. The micro/macro dichotomy is rejected given that routine socially constituted interactions inevitably result in the reconstitution of colonizing social systems, structures, and institutions. Power is viewed as both exercised and imposed. Practitioners are understood as being knowledgeable and having agency, but within constraints. Furthermore, critical reflection is a defining feature of a (de)colonizing praxis, as it is essential for disrupting colonizing mind frames and enabling decolonizing interactions that implicate the dominant discourses, social systems, and institutions.

RESEARCH PROCESS

Given our globalized society, I suspected that Indigenous social workers throughout the world were contending with the borderlands experience. As a result, I attempted to recruit internationally. In the end, I had one international participant and five Canadian participants. Other criteria for participation included comfort and competence in using written English, and in using a secure university-based online research site; self-identification as an Indigenous person (one who is descended from and currently has a historical, social, and cultural affiliation with the original peoples of a territory that was colonized by a Euro-Western nation); formal postsecondary training in social work with a professional designation (certificate, diploma, degree); work experience in a formal social work–related role within the past two years; and self-identification and/or identification by others as being experienced and having expertise in working within social work practice contexts in which worldviews intersect. Five of the participants were interviewed in person for between one and three hours, while one person participated in a one-hour online interview using video conferencing technology.

DECOLONIZING CRITICAL REFLECTION METHOD

A key premise in the research was that we are all culturally socialized into our various ways of knowing, being, and doing. For Indigenous social workers, this means they are socialized within dominant Euro-Western society and often, although not necessarily, socialized within their Indigenous cultures. The dominant perspective also plays out through their socialization within the profession of social work. This means that the minds or perspectives of the participants are likely colonized in varying degrees along with their experiences and contexts. This created a research dilemma given that if I used a traditional interview, I risked not accessing Indigenous worldviews, but instead eliciting colonized data.

As a result, I re-theorized Jan Fook's (2002) critical reflection method into a decolonizing critical reflection research method. This enabled me as a researcher/facilitator to guide the participant through a process of first recalling and then analyzing and remembering an event from their borderland practice. The questions enabled participants to reflect on and reinterpret old events through the new knowledge acquired from an Indigenous-centred and decolonizing framing of the events. Participants identified their Indigenous worldview assumptions, values, and beliefs and the dominant, colonizing worldview influences on their practices. The goal was to identify their practice wisdom that emerges from the borderlands or their knowledge that is created from their experiences.

BORDERLAND STORIES REMEMBERED

Carla: Being in Relationship

Carla arranged for a non-Indigenous social worker to meet with some Indigenous community workers to discuss a child placement issue. The non-Indigenous social worker came to the Indigenous community for the meeting. Carla arrived first and began casually chatting with the Indigenous community workers. When the non-Indigenous social worker arrived, Carla introduced her to the Indigenous community workers, as she believed her role was "to be the bridge." The non-Indigenous social worker then took control of the meeting saying, "Okay then ... let's get to business." She went through the agenda and then said, "Okay seems like we got it all done. Very good, see you." Carla "was really uncomfortable because ... that is not how relationships are built," and the other people at the meeting looked "surprised." She thought about saying something to the non-Indigenous social worker, but when she wasn't asked for feedback, she didn't pursue the issue.

Carla critiqued the non-Indigenous social worker for taking an "expert" stance in the meeting and equated this to a continuation of the colonizing role of non-Indigenous people who come into Indigenous communities. She likened the experience to the history of non-Indigenous store managers, doctors, and teachers who historically came into Indigenous communities and assumed authoritative roles. She stated, "It is the expert coming in again, even if it is more subtle than in the days of 40 years ago." Carla also believed that the non-Indigenous social worker failed to recognize and respect her Indigenous knowledge and practice, as indicated by the non-Indigenous social worker's failure to recognize and honour the relational aspect of Carla's practice.

Carla states, "My assumption is she [the non-Indigenous social worker] thought it was inconsequential women talk ... and we needed to be professional and 'get to work.'" Instead, Carla stressed the significance of relationship-building in Indigenous communities and pointed out that "you can get a lot farther in work if you have spent time on developing the relationships." In terms of borderland practice, she states, "It would benefit people if they came in and watched a little bit what was going on rather than come in and just immediately take control of the situation—without knowing the people or understanding the situation." She stressed that a key value from her Indigenous Nation is "humility," something Carla believed was not demonstrated by the non-Indigenous social worker. Carla also stressed the importance of being a "real person" when interacting with an Indigenous community. Indigenous people want to connect with you on a personal level and you can't attempt to engage in an objective, "empty slate" way. If there is no reciprocity in the relating, people will think there is no way you can understand them or their experience.

Taylor: Dismantling the Role of Grandma

Taylor advocated on behalf of an Indigenous family with two non-Indigenous child protection social workers. Taylor believed that while she understood the Indigenous cultural perspective, the non-Indigenous social workers did not. She stated that "it became a question of what's right and wrong.... And in this case, culture lost." Taylor tried to bring an Indigenous cultural interpretation to the situation, explaining that while "the young mother would take time out from parenting and go partying that grandma was a built-in safety net within the culture." Taylor explained, "This first line, grandma, is built in for a purpose ... to catch." The "safety net" is "built in right across the culture ... it's a different form of knowledge." But from the more powerful Euro-Western perspective, "success was to find the placement for the child, to rescue the child from this terrible situation, and find another home."

In this scenario, Taylor was trying to argue that the child was safe because of the positioning of the grandmother within the culture. But the Euro-Western social workers did not recognize or acknowledge the significance of the grandmother's role within the family and decided to apprehend the child. In addition, grandma didn't have a say during the meeting. Taylor points out the integral role of grandma having some voice and authority, as grandma is an Elder and has authority within the family and community. Grandma should have been positioned to be able to assert her authority, but there was no opportunity for her to do so: "Grandma did not have a say, did not have an opportunity to put down her foot and say 'Stop, you're transgressing … you're crossing the line here, this is how we do things. Go away.' She did not have that opportunity, and the young mom didn't have that opportunity. So you know, it's very unfair, and you know, shameful for social workers to behave like that." Taylor analyzed that in this interaction the social workers were not only ignoring cultural practices and protocols, but actually breaking down Indigenous social structures: "They (the non-Indigenous colonizers) are still dismantling the Indigenous ways of doing things." A core problem was the fact that the non-Indigenous workers were oblivious to the Indigenous ways.

Taylor believes the situation will not change "until we have our own Indigenous social work programming" and all social workers are required to receive training in Indigenous social work, so that they recognize and respect Indigenous cultural practices. Until then, she will find herself working on the outside, feeling powerless, and trying to help people negotiate the Euro-Western way of doing things.

Megan: Consuming Indigenous Trauma

Megan was a support worker for Indigenous students at a high school. She was approached by a substitute teacher who informed her that an Indigenous student left a classroom visibly upset after the regular teacher showed an explicit video on the Indian residential school system. The student was at risk for being penalized for leaving the class and for not completing the assignment associated with the class and the video.

Megan intervened by asking the regular teacher not to penalize the student. She also advocated that at least a disclaimer be made before showing these types of videos in the future. The teacher became upset and defensive explaining that he felt he had done nothing wrong and that it was more important to show the film given that it provides valuable learning for the students in the class. Megan's position was that learning for the non-Indigenous students should not come at the expense of Indigenous people and their suffering. She explained that "there was little thought given to the current-day realities of Indigenous people.… But, like, it's here [in the] present, ongoing, still affecting us today.… This [suffering] is generational." Megan believes that the teacher was taking the Eurocentric position of the detached observer, studying Indigenous people. She said there is "discomfort around feeling like you're singled out and you're studying me and my wounds and I'm the subject of your learning and that's really problematic." She linked this experience to the historical colonial events when Indigenous people were placed in zoos for the curiosity and enjoyment of non-Indigenous people. Megan could empathize with the student based on her own experiences as a student. Unfortunately, Megan described her job as a "mandatory token role" and an "add-on to the cultural program." Her advice to the teacher was only advisory and she was not positioned to make program or structural changes within her organization.

Judy: Spiritual Dilemma

Judy worked with an Indigenous agency. Judy was working with an Indigenous girl who said she heard a voice and that the voice was that of her deceased grandfather. The grandfather gave her advice and she wasn't disturbed by it. The girl reported that her father also hears voices, and a doctor from the community confirmed that the family is known to have this gift of hearing voices from the spirit world. The girl had other problems that required hospitalization. Judy had to write an assessment and address the issue of the voices; her dilemma was how to do this given that she had assessed the girl and did not find any indication of a mental illness.

Judy was aware that some Indigenous families, such as this girl's, were known to have the ability to hear voices from the spirit world. She expected that the hospital system would not be open to a therapist making such an assertion. In the end, she believed that not fighting for Indigenous beliefs would be a betrayal to the girl's culture. So she did write it down in the assessment and luckily the psychologist in the hospital was familiar with this phenomenon and phoned to ask to collaborate with Judy on the case. The girl came back for follow-up therapy with Judy and Judy worked with the voice of the girl's deceased grandfather in providing her with guidance. She would ask the girl, "What would your grandfather tell you to do?" He always gave good advice. But Judy had to be concerned about her credibility as a therapist and the credibility of the Indigenous agency she worked for. She wondered, "What kind of argument can I use that this is working good for her? If asked do you believe in this yourself should I say, 'yes I do'?"

The case scenarios demonstrate that Indigenous social workers enact Indigenous ways of knowing, being, and doing along with decolonizing practices in order to serve Indigenous people. Carla incorporated an Indigenous notion of relationality into her practice and resisted the colonizing role of the authoritative non-Indigenous expert. Taylor used her cultural knowledge to advocate for the recognition and respect of the role of the grandmother in Indigenous societies. She saw her role as assisting her clients in navigating the Euro-Western context. Megan challenged the Euro-Western tendency to assume a stance of objectivity and consume the experiences of Indigenous people. Judy attempted to both protect and assert Indigenous knowledge. She incorporated her Indigenous knowledge directly into her social work practice with her client. This served to respond to and validate her client's beliefs and identity while enriching the knowledge base from which she practised. Thus, the Indigenous social workers in this study integrated their Indigenous values and knowledge and their colonial knowledge into their practices in the face of risks and resistance.

IMPLICATIONS FOR CRITICAL CLINICAL PRACTICE

Indigenous people are often positioned within the borderlands in between Indigenous and Euro-Western worlds and worldviews. Indigenous social workers are challenged with assisting Indigenous clients and colleagues with negotiating and navigating the challenges associated with the in-between. The main challenge is contending with the dominance of the Euro-Western worldview that suppresses and even denies the existence of Indigenous perspectives. There are serious implications for both the Indigenous social worker and Indigenous clients. As evidenced in the case scenarios, Indigenous people are at risk given the replication of colonizing practices that continue to damage Indigenous culture and institutions. Furthermore, these practices often replicate historical colonizing behaviours, such as the imposition of the colonial authority figure on Indigenous communities, the appropriation of Indigeneity, and the disregard for their suffering. However, Indigenous social workers are playing a key role in navigating and negotiating the often treacherous borderlands terrain for the benefit of Indigenous people and the retention of Indigenous ways of being, knowing, and doing. They resist these colonizing perspectives and practices and advocate for the recognition and respect of Indigeneity.

Overall, both Indigenous and non-Indigenous social workers need to be cognizant of the borderlands. Practitioners will not be able to offer the most culturally safe and therefore effective services if they don't account for the borderland phenomenon. They will also put Indigenous people at risk for further colonization by perpetuating colonizing relations and structures.

Ermine (2007) offers a way forward by evoking the notion of an "ethical space" or "a venue to step out of our allegiances, to detach from the cages of our mental worlds and assume a position where human-to-human dialogue can occur" (p. 202). Such detachment is possible, according to Ermine, because in ethical space, "attention is given to understanding how thought functions in governing our behaviors … how hidden values and intentions can control our behavior, and how unnoticed cultural differences can clash without our realizing what is occurring" (pp. 202–203). The goal of this kind of dialogue is to agree on shared values that will collectively guide renewed relationships. Through such ethical dialogue, we have the potential to individually and collectively resist and reconfigure contemporary colonizer/colonized relations by building relationality, an explicit and continuously examined consciousness of our differences and our common ground.

Indigenous social workers are striving to practice with Indigenous people and within Indigenous contexts in a manner that is culturally safe. Yet colonial systems and ideologies within social work practice and social welfare systems continue to dominate and often negate these attempts, resulting in experiences for Indigenous clients and practitioners that are deemed culturally diminishing, even damaging. Social work as a profession must recognize and intentionally and mindfully decolonize its perspectives and practices if practitioners are to genuinely engage in right relationships with Indigenous people that enable a critical clinical approach to practice. Together, we are challenged to create an ethical third space in which our relations are decolonizing, egalitarian, and socially just; in other words, a space in which we can enact our relational accountability in a *good way*. Relational accountability, a core Indigenous principle, means that individually we are intricately connected to and therefore have the responsibility to act in the interest of maintaining our relations with all entities in the natural and spiritual worlds. An Indigenous understanding of a *good way* entails a process that honours tradition and spirit (Flicker et al., 2015).

CONCLUSION

Indigenous social workers are asserting their distinct professional existence as "Indigenous social workers" through their Indigenous social work praxis. They are enacting core Indigenous values such as relationality, responsibility, and respect for Indigeneity. While drawing on mainstream education and training, they also operate through a unique set of perspectives that are not professionally credentialled and therefore are not recognized and valued as legitimate social work. They contend with colonizing power relations, where Euro-Western interpretations and structures typically prevail, while they assist Indigenous people in navigating the dominant Euro-Western reality. This leads to them having to manage dilemmas, including risks to Indigenous knowledges and the risk of being perceived as "unprofessional," in the application of Indigenous knowledge. One's legitimacy and authority as an Indigenous person and as a social worker is often in question. Yet they resist annihilation through enacting their Indigenized practices.

REFERENCES

Anzaldua, G. (1999). *Borderlands/la frontera: The new mestizo* (2nd ed.). San Francisco: Aunt Lute Books.

Chilisa, B. (2012). Situating knowledge systems. In C. Bagele (Ed.), *Indigenous research methodologies* (pp. 1–43). London: Sage.

Ermine, W. (2007). The ethical space of engagement. *Indigenous Law Journal, 6*(1), 193–203.

Flicker, S., O'Campo, P., Monchalin, R., Thistle, J., Worthington, C., Masching, R., ... Thomas, C. (2015). Research done in a "good way": The importance of Indigenous Elder involvement in HIV community-based research. *American Journal of Public Health, 105*(6), 1149–1154.

Fook, J. (2002). *Social work: Critical theory and practice.* London: Sage.

Giddens, A. (1986). *The constitution of society.* Los Angeles: University of California Press.

Jackson, M. G. (2008). *Transformative learning for a new worldview.* New York: Palgrave Macmillan.

Pauktuutit Inuit Women of Canada. (2006). *The Inuit way: A guide to Inuit culture.* Ottawa: Author.

Snelgrove, C., Dhamoon, R., & Corntassel, J. (2014). Unsettling settler colonialism: The discourse and politics of settlers, and solidarity with Indigenous nations. *Decolonization: Indigeneity, Education and Society, 1*(2), 1–32.

Tuck, E., & Yang, K. W. (2012). Decolonization is not a metaphor. *Education and Society, 1*(1), 1–40.

CHAPTER 15

Counterbalancing Life with Chronic Pain through Storying Women's Experiences of (Dis)Ability[1]

Judy E. MacDonald

> Many ill people find they cannot live the story, or just the story, that biomedicine tells of their illnesses; the need for a voice of one's own is a particularity of our times. (Frank, 1997, p. 31)

INTRODUCTION

Sufferers need to find their own voice to testify to the struggles and inequities to which they have paid witness in living with chronic pain. "Chronic pain and (dis)Ability leaves one struggling for 'normalcy,' trying to make sense out of the fundamental operations of one's body, the meaning of suffering, and the social construction of wellness" (MacDonald, 2008, p. 135). Creating a respectful space where sufferers' stories can come forward, ultimately shifting the power differential away from biomedical expertise and toward lived experience whereby the sufferers' stories become vehicles for political and social change, is imperative. The findings in this chapter are based on a narrative testimonio research inquiry where six women (two social workers, two nurses, and two physicians) were interviewed; all were health care professionals living and working with chronic pain. In total, they had 92 years of experience in living with chronic pain, with an individual range from 7 to 25 years. The presenting research question was as follows: How can the stories of women in the helping professions who are sufferers of chronic pain and (dis)Ability inform an anti-oppressive approach to social work practice in working with sufferers? Findings will focus on the emotional experiences of living with chronic pain and the counterstorying narrative processes that critical clinical social workers can guide sufferers through in identifying their coping strategies and building resources of support.

As you read this chapter, ask yourself the following questions:

1. How have women sufferers of chronic pain had their lived experiences denied, including how the biomedical approach has silenced their voices?
2. As critical clinical social workers, what can we do to counterbalance that insult, to help pain sufferers find their voice?
3. What skills are needed for critical clinical social workers to work collaboratively with pain sufferers?
4. How do critical clinical social workers help chronic pain sufferers find counterbalancing ways of coping with their pain and resultant (dis)Ability?

(DIS)ABILITY

In this chapter, disability is written as (dis)Ability: "(dis)" to respect the person's social and physical connection with disability, and "Ability" to highlight the creative and innovative ways of dealing with societal barriers (MacDonald & Friars, 2010, p. 140).

The legitimacy of women's experiences of chronic pain has often been questioned, especially when women are living with conditions such as fibromyalgia, chronic fatigue syndrome, or neuropathic pain (Greenhalgh, 2001; Pryma, 2017a; Wendell, 1996). Pryma (2017a) found that all of the women pain sufferers in her research could recall at least one situation in which their pain legitimacy or resultant (dis)Ability was questioned. Further, she found that the intersection of race added another layer of judgment for the Black women seeking medical treatment for their pain. Repeated research findings have shown that women chronic pain sufferers, regardless of their class position, have had to "battle" to get (dis)Ability benefits, be it through private insurers or publicly funded programs (MacDonald, 2008; Pryma, 2017a). Women sufferers are not listened to as they are often dismissed as malingering or labelled as hypochondriacs, leaving them struggling to prove the existence of their pain to health professionals. One sufferer demands attention: "Listen to me! Hear me speak!" (Pryma, 2017b, p. 156).

SUFFERER

The term *sufferer* was purposely chosen to represent someone living with chronic pain. Sufferer offsets the dominant discourse that questions the authenticity of the person's physical pain experiences, especially when a biomedical diagnosis is difficult to locate. There is no definitive measure for pain, unlike a thermometer that can detect a person's body temperature. When the medical evidence is lacking, physicians tend to revert to psychological causation—the psychologizing of pain (Greenhalgh, 2001; Wendell, 1996). The term *sufferer* legitimizes the person's lived experiences of pain.

Women sufferers who were health professionals working with pain sufferers had their own stories to tell, stories that could potentially disrupt the dominant medical discourse. They wanted to be heard and their fear was that people would not listen. This fear originated from not having their pain experiences heard within the medical community. One sufferer was told her pain was "not that bad." Another was informed she "shouldn't be in that much pain." Yet another recalled the message, "there was nothing wrong with me; I was malingering." And, another felt an "undercurrent of disbelief" when she related her perception of pain. Transcending the sufferers' experiences of not being heard, the women's knowledges and perspectives on living with chronic pain were welcomed and encouraged by the researcher. Through their stories numerous emotions rose to the surface.

EMOTIONS

Pain is an emotional journey as much as it is a physical entity (Barnes, Adam, Eke, & Ferguson, 2018; Mailis-Gagnon & Israelson, 2003). The list of emotions in figure 15.1 was compiled from the interviews with the sufferers and presented to them during the teleconference for verification and discussion. All participants were invited to take part in a teleconference to provide an opportunity for joining and sharing: out of six participants, five were able to attend. In relation to these emotional descriptors, one sufferer noted, "I can identify with each one." The emotions are intimately connected to the sufferers' struggles in living with pain and their appreciation for the supports and pain-controlling mechanisms that greatly add to the quality of their lives. Emotions connected to strife and struggles are depicted, along with emotions associated with hope and

> *Abandoned Afraid Alone Angry Anguish Appreciative Dehumanized Demoralized Denial Desperate Depressed Devastated Distressed Doubtful Driven Embarrassed Empty Exhausted Fearful Fortunate Frustrated Grateful Grief stricken Guilty Happy Helpless Hopeful Hopeless Humoured Meaningful Overcome Overwhelmed Panicked Relieved Resentful Resigned Sad Scared Self-pity Shamed Spirited Spiteful Stoic Stressed Terrorized Thankful Tired Trapped Unhappy Upheaval Vulnerable Wearied Withdrawn Worn Worried*

Figure 15.1: Emotions

gratitude. Contrary to Fordyce's (1990) and Roy's (1988, 1992, 2001) position of claiming that sufferers overstate their pain to family, the sufferers in this study were protective of their loved ones, as one sufferer relates with regard to her relationship with her daughter: "She was taking care of Mom and putting her young life on hold ... I do find myself hiding things from her ... putting on my front."

Other times, sufferers supressed their emotional pain as a defence against the psychologizing of pain (Greenhalgh, 2001; Lumley, Schubiner, Carty, & Ziadni, 2015). A sufferer shared her physician's position: "He was thinking that everything was psychological, he thought I was feeling sorry for myself." Some researchers believe chronic pain stems from unresolved trauma or conflict, aligning pain causation with emotional disturbances (Lumley et al., 2015). Other researchers believe sufferers use avoidance in an attempt to supress complex emotions created by living with chronic pain (Barnes et al., 2018). The physical and emotional connection becomes clear in the sufferer's statement below:

> There were times when I went to get groceries and I would come home without them because I couldn't get out of the car. I would go to bed with my clothes on, because I didn't have the energy to take them off. So going for groceries was pure hell. I couldn't do anything, couldn't do the dishes, I couldn't do anything. I felt desperate.

This was at a particularly difficult time when she was in a flare-up with her rheumatoid arthritis. Her medication was causing her blood levels to drop, resulting in low hemoglobin and platelet counts, which created a drain on her energy. She went on to describe the physical and emotional interconnection:

> Pain comes, then stress, it affects the whole immune system; it affects everything that is connected within us. With chronic stress and chronic pain and never knowing if I would be able to get out of bed and walk again, was overload on my system. But I kept pushing myself to do more anyway. It never seemed as if it would end and depression sets in.

This sufferer's experience challenges the behavioural approach to chronic pain, where the primary focus is on eliminating sick-role behaviour (Bonica, 1990; Fordyce, 1990). In her experience, the pain and immobility came first, thus creating reactions of depression and anxiety particularly when relief was not in sight. Specialists confuse the issue when exaggerated emphasis is placed on treating the emotional effects without addressing the pain (Campbell, 1996; Long, 1996). Mailis-Gagnon and Israelson (2003, p. 10) state, "There is no linear relationship between chronic pain and a particular personality. Chronic pain may provoke personality changes, create negative emotions and alter behaviour."

Difficulty arises when medicine and other health professions doubt the physical origins of the sufferer's pain (MacDonald, 2000). A sufferer questioned the authenticity of her own experience, as she noted, "I was beginning to think I was making this up, I'm not in pain, of course I can do this, I can do that, and I was collapsing." Rosenfeld (2003, p. 287) believes, "as the science and technology of medicine evolve, conditions that were previously dismissed are suddenly revealed to be genuine, and the organic basis for seemingly un-documentable pain is often discovered."

The above exploration primarily deals with the relationship between pain and emotions, while the next section delves into aspects of emotional expression. Through the narrative analysis, two main emotions emerged as being significant in the sufferers' testimonies: sense of loss and fears.

SENSE OF LOSS

In Seers and Friedli (1996, p. 1164), a research participant commented, "pain takes your personality away." Other participants commented along similar lines: "I'm not me anymore" and "I am a much reduced person because of the pain" (p. 1164). Sufferers also make specific comments about aspects of their lives they have lost due to their chronic pain. "One woman indicated her frustration at being physically unable to pick up her grandchildren" and others "missed what could be seen by many to be very mundane activities, such as cooking [and] cleaning" (Brown & Williams, 1995, p. 699). In an expression of exasperation, a sufferer stated, "you lose so much, there is so much you grieve with chronic pain."

Table 15.1 compiles the sufferers' losses. All sufferers testified to numerous losses within their lives attributed to chronic pain. For example, they had to make work adjustments to accommodate their pain, such as retiring or moving to part-time hours, and all had periods where they were physically unable to work, hence creating financial losses. The cumulative effect of their losses could be overwhelming. In a research study with chronic back pain sufferers, similar findings were revealed: "loss of physical and mental abilities, occupational and social activities, job or role ... financial hardship and changes in interpersonal relationships, culminating in loss of self-worth, future and hope" (Walker, Sofaer, & Holloway, 2006, p. 199). Adaptation, coping, and readjustment skills are needed to navigate these emotional experiences. A sufferer testified that if she had received adequate accommodations for her (dis)Ability at work, she might have been able to continue working until her natural retirement.

TABLE 15.1: LOSSES

LOSS	SPECIFICS
Financial	Treatment costs (one sufferer spent $6,000 per year for three years on alternative interventions—with no long-term results); reduced work hours; disability pensions
Avocational activities/ Recreational	Running, hiking, walking through the woods; gardening—can't bend or kneel; painting—can only paint for short periods; travelling— unable to sit for long periods, jarring of car increases pain
Relationships	Some friends withdraw because they find it difficult to be around someone in pain or lack understanding when plans need to be changed because the sufferer is having a painful day
Parenting style	Parentified child—older children have to help care for younger siblings when the parent is having a pain-filled day; parenting happens from a bedside; limited ability to participate in children's activities
Spontaneity	With travel, recreational activities, socializing, parenting, and intimate relations, have to plan ahead yet be flexible within those plans for changing physical condition
Work	Former ways of working often have to be modified: cut back hours, work part-time, redefine types of work, retire, or go on disability pension; secondary loss—loss of work relationships and loss of faith in own profession
Identity	One's identity is often redefined: formerly a runner—now a walker; once a helper—now helped

Two types of loss were portrayed by the sufferers: loss of relationships (counterbalanced by close supports) and loss of control (counterbalanced by rebalancing). The counterbalanced elements are indicators of the sufferers' abilities to adjust, whereby they have been able to acknowledge the loss, work through the related grief, and reinvest in coping strategies. Social workers working from a critical clinical perspective would guide sufferers through this discovery, first by helping the sufferer acknowledge their losses and feel the pain associated with the loss and then find a way forward through the counterbalancing process. Worden's (2009) grief work outlines the beginning stages of this work, where he identifies four tasks of mourning: accept the loss, deal with the pain created by the loss, adjust to an environment in which the loss is evident, and reinvest in life. The stage of adjusting to an environment in which the loss is evident is where the social worker would help the sufferer identify counterbalancing possibilities.

CRITICAL CLINICAL

Critical clinical emphasizes non-pathologizing, deconstructive narratives aimed at unpacking dominant discourses through the creation of counterstories that locate the sufferer as expert of their own body, unsettling the biomedical authority.

Loss of Relationships: Counterbalanced by Close Supports

Sufferers of chronic pain encounter relationship losses. Seers and Friedli's (1996) participants acknowledged that their friends stopped calling, their families were unwilling to discuss their pain, and overall, they were left with feelings of isolation. Rose (1994) identifies the overwhelming nature of the pain building isolation and creating relationship loss: "One woman stated that 'even talking to my husband sometimes seems, well, too big an effort'" (p. 26). These researchers extended the connection from relationship losses to fractured social lives (Rose, 1994; Seers & Friedli, 1996). The chronic pain sufferers in this study noted similar trends of relationship losses. One sufferer shared her experience with trying to juggle friendship commitments and health needs:

> What social life? You don't have anything left, you don't have anything left on the evenings and you don't have anything left on the weekends, for your friends. So out of ten friends you might have eight left . . . let's say of

the now eight friendships there are five who will now call you or include you … and say "how would you like to go for coffee?" And you say, "yes I'd love to," because you have every intention. So what do you do, you do as little as possible all day so that you will be rested up for the evening and about four o'clock you are exhausted, not able to move around. So you make that dreaded call.

This sufferer's partner would often stay at parties after she had to leave. She felt this heightened her isolation and disconnection from her partner and the social group. Further, he would make fun of her medication-induced weight gain, frequently calling her a "fat cow." She eventually asked this partner to leave their home, as she came to realize that his self-involved and abusive demeanour was not supportive of her health and emotional needs.

This sufferer had additional parental responsibilities as her oldest child has developmental and physical (dis)Abilities. When she was in a pain flare, she would need to rely on her daughter to assist with her son's care. In her opinion, her daughter's childhood was cut short because of her health situation. This sufferer expressed her frustration: "I am angry that our relationship, our mother-daughter relationship, although very close, is defined in part by chronic pain." She grieved her daughter's loss of a carefree childhood and struggled with her own guilt in perpetuating this situation.

Another sufferer explored her own frustration with having to convince friends that her pain is genuinely (dis)Abling and that she cannot always be available when they are free:

> If I can't move that day, I can't move. So friends really have a hard time with it and you whittle down to the people you really look forward to, the people who would come at four o'clock in the morning if you can't get out of bed or if you are trapped in the bathtub.

The sufferers in this research knew or learned how to identify genuinely supportive friends and partnerships and each had their own solid support system that helped them navigate through their life with pain. Having a supportive partner, a network of women friends, or an understanding extended family can make a huge difference in breaking through the isolation induced by chronic pain. The sufferers experienced relationship losses—some lost friends, others lost intimate partners—but through renegotiating their relationships (letting go of those who were not accepting of their chronic pain status and the impact it had on their lives), they were able to care for and be cared for by people who were able to accept their (dis)Abilities.

Fundamentally, it was important for the sufferers to recognize their unhealthy relationships and, if positive change was not possible, to grieve their loss. Through grieving their losses, room was made for new, healthy relationships (Worden, 2009). Relationships take time and work and when people are living with chronic pain, they have depleted energy levels. Sometimes they don't have the reserves to go out or even to engage in a phone or online conversation. Having friends that understand the energy ebb and flow so that they don't take last-minute cancellations personally is really important to maintaining relationships. Likewise, friends who can appreciate down times as much as they celebrate your good times are critical to meaningful and supportive friendships for sufferers. A critical clinical social worker would help the sufferer identify what they need from relationships, along with what they can give to relationships. Striking a healthy balance between giving and receiving is critically important for someone living with chronic pain.

Loss of Control: Counterbalanced by Rebalancing

The loss of control or the misperceptions associated with being in control of one's pain often haunt sufferers. Loss of control can result from uncontrolled pain and the sufferer's inability to be in charge of their body, or it can be associated with the effects of chronic pain, for example the loss of employment. The misperception of being in control relates to messages received from health professionals that sufferers should be able to control their pain. According to Wendell (1996, p. 98), "as long as the goal is to control the body, there is great potential in all healing practices for blaming the victims, and for discarding or ignoring all those whose bodies are out of control." A sufferer related the message she received from a specialist: "The message was clear that you are defective and if you would just smarten up you could control it." One sufferer, in her role as a psychiatric nurse, commented, "It's knowing the fear, the doubt, the depression, the sadness, the despair, the pain, the disability, and the emptiness and having no control of a situation. Control, the loss of control was a big issue." Not being able to control the pain or emotional responses at times of greatest vulnerability certainly weighed heavy on sufferers. Loss of control can also be associated with loss of hope. Throughout the sufferers' stories, despair was felt: at times when an intervention was supposed to relieve their suffering and it failed, when hints of relief did not materialize into sustained relief, or through the compounded effects of chronic pain (such as unemployment, relationship losses, and so on). Through these experiences, sufferers felt control slipping away. Leaving a specialist appointment, one sufferer commented: "I came out feeling like not only was my bucket empty, but it had a hole in the bottom. There was no hope left; he was my last hope and it was gone." Another sufferer spoke to her frustration of not being able to control her time or activities: "It's just that limitation of not being able to do the things you want to do when you want to do it. It's huge!" Chronic pain takes one's energy away, it takes longer to do the routine activities of daily living and managing the pain itself takes time: "The biggest impact was that whole energy thing, not being able to do what I wanted to do, not being able to function the way I wanted to function."

Living with chronic pain involves a process of redefining hope and staying hopeful gives one an essence of control. The sufferers in this research continually sought alternative interventions, looking for a glimmer of hope in pain relief. Some interventions proved to be problematic, as in a transverse technique of acupuncture that put a sufferer in a total body flare. But for the most part, problem solving through envisioning alternate paths provided a spark of hope and a reason for sufferers to continue their journey toward pain control. The sufferers were involved in a rebalancing process where they reflected on elements of their lives that had to be altered to accommodate their pain. Their coping abilities helped them redefine aspects of their lives. For example, a sufferer who was athletic could no longer run so she swam and walked. Another could no longer work in nursing, so she took her skills and applied them toward advocating for chronic pain sufferers and promoting chronic pain awareness. Another sufferer got involved in women's healing networks, while she spiritually anchored herself in her gardening. All the sufferers recognized their losses, grieved them for a short time, and moved on to reinvest in alternate ways of doing things. At moments of great vulnerability those losses most likely resurfaced, reactivating the cycle of loss, grieving, and reinvestment (Worden, 2009). Being able to rebalance one's life might signify the difference between succumbing to and surviving life with chronic pain. Having access to a critical clinical social worker who has the political awareness of how invisible (dis)Abilities are dismissed, along with a clinical understanding of grief processes, would guide sufferers in their survival journey.

In a mode of survival, the sufferers found ways to work through their losses. Through active grief work they engaged with the process of letting go and adjusted their lives to accommodate their pain experiences. An ongoing progression, the act of modifying is continual, drawing on creativity, support, determination, and will. This process calls for societal recognition of the rights of sufferers to receive accommodations (Hanes, 2002; Leslie, Leslie, & Murphy, 2003). Critical clinical social workers can help sufferers identify areas in their lives where modifications are needed and then help advocate for appropriate accommodations, such as physical alterations to a work environment or access to flexible working hours, which can make the difference in terms of a sufferer being able to maintain employment. Attitudinal shifts are often needed in recognizing the rights of sufferers to receive accommodations, for sufferers living with chronic pain can experience multiple (dis)Abilities.

FEARS

Fear is defined as "an unpleasant emotion caused by exposure to danger, expectation of pain" ("Fear," 1998). Craig (1999) identifies anger, fear, and sadness as common emotional responses from chronic pain sufferers, whereas Ahern (2002) focuses on anxiety and fear as creating psychological and behavioural disturbances in sufferers, thereby labelling the sufferer as a catastrophizing pain sufferer. Craig normalizes emotional reactions to chronic pain, while Ahern classifies emotional components of chronic pain as psychological pathology. Sufferers' fears need to be measured in proportion to their pain experiences.

Two types of fear were described: the fear of immobility and dependency (counterbalanced by determination to keep going) and the fear of uncontrollable pain (counterbalanced by coping mechanisms).

Immobility and Dependency: Counterbalanced by Determination to Keep Going

One sufferer with chronic back pain has on a few occasions been left totally immobilized, unable to move, confined to bed, and subsequently relying on a relative to attend to her physical needs. She described her worst fear:

> That totally, totally scary place, which for me is my greatest fear, is being unable to look after myself, getting to the point of physical dependence, umm, on anybody or anything. Having been there, those few places, when you can't get up to go to the bathroom or you couldn't turn over in bed, that just, that to me is desperation, that is worse than the pain, that immobility is worse than the pain, that total complete fear that someday, someone will have to be getting me out of bed to go to the bathroom, that's a big scare.

The sufferer described this as a "desperate feeling," as it fills her mind with numerous questions. She asked, "Who would look after me, what would I ever do, how could I cope, how could I function?" Another sufferer, when diagnosed with systemic rheumatoid arthritis, was instructed by the specialist to stop paid work and housework, to literally do nothing until the flare-up settled. She did not comply, partly because she was a single parent and the sole person responsible for her children and partly because she was afraid that if she stopped moving, she would never get moving again and ultimately end up using a wheelchair. She shared her determination and rationale:

> Fear, I never wanted to end up in a wheelchair. I knew I kept moving no matter how much pain, yes, I was doing damage to the joints, so I was told, but on the other hand, I was moving, and I knew movement was good for the joints, was good for the body. I was so exhausted, the more I did the more exhausted I became. I cried, I cried a great deal, but I couldn't give up, I had to keep going.

A critical clinical social worker would deconstruct the gender biases associated with care responsibility where women have socially and culturally been positioned to care for others often at a personal cost. Then the worker would guide the sufferer to locate reciprocal care relationships, for example, physical assistance is forthcoming from a friend and in turn the sufferer provides emotional support. Counterbalancing processes build on each other; close relationships and rebalancing help the sufferer get to a place where their determination surfaces and begins to build.

Uncontrollable Pain: Counterbalanced by Coping Mechanisms

Sufferers identified fear, even terror, associated with the return of their pain or prior health condition. One sufferer who had suffered through cancer pain with multiple surgeries and hot spots (the beginnings of cancer that had moved to other locations) pressing on nerves, relates her reaction when she received a note from the doctor indicating that she would need to be off work for six to eight weeks due to a broken patella: "That struck terror in me. I thought 'oh my God, it's happening again.' That is when … family came and I just did the crying, the crying, it was absolute utter panic." She explained that this pain was different from her cancer pain, for with her cancer she was able to cognitively control the pain. She elaborated on her pain experience:

I can remember lying on my pillow just going out of my skin because of the pain. And that pain, different from my other experience of pain, I had no, I had no sense of control over. I was totally overwhelmed by it, totally! I totally lost it in terms of any sense of control over the pain. The pain was the centre of my universe, I was just consumed. And then the fear, the fear that it was going to be like this forever. Fortunately, it wasn't, and fortunately like after that first week, it improved. This was another acute pain experience and my previous experience with acute pain lasted for seven or eight years.

This sufferer had so effectively used mind control to block her cancer pain, but she was not able to muster up any sense of control over this non-malignant pain. Thankfully, the intensity of her experience was not long-lasting, but for the week while it was so acute, the emotional panic she endured was as great a stress as the physical pain.

Sufferers' experiences can greatly impact their view of returning to uncontrolled pain. I wrote about living with extreme pain caused by reflex sympathetic dystrophy (RSD) over a period of eight years: "Still, tucked away in the corner of my soul is the fear that the RSD might someday come out of remission, returning to the horror of this crippling pain" (MacDonald, 2004, p. 31). Pain is etched in sufferers' memories. What becomes of those memories determines the success of one's ability to cope, for if the sufferer is absorbed with their pain memories, they could become hypervigilant to every pain sensation (Frank, 1995; Wendell, 1996).

Sufferers need to identify the fears associated with their chronic pain. Critical clinical social workers need to help sufferers locate the socio-political-economic context related to their fears, and work toward dispelling the fears by thoroughly exploring their various options and coping strategies. Ultimately, having a contingency plan to address their worst fear will dissipate the intensity of that fear.

EMOTIONAL DISCOURSE

The binary split between the emotional and physical experiences of chronic pain is a false divide (Mailis-Gagnon & Israelson, 2003; Wendell, 1996). Sufferers' believed pain is both a physical and an emotional experience, with their testimonies serving as witness to the emotional struggles embedded in navigating a life in pain. The debate is whether emotional experiences are the "causes or consequences of pain" (Craig, 1999, p. 335). Gamsa and Vikis-Freibergs's (1991) research supports the premise that pain causes emotional reactions in sufferers. In a tone of frustration, one sufferer explained to a psychiatrist, "I wasn't depressed before I had that pain and if you get rid of it, I won't be depressed anymore." He had diagnosed her pain as secondary to her depression, as she struggled to explain that the pain was the primary source of ailment. Another sufferer commented, "My GP was convinced … I suffer from depression and it is the depression that causes the fibromyalgia." This was after she had gone for psychiatric testing for depression at the request of her physician, only to be told by the testing psychiatrist, "You are no more depressed than I am. You have good days and you have bad days just like everyone else and besides that you have excellent coping skills and coping strategies."

The continual association of emotions to pain causation by physicians and pain specialists heightens the chance that sufferers' pain stories will not be believed. Dr. John Sarno (interviewed in Rosenfeld, 2003), a professor of clinical rehabilitation medicine, adamantly states that fibromyalgia is an epidemic of the 21st century due to doctors missing its psychosomatic origins. Four of the six sufferers in this research had fibromyalgia as a primary or secondary diagnosis, and while they acknowledged the emotional effect pain had on their being, they clearly denounced emotions as the cause of pain.

This linear association of emotional stress creating pain responses dates back to ancient times under the classification of hysteria (Jackson, 2002; Mailis-Gagnon & Israelson, 2003). Mailis-Gagnon and Israelson (2003) explore this historical relevance, while placing the debate within a current context.

> Sigmund Freud was the first to establish a psychological language for describing how body symptoms, including pain, may be the result of unresolved conflicts and troubled emotions, which in turn are converted and expressed in somatic complaints. Such a notion has been frequently employed to explain chronic pain symptoms when the doctors cannot find much wrong with a person's body. However, as science progresses and as our horizons widen some symptoms and signs previously attributed to thoughts and emotions are found to have their roots in biology. (p. 11)

Each sense of loss or fear experienced by sufferers was counterbalanced with a coping strategy: for example, the loss of a relationship was counterbalanced by strengthening their supportive relationships. Likewise, their fear of immobility and dependency was counterbalanced by their determination to keep going, resulting in the recalibrating of pacing strategies. If anything, emotional strength was exhibited repeatedly throughout their stories. The debate whether emotions are the cause or consequence of pain needs to be abandoned, while attention is drawn to the emotional impact of living with chronic pain.

COPING STRATEGIES

Frank (2003) suggests that pain has the potential to unmake a sufferer's world. Through the sufferer storying her pain, she can remake her world by changing her perceptions of her pain. As told earlier, one sufferer was able to do this with her cancer pain, cognitively controlling the pain by a process of conscious denial. Frank (2003) does not put the total responsibility upon the sufferer, for he suggests that the physician or clinician has a moral responsibility to truly listen to the sufferer's story, altering how that person is heard and in doing so, how the physician or clinician experiences themself differently. This would suggest a relational quality to coping with pain, transforming a process that has been described by sufferers as lonely and isolating to one based on human companionship and compassion.

Coping strategies fell within one of two categories: personal coping and treatment approaches, specifically medications (both oral and compounding topicals), emotional and mental stressors and stress-relievers, and strategies for navigating through the medical system. One sufferer shared her tactic for bring her family physician on board with pain management options: "There are miraculous things happening in chronic pain research right now, and you have to be very proactive with this stuff and actually go in and say, 'let's do this.'" The sufferers highlighted the benefits of connecting with other chronic pain sufferers, relaying the importance of mutual support structures in coping with chronic pain (Brown & Williams, 1995; Chronic Pain Association of Canada, 2004).

Determination   Drive   Emotional release   Faith   Family   Friends
Gardening   Intellectualization   Mind control   Pacing   Painting
Pets   Self-care   Swimming   Treadmill   Walking

Figure 15.2: Coping Strategies

Personal Coping

The sufferers were very skilful at being able to cope with their pain. Their ability to redefine hope, to reach beyond adversity to find meaning in life, even amongst the pain, vulnerability, and strife spoke to their character. One sufferer articulated, "You are dealing with many, many facets and your life goes on, but you tend to forget you are a person, all you feel you are is pain." Another reflected, "As a person living with chronic pain you are not human. You forget what being human is like because you are just this walking zombie of pain." A further sufferer shared her experience with nightmares of the pain. All the sufferers had difficult journeys, yet they were able to transcend those deep-seated displacements of the human spirit and surface amongst that adversity. A critical clinical social worker needs to work with the sufferer to find those glimmers of hope, creating an alternate story to the overwhelming pain story, and helping sufferers build a "tickle trunk" of resources they can call on when the pain begins to invade their body.

TICKLE TRUNK

A tickle trunk is an imagined trunk designed to hold sufferers' coping mechanisms for dealing with their pain. It would include things such as strategies (meditation, self-hypnosis, pacing), devices (cold packs, TENS units), medications (pain medication, anti-nausea medication, muscle relaxants, topical compounds), physical exercise (exercise bike, swimming, walking), and other items (essential oils, vitamins, over-the-counter topical lotions). Sufferers draw on these items, in various combinations, to help cope with their pain.

Jackson (2002, p. 301) suggests that pain does not fit in the disease paradigm of fighting against, as in battling with cancer, for "pain is more of a collaborator. It's the thing that tunes us inward." Treating the pain allows sufferers to focus outward, relating to the world around them once again. The inward/outward movement shifts in response to pain intensity and the employment of coping strategies. One sufferer spoke passionately about the support she receives from her dog:

My main source of strength and my main coping mechanism is my Labrador retriever. He is my soulmate; my main source of treatment, joy, and everything else in life, is him. When I can't get out of bed he comes and I hang on to, hang on to his fur around his neck and he pulls me out of bed. When I am in really bad pain he comes up and lays his back against my spine, so I have this warm, furry covered hot water bottle laying against me. When you are crying and he licks your tears, he has been my chief source of support. And the days you did not want to get out of bed, you get up because he needs to be fed, he needs to go out. Anyone who has an animal in their life their pain is ameliorated and their life is better.

The unconditional love an animal offers or the ability to care for something distracted the sufferers from their pain experiences, if only momentarily.

The specific combination of distraction, pharmaceuticals, unconditional love, physical activity, meaningful relations and work, emotional expressions, and so forth varies depending on the individual and their specific experience of pain. Each sufferer employed numerous methods, thus demonstrating their determination to manage their pain, as well as highlighting their problem-solving abilities. A critical clinical social worker would acknowledge the sufferers coping ability while working toward additional coping strategies. Sufferers should not be judged for failing to cope, as has been done repeatedly through a biomedical approach to pain, but rather their strengths should be built on in an effort to add more strategies to their tickle trunks. Some of the strategies shared by sufferers included support from family and friends, spirituality, gardening, comfort of pets, sense of humour, pacing oneself, emotional release such as screaming/crying, self-care, withdrawing momentarily, changing priorities, and allowing recovery time with respect to loss of energy.

One sufferer had an amazing ability to use mental processes to cognitively displace her pain:

I made pain an object outside of me; pain was not a part of me. I sort of struggle with the whole concept of living with chronic pain, because it was more for me living beside or having chronic pain as a next-door neighbour, I didn't live with it. I did not choose to co-habit with chronic pain! I kept it separate, it wasn't a part of me, you know it wasn't me; it wasn't part of my definition at all, at all!

Her ability to dislocate her pain outside her physical and psychological experience could be associated with the process of dissociation. Herman (1997, p. 87) suggests that people with this ability are "adept practitioners of the arts of altered consciousness. Through the practice of dissociation, voluntary thought suppression, minimization, and sometimes outright denial, they learn to alter an unbearable reality." Traumatic events, which "generally involve threats to life or bodily integrity, or a close personal encounter with violence and death" (p. 33), are often the precursor to establishing this ability. This sufferer almost lost her life during her eight-hour bilateral mastectomy surgery; she went through years where her life was being threatened by cancer, all the while experiencing horrific pain. For her, this was a creative coping mechanism that from a biomedical lens could have possibly been classified as a psychiatric disorder.

Sufferers are entrapped bodily by their physical experiences of pain; their stories testify to emotional vulnerability and physical, emotional, and spiritual exhaustion. Actively seeking a resolution to this situation seems an appropriate course of action, yet from non-critical interventions sufferers risk the labels of malingering, exhibiting, and benefitting from sick-role behaviour, or attention seeking.

Treatment Approaches

Chronic pain sufferers often believe they will try anything, do anything to lessen their pain: "Most patients with severe pain opt for surgery even when the success rate is estimated to be only 30%" (Campbell, 1996). A sufferer was willing to risk neurosurgery that had a 50 percent chance of leaving her paralyzed. In her own words, "I was quite willing to let them do anything, anything, absolutely anything, they could have amputated me at the waist I would have been happy." At the time of the neurosurgery consultation she was in uncontrollable pain that was undertreated. The same surgeon suggested cutting the sciatic nerve; she inquired if she would then be able to walk, to which he replied, "do you want to walk or do you want rid of the pain?" She did not follow through with this treatment option; however, the surgeon needs to recognize the heightened vulnerability of pain sufferers when their pain is severe and seek an interdisciplinary consult that includes a sufferer advocate.

Surgery has been beneficial for some of the sufferers in this research. MacDonald (2004) attributes her release from intractable pain to having controversial radical surgery. Sufferers in this research identified a variety of treatment modalities with a different combination of strategies employed by each sufferer. Strategies included exercise-relaxation programs such as aquacise, reiki, yoga, and reflexology; physical therapy techniques like craniosacral therapy, massage, TENS (transcutaneous electrical nerve stimulation), hydrotherapy, and stretching exercises; self-reflection activities, such as meditation, self-hypnosis, journalling, and relaxation; and finally, medications, including narcotics, anti-depressants (in low doses as a pain adjunct), anti-convulsants (to change pain perception), anti-inflammatories, and compounding topicals.

Coping Discourse

Sufferers testify to their ability to seek relief of uncontrollable pain. Pain is so devastating and life altering (Mailis-Gagnon & Israelson, 2003; Rosenfeld, 2003) that it demands the total attention of the sufferer. Yet this very attention is identified as a diagnostic criteria leading to the psycho-behavioural classification of sick-role. Fordyce's (1990) assessment is based on excessive consumption of pain medication, inactivity, exhibited pain behaviours, undue focus on pain, and continual utilization of health services. Pain behaviourists have labelled all of these as deviant, dysfunctional behaviours needing immediate correction (Fordyce, 1990; Lumley, Schubiner, Carty, & Ziadni, 2018). If sufferers adhered to the behaviourist theory, their coping abilities could collapse, and the quality of their lives would be compromised. By listening to the stories of sufferers, the assessment criteria can be redefined as potential coping strategies, for example, inactivity viewed as pacing or energy conservation; pain behaviours as adaptive responses; and a focus on pain as finding meaning and purpose in their lives with pain or regaining control. Shifting the power balance away from the medical expert toward the sufferer is the first step in reclaiming control over one's pain and coping strategies; helping the sufferer identify the role and purpose of each strategy is the next step. Critical clinical social workers need to understand the socio-political context in which chronic pain is biomedically housed. They need to validate sufferers in their struggles to cope with pain, displacing blame and transforming it into active coping strategies.

CRITICAL CLINICAL CASE

Rachel, a 28-year-old woman, has been living with intense, unrelenting chronic pain. Her pain developed post-operatively five weeks after having a patellectomy (the surgical removal of a kneecap). Post-surgical recovery was going as expected when, all of a sudden, the nature and intensity of her pain changed.

In Rachel's case, the pain moved from her knee to her entire left leg. Rachel described her experience of pain to the critical clinical social worker she was referred to for pain management:

My whole body is riddled in pain. My left leg feels like a dead weight, lifeless yet incredibly hypersensitive to touch and even vibrations. A clenched fist held in the same position hour-after-hour mimics the tension and stress my entire body feels, with my left leg being amplified 100 times. Pain has become my identity. Loud sounds, bright lights, strong smells are received as direct assaults to my body. It takes every ounce of strength to get through the day, only to have to face a night of sleeplessness. Lightheartedness and being carefree are a distant memory as life has become all too serious.

In hearing Rachel's description of pain, the social worker knew it was critical to work from an interprofessional perspective in helping Rachel. The intensity of Rachel's pain was so great that pain control had to be addressed before emphasis was placed on helping Rachel build her "tickle trunk" of coping mechanisms. In reaching out to physicians and medical pain specialists, the social worker might need to play an advocacy role, as the worker knows that women sufferers have a greater chance of having their pain (1) dismissed or downplayed in severity, or (2) psychologized in that the health professional believes the origins of the pain are manifested in psychological pathology rather than physical causation (Werner & Malterud, 2003). From a sufferer's perspective, "the most important thing that medicine can do is say 'I believe you'" (MacDonald, 2008, p. 144).

The social worker needs to invite Rachel to tell more of her story, as it is important to find out who Rachel was before the pain and what losses she has experienced as a result of the pain. A narrative counterbalancing approach is used to explore emotional entities of loss and fears, engaging in a counselling process that will help the sufferer refocus and redefine hope. Pain can take one's personality away, as expressed by Rachel when she said, "Pain has become my identity." The role of the critical clinical social worker is to help the sufferer regain a sense of self whereby they feel empowered with a renewed sense of control over their life.

Rachel felt the biomedical judgment imposed by the health care system at her very core (MacDonald, 2008; Werner, Widding Isaksen, & Malterud, 2004). She felt her pain story was not believed. She felt judged for her medication usage, feared being admitted to hospital for pain management, and dreaded having to tell her story to yet another pain specialist. She felt her pain experiences were minimized and she was not validated as a sufferer or as a woman who knew her own body. Treating sufferers with respect by communicating an empathetic understanding of their lived experiences of pain and believing their stories (MacDonald, 2008) presents a counterbalance to the dominant medical discourse where expert knowledge belongs to physicians or other health professionals. Rachel was the expert on her own body and her own pain experiences.

The social worker moves through the counselling process, working with the sufferer to identify the various emotional, social, and physical aspects of their life that require counterbalancing, as illustrated in the following example. Rachel had withdrawn from most of her social activities, leaving her feeling isolated and disconnected from her community. The worker explored with Rachel what activities she missed the most and the related meaning to each activity. For example, Rachel used to be an athlete, and she loved playing basketball, field hockey, and softball. In delving a bit deeper, Rachel identified what it was about these activities that brought her joy: physical exercise, connection and interpersonal relationships with teammates, working collaboratively, and socializing after the games. The worker investigated what might be available in their community in respect to wheelchair sports. Rachel was able to join a co-ed ablebodied/wheelchair-user mixed basketball team. While the physical nature of the game changed somewhat, the teamwork and collaboration remained intact and the socializing aspect was even stronger.

The worker helped Rachel begin to build her tickle trunk of coping mechanisms, tapping into Rachel's strengths, likes, and passions, while at the same time acknowledging her fears and guiding her through the grief process. What works for one sufferer might not work for another, and what works in one moment, might not work in the next. In working together with the social worker, Rachel was able to identify multiple coping strategies, realign and counterbalance loss and fear, and acknowledge the emotional toil pain has had on her life (Walker et al., 2006; Werner et al., 2004). She was also able to tap into her strengths and determination to find her own sense of hope—not hope for a cure, but hope that tomorrow will be a better day than today or hope that a new coping strategy will be more helpful.

Initially, Rachel was looking for a diagnosis to validate her pain; however, in working with the critical clinical social worker she was able to restore her sense of self, which prompted her to build on her own strengths in defining coping strategies.

CONCLUSION

Through listening to chronic pain sufferers' stories conveyed in this chapter, the reader's consciousness was raised, ultimately transforming their relationship to the sufferer. Frank (2003, p. 629) describes the location of an illness story listener:

> You are not feeling what the patient feels—it is not that sense of empathy. Rather, you imagine how this story matters for this other person, given who they are and what they face. Listening and responding to patients' stories is a skill, not a technique. This skill may be best described as a moral commitment that becomes a habit, as much who you are as what you do.

Frank calls on the moral obligations of the listener, of the practitioner, to truly hear the sufferer's story. Social workers need to pay witness to the suffering to understand how to respond differently so as not to minimize the pain, by hearing the political nuances depicted in the categories within which the story has been framed.

The sufferers' stories challenge dominant discourses within chronic pain theory and treatment. The category of emotion challenged the binary split between mind-body, emotional-physical experiences of chronic pain, unsettling the medicalization of pain that defines emotional stressors as causal factors. Through the sufferers' stories grows an appreciation for the emotional experiences that are created through living in pain. The category of treatment acknowledged the impact on sufferers of having their knowledges and experiences silenced through a biomedical discourse (Walker et al., 2006; Werner et al., 2004), and called for an immediate disruption of the dominant power structure found within medicine. And, finally, the coping category deconstructed the labelling of a dysfunctional behaviour within sick-role theory, calling for the reframing of behaviours as coping strategies.

The contraindicated dualisms established as meta-narratives in chronic pain assessment and treatment, such as mind versus body, sufferer versus physician knowledge, and psychological pathology versus physiological, need to be dismantled and replaced with an inclusive understanding of the issues from the sufferers' perspectives. Within this chapter, chronic pain sufferers' re-storied their pain in a counterbalancing process whereby the impacts of loss and emotional strife were turned into coping strategies in living their life with pain. Critical clinical social workers can use this knowledge and applied skills to assist pain sufferers in living life with pain.

NOTE

1. Parts of this chapter are drawing on work from a doctoral dissertation entitled *Untold Stories: Women, in the Helping Professions, as Sufferers of Chronic Pain (Re)Storying (Dis)Ability* (2006), supervised by Dr. Joan Pennell.

REFERENCES

Ahern, D. (2002). Psychosocial and behavioral approaches. In J. Ballantzne (Ed.), *The Massachusetts General Hospital handbook of pain management* (2nd ed., pp. 224–236). Philadelphia: Lippincott Williams and Wilkins.

Barnes, A., Adam, M., Eke, A., & Ferguson, L. (2018). Exploring the emotional experiences of young women with chronic pain: The potential role of self-compassion. *Journal of Health Psychology*, 1–11. doi:10.1 177/1359105318816509

Bonica, J. (1990). Multidisciplinary/interdisciplinary pain programs. In J. Bonica (Ed.), *The management of pain* (pp. 197–208). Philadelphia: Lea and Febiger.

Brown, S., & Williams, A. (1995). Women's experiences of rheumatoid arthritis. *Journal of Advanced Nursing, 21*, 695–701.

Campbell, J. (1996). Pain treatment centers: A surgeon's perspective. In M. J. M. Cohen & J. N. Campbell (Eds.), *Progress in pain research and management* (pp. 29–37). Seattle: IASP Press.

Chronic Pain Association of Canada. (2004). Conquer pain. Retrieved from https://chronicpaincanada.com

Craig, K. (1999). Emotions and psychobiology. In P. Wall & R. Melzack (Eds.), *Textbook of pain* (4th ed., pp. 331–340). Edinburgh: Churchill Livingstone.

Fear. (1998). *The Canadian Oxford dictionary.* Toronto: Oxford University Press.

Fordyce, W. (1990). Contingency management. In J. Bonica (Ed.), *The management of pain* (pp. 1702–1709). Philadelphia: Lea and Febiger.

Frank, A. (1995). *The wounded storyteller: Body, illness and ethics.* Chicago: University of Chicago Press.

Frank, A. (1997). Enacting illness stories: When, what, and why. In H. Lindemann Nelson (Ed.), *Stories and their limits: Narrative approaches to bioethics* (pp. 31–49). New York: Routledge.

Frank, A. (2003). How stories remake what pain unmakes. *Progress in pain research and management, 24*, 619–630.

Gamsa, A., & Vikis-Freibergs, V. (1991). Psychological events are both factors in, and consequences of, chronic pain. *Pain, 44*, 271–277.

Greenhalgh, S. (2001). *Under the medical gaze: Facts and fictions of chronic pain.* Berkeley: University of California Press.

Hanes, R. (2002). Social work with persons with disabilities: The world of one in six. In S. Hick, *Social work in Canada: An introduction* (pp. 217–234). Toronto: Thompson Educational Publishing.

Herman, J. (1997). *Trauma and recovery: The aftermath of violence—from domestic abuse to political terror* (Revised ed.). New York: Basic Books.

Jackson, M. (2002). *Pain: The fifth vital sign.* Toronto: Random House Canada.

Leslie, D., Leslie, K., & Murphy, M. (2003). Inclusion by design: The challenge for social work in workplace accommodation for people with disabilities. In W. Shera (Ed.), *Emerging perspectives on anti-oppressive practice* (pp. 157–182). Toronto: Canadian Scholars' Press.

Long, D. M. (1996). The development of the comprehensive pain treatment program at Johns Hopkins. In M. J. M. Cohen & J. N. Campbell (Eds.), *Progress in pain research and management, 7,* 3–23. Seattle: IASP Press.

Lumley, M., Schubiner, H., Carty, J., & Ziadni, M. (2015). Beyond traumatic events and chronic back pain: Assessment and treatment implications of avoided emotional experiences. *Pain, 156*(4), 565–566.

MacDonald, J. (2000). A deconstructive turn in chronic pain treatment: A redefined role for social work. *Health and Social Work, 25*(1), 51–58.

MacDonald, J. (2004). One woman's experience of living with chronic pain: The proclamation of voice. *Journal of Social Work in Disability and Rehabilitation, 3*(2), 17–35.

MacDonald, J. (2006). Untold stories: Women, in the helping professions, as sufferers of chronic pain (re)storying (dis)Ability. Doctoral dissertation, Memorial University of Newfoundland. Retrieved from https://research.library.mun.ca/10944/1/MacDonald_JudyE.pdf

MacDonald, J. (2008). Anti-oppressive practices with chronic pain sufferers. *Social Work in Health Care, 47*(2), 135–156.

MacDonald, J., & Friars, G. (2010). Structural social work from a (dis)Ability perspective. In S. Hicks, H. Peters, T. Corner, & T. London (Eds.), *Structural social work in action* (pp. 138–156). Toronto: Canadian Scholars' Press.

Mailis-Gagnon, A., & Israelson, D. (2003). *Beyond pain: Making the mind-body connection.* Toronto: Viking Canada.

Pryma, J. (2017a). "Even my sister says I'm acting like crazy to get a check": Race, gender, and moral boundary-work in women's claims of disabling chronic pain. *Social Science and Medicine, 181,* 66–73.

Pryma, J. (2017b). Pain, citizenship, and invisibility: A response to Joanna Kempner. *Social Science and Medicine, 189,* 155–157.

Rose, K. (1994). Patient isolation in chronic benign pain. *Nursing Standard, 8*(51), 25–27.

Rosenfeld, A. (2003). *The truth about chronic pain: Patients and professionals on how to face it, understand it and overcome it.* New York: Basic Books.

Roy, R. (1988). Impact of chronic pain on marital partners: Systems perspective. In R. Dubner, G. F. Gebhart, & M. R. Bond (Eds.), *Proceedings of the 5th World Congress on Pain* (pp. 286–298). New York: Elsevier Science Publishers.

Roy, R. (1992). *The social context of the chronic pain sufferer.* Toronto: University of Toronto Press.

Roy, R. (2001). *Social relations and chronic pain.* New York: Kluwer-Plenum Publishing.

Seers, K., & Friedli, K. (1996). The patients' experiences of their chronic non-malignant pain. *Journal of Advanced Nursing, 24,* 1160–1168.

Walker, J., Sofaer, B., & Holloway, I. (2006). The experience of chronic back pain: Accounts of loss in those seeking help from pain clinics. *European Journal of Pain, 10,* 199–207.

Wendell, S. (1996). *The rejected body: Feminist philosophical reflections on disability.* New York: Routledge.

Werner, A., & Malterud, K. (2003). It is hard work behaving as a credible patient: Encounters between women with chronic pain and their doctors. *Social Science and Medicine, 57*(8), 1409–1419.

Werner, A., Widding Isaksen, L., & Malterud, K. (2004). "I am not the kind of woman who complains of everything": Illness stories on self and shame in women with chronic pain. *Social Science and Medicine, 59*(5), 1035–1045.

Worden, W. (2009). *Grief counselling and grief therapy: A handbook for the mental health practitioner* (4th ed.). New York: Springer.

CHAPTER 16

Validating Voice in Critical Clinical Work with Older People

Joan R. Harbison and Donna Pettipas

INTRODUCTION

Our starting point for the discussion of clinical work with older people is an examination of how older people's voices are constrained, and their well-being endangered, by the many manifestations of an embedded, profound, and increasingly complicated societal ageism in many cultural contexts (Cole, 1993; Gullette, 2017; Harbison, 2016). It follows that older people may have difficulty giving voice to what troubles them. We therefore view ageism as central in considering older people's distress in their later years. Our case example illustrates that no matter how this distress is labelled, or by whom, notably by older people themselves, it must be understood through its ageist societal context. Moreover, this context incorporates structural, professional, and interpersonal sites and issues of power. Having introduced the concept of ageism, we go on to examine the many implications for therapeutic encounters that flow from ageist contexts, the thinking and assumptions that inhabit them, and how they might be addressed.

AGEISM

Ageism refers to negative stereotypes and prejudices about aging and older people. Although ageism is also manifest toward younger age groups, it can be argued that its consequences are more profound with regard to those who are older. In a similar way to other forms of oppression, it sets aside facts— in the case of ageism, those demonstrating the diversity of people in late life, especially about how they age, and why, and what they can achieve and contribute to society. As a consequence, ageism results in the devaluation of society's older people. Scholars also point out that, unlike other forms of oppression, ageism persists despite the fact that most people will become old.

The ageist devaluation that pervades society becomes internalized not just by the general public but too often by professionals, and most importantly, by older people themselves. Therefore, the challenge to clinicians in working with older people is to join with them in overcoming their internalized ageism as well as their wariness of the motivations of the helper as "other" and "othering" (van Dyk, 2016). Hence, it is important to lend support to the use of older people's own voices in expressing and validating their needs and wishes. We use an extended case example to illustrate how critical clinical interventions, incorporating the tenets of feminist narrative therapy as described by Catrina Brown (2017), can be crafted in the context of an older woman's circumstances, to support the (re)emergence of the woman's voice through restorying her life. This restorying also supports her in rediscovering old skills and developing new strategies to meet the challenges of being old in her own community within today's society.

"THE OTHER"

"The other" has many meanings. It is used here as it is in postcolonial theory in the sense that "the other" is viewed as a lesser form of the subject and therefore can, through the process of "othering," be legitimately dominated and controlled (Macey, 2001).

As you read this chapter, ask yourself the following questions:

1. What contradictory statements about, and images of, older people do you come across in everyday life? (Consider, for instance, those of governments, professionals, advertisements, and comedy.)
2. How might the label "senior" affect the identity of the older person: how they see themselves and how others perceive them?
3. How might you assist an older person first in unpacking their internalized ageism and then with the construction of a counterstory that reveals or creates a greater awareness of their innate strengths, skills, and contributions?
4. How do you assist an older person in re-examining their life experiences and choices in the context of a societal ageism that may reveal the extent to which they were constrained, and, at the same time, validate this lived experience within their particular cultural, social, and interpersonal context?

AGEISM AND ITS EFFECTS

Beginnings

Acknowledgement of ageism has been ongoing since the term was coined by the pioneering gerontologist and physician Robert Butler in the United States in 1969. Butler (1969, p. 243) referred not only to the "process of systematic stereotyping of discrimination against people because they are old," but also to societies' discomfort with the aging body that heralded death. Most notably, he took the position that this abhorrence affected both older people's social status and the social conditions to which they were allocated. Feminist Margaret Cruikshank added an emphasis on the ideas prominent in Alex Comfort's definition that move our understanding of ageism toward its psychological consequences as well as the social: "People cease to be people, cease to be the same people, or become people of [a] distinct and inferior kind by virtue of having lived a specified number of years" (Comfort, 1976, p. 35, cited in Cruikshank, 2003, p. 13; Bytheway, 1995; Tanner & Harris, 2008).

Around the same time as Butler began to discuss ageism, the work of French feminist philosopher Simone de Beauvoir published in France in 1970 (*La Vieillesse*; English translations: *The Coming of Age* [1972]; *Old Age* [1972]) provided a wide-ranging analysis of old age, and its negative stereotypes, that included philosophical, historical, social, biological, anthropological, and cultural elements. While much has changed in the 50 years since its publication, many of de Beauvoir's comments in *La Vieillesse* remain highly relevant to today's discourse. For instance, speaking from the perspective of a feminist political economy, de Beauvoir says, "the old person who can no longer provide for himself is always [considered] a *burden*" (1972, p. 12). Today, the term *burden* is ever-present in public and private discussions of the aging demographic and older people. In the current rhetoric of the media, and for many policy-makers, this burden represents a "tsunami" that threatens to overwhelm younger generations through its needs for care (Harbison et al., 2016).

Aging, Ageism, and Biomedicine

In large part, this perception of older people as burden has followed from the ongoing dominance of biomedicine in the field of aging. Since Butler named it, the concept of ageism has remained present but not prominent in the study of old age (see, for instance, Bytheway, 1995; McHugh, 2003; Nelson, 2004; Thorpe, 2002; see also Harbison et al., 2016, p. 62). As editor of a text on ageism, Nelson (2004, p. ix) acknowledges in his introduction the general societal "lack of interest" in the topic and declares that researchers should overcome their own ageism to pursue this "long neglected area of research." Yet, that neglect was hardly surprising in an era that saw a surge in attempts to subsume understanding of aging within biomedical frameworks, providing scientific legitimacy through the values and tools of a quantitative empiricism focusing on definition and measurement. Indeed, gerontological knowledge became subsumed within disciplines that ultimately were unable to reflect the true diversity of older people's later years (Katz, 1996). We advocate a different approach to the study of aging and ageism—one that focuses on supporting older people in giving voice to their experiences and opinions (Gubrium, 1993).

BIOMEDICAL

The term *biomedical* in this context refers to subsumption of the concept of aging within the confines of what can be examined and measured through positivist-empiricist research methods. So the study of aging becomes limited to the scientific study of constructed problems of the aging body and mind (Harbison et al., 2016, p. 19).

Notwithstanding the above discussion, not only have the social and psychological sciences contributed to the field of aging, notably through a "critical gerontology," more recently those in the arts and humanities have as well (Kivnick & Pruchno, 2011). Now some worry that this cultural turn may lead away from and undermine "the gains of the Political Economy or Critical Gerontology schools that had emphasized the ways in which old age was socially rather than physiologically constituted" (Twigg & Martin, 2015, p. 355; see also Moody, 1993). This concern about the loss of structural and individual power elements in gerontology is a concern for social work practice in general. We need to provide understandings of people's specific needs that include an awareness of how they are shaped by the current socio-political demands and norms. Within the neoliberal social and institutional context of social work practice today, social work education and practice has increasingly stressed "clinical skills" with a decontextualized emphasis on individual pathology and short-term intervention.

FEMINISTS, AGEISM, AND AGE STUDIES

Some feminists took up the theme of ageism even as many struggled with their own internalized ageism. For instance, Margaret Cruikshank (2003, p. 136) argues that "while women are victims of ageism, they may also be perpetrators." Cynthia Rich too "sees internalized ageism not only within society in general but also within the feminist culture as a major cause of the lack of interest in older women's concerns" (cited in Harbison et al., 2016, p. 23). She also expresses despair that older feminists

> have no idea how to think about our aging and our organizing. They're struggling. Long time feminists … tried to organize a voters' movement called Granny Voters, around their concern for their grandchildren. Granny Voters? These are strong feminists who never would have called themselves Mommy Voters, who never would have ignored the sexism they encountered or fed the stereotype that all women are mothers. (cited in Lipscomb, 2006, p. 4)

Margaret Morganroth Gullette, an American feminist scholar in the arts and humanities who coined the term *age studies* is now a prominent figure in the field. She argues for emancipatory approaches to ageism. She points out that "many observers agree: compared to sexism, racism, or transphobia, ageism is the least censured, the most acceptable and unnoticed of the cruel prejudices" (2017, p. xiii). She also refers to the influence of biomedicine, stating that "'geroscience': that needle-narrow focus on disease is an overwhelming reduction of the meaning of 'aging' … as if there could be human events without sentient subjects" (p. xii).

AGEISM AND THE DIVERSITY OF THOSE IN LATER LIFE

The sharpness with which Margaret Gullette criticizes the reductionism of biomedical approaches to aging has become unusual in recent years (but see, for instance, Phillipson, 2013; Powell & Wahidin, 2006). As we commented earlier in the chapter, the critical gerontology that once based its study of aging on a political-economic analysis now more usually attempts to accommodate biomedical approaches to aging within a field that includes the biomedical, political-economic, social, and psychological, and most recently, the arts and humanities. This mainstreaming of disciplines within the field of aging has lessened the potential for structural critiques of how society perceives and responds to aging. It follows that the lens through which older people are viewed has narrowed even as the field has broadened. So it is that while the arts and humanities are expanding our understanding of aging, much of the interdisciplinary research and writing on older people is reductionist, preoccupying itself with function. The focus is on how to maximize older people's abilities to remain active and meet their own needs (Walker, 2014).

The preoccupation with function leads to the dichotomization of older people's status into those who remain functionally able to be included in the mainstream of society (the third age), and those whose needs for care mean that they are exiled from that mainstream (the fourth age) (Laslett, 1989). Categorization, of whatever kind, in itself is a form of stereotyping that fuels ageism. Most importantly, it fails to address the remarkable diversity of those in old age, which includes the greatest diversity of all age groups. Chronologically older people inhabit a 40-year span. Their culture, education, interests, political views, and financial situations vary widely, as do their physical and mental abilities (McPherson & Wister, 2008; Tanner & Harris, 2008).

OLDER PEOPLE'S RESPONSES TO AGEISM: CHALLENGES TO ACCESSING VOICE

So far we have discussed the ageist social context in which older people must live their lives. We now turn to what this means for older people's voices.

Popular Culture, Ageism, and Older People's Voices

The idea of ageism has now become part of popular culture. Older people's voices may be "heard" through various media: for instance, in books and blogs about ageism and empowerment written by aging feminists (see, for instance, Ashton Applewhite's *This Chair Rocks: A Manifest Against Ageism*, 2016). Yet many older people remain disempowered even as they seek empowerment. For instance, they may embrace their marginalization as "seniors" by having bumper stickers that say "proud to be a senior." When they call in to talk shows or appear on television interviews, they may emphasize their pride in being "seniors" and the fact that they are remaining active. In a CBC radio interview (personal observation), an older woman who had agreed to take part in a national longitudinal study on older people's health said firmly that it was her "duty" to participate in assisting the research group to better understand the aging process.

Older People's Strategies in Addressing Ageism

The sparse research available suggests that many older people attempt to meet the criteria for active and successful aging, or withdrawal from life, that they perceive is expected of them. They bring varying degrees of consciousness to these endeavours. For instance, in our case study Elizabeth believes that she should follow her daughter's wishes for her life and not her own. In this instance, her daughter's expectation was for Elizabeth to decrease her activities and engagement. Others may follow the "successful aging" script that society provides for them, while at the same time remaining highly cognizant of the negative way in which they are viewed and "othered" by the rest of society. Yet others may subvert this stereotyping by developing a number of strategies in response, thus regaining a sense of power (see, for instance, Biggs, 1997; Harbison, 2016; Katz, 2005; Minichiello, Brown, & Kendig, 2000); for example, the Raging Grannies are overtly defiant in challenging the negativity that surrounds them and searching for power, or at least comfort, in communities of like-minded older people (Hall, 2005).

Older People's Understandings of Their Rights and Status

Many older people remain uncertain about their rights. For instance, following a lawyer's presentation on older people's rights to make their own decisions, an older woman came to speak with the lawyer. The woman asked if she and not her daughter could make financial decisions after she was 65 years of age. This woman had understood, apparently from her daughter, that legally things had changed for her when she turned 65. When one takes into consideration that this presentation was made to a well-educated group of older people of whom this woman was one, and that she showed no evidence of mental impairment, this is a striking event. Yet the lawyer in question said that she frequently experienced questions like this after her presentations (Harbison, personal observation and information).

So, despite being of perfectly sound mind, older people (we suspect most often older women) may defer in their judgments to those who are younger, and younger generations may see this as a natural consequence of the aging process. Such views are supported in some professional circles and certainly in much of the care industry. Moreover, it is still the case that in many instances media reports and advertisements act to sustain this assumption. We will see in the case example that follows that such perceptions appear to have influenced Elizabeth's understanding of how she should behave.

We may infer that many older people internalize negative stereotypes of aging in a way that does not support their agency but leaves them vulnerable to dominance by others. This dominance is itself sometimes a consequence of assumptions about aging based on the internalized ageism of its perpetrators. However, as its recipients, older people are encouraged, whether with good intent or not, to give up the struggle for a meaningful life, becoming passive objects of ministrations and, in too many instances, depressed.

COUNSELLING OLDER PEOPLE

Practice Conventions in Working with Older People

The negative stereotypes of aging, named as ageism, have for many years been widely acknowledged in the practice literature focused on work with older people (see, for instance, Holosko & Feit, 1996; McDonald, 2010; Tanner & Harris, 2008). Holosko and Holosko (1996, pp. 23–24) refer to the need for a well-informed understanding of aging processes, one that implies both a broad scope and consideration of ageism. They cite Louis Lowy (1987, p. 40):

> There is increasing consensus that people in their later years have needs and problems that are associated with particular biological, physiological, psychological, social or cultural conditions which are correlated with aging processes or with an interface of personal and social situations, such as retirement, widowhood, or status and role deprivations. As health and social care providers frequently find it hard to come to terms with their own aging, they must learn to cope better with these feelings.

Holosko and Holosko go on to discuss the need to dispel "negative myths and stereotypes about aging" (1996, p. 24). In *Working with Older People*, Tanner and Harris (2008) emphasize the need to think about how older people experience aging, age discrimination, and ageism and how to challenge these. In *Social Work with Older People*, McDonald (2010, p. 94) refers to "ageist assumptions" in "organizational arrangements."

Despite these acknowledgements of ageism over a 30-year period, the authors generally fail to acknowledge how power affects practice. In each of the above-named texts a key component of working with older people is named as the "assessment." This is a term that originates in functionalist, biomedical perceptions of the social work role, one in which power differentials are embedded, and the client is not a partner but the "other" (O'Connor, 2010). In contrast, feminist narrative therapy is intended to offer a different approach and experience to the older person—one that views the self as socially constructed to meet the requirements of particular contexts and circumstances:

> Feminist narrative therapy takes a critical view of the stories people tell about their experiences in life and of the ideas women (and men) hold about how they should behave and think in everyday life.... Feminist narrative practice offers a gendered politicized therapeutic conversation that allows for creating counter-stories. (Brown, 2017, p. 212)

HOW CAN WE ASSIST YOU? THE CHALLENGE OF LIBERATING AN OLDER WOMAN'S VOICE

Elizabeth Jones is a 69-year-old woman who was referred by her family physician, Dr. Hughson, to a family service counselling agency for assistance. The reason for the referral was described on the referral form as follows: "My patient Mrs. Elizabeth Jones, who is in excellent physical health, appears to be suffering a grief reaction following the sudden death from a heart attack of her husband, Jim Jones, five months ago, after 40 years of marriage. She seems unable to make any decisions about her future. Her daughter has become very concerned about her mother's state of mind and whether or not she remains capable of handling her own affairs. Mrs. Jones has therefore agreed to an appointment with a counsellor."

Dr. Hughson is a female physician in a group practice who, unlike her colleagues, rarely makes referrals for counselling as she is more inclined to take a biomedical view of psychosocial problems. The counsellor, Carla Morelli, to whom Elizabeth is assigned, is a woman in her late fifties who for most of her career has worked with those in later life. Carla identifies as a feminist who brings an understanding of the principles of feminist narrative therapy to her work. She immigrated to Canada with her family when she was eight years old. As the daughter of an immigrant family she is very aware of how cultural stereotypes—including those surrounding age—influence perceptions of the self and others. Thus, she also understands people's lives as taking place within a social, cultural, and political context. In her approach, she attempts to ensure that "women's stories are externalized, placing the problem stories outside of the women themselves and within the broader social and historical context" (Brown, 2017, p. 213).

For Carla, the sparse information on the referral form raises a number of immediate questions: What is it that has caused the family doctor, unusually, to see this situation as one in which counselling might be helpful? To what extent is Mrs. Jones a willing, or unwilling, participant in the proposed counselling? In either case, what has motivated her to agree to a meeting? Is her acquiescence intended to meet her doctor's and daughter's needs and wishes rather than her own? Does she view herself as reacting to her grief? Does she see herself as unable to make decisions? Are these decisions necessary in her mind, or in her daughter's, or both? More broadly, what has characterized her relationship with her husband? And with her daughter? How has this been affected by the death of her husband and her daughter's father? What was her daughter's relationship with her father? And how is Mrs. Jones's daughter being affected by the loss of her father?

Essentialism

Carla is well-versed in the widely differing responses of older women to the loss of a long-time spouse. She understands that the dominant societal understanding of that response, one that anticipates an unequivocal sense of loss and grief, may be very far from what emerges for an individual. For instance, it no longer comes as a surprise to Carla that for some women their distress at their feelings about the loss comes from a sense of relief and/or ambivalence that brings with it severe guilt. This, however, can be very sensitive ground to explore.

Carla is also alert to the fact that only five months after the apparently sudden death of her husband of 40 years, Mrs. Jones's uncertainties about her life and inability to make decisions are being viewed as pathological and as needing to be addressed, rather than normalized as a reaction to shock, loss, and disruption in her life.

Carla wonders if Mrs. Jones shares the view that she may not be able to manage her own affairs. What specific concerns does she have? What does she want for herself right now? Are there other issues she feels she needs to take into account around the decisions she makes: for example, as a woman living alone, concerning her age, or her daughter's feelings? Has she internalized the negative, stereotypic societal beliefs about women and aging discussed earlier in the chapter? How might her life experiences reflect knowledge and skills that are readily transferable to her life currently? How aware is she of her own strengths and abilities, often taken for granted or unrecognized? Carla is also interested in knowing what social and psychological supports Mrs. Jones has and if she is aware of sources of support other than her daughter that may be helpful to her.

Carla wonders how Mrs. Jones constructs her relationships with her husband and daughter, thinking that if she offers thin descriptions she might need to encourage her to thicken them in order to have a better sense of how Mrs. Jones understands her roles and abilities, not just in the context of her family, but in the context of society in general. For instance, are roles in her family subject to traditional gender stereotypes? Did she have a career? Does she have interests outside of home and family?

Working with Elizabeth

After greeting Mrs. Jones and both of them agreeing that they will call one another by their first names, Carla shares a simple, accurate, neutral précis of the information that Mrs. Jones's physician provided on the referral form, using lay terms that avoid a pathological construction of grief. Carla comments that Dr. Hughson referred Elizabeth because she thought that counselling support might be helpful following the shock of the sudden loss of her husband. She adds that she wonders if that is Elizabeth's understanding.

Elizabeth's Concerns

Elizabeth shows no hesitation in saying that the loss of her husband was a shock to her as he had always enjoyed good health. She describes feeling a sense of disbelief that he is gone. She talks of how she is struggling to imagine a future for herself without him. Elizabeth then volunteers that she feels overwhelmed when she thinks about the many responsibilities and decisions that now fall solely to her. She says that her worry about managing alone makes it hard for her to concentrate, leaves her feeling "lost" and makes organizing herself, or even making simple decisions on a daily basis, very difficult.

Elizabeth says her daughter, Marilyn, has told her that she is very concerned about her. Marilyn also says she thinks that it would be hard for her mother to undertake the responsibilities of maintaining her home and managing financial matters because Marilyn's father had always looked after these things. Elizabeth says her daughter has spoken to her about moving to a smaller place, an apartment that would offer both less responsibility and less need for maintenance. In response to Carla's inquiry about how Elizabeth feels about this she says that it would be very hard to move away from the suburban community where she spent all of her married life. Yet she emphasizes that she does not want to be a source of worry to her daughter, particularly given that Marilyn has been devastated by the loss of her father with whom she had a very close relationship.

Elizabeth says that she herself is unsure about her ability to manage life on her own as she has never lived alone. Her days have always been busy with family activities and social and community commitments. She can't picture what her life will look like alone. She would like to try to stay in her own home but fears that she could end up creating a greater burden for her daughter if she ran into trouble. She says that this fear has made her reluctant to seek her daughter's support in staying where she is. Elizabeth wonders if perhaps moving to a smaller place would make things easier for her to manage and alleviate her daughter's anxieties. Yet she repeats that the thought of giving up her home and her community is very hard.

Carla notes Elizabeth's emphasis on her daughter's concerns about her abilities and living situation, but is not yet clear about the extent to which these are also Elizabeth's concerns. Carla therefore asks Elizabeth to help her understand her life and relationships with family, friends, and community. By shifting the discussion to Elizabeth's life with her husband, daughter, and neighbourhood, she can revisit their roles in her life.

Elizabeth's Account of Her Life

Elizabeth says she was living at home with her parents when she started working at the bank as a teller. She met her husband there. He was working as a loans officer. Elizabeth left her job with the bank shortly before they were married to become a full-time homemaker. Her husband continued to work for the same bank, gaining promotions until he retired as a senior manager. Her daughter was born two years after they married. They had only one child due to difficulties with the pregnancy, and Elizabeth herself is an only child. In contrast, her husband, Jim, was the eldest of four siblings and liked being head of the family, so they often celebrated family events in their home. Elizabeth says she enjoyed being at the centre of this large family and the work it involved.

Elizabeth was always busy responding to things in the home, including her daughter's busy school, sports, and social schedule, readying her husband for his frequent business trips, and preparing for extended family events. Her husband was so busy that he didn't have time to look after himself. She made his appointments for the doctor or dentist or he would never have gotten there. Elizabeth says that her husband's job included a significant number of customer- and staff-related social obligations that he was expected to respond to. For years they attended or hosted these types of events at least twice a month.

Elizabeth and her daughter were very close when Marilyn was younger, but her daughter and her husband developed a very strong bond as she got older.

Her daughter idolized her father and also chose to pursue a career in banking. After Marilyn broke up with her long-time partner about 10 years ago, father and daughter became "inseparable," at least in her husband's small amount of free time. Elizabeth recalls that they would often have very spirited discussions about politics and finance and would tease her about her lack of interest in those things. Marilyn and Jim also shared an interest in sports, biking, hiking, and boating, and on weekends Jim joined Marilyn and her friends in these activities. Elizabeth said that these were not things that interested her. She preferred to stay home reading. She enjoys participating in a local book club of which she has been a member for 20 years.

Elizabeth says that her daughter's career in banking has been quite successful. Both she and Jim were very happy to see their daughter do so well in her career, but her husband was particularly proud of Marilyn's accomplishments. Despite having a very demanding work schedule, Marilyn has always maintained regular contact with her parents by phone. Not a week went by that she didn't call on her father for advice on sorting out a problem she was dealing with at work.

Carla asks Elizabeth if she took part in other activities outside of the home. Elizabeth replies that her local volunteer work has always been a tremendous source of satisfaction for her. She is a member of the ladies' auxiliary at her church and has held a number of other volunteer positions there over the course of many years. For instance, she was the lead organizer of various annual fundraisers, developed a hospital-visiting program, was responsible for events booking and coordination, and had served as the church's treasurer for six years.

Elizabeth says her husband used to tease her about her job as treasurer, saying that they would be living without electricity if she ever took over the bills at home. Although she views her financial skills as limited, church officers told her that she was a good manager—something she appears not to believe. As Elizabeth sees it, she managed by reading up on being treasurer for voluntary organizations, reviewing the church's financial records, and seeking advice from previous treasurers when she thought it necessary. Elizabeth has not been involved in the administrative or development side of church projects since her husband retired as she wanted to be free to spend time with him. She has missed that and offered to be an "on-call" front-line volunteer for church events and fundraisers when opportunities arose and she could make herself available.

Elizabeth made many good friends through her book club and volunteer work, but has rarely spent time socializing with them outside of scheduled activities, although some others did. Her own home life and commitments were too full. She says that her contact was generally limited to their bi-weekly meetings, to church events, and to meeting for coffee, or by chance since they live in a small community.

Elizabeth's Sense of Loss

Elizabeth says that she had not imagined losing her husband at this point in their lives. She had looked forward to them being able to spend more time together. When he first retired, they went for long leisurely walks each evening and saw more of friends, and Jim sometimes helped her with expanding their vegetable garden. However, besides his time with Marilyn and her friends, Jim had volunteered for a number of projects and fundraisers at the local fire department and his time quickly got taken up with that. Nevertheless, they had more time together than previously, and she was so looking forward to what life would bring them in the coming years.

Elizabeth expresses guilt that she did not urge her husband to retire much sooner. She believes that he would have had a longer life if he had not worked so long in such a stressful job. Elizabeth never imagined their time together would be cut so short. She says that she had hoped that they would have the opportunity to discover each other again.

Carla's Initial Thoughts about Elizabeth's Situation

As Carla sees it, Elizabeth has spent her whole life in the service of others. Her primary concern has been to accommodate and respond to the needs and wishes of her husband and daughter and other family members. She is quick to blame herself for Jim's death. To allay the anxieties of her daughter, Elizabeth now seems prepared to set aside the opportunities for life satisfaction that she has developed over the years through a host of connections within her community. Moreover, Elizabeth has long accepted the version of her abilities constructed by her husband and daughter—one which appears to have undermined the self-confidence of a woman who by her own account is surely socially and functionally competent. Carla also wonders if, despite Elizabeth's portrayal of the perfect marriage and family, her husband contributed much on an emotional level. What has been portrayed is a life filled with busyness. Carla notes too that despite Elizabeth's hopes for greater closeness with her husband when he retired, Jim quickly became involved in new projects outside of their home.

Elizabeth's internalized construction of herself appears very different from Carla's. Carla sees her as a woman who, given her relationships in her community and her good health, has a strong potential for leading an independent and ful-filling life for many years to come. Yet Elizabeth has constructed herself as a woman whose purpose is to serve the needs of others and who doubts her ability to manage her life without the assistance of her husband and now her daughter. Carla's challenge is how to assist Elizabeth in beginning the process of moving beyond these sexist and ageist constructions of her life in the absence of its main focus, her husband, but in the presence of a daughter whose anxieties about her mother are most likely linked to Elizabeth's construction by both father and daughter as an incompetent woman. Moreover, Marilyn is likely in a precarious emotional position given her closeness to her father and her own grief at his loss.

Beginning the Work of Restorying

Carla thinks it best that they begin their work by focusing on practical matters that may alleviate Elizabeth's anxieties by reintroducing her to her management skills, thus giving her a sense of control in her life. Work on emotions may fol-low later, especially if Elizabeth chooses to revisit her existing construction of her marriage and its effects on her life. They begin by reviewing the practicalities of Elizabeth's situation. Her husband's will is not yet probated but its provisions are very straightforward. They leave Elizabeth in possession of the family home, with an adequate income for her personal needs and to maintain the house and garden. The will is being handled by a lawyer and an executor who are friends of her husband's. Both are people that Elizabeth knows well and trusts. Carla and Elizabeth consider what else needs to be done regarding finances, includ-ing paperwork involving pensions, house insurance, and general maintenance, as well as other personal commitments. These matters were well in hand having been organized and kept up to date by both Elizabeth and her husband. There is little that needs immediate attention. Elizabeth expresses relief that what needs to be done in the near future can be managed so easily.

They conclude too that Elizabeth has the financial security to allow her to remain in her own home. She at least has the means to "try" it, to find out if that is what she wants. She can then decide to stay on if she chooses. Carla also draws attention to the shortness of the time since Jim's death and comments that it is generally considered wise not to make quick decisions about major changes in one's life in times of emotional turmoil. Elizabeth seems open to these points of view.

More difficult is how to address Marilyn's wish for her mother to move away from the community that has been Elizabeth's social and emotional lifeline.

Carla decides to raise the possibility with Elizabeth that Marilyn may believe that she should step in for her father and make a plan because Elizabeth has not done so. Carla therefore suggests that it is in Marilyn's best interests for Elizabeth to help Marilyn understand that she, Elizabeth, is clear about what she wants and has the confidence in her own abilities to manage in her home and to seek comfort in the community that has been so important to her. By making her own decisions Elizabeth may therefore relieve Marilyn's anxieties and so lessen the experience of burden that her father's loss brings to her daughter. Elizabeth agrees to these strategies.

Carla's Reflections on Beginning Work with Elizabeth

Carla feels appreciation for the perception of the referring family physician in transcending the stereotype of the aging, bereaved, depressed, and helpless widow. Dr. Hughson had somehow realized that the situation was perhaps not quite as simple as it seemed, and that neither time nor medications would provide an adequate response. Carla hopes that the ongoing positive relationships that she and her agency have cultivated with the group practice have contributed to this very busy doctor's decision to refer despite her usual lack of interest in psychosocial perspectives.

Carla is aware that she must avoid imposing her own feminist perspectives on this marriage in her interactions with Elizabeth. Both Elizabeth and her daughter have protected their image of Jim as the ideal husband and father. To Carla, Elizabeth's serving the family seems to have meant that her own interests and pursuits had to become secondary, and moreover were mostly denigrated by Jim and Marilyn. She has also taken note of the extreme closeness of father and daughter and wonders if that may have stifled Marilyn's ability to fully develop a life of her own.

Carla hopes to assist Elizabeth in sustaining her beginning confidence in her life skills. She wonders if later, as Elizabeth begins to pick up the many threads of her relationships and work in her community, she will begin to question what her marriage offered. Carla will keep alert to this possibility. Carla also questions whether Marilyn will easily be able to allow her mother to grow and whether Marilyn herself may need to seek her own counselling support. With these caveats, Carla believes her work with Elizabeth has made a good beginning.

Carla's work with Elizabeth has followed the principles of feminist narrative therapy, albeit with a caution dictated by Elizabeth's state of grief, and her own and her daughter's adherence to a positive view of her husband and marriage. In reminding Elizabeth of her past demonstrations of her abilities to manage finances and events, Carla has helped her begin the restorying of her life and strengths. She hopes her work with Elizabeth will continue, to support her in beginning a new life, and perhaps eventually to respond to questions that Elizabeth might have about her marriage through counterstorying her past life.

CONCLUSION

Throughout this chapter we have emphasized how the ongoing dominant discourse on aging focuses on a narrow biomedical decline and decay model, one in which aging is assumed as a problem to be treated, by medical or other means. Manifesting ageism, such a construction sets aside the accumulated evidence of diversity in the many dimensions of how people age both mentally and physically. Elizabeth's situation demonstrates not only how this ageism can lead to negative stereotypes and assumptions about an individual, but also how these are too often permeated by longstanding sexism. For clinicians who, like Carla, take a critical feminist approach to clinical intervention, a major challenge is to overcome ageism, as it is internalized in themselves, in other professionals, and in the older people who are their clients. They can then work in partnership with older people to create counterstories that support their clients in moving beyond ageist and sexist constructions of their lives. As with Elizabeth, clients can begin to generate an alternative perspective on their abilities, and to (re)discover their own voices through which to express their needs and wishes.

REFERENCES

Applewhite, A. (2016). *This chair rocks: A manifesto against ageism.* Networked Books, Perfect Paperback Edition.

Biggs, S. (1997). Choosing not to be old? Masks, bodies, and identity management in later life. *Ageing and Society, 17*(5), 553–570.

Brown, C. (2017). Creating counter-stories: Critical clinical practice and feminist narrative therapy. In D. Baines (Ed.), *Doing anti-oppressive practice: Social justice social work* (3rd ed., pp. 212–232). Halifax and Winnipeg: Fernwood.

Butler, R. N. (1969). Age-ism: Another form of bigotry. *The Gerontologist, 9,* 243–246.

Bytheway, B. (1995). *Ageism.* Buckingham, UK: Open University Press.

Cole, T. R. (1993). Preface. In T. R. Cole, W. A. Achenbaum, P. L. Jakobi, & R. Kastenbaum (Eds.), *Voices and visions of aging: Toward a critical gerontology* (pp. vii–xi). New York: Springer.

Comfort, A. (1976). *A good age.* New York: Crown Publishers.

Cruikshank, M. (2003). *Learning to be old: Gender, culture and aging.* Lanham, MD: Rowman and Littlefield.

de Beauvoir, S. (1972). *Old age.* Harmondsworth, UK: Penguin Books.

de Beauvoir, S. (1972). *The coming of age.* New York: G. P. Putman's and Sons.

Gubrium, J. F. (1993). Voice and context in a new gerontology. In T. R. Cole, W. A. Achenbaum, P. L. Jakobi, & R. Kastenbaum (Eds.), *Voices and visions of aging: Toward a critical gerontology* (pp. 46–63). New York: Springer.

Gullette, M. M. (2017). *Ending ageism or how not to shoot old people.* New Brunswick, NJ: Rutgers University Press.

Hall, F. (2005). Old rage and the issue of mistreatment and neglect of older people. Master's thesis, School of Social Work, Dalhousie University, Canada.

Harbison, J. (2016). How ageism undermines older people's human rights and social inclusion: Revisiting advocacy, agency, and need in later life. In P. Naskali, M. Seppänen, & S. Begum (Eds.), *Ageing, well-being and climate change in the Arctic: An interdisciplinary analysis* (pp. 11–29). London: Routledge.

Harbison, J. R., with Coughlan, S., Karabanow, J., VanderPlaat, M., Wildeman, S., & Wexler, E. (2016). *Contesting elder abuse and neglect: Ageism, risk, and the rhetoric of rights in the mistreatment of older people.* Vancouver: University of British Columbia Press.

Holosko, M. J., & Feit, M. D. (1996). *Social work practice with the elderly* (2nd ed.). Toronto: Canadian Scholars' Press.

Holosko, M. J., & Holosko, A. (1996). What's unique about social work practice with the elderly? In M. J. Holosko & M. D. Feit (Eds.), *Social work practice with the elderly* (2nd ed., pp. 21–35). Toronto: Canadian Scholars' Press.

Katz, S. (1996). *Disciplining old age: The formation of gerontological knowledge.* Charlottesville: University Press of Virginia.

Katz, S. (2005). Busy bodies: Activity, aging and the management of everyday life. In S. Katz (Ed.), *Cultural aging: Life course, lifestyle, and senior worlds* (pp. 121–139). Toronto: University of Toronto Press.

Kivnick, H. Q., & Pruchno, R. (2011). Bridges and boundaries: Humanities and arts enhance gerontology [Editorial]. *The Gerontologist, 51*(2), 142–144.

Laslett, P. (1989). *A fresh map of life.* London: Weidenfield and Nicholson.

Lipscomb, V. B. (2006). An interview with Cynthia Rich. "We need a theoretical base": Cynthia Rich, women's studies and ageism. *National Women's Studies Association, 18*(1), 3–12.

Macey, D. (2001). *The Penguin dictionary of critical theory.* London: Penguin Books.

McDonald, A. (2010). *Social work with older people.* Cambridge, UK: Polity Press.

McHugh, K. (2003). Three faces of ageism: Society, image and place. *Ageing and Society, 23*, 165–185.

McPherson, B. D., & Wister, A. (2008). *Aging as a social process: Canadian perspectives.* Don Mills, ON: Oxford University Press.

Minichiello, V., Brown, J., & Kendig, H. (2000). Perceptions and consequences of ageism: Views of older people. *Ageing and Society, 20,* 253–278.

Moody, H. R. (1993). Overview: What is critical gerontology and why is it important. In T. R. Cole, W. A. Achenbaum, P. L. Jakobi, & R. Kastenbaum (Eds.), *Voices and visions of aging: Toward a critical gerontology* (pp. xv–xli). New York: Springer.

Nelson, T. D. (2004). *Ageism: Stereotyping and prejudice against older persons.* Cambridge, MA: MIT Press.

O'Connor, D. (2010). Personhood and dementia: Toward a relational framework for assessing decisional capacity. *Journal of Mental Health Training, Education and Practice, 5*(3), 22–30.

Phillipson, C. (2013). *Ageing.* Cambridge, UK: Polity Press.

Powell, J. L., & Wahidin, A. (2006). *Foucault and aging.* New York: Nova Science.

Tanner, D., & Harris, J. (2008). *Working with older people.* London: Routledge.

Thorpe, D. (2002). Aging, language, and culture. In D. Cheal (Ed.), *Aging and demographic change in Canadian context* (pp. 72–104). Toronto: University of Toronto Press.

Twigg, J., & Martin, W. (2015). The challenge of cultural gerontology. *The Gerontologist, 55*(3), 353–359.

van Dyk, S. (2016). The othering of old age: Insights from postcolonial studies. *Journal of Aging Studies, 39,* 109–120.

Walker, A. (Ed.). (2014). *The new science of ageing.* Bristol, UK: Policy Press.

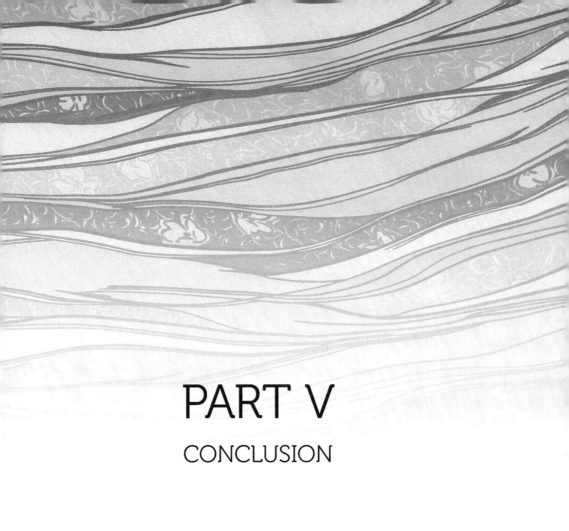

PART V
CONCLUSION

CHAPTER 17

Doing Critical Clinical Work from the Ground Up: Exploring the Dalhousie School of Social Work Community Clinic

Jeff Karabanow, Sarah Oulton, Meagen Bowers, and Cyndi Hall

INTRODUCTION

This chapter highlights the story of the Dalhousie School of Social Work Community Clinic in Halifax, Nova Scotia, paying close attention to its critical and anti-oppressive foundations and the practical teaching approaches we use with our students. Experiential education at the clinic is focused on supporting students to make critical connections between theory and practice while embracing interdisciplinary learning and collaboration.

Our clinical work is deeply entrenched in critical social work theories through feminist, participatory, accompaniment-oriented, and post-structural analyses. This style of intervention will be explored, unpacked, and exposed throughout the chapter—speaking specifically to a clinical practice orientation that is situated within a critical social justice framework. This emphasizes situating the individual's struggles within broader structural dynamics while being critically reflective and reflexive. Engaging with individuals belonging to some of the most vulnerable groups in our community (e.g., low-income households, marginally or precariously housed individuals, lone-parent families, newcomers, individuals with complex histories of trauma, substance use, and mental health), the clinic demonstrates the importance of social justice on a case-by-case basis through the politicization of individual and societal problems. We work with our clients to deconstruct dominant social discourses impacting their lives while understanding that their experiences and stories are unique, varied, and diverse from one another.

This chapter illuminates the clinic's day-to-day work with marginalized populations—through such activities as intakes, assessments, note-taking, record-keeping, referral, advocacy, resource acquisition, counselling, and community outreach—as well as how we make sense of issues related to our work, including use of self, role of the social work practitioner, notions of ethics and power, and the process of developing therapeutic relationships. A range of practice models (i.e., feminist, narrative, trauma specific, crisis intervention, and solution-focused) that support our grassroots and community development techniques and that shape our critical clinical practice orientation will be highlighted. The chapter provides practice insights from our directors, staff, and one of our former BSW students.

As you read this chapter, ask yourself the following questions:

1. What does this chapter tell you about critical clinical practice in the community?
2. What are some of the core characteristics of the clinic that relate to critical clinical practice?
3. How does the clinic make connections between theory and practice on a day-to-day basis?
4. Why are critical reflexive and reflective practices important in community social work settings?

CONTEXT AND HISTORY

Four years ago, in the early spring of 2014, a meeting took place between faculty member Jeff Karabanow and field coordinator Cyndi Hall to discuss a shared dream. We sought to develop a community-based service in Halifax that could provide meaningful support to marginalized populations, while providing a unique space for university health professions students to engage in experiential education rooted in critical and anti-oppressive based theory and practice. Equally important, the vision involved all of this being done through a social justice lens that explores dominant discourses, power differentials, and systemic oppression.

We reflected on the lack of services in the city that provide case management and supportive counselling in an unconditional, immediate fashion to those who are poor, marginalized, precariously housed, or un-housed. The individuals we provide support to are those most often experiencing deep and unresolved trauma and mental health issues. At the same time, we spoke about the frustration around the increasing difficulty in securing quality student placements due to growing competition, enrolment, and organizational fatigue. Sites that are explicit in their social justice work were (and continue to be) scarce. There were very few community-based agencies that operated through a social justice and/or critical lens and that engage in anti-oppressive practice approaches for social work students. Lastly, most interprofessional placement opportunities were within hospital settings and the clinic was seen as a possible way to bring different disciplines together in a community setting.

ANTI-OPPRESSIVE PRACTICE

Anti-oppressive practice refers to a focus on the structural origins of service user issues as well as an orientation toward radical social change. It embodies an egalitarian value system that focuses on reducing the negative effects of the structural inequalities impacting people's lives. It engages in the critical analysis of practice relations with a focus on empowerment of service users (Dominelli, 2002; Healy, 2005).

Four years later, the Dalhousie School of Social Work (SSW) Community Clinic is operating in central Halifax. We have worked with over 500 clients and more than 40 organizations; we have provided practice experiences to approximately 100 undergraduate and graduate students from social work, occupational therapy, psychology, nursing, nutrition, and pharmacy, as well as project-based and service learning opportunities for medicine and management programs at Dalhousie University.

OUR PHILOSOPHY: EXPLORING CRITICAL AND ANTI-OPPRESSIVE PRACTICE

Philosophically, the clinic utilizes postmodern critical social work as an umbrella theory, which incorporates anti-oppressive and post-structuralist feminist theories and practices. Critical social work theories allow us, as an organization, to emphasize the importance of language and discourse in the social construction of both service provider and service user realities (Fook, 2002; Healy, 2005). Such theories highlight how power can operate in various ways and create opportunities for our clients to resist and/or reconstruct dominant ideas about themselves related to oppression or victimization (Briskman, Pease, & Allan, 2009; Foucault, 1980; Fook, 2002). Feminist theory and practice is rooted in the belief that there are dominant social structures that work to privilege and empower certain groups while simultaneously oppressing others (Dominelli, 2002; Turner & Maschi, 2015). Anti-oppressive work involves a commitment to a more socially just society, as well as learning about the complexity of engaging in this work, both as individuals and organizations. As an agency informed by anti-oppressive practice, we strive to commit to using our power in our efforts toward social justice while being mindful of how privilege can make us complicit in the oppression of others (Baines, 2011).

CRITICAL SOCIAL WORK

For our purposes at the clinic, critical social work involves the recognition that structural issues continually impact both social workers and service users on a day-to-day basis, especially those associated with systemic oppression based on race, class, gender, ability, and sexual orientation. It involves a fundamental commitment to co-participatory relationships as well as the implementation of self-reflexive and self-reflective approaches to social work practice. It aims to reduce power differentials between service providers and service users while promoting the co-construction of knowledge in pursuit of social transformation (Healy, 2001).

POST-STRUCTURALIST FEMINIST APPROACHES

Post-structuralist feminist approaches to practice allow us to reconceptualize power in the relationship between service provider and service user while acknowledging that the personal is always political. Client stories and experiences can never be separate from the world in which they are socially constructed. Their experiences are contextualized through their own histories as well as social and political structures working to both oppress and privilege them (Brown, 2007).

From existing research around organizational dynamics of anti-oppressive practice (Barnoff, 2011; Karabanow, 2004; Ramsundarsingh & Shier, 2017; Strier & Binyamin, 2009), we know some key characteristics of anti-oppressive practice organizations, and know that our work at the clinic attempts to align with these principles and practices. Anti-oppressive practice orientations are significant foundations for critical clinical apparatuses. Anti-oppressive organizational structures embrace notions of "locality development"—providing immediate and meaningful services "on the ground" to those in need—in a compassionate and empowering fashion (Karabanow, 2004). We do not close files at the clinic and it is not uncommon for staff and students to reach out to previous clients to see how they are doing. Crisis events (such as a mental health breakdown, the loss of shelter, or the need for food) are triaged and we try to respond urgently to presenting needs. In addition, anti-oppressive practice organizations are committed to ongoing exploration of power and privilege, and ethical use of this privilege (Barnoff, 2011; Ramsundarsingh & Shier, 2017; Strier & Binyamin, 2009). This exploration of power and privilege at the clinic incorporates critical reflexivity and dialogue. These processes are embedded within the clinic through a culture of learning, with a focus on ongoing experiential education and training and an orientation toward innovation, risk-taking, and collaborative work.

Another organizational anti-oppressive practice characteristic that complements critical and feminist social work practice is the notion of expanding beyond individual work and toward social structures and action (Barnoff, 2011; Karabanow, 2004; Mullaly, 2010; Ramsundarsingh & Shier, 2017; Strier & Binyamin, 2009). This fits with an understanding of people's challenges as impacted by societal oppression, and with a commitment to working toward a more socially just society. The clinic works with numerous coalitions/alliances (such as anti-poverty roundtables, income assistance restructuring, and a basic income committee) that are situated within more mezzo/macro explorations of equality and social justice.

Organizations that are centred on critical approaches to practice (anti-oppressive, feminist, anti-discriminatory, etc.) are cognizant of how organizational policies and procedures impact employees. The rationale is that "if the workplace itself is oppressive to the workers, the workers will in turn be oppressive to those whom they are serving" (Ramsundarsingh & Shier, 2017, p. 2321). Some examples of organizational policies that emerge through critical approaches include a commitment toward inclusion and diversity, both in workforce and clientele (Barnoff, 2011), and working toward more egalitarian organizational structures (Strier & Binyamin, 2009). Our clinic strives to structure itself in a non-hierarchical model, fostering collaborative approaches among staff, students, and directors.

THE CLINIC: WHO WE ARE, WHAT WE DO

The clinic employs a critical clinical and case management platform to support our clients who are, for the most part, individuals living in poverty in various communities. Coordinated by MSW graduates from the SSW, the clinic not only complements and supplements existing resources in the Halifax Regional Municipality, but also serves as a field placement site for BSW and MSW students, supervised by our clinic coordinators, and students from other health disciplines, supervised by faculty from their discipline. The "critical" aspect emerges from the clinic's overarching social justice philosophy, which is embedded throughout the student experiences through knowledge sharing, collaboration, mutual learning opportunities, case conferencing, critical reflection, critical reflexivity, and debriefing on cases and article discussion groups.

CRITICAL REFLECTION

Critical reflection at the clinic involves a process of "unearthing deeper assumptions" (Fook & Askeland, 2007, p. 521). Critical reflection explores our own assumptions, values, beliefs, and attitudes about the world around us with the purpose of supporting and improving our social work practice. Practising critical reflection allows us to examine power through our personal and professional experiences through "social, cultural and structural contexts" (Fook & Askeland, 2007, p. 522).

CRITICAL REFLEXIVITY

Critical reflexivity, or critical reflexive social work practice, involves examination of power relations in professional practice as well as the critical questioning of how our knowledge about clients is produced (D'Cruz, Gillingham, & Melendez, 2007). This process of looking inward and outward to explore how we create knowledge through understanding our own beliefs, values, and assumptions is important in allowing us to ethically engage in social work practice (Fook, 2007).

BUILDING AN INTERPROFESSIONAL PLATFORM

As noted earlier, our intention was to develop the clinic's foundation from a critical and anti-oppressive practice community-oriented social work lens and then to bring in other health professionals to support service delivery and student training. Pharmacy was the first profession to integrate into the clinic and has helped lay the groundwork for a model of collaborative interdisciplinary partnership. This collaboration has been supported by existing research, which has shown that rehospitalizations for mental health are reduced when social work and pharmacy work together (Gil, Mikaitis, Shier, Johnson, & Sims, 2013). Building on this model of interprofessional collaboration, in the last two years we have incorporated occupational therapy, psychology, nursing, and nutrition students. We have worked to bring together other professions as our need evolves and are developing meaningful relationships with these professional schools around field experiences and client services.

Through interprofessional rounds, article discussions, and consistent explorations/discussions (critical reflections), we are beginning to see the ways in which we can learn from one another, celebrate the unique contributions of diverse professions, and reflect on how working together can build deeper understandings of social justice work in the community. Existing research notes the benefits of collaboration and integration of multiple professional approaches in the process of working toward a truly interprofessional approach to practice (Wang & Bhakta, 2013). Through interprofessional learning, students can gain greater respect for the contributions of other professions (Dacey, Murphy, Anderson, & McCloskey, 2010).

At times we work together with a client, while at other times one profession takes the lead to support the particular issues presented. Unique to our clinic is that every client is connected with a social work staff member or student—at least initially. It is a very organic, flexible, and adaptive process. We continue to learn as we go. It is our belief that critical (social work) theory is a way forward in engaging in interprofessional practice dynamics and experiential education. The integration of a critical lens with interprofessional practice and education could provide a greater affiliation with social work ethics and social justice. Postmodern critical theory allows for the integration of multiple ways of knowing and understanding the social world (Briskman, Pease, & Allan, 2009). It also contends that professional practice must be grounded in equitable relationships and social justice (Healy, 2005). To engage in this kind of collaborative work there must be some congruence in ideological perspectives regarding how service provision is delivered. Using a critical lens and engaging in critical reflective/reflexive practices could create more space for collaborative knowledge construction and adaptability between professions that historically have been very different in their educational training practices and professional ideals and values (Karban & Smith, 2010).

WORK AT THE CLINIC: CRITICAL CASE MANAGEMENT AND CLINICAL PRACTICE

Critical case management is a continuous and collaborative process where clients, and their community supports, identify needs and goals. Case management within the clinic works to connect marginalized individuals to the social and health care systems from which they are often excluded. Employing a critical clinical case management model, the clinic incorporates system navigation, supportive counselling, crisis intervention, resource support, community outreach, accompaniment, advocacy, and group work, as well as needs assessments. Further, working in partnership with other organizations, the clinic fills in gaps in services while working toward the reduction of the high caseloads and waitlists of existing agencies as discussed earlier in the chapter.

CRITICAL CASE MANAGEMENT

Critical case management involves centring client experiences while affording collaborative provision of services and navigation of resources to meet client needs. It highlights the importance of both process and outcome to advocacy work in order to not only support clients through the acquisition of resources and services, but also to promote client empowerment throughout the advocacy process (Fook, 2002). Critical case management at the clinic also involves clinical therapeutic work, as the majority of clients identify experiencing mental or emotional health concerns and complex trauma histories. Working with these service users requires the development of therapeutic alliances and supportive client-worker relationships. Engaging with our clients requires an in-depth knowledge of trauma-specific approaches and crisis intervention.

Our version of clinical case management involves working to decrease worker-client power differentials through transparency and shared knowledge, promoting client choice and agency in clinic services, providing safety both in the physical space and the working relationship, validating client experiences of strength and resistance while challenging dominant oppressive narratives of self, and exploring structural origins of individual oppression.

Rooted in the "accompaniment" approach to practice, our program serves as a resource centre for marginalized individuals who may not fit into traditional support settings or those who are not yet connected to the existing network of social service agencies in Halifax. Accompaniment is "rooted in an interdependent understanding of psychological and community well-being, not in an individualistic paradigm of psychological suffering" (Watkins, 2015, p. 327). It involves taking a stance to "walk with" or "journey with" those we work with, resisting Western notions of individualism and power-over. This approach helps us reach out and connect to individuals who have experienced barriers accessing services, centring their experience and knowledge, reducing alienation, and fostering connection and hope. This approach espouses the core dynamics of critical clinical orientations.

Much of the current day-to-day work involves supporting clients with applications and appeals concerning Income Assistance and Special Needs, Canada Pension, Disability supports (letters of support, accessing documentation from doctors/nurse practitioners/services, mediation, advocacy, attending annual reviews, and requesting special needs funding for transportation, special diet, medication coverage, and medical expenses), and housing supports (remaining housed, support with landlords and dispute mediation, finding affordable housing, filling out housing applications, viewing apartments, moving support/costs, referring to housing agencies, attending housing meetings, residential tenancies applications and hearings). It also involves crisis intervention and supportive counselling. Many clients have been referred to the clinic from formal mental health services due to not meeting requirements to access care (e.g., acuteness, accessed services in the past, diagnosis). The clinic is able either to bridge a gap while clients are waiting for other formal services or to support those who have been denied access. Engaging in counselling at the clinic involves trauma-specific, narrative, feminist, and solution-focused approaches. Clients are given space and support for their stories and experiences to be explored and unpacked while workers constantly listen for unique outcomes (i.e., the contradictions that arise once a person begins to separate themselves from their dominant or unhelpful stories or the times the issue is not present or not as present in their lives) that highlight strength and resistance (White, 1991). Additionally, clients are offered skill-building options to manage overwhelming emotions (e.g., grounding exercises, deep breathing, visualizations, mindfulness, progressive muscle relaxation).

TRAUMA-SPECIFIC APPROACHES

Trauma-specific and trauma-informed approaches to practice involve a focus on building therapeutic relationships that emphasize safety, collaboration, and power-sharing while focusing on strengths and empowerment (British Columbia Centre of Excellence for Women's Health, 2009; Varghese, Quiros, & Berger, 2018). There is a focus on coping skills and emotional wellness where clients are directly involved in their own service provision and planning.

Students completing practicums at the clinic are able to clearly analyze different system structures and policies and how they affect clients' lives. The broad core goals of field education for students are met through the day-to-day activities in the clinic. In addition, each student develops and works to meet their personal learning objectives, which tend to include:

- observation/shadowing of the intake process and individual needs assessments
- increasing their knowledge of community resources and programs
- participation in case planning and coordination of services among community partners
- advocacy
- crisis intervention
- interviewing skills
- counselling skills
- participation in group supervision
- building critical analysis skills on the impact of formal and informal system operations
- interprofessional collaboration
- self-care

TRANSLATING THEORY INTO PRACTICE

The following section explores how the clinic translates critical and anti-oppressive theory into practice not only in the work we engage in with service users, but also in the experiential education opportunities we provide for our social work students as well as those from other health professions.

Low Barrier Approaches

A practical example of how the clinic offers an alternative critical approach to care involves our commitment to low barrier services. Clients are often referred from other health, government, or community agencies because of rigid policies and mandates that limit the work they can engage in with service users. Service users coming to the clinic regularly report oppressive experiences that make it difficult for them to access services at the institutions designed to help them. Clients are commonly referred to the clinic because they are not "acute" enough to be seen or the organization has a brief model of practice (i.e., the number of sessions is ending).

Seemingly simple tasks such as filling out paperwork to obtain services or compensation are sometimes impossible for our clients for various reasons, such as literacy, mental health, and/or (dis)Ability. The clinic receives several referrals from a number of agencies and organizations for clients to gain support in filling out paperwork for various services such as Workers' Compensation claims, Canada Pension Plan, and/or Income Assistance. There is an existing gap in health and community services where workers are unable to spend time with clients engaging in this kind of work. Being able to spend more time with clients who are identifying a need and engaging in services that they have little or no access to at other organizations provides power, choice, and agency.

Exploring Ethics

Utilizing a "walking with" approach within case management at the clinic can often involve an ethical component that staff and students are tasked with navigating. Recently, a student working at the clinic was responsible for engaging in advocacy to support the acquisition of the disability tax credit benefit. The ethical challenge that arose for the student was navigating Service Canada, which outlined a strict and rigid definition of what living with a (dis)Ability means in order to receive the tax benefit. The student wrote an appeal letter opposing the decision to deny the tax benefit. The letter demonstrated how the client was adhering to the definition of (dis)Ability. The student felt the letter emphasized individual struggles, deficits, and suffering that fit within the institutional definition of (dis)Ability.

In general, work with clients at the clinic focuses on listening to and validating experiences of (dis)Ability, trauma, or suffering while highlighting resiliencies and strengths. The student in this case felt uncomfortable with the language and underlying discourse highlighted in this letter, given the potential for an ethical trespass (see Weinberg, 2005) or harm to the client having to read their experience outlined in such a way. To work through this ethical dilemma, the student engaged in a critical reflection process with the clinic coordinators. Validating this student's feelings of discomfort, social workers are often placed in the difficult role of being both agents of change as well as agents of oppression. Social work practice requires upholding the dignity and worth of persons, but pursuing social justice often requires social workers to manoeuvre within oppressive social systems and structures to access services and resources for clients. Part of moving through this process was exercising transparency with the client in both going over the letter, explaining why it was written with deficit-based language, and seeking approval before sending. This highlights the importance of advocacy work in critical case management through both process (critical reflective and reflexive practice, transparency, and providing the client with the relevant information and final choice over the next steps) and outcome (sending the letter and supporting the client to access government compensation).

Record-Keeping

Social work is a unique profession in the sense that the core values of the profession impact every aspect of social work practice, especially in regard to case note-writing. Clinic staff and students recognize the importance of being critically reflective and reflexive toward any record-keeping or documentation procedures, given the power they can hold over clients. Being aware of language practices that oppress and reinforce dominant discourses for clients is a central part of teaching and learning at the clinic. Intakes, needs assessments, and case notes need to be grounded in critical, feminist, and anti-oppressive principles.

Psychiatric discourse has long been largely accepted as the dominant norm in working in health professions (Strong, 2012; Strong, Gaete, Sametband, French, & Eeson, 2012). Although this terminology is commonly used in mental health services and can sometimes be useful for both assessment and service acquisition, we attempt as much as possible to be conscious of the language used and its contextual place in a medicalized society through recognizing and understanding its foundation in dominant social constructs. Drawing on Fook's (2002) ideas about critical assessment, we resist using categories and labels as totalizing ways of defining the service users we work with. We approach assessment as a means of co-constructing service user narratives, being aware that there is often no one cause of client issues but a number of competing and contradictory factors (Fook, 2002). We keep in mind that, as service providers, we play an active and reflexive role in the narrative created, which could be helpful or harmful to the clients we work with (Fook, 2002).

As such, the information gained in the intake and assessment embodies the client's own language. We are transparent about the information we are recording and are checking in with clients about including certain information such as psychiatric diagnoses. We are also politicizing client experiences in having discussions about diagnosis, powerlessness, and oppression. Many of our clients find this validating and supportive in creating alternative stories about themselves, especially those who have been given multiple diagnoses or feel they have been misdiagnosed.

For the purposes of our work, it is often only helpful to have such labels if we are advocating for other services, resources, or supports that require them. Oftentimes we will record the distressing symptoms and emotions clients are experiencing as opposed to a diagnostic label (e.g., trauma history, panic attacks, sleep disturbances, night terrors, hypervigilance). Our case notes are written using language and discourse that are rooted in empowerment and feminist principles. We write them as if our clients or other health professionals will be reading them, as well as if they could be subpoenaed by the criminal justice system. We are continually aware of how our records could be either helpful or harmful to client situations. We use non-judgmental language, avoid detailed descriptions of trauma histories, and only include information that is relevant to the goals established by the client or that is important for our clinic team to know moving forward.

Crisis Intervention

Crisis intervention at the clinic uses empowerment principles and solution-focused approaches. Drawing on Dass-Brailsford (2007), crisis intervention involves three main steps: (1) pre-intervention (having as much information about the crisis as possible), (2) assessment (exploring safety and providing efficient and comprehensive evaluations that focus on how clients have handled crisis in the past—what worked and what did not), and (3) disposition (allowing clients to lead discussion around their experience of crisis while promoting their active participation in problem-solving or solution-finding). Individuals experiencing crisis situations (e.g., food insecurity, housing, suicidality, violence) require brief and short-term interventions that are going to support their immediate basic human needs (i.e., food, shelter, and safety). The focus is working to provide immediate needs while also implementing ongoing support plans to avoid crisis in the future. Building compassionate and authentic rapport and exploring together next steps are key ingredients to the therapeutic relationship. Staff and students at the clinic regularly discuss during debriefing sessions that clients report "feeling heard for the first time" and "feeling safer being able to share." The clients we work with often report being cut off, belittled, dismissed, and pathologized by formal systems (e.g., health care, mental health, community services). We have found that providing clients with space and time to tell their stories consistently has them leaving the interaction feeling better than when they came in (even if only for a short time). Moreover, knowing that they are free to call and/or come back to speak to a worker whenever they desire helps to alleviate some stress/anxiety. The deep client-centred and safe space (trauma-informed environment) foundations/architecture at the clinic help to provide physical and emotional sanctuary to our clients.

CRITICAL CLINICAL INTERVENTION: POLITICIZING OUR PRACTICE

Samantha, a 56-year-old woman, was referred to the clinic by Mental Health Services in our community after going to the emergency department feeling suicidal during one particularly difficult night. After completing an intake appointment at Mental Health Services, it was determined that she did not qualify and was not at immediate risk; she was provided with community resources and referrals, the clinic being one of them. During her intake appointment with the clinic, she identified that she was seeking counselling because she was having "episodes" and was feeling unsure how to move forward in her current situation. During her "episodes," she described feeling like "she could not breathe" and "feeling an overwhelming sense of dread." Samantha reported an inability to sleep, nightmares, and feeling anxious most of the time. She described her current situation as existing in an "unhappy relationship" where she was experiencing emotional and verbal abuse on a regular basis. She seemed ambivalent about whether or not to remain in her current situation. Samantha is retired and has a fixed income, which would make it somewhat more challenging to live on her own. (It is not uncommon for women in unsafe or detrimental situations to be hesitant to leave due to financial constraints.) Samantha stated that although the night she went to the emergency department she was feeling suicidal, that was the first time she had experienced those feelings and she has not felt that way since. She also reported strong family bonds with siblings and her daughter, as well as friendships outside of the relationship (protective factors).

Using critical feminist, empowerment, and narrative approaches, in the beginning it was important to unpack Samantha's dominant stories about herself to better understand the distressing symptoms she was experiencing (panic, anxiety, and sleep disturbances). The work together was collaborative and involved a process of sharing knowledge (Brown, 2007). In promoting agency and power in the therapeutic relationship, Samantha determined what was most important to discuss and what she was hoping to get out of each meeting (Turner & Maschi, 2015). In telling her story, Samantha recounted feeling most anxious and overwhelmed after negative interactions with her current partner (he would yell, call her names, belittle her, and/or ignore her). She stated that it reminded her of her parents' relationship and hearing them argue when she was a child. As Samantha told her story, she described a few experiences of trauma through sexual and/or physical violence that occurred in her young adulthood. Part of exploring these pieces was asking about how her experiences have made her feel about herself; how she thought her past experiences have influenced her current relationship as well as her expectations of other people; what has been helpful in the past; what has helped her manage her feelings and emotions; how has she been able to manage so well throughout her life despite these experiences; and were there times when things did not seem as bad, and what was happening during those times. Through this exploration, Samantha was able to identify that her current relationship was triggering feelings from other experiences of abuse and violence. She found that "things do not seem so bad" when her partner is away for work. Through this exploration, Samantha made a decision to end the relationship and move in with her sister.

Throughout the therapeutic process, Samantha expressed feelings of guilt, shame, and self-blame around her experiences. She stated that she did not understand why she was feeling the way she was feeling or why she felt it was getting worse. A large part of our discussion in the beginning sessions was around normalizing and contextualizing her feelings given her history and life experiences. Instead of individualizing and pathologizing her "symptoms," we discussed how she was experiencing normal reactions to trauma and that the distressing thoughts, emotions, and feelings she was experiencing made sense (Brown, 2017; Worell & Remer, 1992).

Working with women experiencing shame and self-blame, Brown (2013) suggests that "unless women's stories are unpacked, the self-blame and helplessness within dominant or privileged narratives are simply reconstituted" (p. 24). If we accept the idea that therapeutic interactions are inherently a political process, then they are not exempt from the "politics of gender, class, race and culture" (White, 1994, p. 1). Part of our counselling work at the clinic involves having a socio-political analysis, which provides an avenue to begin having conversations about mitigating dominant stories and privileging alternative ones.

Although a significant piece of the work with Samantha involved highlighting unique outcomes where she demonstrated strength, resilience, and resistance, it also involved challenging unhelpful stories about herself. Dominant discourses about women, gender norms, and rape culture often result in "negative identity conclusions" for women (Brown, 2007, p. 4; 2017). Samantha would often engage in self-blame by making statements such as "Well, I should not have said that to him," "I should not have been there," or "I shouldn't have gotten into the car with him." Covert and overt messaging about women's roles, behaviours, and bodies begins as soon as we start to gain knowledge and understand the world around us. Socially constructed cultural norms related to victim blaming were ingrained in how Samantha viewed herself. Engaging Samantha in discussions about rape culture and societal attitudes toward women and reframing the discussion away from "her choices" and "her behaviour" and toward patriarchal attitudes and behaviours of men that lead to the violence she experienced supported a re-engagement with her own history (White, 2000). During the sessions with Samantha, she would often say, "Well, I never thought of it that way." Samantha was not changing or revisioning her history, rather she was able to "re-engage with [her] personal history on new terms" (White, 2000, p. 36). In this case, challenging patriarchal assumptions focused on women's roles in society and reinforcing alternative stories about women's experiences allowed for stories of manipulation and victimization to become ones of empowerment and resistance.

CONCLUSION

We have much to celebrate at the clinic: its community development roots, its social justice framework, its critical and anti-oppressive emblems, and its accompaniment philosophy. While indeed a work in progress, the clinic signals a social work initiative that can embrace an interprofessional lens, be a bridge between the worlds of community and university, focus on meeting the needs of our marginalized communities, and provide thoughtful and meaningful practice education experiences for emerging health professionals. We are continually working to balance our clinical and case management service delivery platforms with true community development and advocacy orientations of critical and anti-oppressive social work practice. We work hard to maintain our critical lens and engage with our communities to advocate for a more just and equitable society. We are diligent in our efforts to maintain our unique philosophy and offer transformative opportunities for our staff, students, and clients.

REFERENCES

Baines, D. (Ed.). (2011). *Doing anti-oppressive practice: Social justice social work.* Halifax: Fernwood.

Barnoff, L. (2011). Business as usual: Doing anti-oppressive organizational change. In L. Barnoff (Ed.), *Doing anti-oppressive practice: Social justice social work* (2nd ed., pp. 25–47). Halifax: Fernwood.

Briskman, L., Pease, B., & Allan, J. (2009). Introducing critical theories for social work in a neo-liberal context. In J. Allan, L. Briskman, & B. Pease (Eds.), *Critical social work: Theories and practices for a socially just world* (2nd ed., pp. 3–14). Crows Nest, Australia: Allen and Unwin.

British Columbia Centre of Excellence for Women's Health. (2009). *Gendering the national framework: Trauma-informed approaches in addictions treatment.* Vancouver: Author.

Brown, C. (2007). Situating knowledge and power in the therapeutic alliance. In C. Brown & T. Augusta-Scott (Eds.), *Narrative therapy: Making meaning, making lives* (pp. 3–22). Thousand Oaks, CA: Sage.

Brown, C. (2013). Women's narratives of trauma: (Re)storying uncertainty, minimization and self-blame. *Narrative Works: Issues, Investigations and Interventions, 3*(1), 1–30.

Brown, C. (2017). Creating counterstories: Critical clinical practice and feminist narrative therapy. In D. Baines (Ed.), *Doing anti-oppressive practice: Building transformative, politicized social work* (3rd ed., pp. 212–232). Halifax: Fernwood.

Dacey, M., Murphy, J. I., Anderson, D. C., & McCloskey, W. W. (2010). An interprofessional service-learning course: Uniting students across educational levels and promoting patient-centred care. *Journal of Nursing Education, 49*(12), 696–699.

Dass-Brailsford, P. (2007). A practical approach to trauma: Empowering interventions. Thousand Oaks, CA: Sage.

D'Cruz, H., Gillingham, P., & Melendez, S. (2007). Reflexivity: A concept and its meanings for practitioners with children and families. *Critical Social Work, 8*(1), 1–18.

Dominelli, L. (2002). *Anti-oppressive social work theory and practice.* New York: Palgrave Macmillan.

Fook, J. (2002). *Social work: Critical theory and practice.* London: Sage.

Fook, J. (2007). Reflective practice and critical reflection. In J. Lishman (Ed.), *Handbook for practice learning in social work and social care: Knowledge and theory* (2nd ed., pp. 363–375). London: Jessica Kingsley.

Fook, J., & Askeland, G. (2007). Challenges of critical reflection: "Nothing ventured, nothing gained." *Social Work Education, 26*(5), 520–533.

Foucault, M. (1980). *Power/knowledge: Selected interviews and other writings, 1972–1977.* New York: Pantheon.

Gil, M., Mikaitis, D. K., Shier, G., Johnson, T. J., & Sims, S. (2013). Impact of a combined pharmacist and social worker program to reduce hospital readmissions. *Journal of Managed Care Pharmacy, 19*(7), 558–563.

Healy, K. (2001). Reinventing critical social work: Challenges from practice, context, and postmodernism. *Critical Social Work, 2*(1), 1–13.

Healy, K. (2005). *Social work theories in context.* New York: Palgrave Macmillan.

Karabanow, J. (2004). Making organizations work: Exploring characteristics of anti-oppressive organizational structures in street youth shelters. *Journal of Social Work, 4*(1), 47–60.

Karban, K., & Smith, S. (2010). Developing critical reflection within an interprofessional learning programme. In H. Bradbury, N. Frost, S. Kilminster, & M. Zukas (Eds.), *Beyond reflective practice: New approaches to professional lifelong learning* (pp. 170–181). New York: Routledge.

Mullaly, R. (2010). Anti-oppressive social work at the structural level and selected principles of anti-oppressive social work. In R. Mullaly (Ed.), *Challenging oppression and confronting privilege: A critical social work approach* (2nd ed.). Don Mills, ON: Oxford University Press.

Ramsundarsingh, S., & Shier, M. L. (2017). Anti-oppressive organisational dynamics in the social services: A literature review. *British Journal of Social Work, 47*(8), 2308–2327.

Strier, R., & Binyamin, S. (2009). Developing anti-oppressive services for the poor: A theoretical and organisational rationale. *British Journal of Social Work, 40*(6), 1908–1926.

Strong, T. (2012, May). *Talking about the DSM.* Paper presented at Therapeutic Conversations X Conference, Vancouver, British Columbia.

Strong, T., Gaete, J., Sametband, I. N., French, J., & Eeson, J. (2012). Counsellors respond to the DSM-IV-TR. *Canadian Journal of Counselling and Psychotherapy, 26*(2), 85–106.

Turner, S., & Maschi, T. (2015). Feminist and empowerment theory and social work practice. *Journal of Social Work Practice, 29*(1), 151–162.

Varghese, R., Quiros, L., & Berger, R. (2018). Reflective practices for engaging in trauma-informed culturally competent supervision. *Smith College Studies in Social Work, 88*(2), 135–151.

Wang, T., & Bhakta, H. (2013). A new model for interprofessional collaboration at a student-run free clinic. *Journal of Interprofessional Care, 27*(4), 339–340.

Watkins, M. (2015). Psychosocial accompaniment. *Journal of Social and Political Psychology, 3*(1), 324–341.

Weinberg, M. (2005). A case for an expanded framework of ethics in practice. *Ethics and Behavior, 15,* 327–338.

White, M. (1991). Deconstruction and therapy. *Dulwich Centre Newsletter, 3,* 21–40.

White, M. (1994). The politics of therapy: Putting to rest the illusion of neutrality. Adelaide, Australia: Dulwich Centre.

White, M. (2000). Re-engaging with history: The absent but implicit. In *Reflections on narrative practice: Essays and interviews* (pp. 35–58). Adelaide, Australia: Dulwich Centre.

Worell, J., & Remer, P. (1992). A feminist view of counselling and therapy. In *Feminist perspectives in therapy: An empowerment model* (pp. 82–111). New York: Wiley.

CONCLUSION

Practices of Resistance through Counterstorying for Social Justice

Catrina Brown and Judy E. MacDonald

From chapter to chapter within this book, the contributors have identified critical clinical skills that centre on unpacking and deconstructing dominant discourses and the emergence of counterstories that support a social justice approach to practising social work. Dominant discourses that support neoliberal client blaming and pathologization are unsettled in this book. Counternarratives and ways of practising are presented here through many examples: the individualized understanding of women's anxiety described by Gail Baikie; the medicalization and labelling of women's experiences of depression and trauma written about by Catrina Brown, living with chronic pain discussed by Judy MacDonald; the judgment of a mother as a result of her perceived alcohol use, which led to her children being placed in foster care, analyzed by Marjorie Johnstone; and the criminalization of a person for failing to take his HIV medications and thus being deemed a public health risk, as outlined by Eli Manning and MT O'Shaughnessy.

Throughout the book, the authors illustrate how dominant discourses limit speech, render people silent, and often make voicing experiences both difficult and dangerous. To challenge the silencing of lived experience, the authors push back against the mechanisms of power reflected in dominant narratives. Agency and voice become a central element of practice, where the client is supported and encouraged to share their lived experiences. These experiences are unpacked and problem-saturated stories are counterviewed, leading to the creation of preferred alternative stories.

Many of the contributors to this book emphasize the importance of the therapeutic alliance or social work relationship. For example, Marion Brown offers a critical clinical approach to working with youth on issues of sexualized violence. Jeff Karabanow, Sarah Oulton, Meagen Bowers, and Cyndi Hall demonstrate the critical clinical approach taken to work with women in mid-life who find themselves in abusive relationships at the Dalhousie Social Work Community Clinic. Similarly, Joan Harbison and Donna Pettipas's writing on older people dealing with grief and loss after the sudden death of their life partner illustrates how critically important it is to establish a strong therapeutic relationship so that space is provided for the client's stories to be shared, unpacked, and often counterstoried. Indeed, Catrina Brown argues that the therapeutic relationship with women who have experienced complex trauma, such as those women often diagnosed as "borderline," is central to the work as it is a focal point in the re-storying of the possibility of developing relationships that are not harmful and in establishing connection that reduces a sense of aloneness and, often, worth-lessness. Cassandra Hanrahan and Darlene Chalmers offer an understanding of the important role and place of companion animals in people's lives, rec-ognizing the invaluable connection of unconditional love experienced between people and companion animals. This is especially true for those who have ex-perienced marginalization, oppression, and/or relational injury or trauma. The sense of connection between people and companion animals is deeply valuable to people's sense of well-being and mental health. Hanrahan and Chalmers pro-pose a "one-health" perspective that looks at the parallel processes between the social determinants of health of companion animals and humans. They assert that critical clinical social workers need to be aware of the significance of com-panion animals in supporting the health and mental health of clients and have a knowledge base of the services available to support this union, for example, what services are animal-friendly.

Within each chapter, an emphasis is placed on listening respectfully, indeed double listening. By listening beyond the words, we can challenge the influ-ence of normative and often oppressive dominant discourses on people's lives and allow for the development of an alternative or preferred story. For instance, through MacDonald's illustration of Rachel's experience of dealing with dif-ficult pain days, the support she requires from her partner is not pathologized through the medical model's categorization of the "sick-role," which maintains patients' benefit from the pain (through attention or relief of responsibilities). Rather, the counterstory presented demonstrates the supports Rachel and her partner offer each other in a reciprocal relationship. Through case illustrations in this book, we can understand that it is important to move past pathologizing coping strategies to see how they are often creative ways of coping that make sense. Catrina Brown's demonstration of working with Violet and Nancy Ross and Jean Morrison's description of working with Sally reflect a contextualized, non-medicalized, and depathologized harm-reduction perspective that offers a pragmatic, non-judgmental, and non-abstinence-based approach to substance use. Through a socially contextualized harm reduction approach, we can challenge the discourse of personal failure and dominant addiction discourses that are tied to the disease model and its emphasis on abstinence. Feminist approaches to harm reduction are, in contrast, compassionate about people's continued use of substances to cope, and therapeutic conversations centre on the meaning and context of the substance use (Brown, 2017; Brown & Stewart, 2005, 2007).

The role of spirituality among African Canadian women as central to coping with the effects of racism and sexism is powerfully described by Wanda Thomas Bernard, Josephine Etowa, and Barbara Clow. Narrative interviews with African Nova Scotian women demonstrated that "their spirituality and faith created a safe space for hope, comfort, and overall well-being." The authors urged that critical clinical practitioners need to understand the role and place of spirituality, including the action of prayer, in African Canadian women's lives. Spirituality and prayer help African Nova Scotian women cope with the "thousand little cuts" produced by racism (Hunn, Harley, Elliott, & Canfield, 2015). Baikie calls for critical clinical social workers to resist the annihilation of Indigenous ways of knowing and doing through colonialization and to move toward an understanding and respect of Indigenous practices. Ifeyinwa Mbakogu and Sara Torres, Monique Nutter, Donna-Mae Ford, Yvonne Chiu, and Kathi Campbell argue that racism is embedded in child welfare practices and needs to be unsettled, opening up space for relational practices that displace colonial judgments on parenthood. For example, social workers need to understand the communal role of extended family and community members in the raising of Indigenous children, and not be individualistic in looking at the mother as solely responsible for care.

Critical clinical social work practice reflects, integrates, and applies critical theories that are anti-oppressive and support social justice, including feminist and intersectional, postcolonialist, anti-racist, critical (dis)Ability, queer/gender non-conforming and non-binary, political economy, and postmodern. The historical and theoretical anchors of anti-oppressive social work theory and practice extend across practices, which include social movements, community organizing, welfare rights, organizational change, unionization, and decolonization (Baines, 2017). Critical clinical practice is committed to social activism and change through resisting and challenging colonial and neoliberal practices and their oppressive impact. The discursive mechanisms of power are often evident in people's stories of struggles, efforts at coping, and negative identity conclusions (McKenzie-Mohr & Lafrance, 2014). Challenging these discursive mechanisms of power helps to shift meaning that blames and pathologizes individuals and acknowledges the social shaping of these struggles (Brown, 2019). With this approach to understanding people's struggles, including homelessness, living with pain, living with HIV, substance use and eating disorders, dealing with sexualized violence and trauma, having one's children removed by child welfare, and grief and loneliness, we can help to create counterstories toward social justice that challenge oppression and its effects on people's lives.

This book emphasizes the meaning and context of the pain, problems, and struggles people experience, rather than personal failure, inadequacy, or deficit. In contrast, within neoliberalism, people are held responsible for their problems and for their "recovery" from them (Brown, 2019; Morrow & Weisel, 2012). These individualized, decontextualized, and pathologizing approaches fail to address the social and political contexts in which people live; the responsibilization of people to solve their own problems is reflected in the increasingly reduced provision of adequate social welfare services and supports (Baines, Bennett, Goodwin, & Rawsthorne, 2019; Baines & Waugh, 2019; Brown, 2016; Pease, Goldingay, Hosken, & Nipperess, 2016; Pease & Nipperess, 2016). Today, neoliberalism demands significant individual focus on self-management and regulation (Brown, 2014). Neoliberalism's emphasis on individual responsibility co-opts notions of resilience, coping, strengths, and choice, making it appear as though individuals have power when they do cope and deal with their problems on their own. People then blame themselves when they can't cope or are struggling. Within this culture, the stories people tell about themselves and their lives often reflect individual responsibilization. Critical clinical practice does not leave these neoliberal assumptions intact. Instead, it disrupts oppressive discursive assumptions and practices through developing counterstories. This process disrupts and resists existing social relations of power.

REFERENCES

Baines, D. (Ed.). (2017). *Doing anti-oppressive practice: Building transformative, politicized social work* (3rd ed.). Halifax: Fernwood.

Baines, D., Bennett, B., Goodwin, S., & Rawsthorne, M. (2019). (Eds.). *Working across difference: Social work, social policy and social justice.* London: Macmillan International.

Baines, D., & Waugh, F. (2019). Afterword: Resistance, white fragility and late neoliberalism. In D. Baines, B. Bennett, S. Goodwin, & M. Rawsthorne (Eds.), *Working across difference: Social work, social policy and social justice* (pp. 247–260). London: Macmillan International.

Brown, C. (2014). Untangling emotional threads and self-management discourse in women's body talk. In S. McKenzie-Mohr & M. Lafrance (Eds.), *Women voicing resistance: Discursive and narrative explorations* (pp. 174–190). New York: Routledge.

Brown, C. (2016). The constraints of neo-liberal new managerialism in social work education. *Canadian Review of Social Work, 33*(1), 115–123.

Brown, C. (2017). Creating counterstories: Critical clinical practice and feminist narrative therapy. In D. Baines (Ed.), *Doing anti-oppressive practice: Building transformative, politicized social work* (pp. 212–232). Halifax: Fernwood.

Brown, C. (2019). Speaking of women's depression and the politics of emotion. *Affilia: Journal of Women and Social Work, 34*(2), 151–169.

Brown, C., & Stewart, S. (2005). Experiences of harm reduction among women with alcohol use problems. *Canadian Journal of Community Mental Health, 24*(1), 95–113.

Brown, C., & Stewart, S. (2007). Making harm reduction work for women: Restorying dominant addiction discourse. In N. Poole & L. Greaves (Eds.), *Highs and Lows: Canadian Perspectives on Women and Substance Use* (pp. 431–440). Centre for Addiction and Mental Health and the British Columbia Centre for Excellence in Women's Health.

Hunn, V., Harley, D., Elliott, W., & Canfield, J. (2015). Microaggression and the mitigation of psychological harm: Four social workers' exposition for care of clients, students, and faculty who suffer "a thousand little cuts." *Journal of Pan African Studies, 7*(9), 41–54.

McKenzie-Mohr, S., & Lafrance, M. N. (Eds.). (2014). *Women voicing resistance: Discursive and narrative explorations.* New York: Routledge.

Morrow, M., & Weisel, J. (2012). Towards a social justice framework for mental health recovery. *Studies in Social Justice, 6*(1), 27–43.

Pease, B., Goldingay, S., Hosken, N., & Nipperess, S. (Eds.). (2016). *Doing critical social work: Transformative practices for social justice.* Sydney, Australia: Allen and Unwin.

Pease, B., & Nipperess, S. (2016). Doing critical social work in the neoliberal context: Working on the contradictions. In B. Pease, S. Goldingay, N. Hosken, & S. Nipperess (Eds.), *Doing critical social work: Transformative practices for social justice* (pp. 3–24). Sydney, Australia: Allen and Unwin.

CONTRIBUTOR BIOGRAPHIES

EDITORS

Catrina Brown, PhD, is associate professor and graduate coordinator at the School of Social Work and is cross-appointed to gender and women's studies and nursing at Dalhousie University. She is active in the Dalhousie Faculty Association, serving as president in 2014–2015, where she initiated the equity committee. Her work focuses on women's health and mental health issues, including trauma, post-trauma, relational injury, substance use problems, depression, and eating "disorders" within a feminist postmodern/narrative lens. Her work centres on integrating critical theory into direct practice, which is illustrated in her two earlier co-edited books, *Consuming Passions: Feminist Approaches to Weight Preoccupation and Eating Disorders* (with Karin Jasper, Second Story Press) and *Narrative Therapy: Making Meaning, Making Lives* (with Tod Augusta-Scott, Sage). She has been a private practice psychotherapist since 1987 and adopts a feminist, narrative, discursive, and collaborative approach. She has contributed to several edited collections on social justice–based clinical practice and serves on the editorial boards of a number of journals: *Narrative Work: Issues, Investigations, and Interventions*; *Journal of Systemic Therapies*; and *Gender and Women's Studies*.

Judy E. MacDonald, PhD, is professor and director of the School of Social Work and assistant dean of equity and inclusion in the Faculty of Health at Dalhousie University. Her scholarship focuses on access and inclusion within postsecondary institutions for students with (dis)Abilities, autoethnographic and narrative storying of (dis)Ability, anti-oppressive ways of working across abilities, and access and accommodations. She mentors students with (dis)Abilities through research, community development, and the writing of their own experiences. Judy has been co-chair of the Canadian Association for Social Work Education's Persons with Disability Caucus for 18 years, and was previously on the editorial board of the *Canadian Social Work Review* journal, where she served for three years as anglophone co-editor. She has been an invited contributor to numerous books on progressive social work and critical (dis)Ability.

FOREWORD

Donna Baines, PhD, is director and professor of social work, University of British Columbia, where she teaches social justice theory and practice. Donna has recently published in *Gender, Work and Organization, Critical Social Policy*, and *Work, Employment and Society*. Her publications also include the Canadian bestselling *Doing Anti-Oppressive Practice: Social Justice Social Work* (Fernwood, 2017, 3rd companion edition); the co-authored Canadian social work classic text, *Case Critical: Social Services and Social Justice* (with Banakonda Kennedy-Kish, Raven Sinclair, and Ben Carniol, Between the Lines, 2017, 7th edition); and an Australian co-edited book titled *Working across Difference: Social Work, Social Policy and Social Justice* (with Bindi Bennett, Susan Goodwin, and Margot Rawsthorne, Palgrave/Red Globe, 2019).

CONTRIBUTING AUTHORS

Tod Augusta-Scott, MSW, is known internationally for his work with gender-based violence, restorative justice, and narrative therapy. He has worked for a trauma-based community organization for over 25 years. For the past 15 years, he has also worked for the Canadian Armed Forces. He has presented his work across Canada and internationally (in Asia, Europe, British Isles, America). He is the co-founder of the Canadian Domestic Violence Conference. He has taught in the Department of Social Work, Dalhousie University, and continues as a guest speaker on a regular basis. Tod co-edited and contributed to *Narrative Therapy: Making Meaning, Making Lives* (Sage, 2007) and *Innovations in Interventions to Address Intimate Partner Violence: Research and Practice* (Routledge, 2017). Tod was awarded the Distinguished Service Award from the Canadian Association of Social Workers. His work is featured in the documentary *A Better Man* (2017), a film about domestic violence and restorative justice. He serves on the Advisory Council for the Status of Women, Canada. In 2019, he received an Award of Excellence from the Deputy Minister of National Defence for his work addressing sexual violence in the Canadian Armed Forces.

Gail Baikie, PhD candidate, is assistant professor at the School of Social Work, Dalhousie University. Her primary areas of scholarship are Indigenous and decolonizing methodologies and practices, critical reflection, impacts of natural resource development on marginalized populations, and the well-being of urban Inuit. Gail was born and raised in northern Labrador and is of Inuit and settler heritage. She was the second social worker with a BSW from her territory and the first to earn an MSW. She has over 15 years of professional practice experience with Indigenous populations.

Tessa Barrett, MSW, undertook the health and mental health streams at the University of Toronto, where she interned at the Centre for Mental Health and Addictions. She has been working in community-based outpatient mental health and addictions programs across Nova Scotia since 2015. She works specifically with veterans and members of the RCMP for the treatment of operational stress injuries, where her approach to treatment draws from a variety of models including cognitive-behavioural therapy and specific approaches for post-traumatic stress disorder.

The Honourable Wanda Thomas Bernard, PhD, is a social worker, educator, researcher, community activist, and advocate of social change. She was a professor at the School of Social Work, Dalhousie University, for over 25 years and was appointed professor emeritus in 2017. She was appointed to the Senate of Canada in 2016. Much of her research and scholarly work has focused on issues of racism, race equity, health, and Africentric practice. She now uses a race equity and intersectional lens to address anti-Black racism and human rights issues on a national level. She is a founding member of the Association of Black Social Workers (ABSW), which helps address the needs of marginalized citizens, especially those of African descent.

Meagen Bowers, BSW, is a social worker at the Dalhousie Social Work Community Clinic, where she also did her field practicum.

Marion Brown, PhD, is associate professor at the School of Social Work, Dalhousie University, and has a private practice working with individual and collective experiences of violence and discrimination and their effects. Marion has worked in a variety of settings, including community organizing, non-profit agencies, clinical counselling, and assessment services, in roles from front line to supervisory.

Catherine Bryan, PhD, is faculty at the School of Social Work, Dalhousie University. She has a PhD in social anthropology (Dalhousie University), an MSW and BSW (McGill University), and a BA in women's studies and political science (University of Winnipeg). Her research focuses on rural identity and economy, migration, social reproduction, and the long arm of capitalist political economy.

Kathi Campbell, BSW, is the regional director, Edmonton Region, Ministry of Children's Services, Government of Alberta, Child and Family Services. She is a graduate of the University of Manitoba. She was responsible for the development of the multicultural services framework for Edmonton Region, in collaboration with community partners. She has been instrumental in the development of collaboration between Children's Services and the Multicultural Health Brokers Co-op.

Darlene Chalmers, PhD, is associate professor in the Faculty of Social Work, University of Regina. Her interest in the human-animal bond relates to the important role of the integration of animals in social work practice. Her community-based participatory research is concentrated on animal and human wellness at the individual and community levels with a focus on animal-assisted interventions. She was a co-researcher on a team examining the use of equine-assisted learning as a treatment adjunct for volatile substance misuse with First Nations youth in Saskatchewan. Her research is currently exploring the impact of animal-assisted canine programs on inmates' well-being in correctional institutions, where she has been directly involved in these initiatives as a facilitator, dog-handler, and researcher. She is also a co-researcher examining the impact of service dogs in the lives of veterans who problematically use opioids, and she is investigating veterans' experiences of grief associated with the loss of their psychiatric service dog. She has worked with assistance dogs, is a co-founder of the PAWSitive Support Canine Assisted Learning Program, and is certified in facilitated equine experiential learning/psychotherapy for mental health professionals.

Yvonne Chiu is executive director of the Multicultural Health Brokers Co-op. She has over 20 years of experience in community-based program and policy development, as well as working side-by-side with immigrants and refugees. She has participated in multiple research projects in collaboration with academic institutions and has been instrumental in publicizing the multicultural health broker/community health broker model across Canada. She is a member of the Community Health Worker Network of Canada.

Barbara Clow, PhD, has more than 20 years of experience conducting policy-based research on the social determinants of women's and girls' health. She has worked with many marginalized groups, including African Nova Scotian women, Indigenous women, women living in rural and remote communities, lone mothers, and low-income women. For 10 years she served as executive director of the Atlantic Centre of Excellence for Women's Health and she now works as an independent policy and research consultant.

Josephine Etowa, PhD, is professor and past Loyer-DaSilva Research Chair in Public Health Nursing (2012–2019) at the University of Ottawa. She is a senior investigator with the Centre for Research in Health and Nursing at the University of Ottawa, and a founding member and past president of the Health Association of African Canadians. Her research program is grounded in over 25 years of clinical practice in maternal, newborn, and child health and community health nursing with projects funded by local, national, and international funding organizations. Her research addresses health inequities in health and health care with emphasis on the health of African Canadians.

Donna-Mae Ford has worked in the immigrant and refugee sector in Edmonton for almost 20 years. She is currently a project development consultant with Multicultural Health Brokers Co-op, supporting the development, coordination, and evaluation of programming related to health, mental health, education, and Children's Services. Donna-Mae facilitates workshops on interculturalism and is particularly interested in "third space" work, that is, how to foster authentic dialogue and transformation within the tensions of diverse assumptions, values, and power differentials.

Cyndi Hall, MSW, is co-founder/director of the Social Work Community Clinic and field education coordinator at the School of Social Work, Dalhousie University. Her career has included social work practice in government and non-profit social services and health systems. She utilizes various creative approaches to promote the profession and support student learning.

Cassandra Hanrahan, PhD, is associate professor and undergraduate program coordinator at the School of Social Work, Dalhousie University. She teaches courses on social policy and theoretical perspectives in social work, as well as conducting several independent studies on spirituality and social work, and on the positive transformative effects of mutual human-animal bonds on individual and collective well-being. Her research on human-animal interactions in social work urges us to reconceptualize the purpose and practice of social work today. By raising awareness of speciesism and the prescient critique of anthropocentrism in social work, Cassandra suggests new ontologies of being and becoming, inviting individual social workers and the profession into understandings and practices of relational ethics of sustainability for all life.

Joan R. Harbison, PhD, is adjunct professor at the School of Social Work, Dalhousie University. Her scholarship focuses on critical interdisciplinary approaches to aging in both national and international contexts. Her recent work includes co-editing *New Challenges to Ageing in the Rural North: A Critical Interdisciplinary Perspective* (with Päivi Naskali, Joan R. Harbison, and Shahnaj Begum, Springer, 2019), and co-authoring *Contesting Elder Abuse and Neglect: Ageism, Risk, and the Rhetoric of Rights in the Mistreatment of Older People* (University of British Columbia Press, 2016), in collaboration with her interdisciplinary research team from law, sociology, and social work.

Marjorie Johnstone, PhD, is assistant professor at the School of Social Work, Dalhousie University. She has an active research agenda of social justice and equity, Canadian social work history and professionalization, and Canadian multiculturalism. From her front-line work with various marginalized populations over two decades in community mental health agencies, she brings insight into how to integrate social justice and equity issues into front-line practice. Currently, she is teaching both online and offline courses in the BSW and MSW programs for both clinical and social justice–related topics.

Jeff Karabanow, PhD, is professor of social work at Dalhousie University. He has worked with homeless young people in Toronto, Montreal, Halifax, and Guatemala. His research focuses primarily on housing stability, service delivery systems, trauma, and homeless youth culture. He has numerous academic publications in these areas, including *Being Young and Homeless: Understanding How Youth Enter and Exit Street Life* (Peter Lang, 2004), *Leaving the Streets: Stories of Canadian Youth* (Fernwood, 2010), and *Homeless Youth and the Search for Stability* (Wilfrid Laurier University Press, 2018). Jeff is one of the founding members of Halifax's Out of the Cold Emergency Shelter and is co-director of the Dalhousie School of Social Work Community Clinic. He was recently awarded the Senate of Canada 150 Medal.

Eli Manning, PhD, is assistant professor at the School of Social Work, Dalhousie University. Her HIV work began as an advocate for and with people living with HIV, trans people, and queers. As an interdisciplinary academic, her HIV work is an extension of her social work career. Her forthcoming book, *The New War on AIDS: HIV Treatment Adherence and the Treatment as Prevention®️ Empire* (UBC Press), disrupts the seemingly neutral language of treatment as prevention by showing how adherence perpetuates colonialism, racism, and sexism. Her current research examines racism and colonialism in Canadian HIV criminalization.

Ifeyinwa Mbakogu, PhD, is assistant professor and chair of the Diversity and Equity Committee in the School of Social Work, Dalhousie University, with cross-appointment to international development studies. Her research interests include human trafficking, forced migration and displacement, new wars and conflicts, reintegration, African Diaspora studies, and rage and racism in the academy, explored within anti-racist and anti-colonial lenses.

Jean Morrison, MEd, has been an approved supervisor with the American Association of Marriage and Family Therapy. In her 40-year career as a clinician, supervisor, and educator, she has stressed the importance of security in relationships and belonging in community, especially in light of the dislocation that so often accompanies trauma and addiction. Recently, she has focused on the significant role of mindfulness in the treatment of substance use problems and the promotion of mental health.

Monique Nutter has been practising social work for more than 20 years. Her primary areas of practice have been research and evaluation, community organizing, and generalist practice with vulnerable populations, including immigrants, refugees, and other newcomers. She is a consultant with Multicultural Health Brokers Co-op, fostering collaboration between the organization and Children's Services. She believes in putting the voice of lived experience at the centre of decision-making and lifting these learnings into knowledge-driven policy development.

MT O'Shaughnessy is an author and lecturer. Living in British Columbia for the last 25 years, he has been active within the worlds of HIV/AIDS research and activism during that time. He has published articles about representation in fiction and given lectures on identity, HIV criminalization, and disclosure laws. He is a strong advocate of recording the history of the LGBTQA+ community by its own members, as well as the perspectives of community members during the early HIV/AIDS epidemic.

Sarah Oulton, MSW, is a clinic coordinator at the Dalhousie Social Work Community Clinic and has been since the clinic's inception in 2014. In this position, she has engaged in critical and feminist-based counselling and case management practices with individuals and groups who are experiencing marginalization in Halifax, Nova Scotia. Much of her time is spent working with those experiencing poverty, unstable housing, trauma, mental health issues, and grief, as well as facilitating student supervision and interdisciplinary experiential education. Sarah's BSW and MSW degrees were both completed at Dalhousie University, where her research focused on service providers' understanding of the relationship between co-occurring mental health and substance use issues among women.

Donna Pettipas, MSW, was employed by the Nova Scotia government for more than 25 years in a number of capacities, including adult protection and coordinator of program audits in the Disability Support Program. Donna's areas of specialization are human rights, decisional capacity, and abuse and neglect. Donna held a key leadership role in the implementation of the Nova Scotia Personal Directives Act. She has a deep knowledge of the complexities and ethical issues that arise around capacity and consent and acts as a consultant on matters in these areas of practice.

Nancy Ross, PhD, is assistant professor at the School of Social Work, Dalhousie University. Her previous work as a clinical therapist in mental health and addiction services informs her research interests, which include a focus on the role of social work in mental health, gender-based violence, adverse childhood experiences, and resilience. She applies a peace-building and intersectional lens to analysis of justice system responses to domestic violence and systemic and policy responses to adverse childhood experiences. She has produced a short film titled *Women of Substance* that profiled stories of women meeting challenges of substance use, and co-produced a second film titled *I Work for Change*, which explored the complexity of social work while celebrating the profession.

Sara Torres, PhD, is assistant professor at the School of Social Work, Laurentian University. She has over 15 years of experience conducting research and outreach with multicultural and hard-to-reach populations. Her other research interests include the role of community health worker programs in addressing health inequities among immigrant and refugee women in Canada as well as protective factors for children's welfare, and how to prevent the entry or re-entry of children from newcomer, African Nova Scotian, and Indigenous families into provincial care. She is also chair and co-founder of the Community Health Worker Network of Canada.

Merlinda Weinberg, PhD, is professor of social work at Dalhousie University. Before obtaining her PhD in 2004, she was a practising social worker for 25 years. Research interests include ethics in social work practice and the impacts of neoliberalism and diversity on professional ethics. She has a published book, entitled *Paradoxes in Social Work Practice: Mitigating Ethical Trespass* (Routledge, 2016), as well as a website on ethics: http://ethicsinthehelpingprofessions. socialwork.dal.ca/. The Social Sciences and Humanities Research Council of Canada short-listed Merlinda in 2008 as the top new researcher in Canada and she was awarded a senior fellowship at Durham University in 2017.

INDEX